Rescuing Autonomy from Kant

Historical Materialism Book Series

The Historical Materialism Book Series is a major publishing initiative of the radical left. The capitalist crisis of the twenty-first century has been met by a resurgence of interest in critical Marxist theory. At the same time, the publishing institutions committed to Marxism have contracted markedly since the high point of the 1970s. The Historical Materialism Book Series is dedicated to addressing this situation by making available important works of Marxist theory. The aim of the series is to publish important theoretical contributions as the basis for vigorous intellectual debate and exchange on the left.

The peer-reviewed series publishes original monographs, translated texts, and reprints of classics across the bounds of academic disciplinary agendas and across the divisions of the left. The series is particularly concerned to encourage the internationalization of Marxist debate and aims to translate significant studies from beyond the English-speaking world.

For a full list of titles in the Historical Materialism Book Series available in paperback from Haymarket Books, visit: www.haymarketbooks.org/series_collections/1-historical-materialism.

Rescuing Autonomy from Kant

A Marxist Critique of Kant's Ethics

James Furner

Haymarket Books
Chicago, IL

First published in 2022 by Brill Academic Publishers, The Netherlands
© 2022 Koninklijke Brill NV, Leiden, The Netherlands

Published in paperback in 2023 by
Haymarket Books
P.O. Box 180165
Chicago, IL 60618
773-583-7884
www.haymarketbooks.org

ISBN: 979-8-88890-003-1

Distributed to the trade in the US through Consortium Book Sales and
Distribution (www.cbsd.com) and internationally through Ingram
Publisher Services International (www.ingramcontent.com).

This book was published with the generous support of Lannan
Foundation, Wallace Action Fund, and the Marguerite Casey Foundation.

Special discounts are available for bulk purchases by organizations and
institutions. Please call 773-583-7884 or email info@haymarketbooks.org
for more information.

Cover design by David Mabb. Cover art is a detail from *Painting 37, Long
Live the New! William Morris & Co. Hand Printed Wallpapers, Willow Bough
and Kasimir Malevich's Suprematism.* Acrylic on wallpaper mounted on
canvas, (2016).

Printed in the United States.

10 9 8 7 6 5 4 3 2 1

Library of Congress Cataloging-in-Publication data is available.

Contents

Acknowledgements

I would like to acknowledge the SA-UK Bilateral Chair in Political Theory, based in the School of Sciences, University of the Witwatersrand, held by Professor Lawrence Hamilton, for the research fellowship during which time the main draft of the book was written.

I would also like to thank: Komnas Poriazis, for many discussions of the issues; Thad Metz, for helpful comments on Chapters 5 and 6; an anonymous reviewer for the Historical Materialism Book Series; and the reviewers and editorial boards whose advice and editing guided the journal articles listed below to publication.

In the chapters indicated, the book reproduces, revises or expands arguments first presented in:

3: "Can Kant's Formula of the End in Itself Condemn Capitalism?" *Kantian Review*, 24 (1), 1–25. © Kantian Review, 2019.

5: "Kant's Contradiction in Conception Test." *Theoria*, 64 (152), 1–23. © Berghahn Journals, 2017.

6: "Kant's Contradiction in the Will Test." *The Philosophical Forum*, 48 (3), 307–23. © Wiley, 2017.

7: "The Principle of Suitability Interpretation of Kant's Formula of the Law of Nature." *Theoria*, 66 (160). © Berghahn Journals, 2019.

8: "Kant's Argument for the Formula of the End in Itself: A Logical Pluralism Interpretation." *Idealistic Studies*, 47 (3), 171–89. © Philosophy Documentation Center, 2019.

References and Abbreviations

References to works originally written in German or French are first to an original language edition and then, if available, to a published translation; for example,

Bernstein 1899, p. 177; Bernstein 1993, p. 199.

Except for Kant's *Lectures on Philosophical Theology*, which is cited by author: date, and *Critique of Pure Reason*, which is cited by A/B pagination, Kant's writings are referenced using the following abbreviations, followed by the volume and page number in *Kants gesammelte Schriften*, Berlin: de Gruyter, or *Akademie* (*Ak.*) edition:

Anth	*Anthropologie in pragmatischer Hinsicht* (1798)
	Anthropology from a Pragmatic Point of View
GMS	*Grundlegung zur Metaphysik der Sitten* (1785)
	Groundwork of the Metaphysics of Morals
IaG	*Idee zu einer allgemeinen Geschichte in weltbürgerlicher Absicht* (1784)
	Idea for a Universal History with a Cosmopolitan Purpose
KpV	*Kritik der praktischen Vernunft* (1788)
	Critique of Practical Reason
KU	*Kritik der Urtheilskraft* (1790)
	Critique of Judgment
Log	*Logik* (1800)
	Lectures on Logic
MS	*Metaphysik der Sitten* (1797)
	The Metaphysics of Morals
P	*Prolegomena zu einer jeden künftigen Metaphysik* (1783)
	Prolegomena to Any Future Metaphysics
RGV	*Die Religion innerhalb der Grenzen der bloßen Vernunft* (1793)
	Religion Within the Bounds of Bare Reason
TP	*Über den Gemeinspruch: Das mag in der Theorie richtig sein, taugt aber nicht für die Praxis* (1793)
	On the Common Saying: That May Be Correct in Theory, But it is of No Use in Practice
ÜGTP	*Über den Gebrauch teleologischer Principien in der Philosophie* (1788)
	On the Use of Teleological Principles in Philosophy
V-Mo/Collins	*Moralphilosophie Collins*
	Moral Philosophy: Collins's Lecture Notes
WA	*Beantwortung der Frage: Was ist Aufklärung* (1784)
	An Answer to the Question: What is Enlightenment?

ZeF   *Zum ewigen Frieden* (1795)
           Toward Perpetual Peace

As all translations cited include the paginations of the *Akademie* edition, a single reference is provided. The exception is *Idea for a Universal History with a Cosmopolitan Purpose*. For this work, an additional reference to the page number of an English translation is provided.

I tend to use the translation of Kant's *Groundwork of the Metaphysics of Morals* by Mary Gregor and Jens Timmermann. For Kant's other writings, I favour translations by Werner S. Pluhar. If words or phrases appear in square brackets in Pluhar's translation, these brackets are retained. Interpolations by me are distinguished from the former by the addition '– JF'.

Marx's writings are referenced by volume, page number, using the abbreviations:

MECW   *Marx/Engels Collected Works*
MEGA   *Marx-Engels-Gesamtausgabe*
MEJ   *Marx-Engels-Jahrbuch*
MEW   *Marx-Engels-Werke*

If more than one published translation is referenced, the additional translation(s) will follow the reference to MECW.

I occasionally modify the translation of Kant's writings, and translations of Marx's writings are my own. In each case, I have sought to follow the 'Rules of Translation' outlined in my previous book, *Marx on Capitalism* (2018), on p. 58:

(1)   Foreign phrases will be bracketed within citations if and only if it is relevant for an argument advanced in this book to know what phrase is used.

(2)   All and only all the relevant differences between the translations of bracketed foreign phrases, and the official translation(s) referred to in the footnotes, will be noted and explained in the footnote, or, if especially pertinent, in the main text.

(3)   For all translations explained in accordance with (2), if the official translation would more correctly translate a different foreign phrase, that phrase is provided in a footnote, for comparison.

Introduction

We live in a world marked by a variety of divisive dynamics: the concentration of economic wealth in the hands of billionaire capitalists, environmental degradation, a gendered distribution of devalued care work, the hierarchization of political parties and the marginalisation of historically disadvantaged minority cultures. These divisive dynamics are crucial in shaping people's life chances. But another striking thing about them, besides their pervasive impact, is that they go without mention in modern constitutions. There is no constitution in which we can read 'we, the people, give ourselves a capitalist society', or 'we, the people, discount future generations', or 'we, the people, hereby devalue care work and leave most of it to women' or 'we, the people, shall have hierarchical political parties, and an exclusionary dominant culture'. These dynamics are unleashed by constitutionally guaranteed principles and rights. But they are not explicitly affirmed in them. They define our divided lives, but not because a public power acting in our name sets them down as principles to live by.

Where divisive social dynamics have a real but formally unrecognised presence, we lack a kind of autonomy. According to the standard view of freedom as autonomy, to be free is to obey a self-given law. But as social beings, what we must obey, or find our way through, are the various dynamics that define our social arrangements. We can only prescribe these dynamics to ourselves through a public power that affirms them in our name as principles. So, as social beings, we can enjoy autonomy only if our basic social dynamics, to which our lives must adjust, are expressly endorsed as principles in an act of popular sovereignty. If the principles of a public power are to do this, and provide a unifying identity, these dynamics cannot be systematically divisive. We enjoy autonomy at the community level, then, when our fundamental social dynamics are expressly endorsed in co-legislated principles, and are harmonious. This would end the lie of living by a constitution that proclaims one thing, while social reality imposes another. It would allow us to recognise ourselves as free social beings.

As the title suggests, to defend this version of freedom as autonomy is to seek to rescue autonomy from Kant. It is to take a view of autonomy distinct from Kant's: not the autonomy of the individual rational being, but the autonomy of a human community. The argumentative strategy is similar, at least in one way, to Kant's, in that it involves the concept of antinomy.

The project to which this defence of autonomy belongs is Marxist in orientation. Karl Marx identifies the antinomy and outlines the argumentative strategy to which it appeals. On account of its version of autonomy, it also echoes a hope expressed by the Hungarian Marxist Georg Lukács, in *History and Class Consciousness*, for a society in which 'the subject (consciousness, thought) ... moves in a self-created world, whose conscious shape it is, and this world at the same time imposes itself upon it in full objectivity'.[1]

The aim of this book is thus to defend a new way of thinking about the relation of Marx's project to Kant's ethics, namely:

(1) *Critique*. Marxism offers an antinomy-based argument for an ethics of the autonomy of a human community; relatedly, it offers an argument against Kant's ethics of the autonomy of the will.

There are two interconnected themes in this way of thinking. Marxism identifies defects in Kant's moral philosophy, but it offers an ethics that retains certain specific similarities to Kant's. This is a fresh way of thinking about the relation of Marx's project to Kant's ethics, because the *typical*[2] views of this relation are:

(2) *Irrelevance*. Marxism has no ethics (that is, no theory justifying principles of action on impartial grounds) and does need not be complemented by an ethics, whether Kantian or otherwise.[3] Marxists appeal simply to what it is instrumentally rational for the working-class to do, given its class interests.

(3) *Complementarity*. While Marxism has no ethics, Marxists need an ethics, and Kant's ethics is just the kind of ethics that Marxists need to condemn capitalism and defend socialism.[4]

(4) *Incompatibility*. Although Marxism offers (or needs) an ethics, it takes, and can take, nothing from Kant's ethics, because Kant's ethics is not the right kind of ethics.[5] For example, Marxism offers (or needs) a form of consequentialism on which states of affairs are evaluated by the standard of utility,[6] or self-realisation,[7] or capability.[8]

---

1 Lukács 1977, p. 324; Lukács 1968, p. 142.

2 Besides (1)–(4), there is one logically possible but implausible view: (5) *Incorporation*. Marxism incorporates Kant's ethics without modification. The only other possible view is: (6) *Critique and complementarity*. Marxism offers no ethics, but Marxists need an ethics, and a post-Kantian ethics is just the ethics they need. (6) combines elements of (1) and (3). Even if (6) is not implausible, it is not typical. In any event, we need not undermine (6) to persuade those with an interest in Marxism of the need for a critique of Kant's ethics.

3 Heinrich 2005, p. 33; Heinrich 2012, p. 36; Leiter 2015; Wood 1984, p. 15, p. 21; Wood 2004, pp. 128–9.

4 Chojnacki 1924, p. 69, p. 80, p. 145; Nielsen 1989, p. 270; Staudinger 1899, p. iv; Vorländer 1900, p. 2, p. 7, p. 13; Vorländer 1904, p. 14; Vorländer 1911, p. 239.

5 Miller 1981, pp. 342–3; Miller 1984, p. 58.

6 Allen 1973, p. 189.

7 Lukes 1985, pp. 142–4.

8 See Sen 1992, pp. 120–21.

The argument proceeds in three parts. Part I (Chapters 1–4) rejects these three typical views of Marxism's relation to Kant's ethics. It offers a Marxist rationale for critically engaging with Kant's ethics, addressed to proponents of the irrelevance view, the complementarity view and the incompatibility view. Part II (Chapters 5–9) defends the negative part of the critique view. It argues that an agent who adopts any of Kant's formulas of the categorical imperative is committed to a belief in the existence of God, but that Kant offers no good argument for us to believe that God exists. Thus, Kant offers no good argument for us to abide by the categorical imperative. Part III (Chapter 10) defends the positive part of the critique view, by outlining a grounding argument for an ethics of the autonomy of a human community. This ethics is Marxist, in that it offers a basis for condemning capitalism and recommending socialism that is consistent with a class-oriented strategy to achieve socialism.[9] It is post-Kantian, in that it defends a conception of autonomy located at the level of a human community, using a foundational argument that appeals to the need to resolve an antinomy in the social world.[10]

An aside: throughout this work, 'Marxism' is used to denote the theoretical project that Marx founded. In *Marx on Capitalism*, I argued that this project is best conceived as 'commodity form philosophy'.[11] The classic statement of this conception of Marx's project is provided by Georg Lukács in *History and Class Consciousness*: 'the problem of the commodity' is 'the central structural problem of capitalist society in all its expressions of life'.[12] This remains my understanding. But while this conception of Marxism is compatible with the critique view of Marxism's relation to Kant's ethics defended here, it is not entailed by this view.[13] One may accept the critique view without believing that an analysis of the commodity is as central as commodity form philosophy says to the explanatory social theory that Marxism offers. As the aim, here, is simply to defend the critique view, the term 'Marxism' is retained. But it should be borne in mind that if 'Marxism' denotes the theoretical project that Marx founded, the criterion of whether a thesis is Marxist, or can belong to Marxism, is not whether it expresses a position that is fully developed in Marx's writings and/or in subsequent Marxist work; but whether it can belong to a substantive

---

9   For a fuller statement, see ch. 4, sec. 7.
10 Compare ch. 4, sec. 6, and ch. 10, sec. 4.
11 Furner 2018, pp. 85–92.
12 Lukács 1977, p. 257; Lukács 1968, p. 83.
13 Even if *some* traditional rival conceptions of Marx's project, such as Analytical Marxism and Althusserian Marxism, are incompatible with the critique view; see Furner 2018, pp. 406–7.

project that can claim to be inspired by Marx's writings, be it commodity form philosophy, or some other project.

Finally, some aspects of the argument in Part III were suggested in *Marx on Capitalism*.[14] Their presentation here is more closely related to the form of a grounding argument than was possible in that book.

---

14   See Furner 2018, pp. 3–4.

PART I

Three Views of
Marxism's Relation to Kant's Ethics

∴

Introduction to Part I

The aim in the following four chapters is to offer a rationale for conducting a critique of Kant's ethics to those with an interest in Marxism. The typical views of Marxism's relation to Kant's ethics outlined in the Introduction do not allow us simply to assume an interest in this critique, whether among Marxists, or among those broadly sympathetic to Marxism. We need to undermine three typical views – the irrelevance view, the complementarity view and the incompatibility view – to motivate the critique.

Chapter 1 addresses the irrelevance view. The irrelevance view says that Marxism has no ethics – no theory justifying principles of action on impartial grounds – and does need not be complemented by an ethics. On the irrelevance view, it is, at best, *time-wasting* for Marxists to truly engage with moral philosophy, including Kant's. The strategy here is to reject four distinct arguments offered for the irrelevance view. I shall also suggest that in the case of two of them – the ideology argument and the class interests argument – those tempted by them ought to be somewhat persuaded, by a premise of their own argument, not just to reject the argument, but to endorse an ethics of the kind defended here.

Chapters 2–3 challenge the complementarity view. The complementarity view says that, although Marxism has no ethics, Marxists need an ethics, and this ethics is supplied by Kant. On the complementarity view, it is *self-defeating* for Marxists to offer a critique of Kant's ethics. As the complementarity view holds that Marxism and Kant's ethics complement one another, any challenge to this view must show that one or more features of Kant's ethics are irreconcilable with one or more non-negotiable Marxist theses. Two independent arguments against the complementarity view are presented. Either provides a sufficient objection to the complementarity view; and the arguments are compatible.

The first argument, presented in Chapter 2, concerns the question of socialist strategy. The argument here is that the timeless nature of Kant's grounding arguments for the formulas of the categorical imperative is irreconcilable with a Marxist strategy of class struggle. For the purposes of this argument, we take it as given that Kant's ethics can condemn capitalism and justify socialism. We ask whether Kant's ethics is compatible with the means that socialists, in the Marxist view, are to adopt, to replace capitalism with socialism.

The assumption that Kant's ethics can condemn capitalism is questioned in Chapter 3. Here we ask whether Kant's most popular formula of the categorical imperative, the Formula of the End in Itself (FEI), can condemn capitalism. If

FEI cannot condemn capitalism, then all critics of capitalism need an ethics that differs from Kant's. The view that FEI can condemn capitalism has been defended in two main contexts: first, by Kantian socialists at the turn of the twentieth century; and, more recently, by contemporary authors. The chapter assesses these FEI-based arguments against capitalism from the perspective of the issues that arise in interpreting and applying Kant's formula. As this formula's Never Merely as a Means principle can condemn conduct that violates a person's rights, it concludes by asking whether capitalism can be viewed in Kantian terms as a kind of general injustice.

Chapter 4 addresses the incompatibility view. The incompatibility view says that Kant's ethics is not the sort of ethics that Marxism has or needs. It denies that the latter can owe anything to the former. On the incompatibility view, Marxists who engage in a critique of Kant's ethics have *misunderstood* Marxism's ethical demands or needs. The incompatibility view is challenged, therefore, by presenting an interpretive argument about Marx's writings, to the effect that something valuable in them suggests or requires an ethics that draws on at least *some* features of Kant's ethics. The strategy pursued in Chapter 4 is to present evidence for the view that Marx's reflections on post-capitalist society reflect a conception of autonomy: the autonomy of a human community.

Against the Irrelevance View

The irrelevance view says that Marxism neither has nor needs an ethics; if, at times, Marxists express normative opinions, that has nothing to do with their being Marxists. To affirm the irrelevance view, it is not necessary to affirm Marxism. The irrelevance view is a view about Marxism's relation to ethics, whether one affirms or rejects Marxism.

Those who hold the irrelevance view will wonder why a Marxist need really probe any moral philosophy. To interest those who take the irrelevance view in a Marxist critique of Kant's ethics, it is necessary to undermine the arguments given in support of this view. We consider four arguments: the instrumental reasons argument, the false claims argument, the ideology argument, and the class interests argument. Each argument appeals to Marxists' practical or theoretical aims, and attempts to show that the adoption of an ethics is in conflict with, or irrelevant for, these aims.

1   The Instrumental Reasons Argument

The instrumental reasons argument for the irrelevance view says that all ethics is practically irrelevant from a Marxist perspective because Marxists' goal is socialism, and Marxists can be confident that agents will act on instrumental reasons to achieve this goal if and when the time comes. As Brian Leiter puts it, 'Marx takes for granted that, *at the right historical moment*, circumstances will be such that large numbers of people will be motivated to undertake revolutionary change: they do not require a normative theory to help them'.[1] According to the instrumental reasons argument, it is a waste of time, from a Marxist perspective, to engage in ethics: 'normative theory is completely irrelevant'.[2]

Relatedly, in *Self-Ownership, Freedom and Equality*, G.A. Cohen writes that 'two large Marxist factual claims' ensure that normative questions 'do not require investigation, from a socialist point of view'.[3] These 'Marxist factual claims' are that: (i) in capitalism, the number of immiserated and exploited

---

1   Leiter 2015, p. 24.
2   Ibid.
3   Cohen 1995, p. 7.

producers is becoming such a large majority that a transition to a socialist socio-economic structure will become so urgent that there is no need to develop a normative theory to justify it; and (ii) a socialist socio-economic structure will develop productive power to a level that generates such an abundance of goods that there will be no need for people in a socialist society to limit their demands for goods by a sense of what is just.[4] Together, these claims imply that a socialist socio-economic structure can be achieved and sustained without socialists developing a normative theory. Those who believe them can believe that they need not develop a normative theory to advance socialism. Any number of instrumental reasons connected to an individual's own level of welfare (if their situation is so miserable and widespread) will provide sufficient support for socialism, and no degree of instrumental reasoning can destabilise socialism if goods are so abundant that disputes over their distribution need not arise.

Both Leiter and Cohen believe that the Marxist conception of socialist revolution is one on which socialist revolution will come about just as easily without a socialist ethics. To reject the instrumental reasons argument, it is sufficient to undermine this belief.[5] If, on a Marxist conception of socialist revolution, there are grounds for thinking either that socialist revolution requires a socialist ethics, or, more modestly, that socialist revolution may not come about just as easily without one, the instrumental reasons argument is defeated.

We may focus on the second of these two possibilities. No amount of confidence that there will come a time at which actors will bring about socialism for non-normative reasons can exclude the thought that, if an ethical theory gives actors a sufficient reason to bring about socialism, its influence may hasten socialism, or render a transition to socialism less costly. As it would be good, from a Marxist perspective, if socialism is brought about sooner rather than later and with fewer rather than greater costs, no amount of confidence in history can exclude the thought that it is good, from a Marxist perspective, to have an ethics that justifies socialism, if this ethics can give even some actors a sufficient reason to bring socialism about.

In order to defend the instrumental reasons argument in response to this thought, it would be necessary to argue that normative theory cannot be expected to have any significant influence on action. But no convincing argument for this is offered by those who hold the irrelevance view. From the premise (for

---

4   Cohen 1995, pp. 6–8.
5   For a critique of Cohen's second 'Marxist factual claim', see Furner 2018, pp. 50–2, pp. 113–14.

which Leiter offers a bit of evidence) that 'high quality bourgeois moral philosophy does not change the behaviour of high quality bourgeois moral philosophers',[6] we may not infer that socialist ethical theories cannot, through suitable organisations, move some members of subordinate classes in a revolutionary direction. Social organisations possess means of coordination and sanction that render the two processes quite dissimilar. In the absence of a more specific argument that a socialist ethics cannot be expected to have any significant influence on action, even the confidence that proponents of the irrelevance view take Marxists to show in instrumental reason does not imply that a socialist ethics is irrelevant for Marxists' practical aims.

A further problem with the instrumental reasons argument concerns this confidence itself. The confidence that circumstances conducive to a transition to socialism are likely to be circumstances in which instrumental reasoning unambiguously favours this transition seems misplaced. Even if 'large numbers of people'[7] are motivated to undertake revolutionary change, it only takes concessions from a powerful minority to alter what it may be prudent, in the short term, for some people to do, given the risks of revolution. As given preferences alone cannot be expected to provide a stable, unambiguous motive for revolutionary change when resources, and thus the capacity to offer concessions, remain in the hands of a small but capable opponent, some principled reason for socialism that can be given publicly and sincerely is likely to be helpful.

Moreover, in the Marxist conception of socialism, a socialist society treats everyone equally in certain respects. Depending on its level of maturity, a socialist society is either to give each able person the right to means of consumption proportional to productive contribution, or to adopt a policy of distributing means of consumption in proportion to need, no matter whose need it is.[8] If a revolution is to be a vehicle for socialism, it must prepare people attitudinally for a society that treats everyone equally in these respects. Acceptance of this equal treatment can only emerge from a revolutionary process if the latter is itself conducted in some spirit of equality. This is made more likely if it spreads an argument for socialism that everyone affected has a reason to affirm.[9] To the extent that Marxists possess an ethics that sustains an argument

---

6 Leiter 2015, p. 42.

7 Leiter 2015, p. 24.

8 *MEW*, 19, pp. 20–1; *MECW*, 24, pp. 85–7.

9 To provide an argument that everyone has a reason to affirm is not to be blind to the fact that class situation may influence whether people regard a particular interest as an overriding practical consideration. At issue is the kind of public culture that a socialist revolution is to instil, not the existing culture it confronts.

of this kind, they have one more means to further their practical aims than socialists who regard all ethics as irrelevant.

2   The False Claims Argument

The false claims argument for the irrelevance view is advanced by Jeffrey Vogel. Referring to the 'values of a left-wing moralist', Vogel argues that 'moral language has a social meaning that is linked to false claims about how the world works that frustrate the social understanding that is necessary to achieve these values'.[10] According to Vogel, to use moral language is to presuppose that it is possible to 'provide all rational, informed people with the normal range of hopes, sympathies, and emotional responses with impartial and influential reasons for action'.[11] But, Vogel adds, this belief is false, and must be acknowledged as false by Marxists, because its acceptance 'will hinder the necessary class-struggle tactics needed to promote the values'[12] that Marxists hold.

The objection to the false claims argument is that it overstates the presuppositions of using moral language. Because the use of moral language presupposes less than Vogel suggests, the use of moral language need not commit its user to claims that Marxists must disbelieve, to promote their values consistently.

The exaggeration results from the inclusion of the words 'and influential' in the belief that, Vogel says, is presupposed by the use of normative language. We can distinguish between: (a) impartial reasons for action; and (b) social conditions under which impartial reasons will be influential among *all* informed people with the full range of psychological experience. To use normative language is to presuppose (a), not (b). As such, its use need not presuppose a belief in conflict with Marxism, according to which socialist values are promoted through class struggle, rather than through rational reflection spread evenly across a population.

To be sure, the space for denying that the use of normative language presupposes (b) has narrowed slightly, given the above reply to the instrumental reasons argument. We cannot deny that the user of normative language presupposes (b) on the grounds that existing conditions prevent *anyone* from acting on impartial reasons, for that would preclude the above rebuttal of the instru-

---

10   Vogel 1994, p. 562.
11   Vogel 1994, p. 545.
12   Vogel 1994, p. 549.

mental reasons argument. But there is no need to say anything this extreme to deny that the use of normative language presupposes (b). It is sufficient to insist that it is consistent to use normative language, and to believe that existing conditions make it foolhardy to expect that all informed people with the full range of psychological experience will be influenced by impartial reasons. There is a point to using normative language even if only *some* people can be expected to be influenced by impartial reasons.

To use normative language to communicate with someone for practical purposes presupposes a belief that normative language can influence how that person will act. It is pointless to use normative language to communicate with someone for practical purposes if one believes that normative language will not influence how they will act. An impartial reason to act is a reason that everyone has a reason to accept. So, to use normative language to communicate with someone for practical purposes presupposes a belief that *that person* can be influenced in how they will act by an argument that *they* regard as one that everyone has a reason to accept. It does not presuppose that this person believes that everyone else will find this argument sufficiently weighty as to override any other practical considerations that they may have. To be persuaded of an ethical injunction, a person does not have to believe that everyone else will act on it.

The test of whether a user of normative language presupposes that impartial reasons will be influential among all informed people with the full range of psychological experience is not *that* they use this language, but *with whom* they use it. If a person uses normative language to communicate for practical purposes with people from across *all* social groups in *equal* measure, their use of normative language may be said to presuppose a belief that all rational, informed people will be influenced by impartial reasons. But users of normative language may be more selective in their use of it than this.

The relevant test in the case of *Marxist* users of normative language is whether Marxists use normative language to communicate for practical purposes with people in equal measure, *no matter their class*. Only if their use of normative language is not discriminating in this way are they committed to a belief that existing social conditions enable individuals, no matter their class, to exhibit an equal preparedness to act on impartial principles; and only *this* belief would sit uneasily with an adherence to class struggle tactics. More discriminating Marxist users of normative language do not face this problem. It is perfectly consistent for Marxists to affirm an ethics and to adopt class struggle tactics, such as by spreading impartial arguments for socialism among the members of the classes who they regard as its main agents.

3   The Ideology Argument

The ideology argument for the irrelevance view, advanced by Allen Wood, is that Marxists must reject morality because moral motivations involve a lack of self-understanding. The ideology argument proceeds from the premise that 'Marx regards morality, along with law, religion and other forms of social consciousness, as fundamentally ideological'.[13] By calling morality 'ideological', Wood means to say that, for Marxism, morality is (to use Friedrich Engels's term) a form of '"false consciousness"'.[14] Actors have false consciousness if they lack a certain kind of awareness about their actions. Religious, philosophical or moral motivations are forms of false consciousness insofar as they leave actors unaware of the relation of their actions 'to the social life of which they are a part'.[15] As Marxists regard morality as a form of false consciousness, they must avoid it to retain self-understanding: '[w]hen they are motivated by ideologies, people do not understand themselves'.[16]

Self-understanding of one's actions is practically important, because, to shape society as one wishes, it helps to be fully aware of alterable features of the world that affect human lives. Marxist theory offers a particular account of these features. It emphasises the alterable fact of class oppression. This emphasis informs the Marxist account of false consciousness. False consciousness, on the Marxist account, consists in a lack of awareness about the class basis of action: 'the chief illusion in any ideology is an illusion about its own class basis'.[17] Morality is a form of false consciousness, on the Marxist account, because moral motivations leave actors unaware of the fact that they are 'promoting the interests of one social class as opposed to others'.[18] Actors motivated by religion, philosophy or morality, Wood says, 'do not act with the intention of promoting the interests of one social class as opposed to others; but they go right on doing so'.[19]

---

13   Wood 1991, pp. 515–16. The correct phrase is 'social forms of consciousness'; see Furner 2018, p. 49.

14   Wood 1991, p. 514, citing Engels's remark (after Marx's death) in a letter to Franz Mehring dated 14 July 1893 at *MEW*, 39, p. 97; *MECW*, 50, p. 164. The term 'false consciousness' is sometimes attributed to Marx, for example, by Rawls 1980, p. 539, and Sen 2009, p. 164. There is no evidence Marx used it, however.

15   Wood 1991, p. 514.

16   Ibid.

17   Ibid.

18   Ibid.

19   Ibid.

What is it about morality that explains this result? Wood suggests that '[w]hatever the theory, morality is depicted as the standpoint of impartial or disinterested well-wishing ... It is this feature of morality which renders it fundamentally ideological'.[20] On Wood's account of the Marxist position, we are faced with moral ideology whenever we encounter an appeal to do something because there are 'good (impartially based) reasons for doing so'.[21] Morality is a form of false consciousness, on the Marxist account, because actors motivated by impartially based reasons are left unaware of the fact that their actions are serving to promote class oppression (or, perhaps, to undermine it, as the case may be).

Here I shall raise two objections to the ideology argument. Both objections come down to the thought that the ideology argument does not give Marxists a reason to reject all morality. The ideology argument can at most give Marxists a reason to reject *some* moral arguments. As the ideology argument does not give Marxists a reason to reject morality as a whole, it does not stand in the way of a critical engagement with Kant's ethics.

The first objection is that there is at least one form of moral argument of appeal to Marxists that does not count as false consciousness. Consider an argument of the form: existing society ought to be revolutionised, because the class oppression in it is in one way[22] bad for everyone. An argument of this form uses impartial reasoning, and is alive to class oppression. It is not a form of argument in which 'class warfare is being simultaneously waged and disguised'.[23] It does not disguise existing class oppression. Nor, if it inspired socialist revolution, would it disguise the fact that the action it motivated was serving to abolish existing class oppression. Hence, it is not a form of argument that, in motivating actors, must leave them unaware of the contribution of their actions to the class nature of the society of which they are a part. It is a form of moral argument that is not false consciousness in the Marxist sense. Not all morality is false consciousness in the Marxist sense.

---

20 Wood 1991, p. 518.

21 Ibid.

22 The phrase 'in one way (good/bad)' indicates that the 'ought' is a *pro tanto* ought. A *pro tanto* ought is a final ought if there are no other normative considerations. But a *pro tanto* ought can be outweighed by other normative considerations. A *pro tanto* ought is therefore distinct from an all-things-considered ought. It is also distinct from a *prima facie* ought. While a *pro tanto* ought can be outweighed by independent and weightier normative considerations, a *prima facie* ought is a final ought unless it is undermined; it functions like a rebuttable presumption. For a discussion of *prima facie* oughts and *pro tanto* oughts, see Reisner 2013.

23 Wood 1991, p. 516.

The second objection is that, viewed as an argument against all morality, the ideology argument is self-undermining. This is because any proponent of the ideology argument must acknowledge that there is an impartial reason to institute social arrangements that reduce or eliminate false consciousness. Yet this is to acknowledge an impartial reason, the very quality that is said to make moral motivations ideological. One cannot argue against all morality by appeal to an argument that commits to a moral claim.

The ideology argument urges Marxists to reject morality because morality is a form of false consciousness. It presupposes that a Marxist is not willing to countenance that Marxist theory leads to false consciousness. A Marxist will be unwilling to countenance this if they believe both that theory that leads to false consciousness is defective, and that Marxist theory is not defective.

Consider what the first of these two beliefs commits them to. On the Marxist account, false consciousness consists in a lack of awareness that one's actions are promoting class interests. However, Marxists must concede that this is a Marxist way of filling out what is, in principle, a more general idea. The general idea of false consciousness is the lack of awareness of the relation of one's actions to the social life of which they are a part. This is a general idea of false consciousness, because it allows for the fact that non-Marxist theories, which may take a different view of social life as a whole, may have a different (less class-focused) view of what actors lack an awareness of when their consciousness is false. A Marxist presupposes this general idea of false consciousness insofar as they believe, in respect of all theories, that theory that leads to false consciousness is defective. If a Marxist can only be moved by the ideology argument because they have this belief, any Marxist it moves must acknowledge that there is a sense in which it is true to say that everyone has a reason to accept that theory should not lead to false consciousness. This is so, even if a Marxist *also* additionally believes that it is Marxists who give the best account of what false consciousness disguises (namely, that it disguises class interests).

Any Marxist tempted by the ideology argument is therefore committed to a form of moral argument. Consider an argument of the form: social arrangements that reduce or eliminate false consciousness ought to be adopted, because false consciousness is in one way bad for everyone. This is a form of moral argument: an impartial reason is to be offered in support. The impartial reason to adopt such arrangements is that everyone has a reason to want to understand their actions. This reason is impartial, so long as no Marxist assumptions about what constitutes false consciousness or self-understanding are smuggled in. As Marxists and non-Marxists employ different theoretical frameworks, they will have different understandings of the benefits of avoiding false consciousness. But that does not alter the fact that the reason given for avoiding false consciousness is impartial. Wood, who devised the ideology argument, claims in the same piece that, for Marx, 'the task of human emancipation is to build a human society on rational self-transparency'.[24] Does this claim not imply that Marx is committed to an impartial argument for a 'human society' that rests on the value of rational self-transparency?[25]

Again, we find that the ideology argument cannot be employed to reject all morality. If the first objection is that the ideology argument does not count against a form of moral argument that acknowledges the fact of class oppression, the second objection is that those who wish to use the ideology argument to reject morality are committed to endorsing a moral argument for instituting social conditions that promote rational self-transparency.

The second objection ties in with the argument for an ethics of the autonomy of a human community. We social beings enjoy autonomy if the fundamental dynamics of our society are harmonious, and expressly endorsed in co-legislated constitutional principles. For then, by navigating our way through these dynamics, we are obeying a self-given law. Of relevance, here, is that the conditions of the autonomy of a human community are conditions for rational self-transparency. If constitutional principles expressly endorse social dynamics, knowledge of the former enables actors to be aware of the contribution of their lawful action to the social life of which it is a part. This is not presently the case. Actors cannot know, from a constitutional right to private property, that its lawful employment is serving to sustain capital accumulation on the part of mega-rich capitalists. If the express recognition of social dynamics in co-legislated public principles can only be achieved in a classless society, free from aggressively competitive sub-groups, Marxists tempted by the ideology argument may in fact look sympathetically on the argument for autonomy defended in Part III.

4   The Class Interests Argument

The final argument for the irrelevance view, also offered by Allen Wood, is the class interests argument. The class interests argument is that morality contra-

---

24   Ibid.

25   That Wood does not see this can be explained, I think, by the fact that he does not explicitly distinguish between the class-based elaboration of false consciousness by Marxists, and the more general idea of false consciousness that this elaboration presupposes. Once this distinction is made, it is apparent that the ideology argument commits to a moral claim.

dicts practical recognition of a core Marxist thesis about how structural socio-economic change comes about. According to Wood,

> Marx believes that our actions are historically effective only insofar as they involve the pursuit of class interests, and that the historical meaning of our actions consists in their functional role in the struggle between such interests. Let us call this Marxian belief the 'class interests thesis'.[26]

The class interests argument is that 'practical recognition of the class interests thesis excludes rational historical agents from taking justice as their fundamental goal',[27] where 'justice' denotes any attempt to justify 'the distribution of some chosen variables ... from an impartial or disinterested standpoint'.[28]

Let us start with what we shall grant to proponents of the class interests argument. We shall grant that the class interests thesis, as defined above, is a core Marxist thesis. It is a core Marxist belief that attempts to transform the socio-economic structure only stand a chance of success insofar as they 'involve the pursuit of class interests' in class struggle. From this, it follows that it is irrational for a Marxist to embark on or recommend actions to transform the socio-economic structure that do *not* 'involve the pursuit of class interests'. To do so would display a lack of 'practical recognition of the class interests thesis'. If advocates of structural socio-economic change are required, insofar as they affirm an ethics, to try to transform the socio-economic structure by actions that do not involve the pursuit of class interests, then it is irrational for Marxists to affirm an ethics.

Socialist revolutionaries who affirm an ethics are not required to do any such thing, however. To affirm an ethics is to adopt an impartial standpoint on outcomes and/or processes. It is possible both to affirm an outcome or process on impartial grounds, and to recognise that it can only be brought about by actions that involve the pursuit of class interests in class struggle. It is possible, without inconsistency, to affirm an ethics, and to accept the class interests thesis, as above defined. No contradiction is contained in a statement of the form: it is necessary for the working-class to pursue its class interests in class struggle in order for justice, which requires structural socio-economic change, to be realised. The class interests argument is misconceived: practical recognition of the class interests thesis and of justice as a fundamental goal are not mutually exclusive.

---

26   Wood 1984, p. 19.
27   Wood 1984, p. 20.
28   Ibid.

Wood confuses a statement of condition with a statement of motivation. The class interests thesis, as formulated above, states a *condition* under which actions are historically effective ('only insofar as they involve ...'). It does not stipulate how historically effective actions are *motivated*. The class interests thesis says that structural socio-economic change cannot be brought about other than by means of the pursuit of class interests in class struggle. But it does not deny that people can engage in class struggle in order to realise what is impartially good. *If* the class interests thesis said: structural socio-economic change occurs only insofar as actors seek to realise class interests as particular interests; *then* it would deny that impartial considerations motivate historically effective actions. But that is not what the class interests thesis says.

Shortly after introducing the class interests thesis, Wood misrepresents what this thesis says. Having introduced the class interests thesis in the above terms, Wood says: 'according to the class interests thesis, no effective historical action ever takes the form of pursuing what is impartially or disinterestedly good'.[29] The class interests thesis does *not* say or imply this. By confusing this misrepresentation of the class interests thesis with the class interests thesis itself, Wood adopts a view of what Marxists believe for which Wood offers no argument.

Recall that the thought behind the objections to the ideology argument was that the ideology argument can at most give Marxists a reason to reject *some* moral arguments. A similar objection applies to the class interests argument. One can imagine *a* form of fundamental ethical concern that it would not be rational for historical agents who recognise the class interests thesis to share. But this form of fundamental ethical concern is not the only form of fundamental ethical concern.

Suppose that Marxist agents affirm an ethics that prizes a classless society, *but* this ethics also imposes constraints on action in the present that preclude any class-interest-pursuing, impartial-good-seeking strategy necessary to achieve a classless society. Marxist agents who treat *this* ethics as fundamental do refuse to be 'rational historical agents'. They are bound to fail to realise the goal that they prize, all because they knowingly refrain from the actions for bringing it about.

This is not the only way for Marxist agents to show a fundamental ethical concern, however. Marxist agents can show a form of fundamental ethical concern by combining two types of conduct: (i) prioritising participation in a class movement that aims to abolish class society, as the condition under

---

29   Ibid.

which a community *can* make justice a fundamental concern; (ii) choosing the course of action that an ethics recommends if two or more courses of action are each effective means of this movement, or if neither bears on its success. This form of fundamental ethical concern is consistent with Engels's remark in *Anti-Dühring* that communists struggle for a classless society in which a 'really human morality ... will first become possible'.[30]

To be sure, Wood raises a specific objection to the idea that Marxist agents can maintain the form of fundamental ethical concern suggested by Engels. In response to Engels's remark in *Anti-Dühring*, Wood claims that the moral principles of a future society are 'as unknowable by us as the scientific truths which will belong to some future theory which lies on the far side of the next major scientific revolution', and so they are 'not something available to us'.[31] This claim rests on the idea that moral principles concerning socio-economic structures cannot be known until they are implemented. As the moral principles of a classless society cannot be implemented until after capitalism is abolished, it follows that they are unknowable to agents in capitalism. A fundamental ethical concern on the part of agents in capitalism therefore cannot take the form of a commitment to a movement to realise a future classless society conceived of as moral, Wood objects. Such agents are not able to understand the principles behind any morality that a classless society may exhibit.

One problem with this objection, however, is that it conflicts with thinking about revolution that Wood correctly attributes to Marx, as distinct from Hegel. 'Hegel', Wood says, 'has a "great man" theory of history in the sense that he thinks that a new principle of spirit first shows itself through the action of individual political or military leaders', but 'they do not serve it intentionally'.[32] The principle of a new age 'cannot be grasped reflectively in its determinacy until much later in history, after it has been actualized'.[33] As, for Hegel, the normativity of a new order must remain unclear to contemporaries of the leaders through which it first shows itself, and these leaders act contrary to the principle of the existing order, it is impossible for revolutionary deeds to be appreciated in normative terms during the period of revolution itself. The place of justice is 'within the scope of an existing ethical order'.[34] On Hegel's view of history, Wood says, transformations initiated by world-historical individuals

---

30   *MEW*, 20, p. 88; *MECW*, 25, p. 88.
31   Wood 1991, p. 522.
32   Wood 1993, p. 430.
33   Ibid.
34   Wood 1993, p. 431.

'can never be self-transparent, since self-transparency is possible only for social forms that have reached maturity'.[35]

Marx's view of emancipatory social transformation departs from Hegel's view of history on this point. Marx states in his *Critique of Hegel's Doctrine of the State*: '[t]hat the rational is actual is proven by the contradiction of irrational reality'.[36] Normative principles are known to be valid if they are recognised to resolve contradictions in an existing social structure that precedes the one in which they can be implemented. This entails some insight into the nature of these principles themselves, prior to their implementation in a new order. Marx continues in this vein when, as a co-editor of the *Deutsch-Französische Jahrbücher*, he characterises 'the tendency of our journal in *one* word: the self-clarification (critical philosophy) of an age about its struggles and yearnings'.[37] Marx's *Economic and Philosophic Manuscripts of 1844* similarly say of communism that it is 'the riddle of history solved, and knows itself as this solution'.[38] *The Communist Manifesto* says of 'communists' that 'theoretically, they are in advance of the remaining mass of the proletariat in their insight into the conditions, course and general results of the proletarian movement'.[39] As Wood correctly observes of Marx's thinking on communist revolution in the latter passages, its 'revolutionary practice will be self-transparent'.[40] According to Marx, communist revolutionaries can achieve some insight into the nature and validity of the principles of structural socio-economic change that they advocate, prior to their actualisation in a new order.

This undermines Wood's claim, elsewhere in the same piece, that Marx and Hegel 'have similar attitudes to the role of right, morality, and ethical values in periods of radical change. Valid ethical principles depend on actual social structures'.[41] Marx and Hegel have *dissimilar* attitudes to the validity of ethical principles. At one point, Wood draws a distinction that can support the crux of this difference: the self-transparency of communist revolution. Wood says that people can have 'a rational knowledge of the fact that they are creating a new and higher social order' provided that self-transparency 'does not depend on a determinate conception of the social order they are creating'.[42] Wood relies

---

35   Wood 1993, p. 437.
36   *MEW*, 1, p. 266; *MECW*, 3, p. 63. On the translation of this phrase, see Furner 2018, pp. 54–5.
37   *MEW*, 1, p. 346; *MECW*, 3, p. 145.
38   *MEW*, 40, p. 536; *MECW*, 3, p. 297.
39   *MEW*, 4, p. 474; *MECW*, 6, p. 497.
40   Wood 1993, p. 438.
41   Wood 1993, p. 434.
42   Wood 1993, p. 440.

on this distinction when he affirms that Marx thought that communist revolution can be self-transparent, but ignores it when he denies that Marx's thinking on revolution differs from Hegel's. Wood's objection to Engels's remark in *Anti-Dühring* also ignores this distinction. If we retain the distinction, Wood is left with no objection to the form of ethical concern suggested by Engels's remark.

Let us recap on the three main points advanced thus far. First of all, Wood misrepresents the thesis he attributes to Marx, by confusing a statement of condition with a statement of motivation. Second, the class interests thesis is in fact compatible with a fundamental ethical concern. A rational historical agent is simply required to reject one form of fundamental ethical concern. Third, Wood's more specific objection to a form of fundamental ethical concern that the class interests argument itself does not discredit ignores the fact that (as Wood elsewhere recognises) Marx's thinking on revolution plausibly differs from Hegel's.

For all the class interests argument shows, Marxists can consistently affirm an ethics. All the class interests thesis implies is that the ethics that Marxists affirm must allow them to account for why present circumstances are not ones in which impartial considerations preclude a strategy necessary to achieve socialism. An ethics can do this, if it can support the judgments that capitalism is unjust and socialism is just. For if capitalism is unjust and socialism is just, the impartial reason to permit a strategy necessary for replacing capitalism with socialism is that strategies necessary to abolish injustices are permitted. A class struggle strategy necessary to achieve socialism is permitted, just as self-defence can excuse action necessary to repel a wrongful aggression, including action that would be wrong in the absence of a wrongful aggression.[43] Indeed, if capitalism is unjust and socialism is just, then there is an impartial (pro tanto) reason for regarding any strategy that replaces capitalism with socialism as permissible; namely, that strategies that abolish injustices are permitted.

---

43 To argue for the compatibility of the class interests thesis and an ethics, an impartial reason must be offered for the permissibility of a class struggle strategy that is viewed as necessary to achieve socialism (for example: strategies necessary to abolish injustices are permitted). However, it is not necessary, simply to establish this compatibility, to claim that no normative considerations can ever outweigh this reason. The class interests thesis says that *only* the pursuit of class interests in class struggle can succeed in transforming a socio-economic structure. It does not say that class interests must be pursued in class struggle *whenever* a transformation of the socio-economic structure will result, irrespective of the overall consequences. A rational historical agent who believes in a just cause is not committed to transform a socio-economic structure if this will lead to something more unjust.

We may add one final point that parallels an earlier objection to the ideology argument. The ideology argument, we said, is self-undermining, because its proponents are committed to regarding social conditions that promote rational self-transparency as good, from an impartial point of view. The class interests argument is also self-undermining, if it commits its proponents to affirm an impartial good. This is what Wood implicitly confesses.

The class interests argument appeals to what it is rational for historical agents to do, once they accept a certain view of how structural socio-economic change can come about. It therefore rests on a premise about rational historical agency. This premise, Wood says, is that 'we want (and rationally ought to want) a unified and harmonious conception of ourselves as historical agents'.[44] This premise suggests an impartial good.

To want a unified and harmonious conception of ourselves as historical agents is to want to be able to regard the various ways in which we contribute to shaping historical processes and events as accomplishments that we can affirm from a single standpoint, as reinforcing (rather than undermining) one another. It is 'rational' to want this, if it is rational to want to look positively on our achievements as amounting to something as a whole. But if it is rational for each of us to want this, that suggests a moral argument of the form: social arrangements that promote a unified and harmonious self-conception ought to be adopted, because they are in one way good for everyone. If proponents of the class interests argument are committed to Wood's premise, then they are committed to a form of moral argument.

A moral argument of this form can be used to defend socialism, if socialism realises the value of the autonomy of a human community. To realise this version of autonomy, co-legislated principles must expressly endorse a society's harmonious dynamics. The conditions of this autonomy are thus conditions that promote a unified and harmonious self-conception. For if social dynamics are harmonious and expressly recognised in the co-legislated principles of a public power, it is possible for all agents to enjoy a unified and harmonious self-conception. If, by contrast, social dynamics instead pit one aggressively competitive sub-group against another, a unified and harmonious self-conception can only be pursued at the expense of its enjoyment by others. As the class interests argument rests on a premise regarding rational agency that survives the objection to this argument, those tempted by the argument have a reason to look favourably on an ethics of the autonomy of a human community.

---

44   Wood 1984, p. 27.

5   Summary

These replies to the arguments for the irrelevance view carry certain commitments regarding the ethics that Marxists need. The reply to the instrumental reasons argument implies that this ethics includes the value of equality, and must be communicable publicly and sincerely. The reply to the false claims argument requires that it be communicated to the members of those social groups who can be expected to be influenced by it. These points are general enough that they require no further emphasis. By contrast, the commitments arising from the replies to the ideology argument and class interests argument are more specific. The reply to the ideology argument implies that the ethics that Marxists need must support at least one of the following two claims: (i) existing society ought to be revolutionised because the class oppression in it is in one way bad for everyone, or (ii) social arrangements that promote rational self-transparency ought to be adopted because false consciousness is in one way bad for everyone. The reply to the class interests argument implies that this ethics must be able to condemn capitalism as unjust and recommend socialism as just, so as not to preclude the adoption of a class struggle strategy necessary to achieve socialism.

Against the Complementarity View, Part 1: Socialist Strategy

In Chapter 1, we rejected the arguments for why Marxists do not need or should not adopt any ethics. It is a further question, however, where the ethics that Marxists need is to be found. The complementarity view says that the ethics that Marxists need is not part of Marxism, but is provided independently of Marxism, by Kant.

Like the irrelevance view, the complementarity view is a view about Marxism's relation to ethics. Even if most historical proponents of the complementarity view have affirmed both Marxism and Kant's ethics, it is not necessary to affirm either Marxism or Kant's ethics, to adopt the complementarity view.[1] Perhaps Kant's ethics condemns capitalism and justifies socialism, but it and/or Marxism is subject to fatal objections.

The need to discuss the complementarity view relates, once again, to the task of motivating a Marxist critique of Kant's ethics. A rebuttal of the irrelevance view will not persuade those who affirm the complementarity view of the rationale for a Marxist *critique* of Kant's ethics. On the complementarity view, any such critique is self-defeating. It can only undermine the ethics that Marxists need. We need to persuade those who regard Kant's ethics as satisfying Marxists' need for an ethics that Kant's ethics and Marxism are incompatible.

The complementarity view is undermined, if it leads to contradiction. It leads to contradiction if it requires a Marxist to take an ethical position that contradicts a thesis that unquestionably belongs to Marxism. The claim defended in this chapter is that combining Kant's ethics with Marxism produces a contradiction in socialist strategy. The socialist strategy flowing from the timeless nature of Kant's grounding arguments for the formulas of the categorical imperative contradicts the socialist strategy flowing from the Marxist view of the role of class struggle. If so, it is contradictory for a Marxist to affirm Kant's ethics, and a Marxist critique of Kant's ethics cannot be resisted as self-defeating.

Challenging the complementarity view in this way provides a chance to highlight the origin of the suggestion that Marxists display a problematic atti-

---

1   One example is Chojnacki 1924.

tude to the idea of justice. The roots of this suggestion appear to reach back
to interpretations of Marx's writings published shortly after Engels's death, by
philosophers indebted to Kant in their conception of ethics.

1   The Complementarity View: Stammler, Staudinger, Vorländer

First of all, we must sketch how, on the complementarity view, Marxism and
Kant's ethics complement one another. According to the complementarity
view, Kant's ethics is just the type of ethics that Marxists need to justify their
condemnation of capitalism and defence of socialism. Marxism itself has no
ethics, on the complementarity view, because it is a non-normative theory of
history. It is just a tool of causal explanation. As a theory of history that is more
or less deterministic, Marxism includes a claim of the form that it is necessary,
or likely, or possible, that capitalism will be replaced by socialism. But Marxism
does not just for this reason also include the claim that it is *good* to replace capitalism with socialism. Marxism tells us *that* socialism will (definitely or likely
or possibly) be brought about, *why* it will be brought about, and *how* it will be
brought about (if it is brought about). But it does not *justify* the replacement of
capitalism by socialism, that is, say why socialism *ought* to be brought about.[2]
On the complementarity view, Marxists need Kant's ethics to supply this normative argument.

The distinction between these two viewpoints, the one purely causal and
the other normative, is emphasised by the neo-Kantian Rudolf Stammler in
Wirtschaft und Recht nach der materialistischen Geschichtsauffassung (*Economy and Law in the Materialist Conception of History*) (1896). According to
Stammler, 'the materialist conception of history ... provides, in its logically
purified and conceptually clarified form, a suitable general method for sup-
plying the *material* of social experience'.[3] However, Stammler continues, 'if
the method of social materialism provides only the material, and not its lawful determination in terms of a basic law of social life, a social movement
that is *objectively justified* in its content cannot be supported by it *alone*'.[4] The
normative justification of the content of a social movement requires a critical
exposition of a 'universally valid goal' of social life, or '*universally valid formal
principle*',[5] against which the validity of this content can be assessed. According

---

2   Stammler 1896, pp. 478–9; Chojnacki 1924, p. 69.
3   Stammler 1896, p. 482.
4   Stammler 1896, p. 483.
5   Stammler 1896, p. 465.

to Stammler, this exposition falls outside the bounds of Marxism, understood as a causal account of history. Stammler describes the required exposition in Kantian terms, as the exposition of an objective and a priori final end:

> *Ought* denotes merely a scientific insight into the possible unity in the determination of the end and into the subjectively unconditioned final end as the moment that constitutes the lawfulness of the individual representations of ends. In the moral law there is, in itself, nothing of empirical effect.[6]

A similar distinction informs Franz Staudinger's explicit plea to combine Marx with Kant in *Ethik und Politik* (1899):

> both endeavours are merely sides of a single indivisible unity. Only when we possess scientific insight into the connection of causes and effects can we form ends. And only when we know the law of end-formation as the law of unity, and submit ourselves only to it even in our ultimate strivings, is the purposeful application of that knowledge possible. Insight into the law of end-formation rests on the studies of Kant; insight into the laws of previous economic development, on the studies of Marxism.

> As long as Marxism studies social evolution scientifically, according to the causal point of view, it is of service, and is always able to correct possible errors through a scientifically unified method. But as soon as it adopts the *conscious and methodical* transformation of what is given as its aim, it cannot find the criterion for this in its causal evolution. Marxism thus runs into the danger of confusing particular ends, such as the socialisation of production, with the abiding end of a unified regulation of the human community; and it thereby confounds, in eclectic fashion, the methods of the old ethics with the methods of its own ethics. As soon as Marxism becomes aware of this, it is led, through the consistent pursuit of its own principle, to Kant.

> And contrariwise, the Kantian must find himself in an internal conflict if he derives rights and duties immediately from the abstract law of unity. For while he can then present them as beautiful ideals, he cannot make them fruitful for the praxis of life. The laws of end-formation are an empty

---

6 Stammler 1896, p. 376.

schema once the natural laws of everyday life do not provide the foundation. As soon as the Kantian sees this clearly, he is led by the consistent
development of his own fundamental thoughts to Marx.[7]

Relatedly, Karl Vorländer writes in *Kant und Marx* (1911):

The basic assumption of Marx and Engels 'that the development of
human society is necessarily conditioned by economic development, and,
in societies with various opposed classes, by the class struggle that arises
from economic relations' (as per Kautsky's formulation) seems to me
to bear a thoroughly scientific character. Similarly, there can be just as
little objection, from a scientific standpoint, to the fact of the application
of this hypothesis to the study of the laws of development and laws of
motion of the existing mode of production ...

But now to what, in our view, is the crux of the whole problem, which also
returns us to Kantian philosophy. We have in mind the thought – which is
really the animating one for Bernstein as well, but which has yet to receive
a correct solution from him – that *socialism is not entirely resolved into natural science* (in the widest sense of the word), i.e. *into the genetic-causal
explanation of what exists* or *conjecture about the future*. Socialism, in our
opinion too, can never be grounded entirely sufficiently, with unconditioned necessity, *simply* by means of the natural-scientific method. For
socialism in fact carries within itself, whether it is aware of it or not, an
element – not, as Bernstein says, of speculative idealism, for that arouses
the thought of an unscientific metaphysics – of *rational purposeful willing*. The basic mistake that Bernstein and most of his socialist critics make
is that they restrict the name and concept of science one-sidedly to causal
explanation. The will is excluded from the sphere of what is 'scientifically identifiable'. 'Systems of demands are not sciences'. To achieve his
aims, Bernstein admittedly requires 'the directing guidance of a science
of the powers and interconnections of the social organism, of cause and
effect in social life'; but the aim itself is not to be grounded scientifically.
The greatness of what Kant's philosophy has achieved for us, however, is

---

7   Staudinger 1899, p. 159. Vorländer repeatedly cites parts of this passage, and expresses his
    agreement with it; see Vorländer 1900, p. 31; Vorländer 1911, p. 144; and Vorländer 1920, p. 42.
    The sentiment expressed in the middle paragraph is echoed in John Dewey's reply to Trotsky;
    see Dewey 1973, pp. 70–1.

precisely to have demonstrated, very methodically, another point of view besides the mathematical-physical point of view of *why?* It has shown that rational volition, the *where to?*, the realm of ends, also admits of a lawfulness *of its own*, and hence also allows of an independent, scientific treatment.[8]

According to the above authors, Marxism is only one part of the theory that socialists need. Marxism is a tool for studying causes and effects in social life. It offers a conceptual apparatus that directs our attention to economic factors as the causes of effects. It uncovers the economic facts that explain why, for example, the legal order is as it is, or why common moral judgments are as they are. Engels's claim that 'socialism became a science' through Marx's two 'great discoveries' of the 'materialist conception of history' and 'the revelation of the secret of the capitalist production through surplus value'[9] is a likely influence on these authors' understanding of Marxism.[10] To value Marx's writings for these two achievements, it is not necessary to see in Marxism anything more than the study of empirical fact. But for the above authors, socialists need more than this. They need an ethics that justifies, in normative terms, the socialist society that they aim to bring about.

For the above authors, the contribution of Kant's ethics to socialism is that Kant's ethics provides a basis for arguing that the law ought to be used to institute a socialist form of production. The occasions on which laws are decided are as subject to moral duty as any other occasions; and, if the law is used to replace

---

8   Vorländer 1911, pp. 186–7, citing Kautsky 1901, p. 359 and Bernstein 1901, p. 22, pp. 35–6; see, similarly, Vorländer 1920, p. 42. Vorländer's judgment in the second edition of *Kant und Marx* (Vorländer 1926, p. 282) is the same. Vorländer's critical view of Bernstein is instructive, as Anglophone Marxist literature tends to associate attempts to combine Marxism and neo-Kantian ethics with 'Eduard Bernstein's revisionism' as well as 'Austro-Marxism' (Callinicos 2006, p. 221). Stammler, Staudinger and Vorländer – whose main works remain untranslated into English – do not really belong to either trend. Their writings, along with those of Hermann Cohen and Paul Natorp, provide the focus of Pierre Chojnacki's dissertation on Kant's ethics and socialist ethics (Chojnacki 1924). In German language scholarship, Staudinger and Vorländer are considered the '"red Kantians"' (Grau 2017, p. 124). For a critique of Vorländer's attempt to synthesise Kant and Marx, see Giesecke 1991, pp. 167–203.

9   *MEW*, 19, p. 209; *MECW*, 24, p. 305; and *MEW*, 20, p. 26; *MECW*, 25, p. 27.

10   Engels's claim is questionable, because it raises the question as to where exactly in Marx's writings we are to find the kind of *systematic* presentation and defence of a 'materialist conception of history' that alone could justify the claim that socialism became a science through Marx's discovery of it; see Chojnacki 1924, p. 55. A preface – such as Marx's 1859 Preface to *A Contribution to a Critique of Political Economy* – hardly qualifies.

capitalist production with a socialist form of production, agents will be better enabled to conform to the moral law. In other words, they will be better enabled to act at least with what Kant called '*legality*', as distinct from morality.[11] Hence, the law ought to be used to replace capitalism with socialism. Kant's ethics is held to ground this 'ought', while Marx's theory of history is said to explain the succession of social forms of production in history and their conditions, and so to explain when and on account of what social mechanisms the application of the moral law requires socialism.

2   An Objection to the Complementarity View

Even on the complementarity view, there are limits on how Kant's ethics and the Marxist theory of history can combine. Considered together, the nature of these limits suggests an objection to the complementarity view.

There are two limits to focus on. The first limit is a limit on what Marxism is taken to be able to say regarding morality. Understood as an approach to the empirical study of causes and effects, Marxism can include an explanation of why particular moral judgments are held at a given time and place. But what it cannot include, according to the complementarity view, is an explanation of the validity of any categorically binding imperative which is regarded as timeless. The second limit is a limit on what it is about socialism that Kant's ethics is taken to justify. Its service is to ground a categorical imperative to which action may or may not conform, such that a fully constructed socialist society can be presented as a condition for promoting action that at least conforms to morality. This is a moral defence of socialism, and only indirectly a defence of the movement for socialism. In Staudinger's terms, it is a defence of the 'rights and duties'[12] that regulate a human community in which production is socialised. It is a defence of what Stammler refers to as the 'content'[13] or goal of a socialist movement, not this movement itself. It stops short of directly justifying a strategy by which socialists can assume the power to institute a socialist form of production.

---

11   The distinction is drawn at *KpV*, 5: 71: '[i]f the determination of the will, although occurring *in conformity with* the moral law, does so only by means of a feeling – of whatever kind – that must be presupposed in order for that law to become a sufficient determining basis of the will, and hence does not occur *on account of the law*, then the action will indeed contain *legality* but not *morality*'.

12   Staudinger 1899, p. 159; see above. Vorländer's defence of socialism is discussed in Chapter 3.

13   Stammler 1896, p. 483; a fuller statement is cited above.

These two limits suggest the following problem: how can the view that socialism is to be brought about by class struggle, by an alliance led by the working-class against the capitalist class, not be compromised by a justification of socialism in terms of a categorical imperative that is grounded by a timeless argument, and that therefore constrains, no less than any other action, action against groups that obstruct the passage to the society that this imperative recommends? If the timelessly grounded categorical imperative that justifies socialism applies with exactly the same stringency to the antagonistic context in which mobilisation for socialism takes place, might it not rule out the class-interest-pursuing, impartial-good-seeking actions that Marxists regard as necessary for bringing socialism about?

The focus of this problem differs from the focus of the ideology and class interests arguments for the irrelevance view, examined in Chapter 1. Both of the latter focused on the tension between class oppression or class interests, and the *impartial* nature of moral arguments. Of present concern is not a tension between class struggle and the impartial quality of the moral law, but between class struggle and the *timeless* quality of Kant's grounding arguments for the formulas of the categorical imperative. As these grounding arguments do not rest on facts about a form of society, they do not rest on any facts that could qualify their application to a context of class antagonism any more than to any other context.

The problem is significant, because it is an essential thesis of Marxism that class struggle is the key mechanism by which one form of society is replaced by another. *The Communist Manifesto* begins: 'the history of all hitherto society is the history of class struggles'.[14] In particular, Marx envisages that a working-class movement will be essential to the abolition of capitalism and the construction of socialism. *The Communist Manifesto* ends: '*workers of all countries, unite!*'.[15] If Kant's ethics and Marxism are truly complementary, then the agency implications of Kant's grounding arguments for the formulas of the categorical imperative must be consistent with the role that Marxists assign to working-class struggle in the achievement of socialism.

Indeed, Marxists see themselves as actively relating to the class struggle that brings socialism about. They see themselves as offering ideas and resources to participants in a working-class movement that strengthen their resolve, and form an effective socialist strategy. This imposes a test on any moral defence of socialism that they can consistently adopt. If an ethical theory unambiguously

---

14   *MEW*, 4, p. 462; *MECW*, 6, p. 482.

15   *MEW*, 4, p. 493; *MECW*, 6, p. 519.

condemns capitalism and justifies socialism, it must be possible to conceive of actors in capitalism who adopt it and who act to bring socialism about because they agree with it. The test imposed on any ethics that Marxists are to adopt, in light of how they see themselves as relating to a working-class movement for socialism, is as follows. Is the action that socialists perform if Kant's ethics inspires them to bring socialism about in line with the action that socialists perform in the Marxist belief that class struggle brings socialism about?

This is not a test that Stammler, Staudinger (at least in *Ethik und Politik*) or Vorländer pose. But judging by the foregoing passage from Vorländer's *Kant und Marx*, it is not a test that they could dismiss. Vorländer grants that it is one of the basic assumptions of Marxism that historical development occurs by means of class struggle. If this is granted, then, to seek to combine Marxism with Kant's ethics, a process by which Kant's ethics motivates a transition to socialism must be conceived of as consistent with a process by which class struggle brings socialism about. The objection to the complementarity view, however, is that it cannot pass this test. The agency implications of Kant's timeless grounding arguments for the formulas of the categorical imperative, and the Marxist focus on working-class struggle as a key agent of socialism, are out of line.

We may say a bit more, at this point, about what makes a grounding argument timeless. A timeless grounding argument is a grounding argument that is either entirely a priori, or else whose only appeal to empirical facts about human beings is to empirical facts about human beings that are true throughout human history. In either case, no facts about a specific historical context are appealed to, to ground the value. No claims about a historically specific form of society need to be advanced, to know what value is ethically valid. Stammler insists on the timelessness of any grounding argument for an ultimate value when he claims: 'unity in the sense of the unconditioned fundamental thought of all social regulation cannot be supplied by history'.[16] Or as Gotthold Ephraim Lessing put it in *On the Proof of the Spirit and of Power* (1777): '*contingent truths of history can never become proofs of necessary truths of reason*'.[17] Staudinger and Vorländer share this view in the passages cited above when they take Kant to reveal the 'law of end-formation' as an 'abstract law of unity'[18] or claim that Kant provides a 'scientific treatment' of 'rational volition'.[19] It is this view of

---

16   Stammler 1914, p. 467, improving on the formulation in the first edition, at Stammler 1896, p. 481.

17   Lessing 1777, p. 9; Lessing 2005, p. 85, paraphrased at Stammler 1896, p. 469.

18   Staudinger 1899, p. 159.

19   Vorländer 1911, p. 187.

what a grounding argument must look like that also appears to lie behind G.A. Cohen's belief that 'historical materialism ... ha[s] nothing to say about what justice (timelessly) is'.[20]

The timelessness of a timeless grounding argument is thus a characterisation of the a priori or general nature of the considerations that are offered for accepting an ultimate value. It is not, directly, a characterisation of the time for which the value is valid, although it clearly has implications for this. If the grounding argument for a value is timeless, its application will also be timeless. In other words, it will apply either to all rational beings, or else to all human beings throughout history. It will not apply only to one specific form of society. By contrast, if the grounding argument for a value is not timeless, then it is hard to see how it could apply timelessly. Suppose, for argument's sake, that there were impeccable grounds to accept that our highest moral duty is to execute God's will, and that these grounds appealed to a miracle that was said to have occurred at a particular place and time. Such an argument would not be timeless, in the current sense. It could also not establish that the moral duty of all human beings is always to execute God's will. It could hardly ground this duty in the case of human beings who lived and died before the miracle was alleged to have occurred.

A timeless grounding argument for a moral principle has implications for moral agency that are summarised well by Jean-Paul Sartre's remark (with Kant in mind) in *Notebooks for an Ethics* that in 'bourgeois ethics ... moral activity is held to be independent of historical circumstances. It is pure positivity and can occur anywhere'.[21] If the grounding argument for a moral principle is timeless, then the determination of a moral agent's will in acting morally is also timeless. In Kant's case, an agent's will is morally determined if it determines itself a priori, purely out of respect for the moral law. If so, no historical or social circumstance can be thought to preclude moral action. Any agent, no matter their circumstance, can always act morally, by applying a formula of the categorical imperative over all empirical grounds. But if no circumstance can be thought to preclude moral action, then any one agent is as bound by the categorical imperative as any other. Any agent who lives in circumstances which must be strongly disvalued, in terms of the categorical imperative, is as bound by it as any agent who lives in circumstances more conducive to it. So, a moral agent is fully bound by a timelessly grounded categorical imperative even when it puts them under an obligation to remove a state of affairs unconducive to mor-

---

20   Cohen 1995, p. 3.
21   Sartre 1983, p. 173; Sartre 1992, p. 165.

ality. In being fully bound by this imperative, a moral agent is bound not just to remove this disvalued state of affairs, but also to positively conform to this imperative in any action to remove it. This may preclude action to remove a disvalued state of affairs, if the obligation to conform to a categorical imperative even in a course of action to remove a disvalued state of affairs rules out a strategy that is necessary to remove it.

The constraints imposed by Kant's timelessly grounded categorical imperative preclude the class struggle strategy that Marxists see as necessary to achieve socialism. A socialist who holds that Kant's ethics justifies socialism is led, by Kant's a priori grounding argument for the Formula of the End in Itself, to proselytise for socialism in a way that respects all rational beings: '[s]o act that you use humanity, in your own person as well as in the person of any other, always at the same time as an end, never merely as a means'.[22] This formula need not require a Kantian socialist to treat members of the capitalist class as ends by promoting their happiness in their capacity as capitalists, *if* it can condemn capitalism. We are not obliged to aid others in their achievement of immoral ends. But even if so, it still requires a Kantian socialist never to treat themselves or others merely as means. This principle precludes not just lying[23] (even to a professional hierarchy of clever liars) but also tailoring demands, or a strategy, to short-lived vulnerabilities or weaknesses of members of an otherwise powerful and wealthy class.[24] By contrast, a socialist guided by a Marxist belief in class struggle cannot see a barrier here.[25] To aid a working-class movement for socialism through class struggle constitutively involves disrupting or blunting the initiatives of the capitalist class, including by playing on its members' vulnerabilities or weaknesses. The two approaches are strategically out of line.

It is to Staudinger's credit that he came to recognise this. As we have seen, *Ethik und Politik* (1899) offers a defence of the complementarity view. Staudinger there suggests that Marxism and Kant's ethics can be combined, to mutual benefit; in particular, that Kant's studies reveal the 'law of end-formation' as an 'abstract law of unity'.[26] But in a later work, *Wirtschaftliche Grundlagen der Moral* (*Economic Foundations of Morality*) (1907), Staudinger changes

---

22   *GMS*, 4: 429.

23   *MS*, 6: 430–1.

24   Compare the discussion of the vulnerability argument in ch. 3.

25   Socialists should be 'very pleased', Trotsky implies, to see 'how the workers arose … and caught their exploiters unawares' (Trotsky 1973, p. 41). He adds that '[t]he life-and-death struggle is unthinkable without military craftiness, in other words, without lying and deceit. May the German proletariat then not deceive Hitler's police?' (Trotsky 1973, p. 44).

26   Staudinger 1899, p. 159.

tack. In this work, Staudinger claims that '[m]*orality is only actual and possible insofar as community exists*'.[27] Relatedly, Staudinger criticises Kant in the following terms:

> Kant's essential, fundamental mistake consists in this. His categorical imperative does not say: act so that an always more complete community is produced; but rather: 'so act that the maxim of your will could always hold at the same time as a principle of a universal legislation' ... he requires simply that one ask, for every action, whether, if thought universally, it conforms to the principle of a universal legislation ...

> The worst thing about this is that even Kant's moral demand is exquisitely suited, by its rigidity, to become a shackle morality. The domineering man can do what he wants with me when he knows that I am chained by a tie of conscience to such morality.[28]

This prompts Staudinger to remark in respect of the 'rule for community-based human coexistence' that

> When this rule is abstracted, and tied around our decision of the will as a leash even where no relation of community is present, and where it perhaps hinders our aim of community, there it is an alarming imprisonment of man.[29]

If the moral law applies whether or not human beings stand in relations of community to one another, then, Staudinger reasons, those who seek to bring community about will be hindered from doing so by the morally unscrupulous, who use others' virtuous characters to trap them in situations where they can be taken advantage of.[30] This recalls Marx's remark in an article on Lord Palmerston for the *Neue Oder-Zeitung*:

> 'Clever' is an untranslatable property, full of ambiguity and rich in connotations. It embraces all the qualities of a man who knows his own

---

27   Staudinger 1907, p. 10.
28   Staudinger 1907, pp. 87–88, citing *KpV*, 5: 30.
29   Staudinger 1907, p. 90.
30   Staudinger extends this criticism to the ethics of Hermann Cohen; see Staudinger 1906, p. 322.

appeal, and who understands his own advantage as keenly as others' loss. Moral and respectable as the English bourgeois is, he still admires above all the man who is 'clever'; who, unperturbed by morality, and undeceived by respect, regards principles as traps in which to ensnare his neighbour.[31]

Staudinger therefore concludes:

> In practice, Kant's morality in its entirety is therefore useless, suited at most as a moral shackle for those who have already grown out of the religious shackle. To make Kant's moral law useful, a correlate must be added that displays to human beings the community itself as the foundation, and says: where community links you with other human beings, act on Kant's imperative; but where there is as yet no community, seek to create it.[32]

Kant's formulas of the categorical imperative rely on value conceptions that do not survive the revision that Staudinger seeks, however. As, for Kant, freedom of the will is its determination a priori, Kant is unable to insist that a social condition, such as relations of community, must first be brought about before moral action can occur. If an ethics only fully applies on the condition that relations of community prevail, its grounding argument will not be timeless. Staudinger's criticisms of Kant in *Wirtschaftliche Grundlagen der Moral* thus mark out a *post-*Kantian direction of thought. No longer are socialists urged to combine Kant's ethics and Marxism, as the complementarity view holds. Rather, socialists are urged to combine Marxism with a more conditional ethics that nevertheless retains some features of Kant's ethics. This may make Staudinger, for Marxists, the most interesting of the ' "red Kantians" '[33] in this period, but only insofar as Staudinger distances himself from his earlier advocacy of the complementarity view.

The complementarity view is subject to an objection of contradictory strategies. It is a core Marxist thesis that class struggle is key to bringing socialism about. Marxists see their primary practical task as that of offering ideas and resources to a working-class movement in its confrontation with a powerful and hostile ruling class. The complementarity view holds that Marxists have a reason to endorse Kant's ethics, to be able to condemn capitalism and jus-

---

31   *MEW*, 11, p. 92; *MECW*, 14, p. 50.
32   Staudinger 1907, pp. 90–1.
33   Grau 2017, p. 124.

tify socialism. Yet this creates a problem, stemming from the fact that Kant's ethics is an ethics with timeless grounding arguments. Insofar as Marxists adopt Kant's ethics, they will be led, by the implications of its timeless grounding arguments, away from what, as Marxists, they must see as their primary practical task. The socialist strategy arising from Kant's ethics is incompatible with the socialist strategy arising from Marxism. The former is constrained to treat all existing human beings with equal respect regardless of the goal to be achieved, while the latter is to promote class-interest-pursuing, impartial-good-seeking actions by a working-class movement to weaken a conniving capitalist class. As Kant's ethics and Marxism imply incompatible strategies in pursuit of the socialist cause, they are not complementary.

This objection to the complementarity view does not deny Marxists' need for an ethics. It is compatible with a rejection of the irrelevance view. Nor does it put up an insurmountable barrier to the formulation of an ethics that suits Marxists' needs. The objection implies that a Marxist can adopt an ethics, *provided* that its grounding argument for an ultimate value is not timeless, but appeals to a fact (or facts) about capitalism. A grounding argument may appeal to such facts, if it can be shown that capitalism is a necessary form of society for human freedom, such that we are bound to think about freedom in terms that resolve an irrationality that it contains. If the requirement to resolve this irrationality commits agents to a negative principle with which to condemn an existing state of affairs, and if an ultimate value is grounded only because it must be thought to underlie this principle, its grounding argument may allow that action to remove a disvalued state of affairs need not be bound to exhibit the value positively. In this way, a non-timeless grounding argument may commit agents to transform an existing society without committing them, in its transformation, to uphold all the standards of ethical conduct exhibited in the ethically best society. Such an argument may justify class-interest-pursuing, impartial-good-seeking actions to promote socialism, without imposing positive duties that preclude it.

To argue that the grounding argument of an ethics need not be timeless is *not* to deny the distinction between causal and normative viewpoints. Rather, it is the lack of sensitivity to the fact that these two issues are distinct – the difference between a causal and a normative viewpoint, and the timelessness or not of a grounding argument – that is the problem.

To highlight this problem, consider a pair of remarks by the Catholic philosopher Theodor Steinbüchel in *Der Sozialismus als sittliche Idee* (*Socialism as an Ethical Idea*) (1921), which examines the work of Stammler, Staudinger, Vorländer and others. In the first, Steinbüchel describes what he refers to as the 'dualism in the justification' of socialism offered by these thinkers:

For the purely causal course of history is, as such, ethically entirely neutral, and nor can it give any cause to an ethical evaluation. The judgment of the aim of this social process proceeds from an entirely other point of view, from the standpoint of the ethical ideal.[34]

There is little to object to in this remark. The fact that X follows Y in history is no reason for thinking that X is good or better than Y. Hence, no claim about the historical inevitability of the fact that X will follow Y can provide a normative justification of X. Even if, for the sake of argument, we suppose that it is inevitable that socialism will replace capitalism, it does not follow just from this that it is *good* that socialism will replace capitalism. To this extent, causal and normative viewpoints are distinct.

It does not follow from their distinction, however, that the standards belonging to a normative viewpoint are justified by a timeless grounding argument. Steinbüchel makes this assumption when, in explanation of 'how little the materialist conception of history can deal adequately with ethics', Steinbüchel remarks:

> While it may be commendable to identify the historically conditioned nature of ethical standards of value, this service is only ever a preparation for the ethical evaluation itself, which now begins to apply, to historical ethical intuitions, ideals and norms, its standards of value, which are won by entirely other means than by historical observation.[35]

The complementarity view rests on a strict separation of history and ethics. It holds not only that normative justification is distinct from historical sequence/inevitability, but also that the standards of normative justification are grounded by a timeless argument. It assumes that any ethical evaluation employs 'standards of value, which are won by entirely other means than by historical observation'. Among socialists, this attitude to the relation of history to ethics is perhaps a reaction to the mistaken belief that socialism's historical inevitability proves its moral superiority. But to avoid the normative error in this mistaken belief, it suffices to acknowledge that statements of fact differ from statements of value, and that no statement of value can be inferred *merely* from statements of fact. It is not necessary to insist that the standards employed in normative argument are grounded *without* appeal to statements of fact.

---

34   Steinbuchel 1921, pp. 156–7.
35   Steinbuchel 1921, p. 150.

To be sure, a grounding argument must appeal to some general starting point, some rational requirement on everyone who is to be obligated by the principle that is to be grounded. This general starting point cannot, therefore, include facts about a specific form of society *if* it is to ground a principle that is to obligate all rational agents throughout history, including those rational agents who lived prior to this form of society. But a normative theory need not set out to ground a principle that is to obligate every rational agent (of human history). John Rawls's theory of justice as fairness is one example. Rawls offers his theory specifically for the human subjects of a liberal society. Its 'content', Rawls says, is to be 'seen as implicit in the public political culture of a liberal society'.[36] Marxists have no need for an ethics that obligates everyone in human history. In the Marxist view, Marxism only became possible at a certain stage of history, once capitalist production was underway.[37] So, even if Marxists have always required an ethics, they have never required a normative principle of such range that it had to be grounded by an argument that avoids appeal to facts about capitalism. The starting point of the grounding argument for the ethics that Marxists need is sufficiently general, even if it rests on general facts about capitalism.

3 The Deficient Self-Understanding Claim: A Critique

The above critique of the complementarity view provides an opportunity to highlight the origin of the suggestion that Marxists display a problematic attitude to justice. It is said that, in practice, Marxists often condemn capitalism on normative grounds; and yet Marxists believe that they do not offer normative arguments. As a result, Marxists deny that they do in fact condemn capitalism on normative grounds. As such, in respect of the idea of justice, Marxists suffer from 'deficient self-understanding'.[38] Indeed, for G.A. Cohen, 'Marx did not always realize that he thought capitalism was unjust'.[39] Norman Geras later popularised this view: 'Marx did think capitalism was unjust but he did

---

36   Rawls 1993, p. 37.
37   Marx writes in *Capital* Volume I: 'The secret of the expression of value ... can only be deciphered once the concept of human equality already possesses the firmness of a popular prejudice. But that is only possible in a society in which the commodity form is the general form of the product of labour, hence also where the relation of human beings to one another as commodity possessors is the dominant social relation' (*MEW*, 23, p. 74; *MECW*, 35, p. 70; Marx 1976, p. 152).
38   Cohen 1981, p. 12.
39   Cohen 1983, p. 444; see, also, Cohen 2013, p. 12.

not think he thought so'.[40] A significant number of commentators have since endorsed Cohen's or Geras's claim,[41] or articulated their own version of it.[42]

The foregoing discussion suggests that this is an understandable suggestion to make, as soon as it is assumed both that Marxists offer a causal theory of history that assigns importance to class struggle, and that any normative theory rests on a timeless grounding argument, which must trouble a class-based strategy to achieve the good society. For on these assumptions, if Marxists recognise that their condemnations of capitalism and recommendations of socialism (which their revolutionary activities lead them to offer, for the reasons outlined in response to the instrumental reasons argument for the irrelevance view)[43] presuppose a normative theory, then they must find that the grounding argument of any such theory is timeless. If a timeless grounding argument must invite a doubt in regard to a class struggle strategy for achieving socialism, Marxists' search for a basis for the normative views that they express must lead them to withdraw from normative theory, and to deny that they express the normative views that they express.

As these assumptions were widespread among socialists at the turn of the twentieth century, the deficient self-understanding claim does not – contrary to their self-understanding – originate with Cohen and Geras. It originates from the same historical context that gave rise to the complementarity view. In the year immediately following Friedrich Engels's death in 1895, Stammler argued:

> It is not without interest to establish how, at the slightest attempt to elaborate on and present its thoughts more exactly, the doctrine of the materialist conception of history is pushed, involuntarily and on occasion even contrary to its intention, in the direction of *teleological* considerations and onto the basis of the fundamental law that is valid in the social *pursuit of ends* ...

> Marx – without really wanting to – moves entirely onto the sphere of teleological considerations in recognising, as justified social endeavours, those that are based on the firm decision to consciously follow a recognised development. Yet he still claims to have kept to a consistent social

---

40   Geras 1985, p. 70, repeated in Geras 1992, p. 65.
41   Callinicos 2013, p. 275; Lukes 1982, p. 197; Nielsen 1989, p. 119; Peffer 1990, p. 339; Rawls 2007, p. 336; Reiman 1991, p. 148; Wood 1989, p. 78.
42   Elster 1983, p. 290; Gilabert 2017, p. 563; Leopold 2007, p. 156; Lukes 1982, p. 197; Schwartz 1995, p. 164.
43   See ch. 1., sec. 1.

materialism that recognises nothing other than causal observation as scientific. That is a misapprehension.[44]

Marx, Stammler suggests, evaluates working-class attempts to hasten the abolition of private property as justified social endeavours; and yet Marx still thinks of his studies as operating from a purely causal viewpoint.[45] These remarks in Stammler's *Wirtschaft und Recht* (1896) may well be the earliest statement of the deficient self-understanding claim.

Similar comments can be found in Ludwig Woltmann's *Der historische Materialism* (1900). In respect of whether 'Marxism' has an 'ethical foundation', Woltmann says:

> One should not be led into error in this respect by the contrary statements of Marxists and even by Marx's mode of presentation. The apparently tendentious and often ironic dismissal of all ethical reflections is provoked by the shallow moral prescriptions of opponents. In the heart of Marx's philosophy glows the pure flame of a higher human morality that constantly attempts to break through the outer shell of the presentation with the powerful force of enlightenment and liberation.[46]

In *Ethik des reinen Willens* (*Ethics of the Pure Will*) (1904), Hermann Cohen argues in the same vein:

> It may certainly be the case that, in fervour and indignation over a hypocritical use of ethical ideas, one points to unethical power relations, in order to uncover in them the driving force of previous history. But then it would not be materialism, but a reticent idealism, that guides this view of history.[47]

> When, from its high historical vantage point, the socialism of *Marx* seeks to make vivid the compelling power of material circumstances, he unintentionally turns into a satirist. The ethical fiery spirit drives all his great achievements, both the theoretical and the practical.[48]

---

44   Stammler 1896, p. 430.
45   Stammler 1896, p. 431.
46   Woltmann 1900, p. 367.
47   Cohen 1904, pp. 34–5.
48   Cohen 1904, p. 296.

Leonard Nelson says in lectures on Kant's *Critique of Practical Reason*, published in 1917:

> And indeed, it is only on account of the ethical deficiency of the prevailing exploitation and disenfranchisement of the working-class in the capitalist economic order that the MARXist wishes for the greatest possible acceleration of the process of dissolution of this economic form, and so, too, the most uninhibited exacerbation of class conflicts. The theory of the natural necessity of this economic process is, in the MARXist's case, merely the belated attempt to provide an economic basis for the ethical idea that guides him, because he lacks the confidence to ground it as such scientifically.[49]

We may also add the Ph.D. dissertation of Pierre Chojnacki, entitled *Die Ethik Kants and die Ethik des Sozialismus* (1924) (*The Ethics of Kant and the Ethics of Socialism*). It concludes:

> If we have described socialism's method of justification as 'amoral', then we do not thereby intend to deny that it contains ethical leanings beneath the surface, so to speak. The socialism of Marx and Engels operates with the concept of justice; it criticises the degradation of the worker into a tool of work, or means, and struggles against this. It sets as its aim an 'association, in which the free development of each is a condition for the free development of all'. The ethical quality of these endeavours cannot be disputed. But the fundamental inconsistency of 'scientific' socialism also cannot be overlooked, for these ethical concepts constitute 'a real remnant of utopianism in Marx's system'.[50]

None of the afore-cited works have been translated into English. Presumably, neither Cohen nor Geras acknowledge them as precursors because they were unaware of them. These passages do not just clarify that the deficient self-understanding claim that they put forward is far from new, however. They also suggest its premises. The deficient self-understanding claim is popular, because – for reasons having nothing to do with Marx interpretation – a premise about normative judgments is popular; namely, that normative judg-

---

49   Nelson 1917, p. 35.
50   Chojnacki 1924, p. 138, quoting *MEW*, 4, p. 482; *MECW*, 6, p. 506, and Bernstein 1899, p. 177; Bernstein 1993, p. 199.

ments rest on an ethics whose validity is grounded by a timeless grounding argument.

In support of this last suggestion, consider the drawbacks of G.A. Cohen's own explanation for what he takes to be the Marxist attitude of deficient self-understanding. In a paper from 1981, Cohen says: 'revolutionary Marxist belief often misdescribes itself, out of lack of clear awareness of its own nature, and Marxist disparagement of the idea of justice is a good example of that deficient self-understanding'.[51] Marxists who disparage the idea of justice are said to be mistaken in two respects: they are mistaken about the 'nature' of revolutionary Marxism, which includes an idea of justice; as a result, they are also led to falsely describe their own beliefs. Cohen's explanation for these mistakes is that Marxists who disparage the idea of justice do so 'because of ill-conceived philosophical commitments'.[52]

We know that these 'ill-conceived philosophical commitments' do not, for Cohen, belong to Marxism. Otherwise, Marxists who disparage the idea of justice would not be mistaken about the nature of revolutionary Marxism. Cohen explicates them in a later work, *If You're An Egalitarian, How Come You're So Rich?* (2001), which argues that 'classical Marxism was dominated by an *obstetric* conception of political practice'.[53] This conception of political practice, Cohen says, 'descends from a Hegelian idea which few would now regard as consonant with the demands of rigorous science'.[54] Thus, according to Cohen, Marxism was born impure. In its classical form, Marxism contains a foreign, unscientific element. The root cause of this impurity is the acceptance of Hegel's 'dialectical idea' that

> every live thing, including not only the literally living things studied by biology but also live systems of ideas or trends in art or smoothly functioning societies or vigorous families – every such thing develops by unfolding its inner nature in outward forms and, when it has fully elaborated that nature, it dies, disappears, is transformed into a successor form precisely because it has succeeded in elaborating itself fully.[55]

Cohen's claim is that, by adopting this philosophical idea and applying it in its historical studies, classical Marxism ended up with an obstetric conception of

---

51   Cohen 1981, p. 12, reprinted in Cohen 1988, p. 297.
52   Cohen 1981, p. 13.
53   Cohen 2001, p. 43.
54   Cohen 2001, p. 64.
55   Cohen 2001, p. 46.

political practice. An obstetric conception of political practice assumes that, on the occasion of dysfunctionality in a type of socio-economic structure, the latter will have itself developed the means for its replacement, just as midwives 'deliver the form that develops *within* reality'.[56] Cohen infers that, in its political practice, classical Marxism presents itself as 'the consciousness of a struggle within the world, rather than as a set of ideals proposed to the world'.[57]

To summarise Cohen's explanation: the influence of Hegel's dialectical philosophy on Marxism's founders led Marxist science to be born impure, and those who accept this form of Marxism, with its obstetric conception of political practice, overlook the idea of justice that Marxism contains, and so falsely describe their own beliefs. Marxists who adopt an obstetric conception of political practice are led to view the historical transition from capitalism to socialism as independent of normative ideals. But as Marxists are also revolutionaries, they condemn capitalism in practice. Those who accept this form of Marxism therefore suffer from deficient self-understanding. They believe that they fully grasp Marxism though they do not, and they do not think that they condemn capitalism although they do.

Before suggesting why Cohen's explanation is unconvincing, we may note that it, too, is not original. Steinbüchel attempted the same diagnosis over a hundred years ago:

> While the repression of ethical appraisal in Marxist literature over the decades is a fact, it is nonetheless understandable historically. It is sufficiently explained by the explicit aversion of Marx and Engels to any ethical reflection that appeared to bring them into uneasy proximity with the socialist utopianism of Saint-Simon, Fourier and Owen, and which they believed to have directly surpassed with their 'materialist' conception of history. In contrast to this utopian socialism, which exhausts itself in constructing, conceptually and through ethical postulates, future forms of society in accordance with a communist ideal, and which at the same time expects a real new ordering of society from the insight into these future designs' conformity to reason; *Marx* seeks to derive, from an actual, given form of society, the socialist form of society, whose development rests on a realistic foundation, and is tied to given elements within the existing order of society. Marx's 'scientific' socialism does not appeal to individuals' knowledge and good will; rather, it is backed by historical

---

56   Cohen 2001, p. 50.
57   Cohen 2001, p. 102; see also p. 77.

necessity. The development of society itself leads, with unconditional necessity, to socialism, which is no longer in need of mere postulation. To Marx the *historian*, the socialist order is a social result of development; not an ethical ought, but a must of natural necessity, just as it already struck him in 1843 in a letter to Arnold Ruge 'not to anticipate the world dogmatically, but to find the new world from out of a critique of the old' ... Despite the sociological orientation of his scientific thinking, Marx nevertheless cannot deny his intellectual father, *German idealism* ... which is amply felt in Marx's application of the dialectic, the value-based 'realm of freedom' Marx expected as well as the 'really human morality' that Engels proclaimed, and which lives on in the socialist idea of community.[58]

According to Steinbüchel, the cause of Marx's deficient self-understanding is an overreaction to utopian socialism, which led him to embrace an obstetric conception of history on which socialism's historical inevitability is independent of normative ideals. To substantiate this, Steinbüchel cites the same passage from Marx's *Letters from the Deutsch-Französische Jahrbücher* that Cohen would later cite,[59] and the same phrase from Engels's *Anti-Dühring*.[60] Little separates Cohen's claim that 'Marxism has lost much or most of its carapace, its hard shell of supposed fact ... To the extent that Marxism is still alive ... it presents itself as a set of values'[61] from Steinbüchel's claim that 'contemporary socialists have lost belief in sheer development; they conceive socialism fundamentally as a *problem of education*'.[62]

The Steinbüchel/Cohen explanation for the Marxist attitude of deficient self-understanding is unconvincing, for two separate reasons. First and most damagingly, an obstetric conception of political practice is compatible with ethics. Capitalism may develop the means for its replacement in part because principles for organising a new society are exhibited in or suggested by struggles prompted by its dysfunctionality. If capitalism prompts class struggle of a form that suggests an ethical principle, attention to this ethical principle is part of what an existing capitalist structure develops within reality; one of the outward forms it produces as it develops. So, if classical Marxism includes an

---

58   Steinbüchel 1921, pp. 2–3, quoting (i) *MEW*, 1, p. 344; *MECW*, 3, p. 142; (ii) *MEW*, 25, p. 828; *MECW*, 37, p. 807; Marx 1981, pp. 958–9, and (iii) *MEW*, 20, p. 88; *MECW*, 25, p. 88.

59   See Cohen 2001, pp. 66–7. For the full passage and an alternative interpretation, see ch. 10, sec. 2.

60   See Cohen 1995, p. 2.

61   Cohen 1995, p. 6.

62   Steinbüchel 1921, p. 269.

obstetric conception of political practice, that by itself cannot explain any disparagement of the idea of justice by classical Marxists.

A shared assumption about ethics is likely to have led Steinbüchel and Cohen to overlook the possibility of this response. As noted above, Steinbüchel and Cohen both assume that any grounding argument for an ultimate value will be timeless. If grounding arguments must be timeless, then it is natural to read Marx's remark about finding 'the new world from out of a critique of the old' as precluding an ethics. To provide a 'critique of the old' world, in this context, is to provide a critical account of capitalism. According to Steinbüchel's and Cohen's assumption about grounding arguments, no facts about specific forms of society form part of any grounding argument for an ultimate value. No 'critique of the old' world can form a part of a grounding argument for the validity of a value. Steinbüchel and Cohen must understand Marx's aspiration to find 'the new world from out of a critique of the old' as the declaration of a project to realise socialism without an ethical principle. They both overlook the possibility that obstetric conceptions of political practice allow for an ethics because they assume that grounding arguments must be timeless. But this is just an external prejudice that they bring to Marx interpretation, without any basis in the matter itself.

The second reason that the explanation is unconvincing is the jump from irrelevance to disparagement. Let us assume, for the sake of argument, that classical Marxism contains the view that capitalism develops the means for its replacement, for reasons having nothing to do with ethical principles. This view would still not explain why classical Marxists 'disparage the idea of justice'. All it implies is that they would regard justice as practically irrelevant. However, irrelevance is distinct from disparagement, and it is disparagement that Cohen has to explain, on his account of the deficient self-understanding claim. For all that is implied by the practical irrelevance of the idea of justice, it is possible for classical Marxists to believe that the idea of justice, while not causally efficacious, nonetheless recommends socialism. Moreover, no deficient self-understanding is implied by expressing beliefs that are regarded as lacking causal efficacy (and if it were, this would be a different type of deficient self-understanding to the one that Cohen identifies and seeks to explain). So, even if we put aside the fact that an obstetric conception of political practice does not preclude an ethics, an obstetric conception of political practice does not commit to disparagement of what it merely renders irrelevant. The idea that classical Marxism has an obstetric conception of political practice is of no use in explaining the deficient self-understanding that Cohen seeks to draw attention to.

Let us recap on what this section has tried to show. Firstly, we have provided evidence that the deficient self-understanding claim has existed for far longer than its recent proponents assume. It begins not with Cohen and Geras, but a matter of months after Engels's death. We have also exposed the premises from which it arises. These premises are not exhausted by premises about what Marx or Marxists say. The deficient self-understanding claim also rests on the external premise that any ethics requires a timeless grounding argument. Further, we have argued that deficient self-understanding cannot be explained by an obstetric conception of political practice, for two reasons: obstetric conceptions may be ethical conceptions, and irrelevance does not imply disparagement. Cohen, like Steinbüchel before him, overlooks the first objection, for, like proponents of the complementarity view, he assumes that grounding arguments must be timeless. All this suggests that Marxists can root out any attitude of deficient self-understanding that they may display, and thus dispel the appeal of the deficient self-understanding claim, by developing an ethics with a grounding argument that is not timeless. A critique of Kant's ethics can serve in this project.

Against the Complementarity View, Part 2: Can Kant's Formula of the End in Itself Condemn Capitalism?

In Chapter 2, the complementarity view was criticised from the side of socialist strategy. We now address the question of aim. Putting aside the incompatibility of Kant's ethics with the strategy of class struggle, can Kant's most popular formula of the categorical imperative, the Formula of the End in Itself (FEI), be applied to condemn capitalism? If we find that FEI cannot condemn capitalism, then all critics of capitalism, Marxist or not, need an ethics that differs from Kant's.

Various commentators have thought that FEI can condemn capitalism. This chapter assesses their arguments from the perspective of the issues that arise in interpreting and applying Kant's formula:

> The Formula of the End in Itself (FEI)
> *So act that you use humanity, in your own person as well as in the person of any other, always at the same time as an end, never merely as a means.*[1]

From one angle, the idea that FEI can be applied to condemn capitalism may seem farfetched. Kant himself offers no such application; and FEI attracts those who see in it a principle of consent, which a capitalist employer may certainly respect. Viewed in this light, FEI seems unsuited to condemn what critics of capitalism regard as its systematic failings. Socialist thinkers in two distinct historical contexts have argued otherwise, however. Kantian socialists at the turn of the twentieth century, as well as contemporary authors seeking a socialist principle of morality, have both turned to FEI to condemn capitalism.

It is understandable, given two basic pre-philosophical views, why critics of capitalism might appeal to FEI to couch their criticisms. It is a widely-held view that there is something inhumane about capitalism. You do not have to be a Marxist (or even an anti-capitalist) to sympathise with Marx and Engels's statement in *The Communist Manifesto* that 'the bourgeoisie ... has resolved

---

1 *GMS*, 4: 429.

personal dignity [*persönliche Würde*] into exchange-value'.[2] The idea that the treatment of people in capitalist economic relations has been governed by considerations of making a return on an investment is hard to deny. Moreover, it is one of the most widely known facts about moral philosophy that Kant said 'don't treat people merely as a means'. It is understandable, therefore, that many people who are not specifically trained in Kant's philosophy will form the intuition that FEI ought to be able to condemn capitalism, on account of the thought that to treat someone just as a commodity is to treat them merely as a means.[3] FEI is a natural reference point for humanist anti-capitalists, especially in the absence of a systematic moral philosophy from a major socialist or anarchist theorist of capitalism.

Before proceeding, three limitations may be indicated.

First, the chapter addresses the question: can FEI *condemn* capitalism? To condemn *x* by FEI is to assert that *x* is contrary to a duty, which is compulsory. It is not merely to assert that *x* is contrary to supererogatory conduct. To argue that FEI can condemn capitalism gives urgency to the moral case for seeking out alternatives. A condemnation is also an absolute judgment. It finds fault with *x* independently of a judgment about alternatives to *x*. To condemn capitalism by FEI, it is necessary to identify a type of conduct essential to capitalism that is contrary to a duty. The judgment of alternatives to capitalism can be put to one side. The finding that capitalism is to be condemned is the sort of finding that encourages a search for an alternative to capitalism. But it does not presuppose that an alternative has already been found.

Second, the chapter considers the *substantive* question of whether FEI can condemn capitalism. The answer to this question does not depend on Kant's *historical* influence on critics of capitalism, such as Marx.

Third, the chapter asks whether FEI can offer a *Kantian* condemnation of capitalism. There are a variety of everyday notions of treating someone as a 'mere means' or 'just using' them. Not all such notions are Kantian, in the sense of giving expression to the absolute value of rational nature. This chapter examines the critical potential of *Kantian* conceptions of FEI, as distinct from any 'just using' principle. It is only on this condition that one might claim to depart from Kant in the spirit of Kant.

Finally, a clarification as to what is meant by capitalism. One now familiar conception of capitalism defines it in terms of *differential private ownership* of

---

2 *MEW*, 4, p. 465; *MECW*, 6, p. 487. *MECW* renders '*Würde*' as 'worth' (which could translate: '*Wert*'). 'Dignity' is a more literal translation.

3 For remarks to this effect, see Steinbückel 1921, p. 185, and Chojnacki 1924, p. 33.

the means of production.[4] On this conception, a society is capitalist if the typical producer owns their labour power but 'none' of the 'means of production he uses', because the latter are owned by 'superiors' who 'do not produce for' producers.[5]

Yet 'capitalism' is, literally, a system of capital. This permits a conception of capitalism as commodity production subject to a dynamic of *capital accumulation*.[6] By means of the production of commodities, a smaller and smaller number of individuals gain control of a greater and greater proportion of the value of the total social product.

One difference between these conceptions is that only the former takes as definitive the differentiation of a group that produces for others from a group that does not. Even if, as Marx says in the *Grundrisse*, the separation of free producers from the means of production is one of the 'historical conditions' of 'capital',[7] it is not, just by virtue of that, a logical condition. On the latter conception, a system of profit-maximising cooperatives is a form of capitalism if commodity production subject to a dynamic of capital accumulation shapes the kinds of product produced, the techniques employed, the amount of time devoted to labour, and any occurrence of crises, even without class division.

As historically existing capitalism satisfies either conception, moral critics of capitalism may have one particular conception or either conception in mind. For example, in the space of a few pages, Karl Vorländer appeals to FEI to condemn both 'the rule of private capital',[8] and the 'planless anarchy of value production'.[9] This is not the place, however, to assess whether one of the above conceptions of capitalism is superior to the other. As both conceptions have been defended by Marxists, the disagreement does not mark a distinction between Marxism and other theories. It is therefore immaterial to the assessment of the complementarity view. The question in this chapter is whether or not FEI can

---

4   Roemer 1982, p. 7.

5   Cohen 1978, pp. 68–9.

6   The two conceptions are distinguished at Cohen 1978, p. 181; see also Cohen 1978, pp. 314–15. Postone 1993 offers a Marxist critique of the former conception.

7   *MEW*, 42, p. 383; *MECW*, 28, p. 399; Marx 1973, p. 471.

8   Vorländer 1904, p. 21.

9   Vorländer 1904, p. 15. Of the other arguments assessed below, the division of labour argument and the capital accumulation argument could be directed at either conception of capitalism, while the co-legislation argument, the vulnerability argument, the freedom in production argument and the veil of ignorance argument are directed at the differential private ownership conception. The general injustice argument discussed in sec. 6 is directed at the differential private ownership conception.

condemn a type of conduct[10] essential to one or both of the above conceptions of capitalism. If FEI can be used to condemn a type of conduct essential to at least one of these conceptions, it can be used to condemn our existing economic system in a way that some Marxists aim to do.

Section 1 presents seven arguments given for why FEI can condemn capitalism. Section 2 elaborates the part of FEI to which these arguments appeal: the command never to treat humanity in a person merely as a means. Section 3 defends a version of the claim that every derivation of a duty from FEI rests on an intermediate premise, and draws out some implications of this. Section 4 notes some strategies that might allow FEI to yield a judgment that Kant did not endorse. Section 5 evaluates the arguments presented in section 1. Finally, section 6 considers whether FEI can condemn capitalism once it is combined with Kant's doctrine of general injustice.

1 FEI-Based Arguments against Capitalism

There is, at present, no overview of the arguments given for why FEI can condemn capitalism. This overview is organised historically, and is confined to literature available in German or English.[11]

FEI was first applied critically to capitalism by Hermann Cohen, founder of the Marburg school of neo-Kantianism, in a study of Kant's aesthetics entitled *Kants Begründung der Aesthetik* (1889). For Cohen, FEI expresses the thought that 'each individual is, as a moral person, the final end of all things'.[12] As such, FEI condemns the 'statistical causality under which human beings, as values

---

10 The types of conduct are specified in sec. 3.

11 Bare assertions that FEI condemns capitalism (for example, Mehring 1898, p. 284 or Goldmann 1971, p. 176) are ignored. There is no mention of Otto Bauer and Max Adler, the main figures of Austro-Marxism, as neither offers an argument from FEI against capitalism (see Bauer 1906, and Adler 1912, p. 188, where Adler simply endorses the view, which he attributes to Hermann Cohen, that FEI expresses 'the political idea of socialism'). The most recent collection of essays on Kantian socialism in German (Holzhey 1994) contains no new argument specifically from FEI against capitalism. I do not discuss David Ellerman's argument from FEI for a 'labor-managed firm' (Ellerman 1988, pp. 1110–19), because an argument for a 'labor-managed firm' is not an argument against capitalism, on either the differential private ownership conception of capitalism or the capital accumulation conception of capitalism. Labour-managed firms do not preclude either the renting of productive facilities from a non-producing class, or profit-maximising market competition.

12 Cohen 1889, p. 140.

of labour, have languished'.[13] To treat producers with the attitude 'if producers work for time t, then they will produce monetary value m', is to ignore their value as persons:

> As long as we figure merely as values of labour, we belong solely to the mechanism of social economy in which each natural being, as if it were only part of a machine, operates as a means, and is used up and devoured as a means. Here there is no individual, and no value, that exceeds that of a mere means.[14]

Cohen implies that, to treat producers as persons, the work that they are offered must have a quality that serves a purpose beyond monetary value.

This claim rests on a premise made explicit in *Ethik des reinen Willens* (*Ethics of the Pure Will*) (1904). In this work, Cohen asks what it would take to treat producers as persons, on the premise that 'the vocation for morality cannot be fulfilled except on the basis of scientific insight'.[15] Scientific insight may alert agents to the occasions of a moral end, and so enable them to fulfil their moral vocation.[16] As persons ought to fulfil their moral vocation, then, by the principle of ought implies can, everyone must be able to partake in intellectual life. Our problem is that 'man ... has not come to partake in intellectual labour'.[17] Producers are consigned to menial machine labour by the constraints of '*market price*'.[18] If the nature of capitalism sustains general claims about the monetary value that the capitalist seeks by employing producers, and the menial type of labour and long hours this often requires, then, if this type and amount of labour hinders those who perform it from acquiring scientific insight (by exhaustion or by dulling their minds), capitalism hinders (some) producers from fulfilling their moral vocation as persons. We can call this FEI-based argument against capitalism the *division of labour* argument.

Karl Vorländer first argues that Kant's ethics provide a justification for socialism in *Kant und der Sozialismus* (1900). In this text, Vorländer claims that FEI formulates 'the basic idea of socialism, the thought of community'.[19] If the basic

---

13   Cohen 1889, p. 138.
14   Cohen 1889, p. 139.
15   Cohen 1904, pp. 477–8.
16   '[A] person who has an end must both take action to promote it and also be alert to its occasions' (Korsgaard 1990, p. 239).
17   Cohen 1904, p. 478.
18   Cohen 1904, p. 305.
19   Vorländer 1900, p. 7.

idea of socialism is 'the thought of community', then, in Vorländer's view, that means that socialism is related to Kant's ethics, as distinct from Kant's 'political ideal'. The latter, Vorländer says here, 'remains primarily determined by the thought of freedom'.[20] FEI, in giving expression to the thought of community,[21] commands us to treat humanity in the person of even 'the poorest day labourer'[22] as an end in itself. Indeed, Vorländer holds against Kant that he

> was yet to grasp the full implications of his categorical imperative, which modern socialism draws out by holding that the real precondition of political independence, *economic* independence [*Selbständigkeit*],[23] i.e. freedom from economic servitude, is to be enabled for all not merely ideally, but in fact.[24]

This (as we might call it) *community argument* from FEI against capitalism has the structure: FEI expresses the thought of moral community; moral community presupposes universal political independence; and universal political independence presupposes universal economic independence, which capitalism denies to producers.

Consider the step from moral community to universal political independence. If we suppose that universal political independence, understood as universal rights of active citizenship, can guarantee for all the opportunity to assess and decide on principles that ought to be publicly declared and enforced, and that political life is thus, at least potentially (when universal political and economic independence are combined), a sphere in which everyone can develop the ability to judge and act on principles; then we may view universal political independence as a necessary preparation[25] for all agents to cultivate the

---

20   Vorländer 1900, p. 13. In a later text, Vorländer offers an argument for socialism related to Kant's 'political ideal' (Vorländer 1920, p. 45). This argument is discussed separately, in sec. 6.

21   On this point, see, also, Natorp (1923, p. 96), who says of FEI: 'one serves the other; that is, he does not refuse at any time also to be a means for promoting the other's true ethical final ends; not a mere means, but in turn also itself an end, that is, reciprocally each for the others. That is precisely the *concept of community* that is community of individuals'.

22   Vorländer 1900, p. 13.

23   '*Selbständigkeit*' is distinct from '*Unabhängigkeit*'. The latter term is the one Kant uses to elaborate freedom in the context of 'original right' (MS, 6: 237). Although '*Selbständigkeit*' is translated here as 'independence', this should not be taken as a sign that Vorländer appeals to Kant's doctrine of right at this point.

24   Vorländer 1900, p. 14.

25   Compare Kant's remark that 'the good moral education of a people is to be expected from

moral disposition that they must exercise in promoting one another's permissible ends as members of a moral community.

Vorländer elaborates on the final part of the community argument in a slightly later text, *Kant und Marx* (1904):

> The freedom of the individual is merely apparent as long as the grinding rule of private capital makes him a mere means of labour in the hands of the possessor. Freedom is in fact first secured by a state of affairs in which it is also economically the case that no one is entirely dependent on another, but rather the one serves the whole, others, of their free will, just as this one is supported by them. Only when the *free development* of one's capacities is enabled for *each* not just in words, but by real institutions; only then have we arrived at Kant's realm of ends, in which no human being is any longer a mere means, but rather is always also an end in itself.[26]

This text permits two accounts of why universal active citizenship that is morality-preparing rests on universal economic independence. The first is that, if, in virtue of inequalities of private wealth, there is a lack of reciprocity between producers and possessors, then political life can be expected to cultivate acquiescence in an order by which possessors are enabled to exempt themselves from rules that producers must follow. Universal active citizenship will then not serve to prepare a moral disposition.

A second account is suggested by the thought that freedom requires each to serve 'the whole', and by Vorländer's rejection of the 'planless anarchy of value production'.[27] The idea would seem to be that, if separate units of production compete to maximise profits at each other's expense, that will encourage a disposition to seek and bend public enforceable principles in one's own favour. By implication, a moral disposition can only be enabled in a political community whose economic institutions allow citizens to pursue a *common* aim in their working lives. In the first version of the community argument, the problem with a capitalist economy is the lack of reciprocity, which might be possible to secure in an egalitarian market economy. In the second version, the problem is that any one person's opportunity to work and acquire means of life remains

---

a good state constitution' (*ZeF*, 8: 366), rather than the other way around. After citing this remark, Vorländer likens Kant approvingly to a 'staunch historical materialist' (Vorländer 1911, p. 14).

26   Vorländer 1904, p. 21.
27   Vorländer 1904, p. 15.

under the control of an aggressively competitive sub-group, which a form of planning would have to replace.

The final figure in this period to offer a distinctive FEI-based argument against capitalism is the Russian economist Mikhail Tugan-Baranowsky, who offers a *capital accumulation* argument. According to Tugan-Baranowsky, FEI formulates the 'fundamental ethical norm' with which 'capitalism' stands in 'contradiction'.[28] Capitalist production turns a producer into a 'mere economic means', for while human labour is the most important economic means of capitalist production, it is a mistake to believe that the producer's consumption is 'one of its ends'.[29] Tugan-Baranowsky's defence of this last premise relates to his claim that '[t]he decrease of social consumption and the simultaneous extension of social production is no economic contradiction from a capitalist standpoint'.[30] Tugan-Baranowsky defends this claim in an earlier analysis of capitalist reproduction as a whole.[31]

In this earlier analysis, Tugan-Baranowsky presents a social reproduction scheme that illustrates the possibility for social consumption to decrease at the same time as output expands (at a constant level of productivity).[32] This can happen if capitalists invest a part of the surplus that they would otherwise use for their personal consumption in other areas of production.[33] But social consumption can also decrease in virtue of a decrease in the part of social consumption represented by producers' personal consumption, at the same time as output expands (at a constant level of productivity). Producers may be paid less for more labour (without presupposing a disturbance of demand and supply)[34] if production of items that do not enter into personal consumption increases (for example, destructive weapons); or if, on account of the depletion of natural resources, means of production that require longer to produce are now required in production processes that produce means of consumption. In any event, whatever the exact cause of a decrease in social consumption, Tugan-Baranovsky regards the possibility for this decrease to occur simultaneously with an expansion in output as proof that, in capitalism, 'production as a technical moment in the creation of capital' is an '*end in itself*'[35] that demotes producers to the status of mere means.

---

28 Tugan-Baranowsky 1905, p. 237.

29 Tugan-Baranowsky 1905, pp. 237–8.

30 Tugan-Baranowsky 1905, p. 238.

31 Tugan-Baranowsky 1901, pp. 18–27, p. 229.

32 '[T]echnical progress' is 'ignored' (Tugan-Baranowsky 1901, p. 27).

33 Tugan-Baranowsky 1901, pp. 22–3.

34 This is one of Tugan-Baranowsky's assumptions; see Tugan-Baranowsky 1901, p. 25.

35 Tugan-Baranowsky 1901, p. 27; compare p. 229.

Moving now to the Anglophone context, Harry van der Linden offers an *institutional co-legislation* argument. Van der Linden interprets FEI from within a broader account of Kant's ethics as 'a *social ethics*', that is, an ethics that includes 'the demand that we *actively* seek the realization of ideal institutions'.[36] Ideal institutions are institutions that include 'all' participants as 'legislative members', and that aim 'at the satisfaction of the ends' of all their participants.[37] A social ethics requires us to direct our efforts to realise a world in which all our institutions instantiate these features.[38] For if human beings can only do all they can to promote a goal if they 'coordinate and optimize'[39] their efforts by institutional means, the realisation of a moral ideal among human beings must include the bringing into line of these institutions with this moral ideal.

FEI is a formula of a social ethics, for van der Linden, because humanity is a 'task-setting idea'; 'the idea of humanity does not refer to humanity as it now exists but to humanity as it *ought* to exist'.[40] Humanity only exists as it ought if institutions promote the highest good by making all participants legislative members and by aiming as far as possible to satisfy individuals' ends. For van der Linden, 'to treat humanity in other persons as a means only is to act contrary to the demand that we should create a society of legislators who seek to promote one another's personal ends'.[41] He concludes: '[t]he cooperative fulfils this command, whereas the capitalist private enterprise violates it'.[42] The employment contracts offered by capitalist private enterprises do not make a worker a co-legislator. Rather, 'his will is determined by another will – the will of the capital owner', and so the worker 'is treated as means only'.[43]

Allen Wood suggests an argument from FEI against capitalism that condemns playing on another person's *vulnerability* for one's own ends. For Wood, FEI requires us 'to give the equal absolute worth of every human being its due'.[44] Wood then adds that, 'when a social order treats some people better and some worse in ways that they themselves regard as essential to their self-worth, there is a presumption, based on [FEI] itself, that this social order fails to respect the

---

36   Van der Linden 1988, p. 4.
37   Van der Linden 1988, p. 31.
38   Van der Linden 1988, pp. 163–4; van der Linden 1994, p. 155.
39   Van der Linden 1988, p. 163.
40   Van der Linden 1988, p. 29.
41   Van der Linden 1988, p. 30.
42   Van der Linden 1988, p. 225.
43   Van der Linden 1988, pp. 225–6.
44   Wood 1995a, p. 316.

humanity of those who receive worse treatment'.[45] A social order may fail in this regard if 'untrammelled external freedoms in the economic sphere lead to large inequalities in wealth and status between human beings which are degrading to those placed in an inferior position'.[46] In capitalism, workers are degraded by their bargaining interactions with capitalists in virtue of the fact that workers' lack of means of production ensures that they 'have no acceptable alternative'[47] to working for a capitalist. The capitalist's use of the worker's vulnerability is degrading, because '[p]roper respect for others is violated when we treat their vulnerabilities as opportunities to advance our own interests or projects'.[48] 'Kant's principle that we must not treat others merely as means'[49] may account for this objection, Wood suggests. The presumption that FEI condemns capitalism can be rebutted only if such treatment is necessary to avoid conduct even more damaging to workers' self-worth; and if capitalism avoids this conduct.[50]

Justin Schwartz suggests a *freedom in production* argument. To understand this argument, we need to understand that for Schwartz, exploitation denotes '*forced* transfer'.[51] Exploiters are recipients of goods that others were forced to transfer. Capitalists are exploiters, according to Schwartz, if workers must transfer some product of their labour to capitalists 'because they lack productive assets and so must sell their labor power to live'.[52] Schwartz then suggests that capitalist 'exploiters' treat workers 'merely as means', because they use workers for their own purpose, appropriation of the product, 'in a way that prevents them [workers – JF] from setting and acting on their own purposes'.[53] If capitalists own all means of production, they prevent workers from acting on ends that require exploitation-free access to productive assets. To prevent workers from acting on such ends is to deny them 'the sort of "positive" freedom involved in having the resources to do as they might, to exercise their options'.[54] Insofar as capitalists deny workers this freedom, they treat them merely as means, according to Schwartz.

---

45   Ibid.
46   Wood 1995a, p. 316; see also Wood 2014, p. 267, pp. 296–8.
47   Wood 1995b, p. 149.
48   Wood 1995b, pp. 150–1.
49   Wood 1995b, p. 151.
50   Compare Wood 1995a, p. 316.
51   Schwartz 1995b, p. 160.
52   Schwartz 1995b, p. 159.
53   Schwartz 1995b, pp. 176–7.
54   Schwartz 1995a, p. 300.

Finally, Jonathan Wolff (in the name of a Marxian account of exploitation) suggests that FEI can condemn capitalism if its Never Merely as a Means principle is elaborated with a version of a Rawlsian *veil of ignorance*.[55] Wolff suggests that to exploit a person by treating them merely as a means is to leave them 'worse off' than if the transaction's terms were settled by what its parties could accept if each was in 'ignorance of [their – JF] position in the transaction'.[56] So elaborated, FEI can condemn capitalism, Wolff suggests, once we give due attention to a fact about the history of capitalism; namely, that 'capital' has 'invariably' been accumulated through 'illegitimate means'.[57] Giving due attention to this fact, parties behind a veil of ignorance would agree that there is 'no moral entitlement to private property' in productive assets.[58] Hence, from behind a veil of ignorance, 'neither side' of a transaction would agree to a transaction in which private property ownership enabled its owner 'to extract surplus labour'[59] from a producer, that is, to extract labour beyond what is necessary to produce an equivalent for the producer's wage. Insofar as the parties would also agree behind a veil of ignorance that some of this surplus labour ought to benefit the producer, the capitalist leaves the producer worse off than what the parties could accept behind a veil of ignorance. By appropriating this surplus labour, the capitalist treats the producer merely as a means.

2   Kant's Never Merely as a Means Principle

An agent violates FEI by failing to treat humanity in a person not merely as a means, or by failing to treat humanity in a person as an end. One common feature of the above arguments against capitalism is that they all appeal to the Never Merely as a Means principle. This reflects a sound intuition. If one seeks to condemn capitalism by appeal to FEI, there is reason to focus on the Never Merely as a Means principle, at least as distinct from the Always as an End principle.

Kant's statement of FEI reflects his distinction between strict (or narrow) duties, and wide duties.[60] A strict duty is one that an agent has no latitude in observing. A wide duty is one that an agent is afforded latitude in fulfilling: the

---

55   Wolff 1999, p. 114.
56   Wolff 1999, pp. 113–14.
57   Wolff 1999, p. 118.
58   Wolff 1999, p. 119.
59   Ibid.
60   *GMS*, 4: 424; *MS*, 6: 390.

agent may decide on the degree to which, and how, they fulfil a wide duty, for they may be obliged to limit its perfection by another duty. The Never Merely as a Means principle grounds strict duties: an agent is unconditionally necessitated to refrain from action that disrespects the status of humanity in a person as an end. The Always as an End principle grounds wide duties: an agent is not unconditionally necessitated to any specific action that respects the status of humanity in a person as an end.

Suppose that there is a type of conduct that falls under a wide duty that a type of agent essential to capitalism cannot perform, at least in a certain context. Its absence may not be sufficient to condemn capitalism. It may be that the agent cannot treat humanity in a person as an end in that respect while also fulfilling another duty, which capitalism enables them to fulfil. Its absence is then a permissible limitation of one duty by another. Capitalism is not thereby characterised as wrong. It is characterised as imposing a specific direction on how its agents can act morally.

It might be thought that the Always as an End principle can conclusively condemn capitalism by condemning conduct within it that consists in the adoption of a maxim *never* to fulfil a wide duty towards an agent or class of agent, e.g. a maxim never to come to the aid of workers in one's employ. There are two problems here. Firstly, this maxim is one that an agent has no latitude not to adopt. As such, it is condemned by the Never Merely as a Means principle. But in any case, such a maxim is not the sort of maxim that defines capitalism. A capitalist economy enables and constrains certain types of conduct. For instance, each unit of production is constrained by competition to make and reinvest as much money as it can, because competition attaches future disadvantages to non-accumulation. A capitalist economy cannot, however, constrain *every* type of conduct in which capitalists engage in relation to their workers. Expressed in terms of the characters of Dickens's novel *A Christmas Carol*: even if competition constrains Scrooge to keep Cratchit's wage down, Scrooge may decide, without compromising his firm's profitability, to pay for Tiny Tim's medical insurance with his own income.

It is also crucial to note that the Never Merely as a Means principle says: never treat *humanity* in a person merely as a means. For Kant, humanity is a set of rational capacities distinct both from animality (a living being's capacities for self-preservation, propagation and community) and from personality (the capacity for moral action).[61] Most basically, humanity is the capacity for setting ends: '[t]he capacity to set oneself an end – any end whatsoever – is what char-

---

61   *RGV*, 6: 26–7.

acterizes humanity'.[62] Humanity also includes any capacity whose exercise is a rational requirement of setting ends. It includes the capacity to order ends, and to select means to an end.

However, although this view of humanity has support in Kant's writings, it is not the only one used to interpret FEI. Vorländer and van der Linden speak in this connection of 'the idea of humanity'.[63] For them, the idea of humanity includes the institutional preconditions of what Kant refers to as the 'perfection'[64] of one's own humanity; that is, the cultivation of a virtuous disposition. Van der Linden, as we have seen, takes 'the idea of humanity' to include institutions that make all participants legislative members. Similarly, Vorländer says that 'the idea of a moral realm or realm of ends' that we are to realise, and that institutions are required to enable, is 'constituted by the idea of humanity', and that FEI rests on this idea.[65] Yet if, as Kant says in *The Metaphysics of Morals*, the ground of agents' duties to perfect their humanity in their 'deeds' is to 'be worthy of the humanity that dwells within'[66] them, a social ethics based on FEI will emphasise that the humanity that 'dwells within' agents is the ground of their duty to realise ideal institutions. That differs from basing this duty in FEI interpreted as a command 'to strive for humanity as it ought to be'.[67]

Further, the Never Merely as a Means principle commands us never to treat humanity *in a person* merely as a means. A person is a being with personality, that is, the capacity to subject one's conduct to the moral law, and to act for duty's sake.[68] In the *Groundwork*, Kant writes that 'morality is the condition under which alone a rational being can be an end in itself'.[69] If a capacity for moral action is the condition under which a rational being can be an end in itself, we can only be required to treat humanity in *persons* never merely as a means. FEI does not directly constrain action toward beings of a kind whose nature is such that their ends are 'always wrong',[70] or whose nature is such that they can only comply with duty on heteronomous grounds. The relevance of this point for applying FEI beyond Kant will be made evident in section 4.

---

62   *MS*, 6: 392.
63   Vorländer 1900, p. 7; van der Linden 1988, p. 29.
64   *MS*, 6: 386.
65   Vorländer 1900, p. 7.
66   *MS*, 6: 386–7.
67   Van der Linden 1988, p. 31.
68   *RGV*, 6: 27.
69   *GMS*, 4: 435; see also *KpV*, 5: 131–2; *KU*, 5: 431.
70   Ameriks 2003, p. 200.

What remains clear in any case is that the Never Merely as a Means principle requires us never to disrespect the worth of humanity in a person that gives it the moral status of always being an end. What gives humanity in a person this moral status, Kant claims in arguing for FEI, is that only humanity in a person is 'something the existence of which in itself has an absolute worth'.[71] We therefore require an analysis of exclusive absolute worth.

The *Groundwork* leads us to believe that absolute worth contrasts with 'relative'[72] worth. One way to begin to think about the absolute worth of humanity in a person is suggested by Scanlon: 'seeing something as an end in itself is seeing it as having value that is not derived from any other source'.[73] By contrast, 'to regard something merely as a means is to see it as having no value except for what may be conferred on it' by something else.[74] This suggests the following analysis: something exists with exclusive absolute worth if it exists with *non-derivative* worth.

This suggestion is not yet adequate, however. If X has *some* non-derivative worth, but X's non-derivative worth cannot equal Y's non-derivative worth, then, as a thing of lesser value than Y, X may be treated as a mere means with respect to Y's worth. So, to say that X has non-derivative worth does not imply that X ought always to be treated as an end. What needs to be added is the notion of *transcendent* worth. Y has transcendent worth if no amount of anything that is not Y can have a value equal to Y.[75] If Y's non-derivative worth is a transcendent worth, Y ought always to be treated as an end.

By itself, transcendent worth does not suffice for absolute worth, for transcendent worth may still be derivative. Y has transcendent but derivative worth if Y owes its transcendent worth to an external source, Z. If this external source is cut off, Y may continue to exist, just not with transcendent worth. Something of transcendent worth only always exists with absolute worth (and so must always be treated as an end) if it is also its own source of worth, that is, if it has non-derivative worth. On this analysis, the Never Merely as a Means principle requires us never to disrespect the non-derivative and transcendent worth of humanity in a person. This finally puts us in a position to gain more clarity regarding the problem of applying FEI to the case of capitalism.

---

71   *GMS*, 4: 428.
72   Ibid.
73   Scanlon 2008, p. 92.
74   Ibid.
75   See Kerstein 2013, p. 129.

3   Applying FEI: Some General Considerations

First it is important to consider the general form of argument by which a duty may be derived from FEI. A good place to start is Allen Wood's claim that every derivation of a duty from FEI 'depends on an intermediate premise, logically independent'[76] of FEI itself. In Wood's view, if FEI requires us to treat humanity in a person always as an end and never merely as a means, then, to conclude that FEI imposes a duty on us (say, not to y), it is necessary to defend a premise that says: to y is to treat humanity in a person merely as a means, or to fail to treat it as an end. An 'intermediate premise' of this form is said to be logically independent of FEI because it is 'possible without contradiction'[77] to deny it while affirming FEI.

One drawback of Wood's view, however, is that, if rational nature is something about which it is possible to have knowledge,[78] then it ought not to be possible, without contradiction, to deny that FEI imposes *any* given duty on us, while affirming FEI. *Some* duties on us derived from FEI ought to be incontrovertible. Our affirmation of FEI ought to commit us to at least some duties, even if other duties remain controversial.

Fortunately, it is not necessary, while affirming FEI, to deny that FEI imposes any given duty on us, in order to hold that every derivation of a duty from FEI rests on a premise logically independent of FEI. For the form of this premise may be altered to: 'in the context of x, to y is to treat humanity in a person merely as a means, or to fail to treat it as an end'. Any premise of this form can be used, with FEI, to derive a duty (not to y). A premise of this form is also logically independent of FEI, for one may conceive of a hypothetical world in which x is not a possible context, and so deny that the premise is relevant to moral deliberation in that world, while holding that FEI remains valid for it. For example, one may conceive of a one agent world in which no context in which an agent invites another person to act is possible, and so deny that the avoidance of false promising is a duty in it (there being no duty not to do something that is causally impossible), while holding that FEI remains valid in that world. As a premise of the above form can be used, together with FEI, to derive a duty, it is not necessary, while affirming FEI, to deny that FEI imposes any given duty on us, in order to hold that every derivation of a duty from FEI rests on an intermediate premise logically independent of FEI.

---

76   Wood 1995a, p. 313.
77   Wood 1995a, p. 314.
78   Wood 1995a, p. 315.

The form of argument for deriving a duty from the Never Merely as a Means principle can be illustrated with the *Groundwork*'s example of a lying promise to obtain money. Kant says that someone who makes a false repayment promise uses another merely as a means, for 'the one I want to use for my purposes by such a promise cannot possibly agree to my way of proceeding with him and thus [*also*] himself contain the end of this action'.[79] The 'thus' in this statement is crucial. If *A* makes a false repayment promise to *B*, *B* cannot will to contribute to *A*'s end *by virtue* of being given a chance to do so *by A*. *A* fails to give *B* this chance, by inviting *B* to act on reasoning about *A*'s end in respect of *B* that *A* must believe is false (namely: 'if I give *A* this money, *A* will repay me'). As it is part of *A*'s end to get *B* to act as *B* would not otherwise act, *A* is obliged to invite *B* to act on a sound piece of reasoning about *A*'s end in respect of *B*. To invite *B* to act on reasoning about *A*'s end in respect of *B* that *A* must believe is false (that is, to make a false promise) is to do the contrary of this.

The argument can be represented as follows:
(1)   Never treat humanity in a person merely as a means
(2)   In the context of inviting another person to act as they otherwise would not, it treats their humanity merely as a means not to give them the chance to act on reasoning about one's end in respect of them that one believes is true
      Therefore:
(3)   It is a strict duty not to make a false promise to another person
(1) is Kant's Never Merely as a Means principle. (2) is a premise that concretises (1) in a certain context. (3) states a specific duty. If (1) and (2) are true, (3) is true. On the analysis defended in section 2, the argument for (2) is to take the form of arguing that the conduct in (2) disrespects the non-derivative, transcendent worth of humanity in a person.

One general point to note is that the contextualising premise (2) must relate FEI to the act and end of a type of conduct. FEI begins '*so act ...*', and commands us always to treat humanity in a person '*as an end*'. It is impossible to judge whether a piece of conduct treats humanity in a person as an end, and whether it treats it merely as a means, without subsuming it under a contextualising premise that relates FEI to an end to which an act is oriented.

The idea that every derivation of a duty from FEI rests on a contextualising premise of this kind raises a number of issues. Two may be mentioned here.

First, the description of conduct to choose when subsuming it under a contextualising premise must state the agent's *end*, or reason for action. It does

---

79   *GMS*, 4: 429–30.

not suffice for it to report an action's *consequences*. Suppose *A* defends herself against an unprovoked violent attack by *B*. In applying FEI to *A*'s conduct, it would be mistaken to look for a contextualising premise under which to subsume a description such as: *A* injures *B*, and thereby damages *B*'s humanity. This description does not state *A*'s end, to defend herself from *B*.

Second, if the contextualising premise relates FEI to an act and end, a charge of treating humanity in a person merely as a means must rest *entirely on the conduct of the agent(s) against whom the charge is levelled*. There must be an agent (or associating agents) against whom the charge can be levelled, because only agents can act on an end; and third party influences that impact on the *addressee*'s *overall situation* are not relevant just by virtue of that, for they are caused by parties unrelated to the agent(s) whose conduct is under evaluation.

Take *A*'s false repayment promise to *B*. *A* cannot be saved from a charge of treating *B* merely as a means by the fortuitous fact that *B* may know what is going on from *C*, who informs *B* of *A*'s plan to deceive *B*, and so puts *B* in a position to choose whether or not to contribute to *A*'s end, e.g. after *B* considers whether they want to 'revel in the demise'[80] of *A*'s reputation as a result of *A* achieving *A*'s end of obtaining money from *B* by a false promise.

Contrariwise, if *B* is falsely convinced by a third party, *C*, that what *A* proposed to *B* differs from what *A* said to *B*, e.g. *C* convinces *B* that *A* spoke to *B* in code, that does not mean that *A* treats *B*'s humanity merely as a means, even if the confusion sown by C leaves *B* unable to will to contribute to *A*'s end. Similarly, if *B* is powerless to decline *A*'s offer by virtue of conduct by a third party, *C*, that *A* is unaware of (*C* has, say, hypnotised *B* to say 'yes' whenever *B* wants to say 'no'), that does not mean that *A* treats *B*'s humanity merely as a means by making *B* an offer.

In short, the Never Merely as a Means principle only condemns conduct, rather than its addressee's overall situation; and it need not condemn conduct whose efficacy depends on its addressee's ignorance or powerlessness. For in neither of the latter cases does *A* treat *B*'s humanity merely as a means if it is also assumed that *B* would certainly decline *A*'s offer if *B* knew that *A* was not speaking in code, or if *C* had not hypnotised *B*. If the 'nature *and* efficacy'[81] of conduct depends on its addressee's ignorance or powerlessness, *then* it will count as treating her merely as a means.

Two related points pertain to applying FEI to condemn capitalism. First, when applying FEI to condemn capitalism, the description of the type of

80   Kerstein 2013, p. 61.

81   Korsgaard 1996, p. 139; emphasis added.

conduct essential to capitalism that is to be subsumed under a contextual-ising premise must state its act and end (not a mere consequence). Second, any charge that an agent (or associating agents) treats the humanity in a worker's person merely as a means must rest entirely on the conduct of the agent(s) against whom the charge is levelled. This agent may in principle be a capitalist, an association of capitalists, or a capitalism-guaranteeing gov-ernment. (Depending on the conception of capitalism, a capitalist is a mem-ber of a class of private owners of means of production, or a representat-ive of a profit-maximising unit of production.) A capitalist's end in hiring a worker is to obtain the power to put the worker to work on the agreed terms. A capitalist's end in putting a hired worker to work on the agreed terms is to appropriate the product. If FEI is to condemn capitalism, a duty must be derived from FEI's Never Merely as a Means principle, by the form of argu-ment outlined above, that *either* prohibits one of these two types of conduct, *or* prohibits a type of conduct (including by an association of capitalists or a capitalism-guaranteeing government) that is a necessary condition of either of them.

4   Applying FEI beyond Kant

I begin by noting that a Kantian might use FEI to condemn conduct that Kant did not use FEI to condemn by adopting one or more of the following strategies:[82]

(1)   Revise a value criterion in Kant's *a priori* argument for FEI as a categorical imperative, to strengthen the justification of FEI as a formula of a moral law whose principle is autonomy of the will (that is, argue that a value cri-terion other than '*existence* [having] absolute worth' qualifies something, and only that thing, as an obligatory end, or reason for acting).[83]

(2)   Revise Kant's statement of FEI, to better capture the value of rational nature to which FEI is to give expression (for example, to: treat humanity in a *being* always as an end, never merely as a means).

(3)   Affirm a contextualising premise that Kant did not affirm.

(4)   Subsume under a contextualising premise a description of conduct that Kant did not consider.

---

82   Strategies (1)–(4) are independent of any appeal to Kant's doctrine of right. A further strategy that appeals to this doctrine is discussed in sec. 6.

83   On the concept of an end ('*Zweck*') as a reason for acting, see Wood 2014, p. 149.

As we shall see, the arguments from FEI against capitalism presented in section 1 can all be understood as attempts to pursue one or more of these strategies. (They all pursue strategies (3) and (4).) The aim of the following evaluation is to show that, even if *plausible* versions of these strategies are *permitted*, none of the arguments presented above allows FEI to condemn capitalism. To anticipate: one group of arguments (the institutional co-legislation, division of labour and community arguments) rewrite FEI so as to be unrecognisable as arguments from an obligatory-ends-based formula of a moral law whose principle is autonomy of the will; the veil of ignorance argument models a thought that conflicts with FEI; and, finally, the capital accumulation, vulnerability and freedom in production arguments rely on a description of conduct in capitalism to which FEI cannot be applied.

5   Evaluation of the Arguments

The Institutional Co-legislation Argument

The institutional co-legislation argument interprets FEI as a command 'to strive for humanity as it ought to be'.[84] The institutional co-legislation argument thereby abandons Kant's own argument for FEI. Kant argues for FEI by arguing that only humanity in a person is '*something the existence of which in itself* has an absolute worth'.[85] After introducing this value criterion, Kant writes: 'I say: a human being and generally every rational being *exists* as an end in itself'.[86] Humanity as it ought to be is not a possible candidate for something that exists with absolute worth, or exists as an end in itself. If FEI is interpreted as a command to promote humanity as it ought to exist, and the failure of capitalist firms to treat their workers as co-legislators is condemned by FEI on this basis, we require a different value criterion for an obligatory end, in virtue of which an obligatory end can be something to be brought about. We can then argue that humanity as it ought to exist is this something that it is obligatory to bring about. One question to ask of the institutional co-legislation argument, therefore, is whether this particular version of strategy (1) is plausible. It is not plausible if nothing to be brought about can be an obligatory end in a formula of a moral law whose principle is autonomy of the will.

---

84   Van der Linden 1988, p. 31.
85   *GMS*, 4: 428.
86   Ibid.

A categorical imperative, as an *imperative* form of the moral law, is only possible if it is possible for there to be a kind of *finite* being capable of acting on it. So, suppose it is inconsistent with the thought of a kind of finite being capable of acting on a categorical imperative that nothing that already 'dwells within'[87] such a being is an obligatory end. If so, then, if there is a categorical imperative, and hence an obligatory end, this end, or obligatory reason for acting, will be provided by something existent. An obligatory-end-based formula of a categorical imperative could not then declare something that it is obligatory to bring about – for example, humanity as it ought to exist – to be the obligatory end. Acting to honour the absolute worth of something that is conceived of as existing independently of action may in a given context require an agent to refrain from bringing about a certain state of affairs.

Now, it is inconsistent with the thought of a kind of finite being capable of acting on a categorical imperative that nothing about it is an obligatory end. A categorical imperative is an imperative form of a moral law whose principle is freedom as autonomy of the will. An agent can only regard themselves as free qua autonomous in being bound to adopt an end for its own sake if what grounds this obligatory reason for acting is some valued part of them. If what grounds this obligatory reason for acting is the value of something else, a categorical imperative to honour its value by treating it as an end in itself would imply that any agent bound by this imperative was merely of instrumental value. No such agent could recognise this imperative as categorical *and* regard themselves as free *qua* autonomous. So, if there is an obligatory end in itself, the object that provides the agent with this obligatory reason for acting must be taken to exist, with absolute worth.

For a utilitarian, to act morally is to intend to bring about the state of affairs that has moral value on that theory. FEI is not a command of this kind. Humanity in a person is not something to be brought about, but the reason to bring about what respect for humanity in a person requires in a given context. As the institutional co-legislation argument rests on a version of a social ethics that requires a teleological ('task-setting') rewriting of FEI, it departs from Kant in a non-Kantian spirit. Any condemnation of capitalism it sustains is independent of FEI, as a formula of an imperative reflecting the principle of autonomy of the will.

---

87   *MS*, 6: 386–7.

The Division of Labour Argument

The division of labour argument may be represented as follows:

(1) Never treat humanity in a person merely as a means.

(2) In the context of employing another person, it treats their humanity merely as a means not to give them the chance to perform intellectually creative work, by giving them only menial machine labour to perform. Therefore:

(3) It is a strict duty not to employ a producer only for menial machine labour. Yet:

(4) The capitalist employs some workers exclusively for menial machine labour, to appropriate the product. Therefore:

(5) Insofar as capitalists employ workers exclusively for menial machine labour in a statistically significant number of employment relations in all capitalisms, FEI condemns all capitalisms

Central to Cohen's defence of (2) is the claim that 'the vocation for morality cannot be fulfilled except on the basis of scientific insight'.[88] In itself, this claim is unobjectionable. A problem arises, however, if it is used to defend (2). For it then presupposes a teleological rewriting of FEI.

Suppose FEI is *not* rewritten along teleological lines. The division of labour argument would then have to be: humanity in a producer's person is disrespected when a producer is only given menial machine labour to perform, because performing only menial machine labour thwarts their acquisition of the scientific outlook they require to fulfil their moral vocation. This argument implies that humanity in a person is disrespected when it is not promoted (through the offer of intellectually creative work) *for the sake of a further end*, the fulfilment of a moral vocation. If the point of not disrespecting humanity in a person is a *further end*, however, humanity in a person is not *always* to be respected. It is to be respected only when its respect is a means for that further end. If it is necessary to disrespect humanity in a person to promote the fulfilment of a moral vocation (for example, to lie to *A* to get *A* to develop a scientific outlook), then humanity in a person is not to be respected. In this form, the division of labour argument implies that humanity in a person lacks the absolute worth that it must have if FEI is to be grounded as a possible categorical imperative in the first place.

The division of labour argument presupposes that the Never Merely as a Means principle is rewritten as: never hinder the promotion of a person's moral

---

88   Cohen 1904, pp. 477–8.

vocation. This rewriting of FEI implies that the end it commands is something to be brought about, however. Like the institutional co-legislation argument, the division of labour argument rests on an implausible version of strategy (1). Unless an obligatory end can be taken to be provided by the value of something that exists in finite rational agents, there can be no obligatory-end-based formula of an imperative reflecting a moral law whose principle is autonomy of the will. Whatever condemnation of capitalism can be rescued from the division of labour argument will be unable to show that FEI can condemn capitalism.

The Community Argument

The structure of the community argument is from moral community to a morality-preparing form of universal active citizenship as its condition, and from the latter to universal economic independence as its condition. The final part of the argument admits two versions: economic independence may be taken to consist either in (i) the opportunity to work and acquire means of life in circumstances of classless reciprocity, as a condition for principles of political life to be assessed and decided upon free from class bias; or in (ii) the opportunity to work and acquire means of life by using resources held in common for a common aim, as a condition for principles of political life to be assessed and decided upon in an impartial manner. In what follows, I focus on (ii), although what is said in response to (ii) also applies to (i).

One complication with both versions of the argument is that a general state of affairs – 'the rule of private capital' or 'planless anarchy of value production' – is presented as the object of condemnation. FEI is a formula of a moral law that condemns conduct. If a state of affairs is to signal a FEI-based objection to capitalism, an agent within capitalism must possess the capacity to set and pursue this state of affairs *as an end*. As only a lawmaker or policy-maker has the capacity, in capitalism, to bring about a *general* state of affairs, the community argument must be revised so that it relates FEI to the context of conduct by a lawmaker or policy-maker. Version (ii) of this revised community argument would have to run as follows:

(1)   Never treat humanity in a person merely as a means.

(2)   In the context of lawmaking, it treats humanity in a person merely as a means to omit to relieve the producer's dependence on employment in a unit of production that pursues its particular interests at others' expense. Therefore:

(3)   It is a strict duty for a lawmaker to relieve the producer's dependence on a unit of production that pursues its particular interests at others' expense. Yet:

(4)   In capitalism, the lawmaker omits to relieve the worker's dependence
      on a unit of production that competes to maximise its profits at others'
      expense, to avoid antagonising profit-maximising units of production.
      Therefore:

(5)   Insofar as lawmakers in all capitalisms omit to relieve this dependence,
      FEI condemns all capitalisms.

A form of argument linking moral community to universal economic independence as its condition was outlined above; and an omission of action can be
attributed to an agent with the capacity to perform it. A lawmaker has the capacity to relieve the worker's economic dependence on a profit-maximising unit
of production by offering employment in not-for-profit public works schemes,
or by nationalising productive assets and initiating not-for-profit production
with them. It is hard, moreover, to deny that (4) is true of all capitalisms.

The problem with the revised community argument, however, is that it
requires a teleological rewriting of FEI. If FEI is *not* rewritten along teleological lines, the argument would have to be: humanity in a worker's person is
disrespected when the lawmaker omits to relieve the worker's dependence on
a profit-maximising unit of production, because this dependence thwarts the
political life that is necessary for preparing agents to cultivate a moral disposition. Yet *this* defence of (2) implies that humanity in a person is disrespected
when it is not promoted (by uprooting economic dependence) *for the sake of
a further end*, the cultivation of a moral disposition. But then humanity in a
person is not *always* to be respected. If it were necessary to disrespect humanity in a person to promote the cultivation of a moral disposition (for example,
to disrespect the humanity of a person who opposes a lawmaker's attempts to
promote universal economic independence), then humanity in a person is not
to be respected. On this defence of (2), humanity in a person lacks the absolute
worth that it must have if FEI is to be grounded in the first place.

The revised community argument presupposes that Kant's Never Merely as
a Means principle is rewritten as: never hinder the cultivation of a moral disposition. But as we have seen, a teleological rewriting of FEI is not a plausible
version of strategy (1). The obligatory end in a formula expressing, in imperative form, a moral law whose principle is autonomy of the will, cannot be an end
to be brought about. Even a revised community argument does not show that
FEI can condemn capitalism.

The Veil of Ignorance Argument

The veil of ignorance argument adopts strategy (2). If the Never Merely as a
Means principle is elaborated by appeal to what would be decided from behind
a version of a Rawlsian veil of ignorance, it cannot refer to persons. Agents

behind a version of a Rawlsian veil of ignorance do not possess (or assume one another to possess) the capacity to obey principles for the sake of duty. They have the capacity to abide by the principles they choose, and, in selecting principles, they presume that compliance resulting from the exercise of this capacity will generally be forthcoming.[89] But compliance to principles (for whatever motive) does not suffice for personality. As agents behind a version of a Rawlsian veil of ignorance do not possess (or assume one another to possess) personality, what they can agree to is not a device for representing the absolute worth of humanity in a person. Nor can agents behind a version of a Rawlsian veil of ignorance rationally endorse FEI, as the principle of always treating humanity in a person as an end. They have no reason to endorse a principle whose only upshot is to subordinate themselves to another species of being. The veil of ignorance argument must therefore re-write the Never Merely as a Means principle as: never treat humanity *in a being* merely as a means.[90]

Suppose that we make this revision. We must then reject, on Kantian grounds, Kant's claim that 'morality is the condition under which alone a rational being can be an end in itself',[91] and thereby reject, on Kantian grounds, the whole notion of moral autonomy. Even if this did result in a better understanding of the value of rational nature, the problem would remain that a *transaction-based version* of a Rawlsian veil of ignorance will tend to lead to decisions that violate this principle (as well as Kant's).

A transaction-based original position will tend to violate either Never Merely as a Means principle, because only participants are represented in it. As only participants are represented in it, only their interests are taken into account. The veil of ignorance argument does not only rely on the idea that participants in a capitalist wage bargain would agree from behind a veil of ignorance that no participant should benefit from surplus labour performed by any one of them just on account of owning property acquired through illegitimate means. It also relies on the idea that, from behind a veil of ignorance, participants would agree that all such surplus labour is to benefit only the participants themselves.

---

89 Besides the 'assumption of mutually disinterested rationality ... [t]here is one further assumption to guarantee strict compliance. The parties are presumed to be capable of a sense of justice and this fact is public knowledge among them. This condition ... means that the parties can rely on each other to understand and to act in accordance with whatever principles are finally agreed to' (Rawls 1971, p. 145). '[E]lements of social solidarity and good will' are expressly rejected as a motivation of parties in the original position at Rawls 1971, p. 146.

90 This is a simplification, because the comparative aspect of humanity is not represented behind a Rawlsian veil of ignorance either; see sec. 6 below.

91 *GMS*, 4: 435; see also *KpV*, 5: 131–2; *KU*, 5: 431.

In determining whether a producer is in actual fact 'worse off'[92] than if the transaction's terms are settled behind a veil of ignorance, the only alternative distributions to be considered are distributions in which participants in the transaction are the only recipients.

The problem this raises is that mutually disinterested beings with humanity who know that they have a position in a transaction will prefer any arrangement that leaves all participants in their transaction better off over any arrangement that leaves all participants worse off, even if the former arrangement treats humanity in the being of a non-participant merely as a means by virtue of omission.[93] From behind this veil of ignorance, mutually disinterested beings are unconcerned if non-participants are adversely affected. They have no reason not to agree to an arrangement that treats a non-participant merely as a means, if that is to the advantage of all participants, as it will be, under capitalism. For market competition tends to ensure that capitalists do not all have equal amounts of illegitimately acquired property, and that workers do not all have equally advantageous combinations of valued skills and inexpensive needs. If non-participants cannot be recipients of any surplus labour performed by participants, some claims will be inappropriately ignored. It is a fatal objection to the veil of ignorance argument that the device it recommends will tend to violate the version of the Never Merely as a Means principle that this device is used to elaborate.

The Capital Accumulation Argument

The capital accumulation argument, which adopts strategies (3) and (4), is that, if it is possible, in capitalism, for output expansion to be accompanied by an absolute decrease in social consumption, social consumption is not one of the ends of capitalist production; but if social consumption is not one of the ends of capitalist production, workers in capitalism are treated merely as means. There are various problems with this argument.

One problem is that the argument has gaps. We need to know why a form of production only treats humanity in the person of its producers as an end if social consumption is one of its ends. The general category of 'social consumption' does not appear to require a particular distribution of means of consumption, or a focus on items whose consumption is moral rather than immoral. A more fine-grained account of consumption and its value is required, if the capital accumulation argument is to count as an argument from FEI.

---

92   Wolff 1999, p. 113.
93   Compare Kant's notion of general injustice, discussed in sec. 6.

A second problem is that Tugan-Baranowsky does not seem to target a spe-cifically capitalist feature of capitalist production. Tugan-Baranowsky says of the social reproduction scheme that he presents, and that illustrates the pos-sibility for social consumption to decrease at the same time as output expands (at a constant level of productivity and without a disturbance of demand and supply), that it illustrates the possibility for this decrease to accompany 'the accumulation of capital'.[94] This does not seem right. Capital accumulates from T_1 to T_2 if all profit-maximising firms taken together can purchase a greater proportion of the total social product at T_2 than at T_1, and all workers taken together can only purchase a lesser proportion of the total social product at T_2 than at T_1. If output expands at a constant level of productivity owing to a decrease in social consumption, no capital accumulation need have taken place. The decrease in social consumption could occur due to a decrease in cap-italists' personal consumption. The proportion of the total social product that could be purchased with the total income of workers could remain unchanged.

To be sure, capital accumulation can be accompanied by a relative decrease in consumption by workers. It can proceed in tandem with technical advance reflected in a capacity to produce, at T_2, the total social product of T_1 in less overall time than at T_1. The proportion of total labour time expended in produc-ing commodities other than workers' means of consumption at T_2 may then exceed the proportion at T_1.

However, even if it is argued, on the basis of this different claim, that workers' consumption is not one of the ends of production subject to capital accumu-lation, and that it ought to be of value, the problem remains that the argument does not rest on a descriptive premise to which FEI can be applied. A claim about capital accumulation cannot be translated into an *end* on *anyone's* part. There is no content to the notion of being treated merely as a means that is not resolvable into the notion of an agent (or associating agents) acting in pursuit of an end so as to treat someone merely as a means. But no capitalist (or group of capitalists) pursues the end of capital accumulation by means of a relative decrease in workers' consumption. Rather, each capitalist seeks to maximize their *own* profit, by producing and selling *whatever* type of commodity can be expected to maximize returns, whether or not it is an item of consumption by workers. Insofar as capital accumulation and a relative decrease in workers' consumption is the unintended macro-level consequence of actions by *inde-pendent* capitalists, no objection to capital accumulation can be formulated in terms of FEI.

---

94   Tugan-Baranowsky 1901, p. 27.

The Vulnerability Argument

The vulnerability argument, which adopts strategies (3) and (4), can be represented as follows:

(1)   Never treat humanity in a person merely as a means.

(2)   In the context of seeking one's own advantage (and where people regard the treatment of their capacity to work as essential to their self-worth), it treats humanity in the person of poor producers merely as a means for the wealthy to play on their vulnerability.

Therefore (given an assumption about self-worth):

(3)   It is a strict duty for the wealthy not to play on poor producers' vulnerability for their own advantage.

Yet:

(4)   The wealthy capitalist plays on the poor worker's vulnerability to hire the worker on terms favourable to the capitalist (even though workers in capitalism regard the treatment of their capacity to work as essential to their self-worth)

Therefore:

(5)   Insofar as wealthy capitalists in all class divided capitalisms play on poor workers' vulnerability for their own advantage, FEI condemns all such capitalisms.

Before assessing the vulnerability argument, it is necessary to say something more about vulnerability. Wood suggests that vulnerability in the context of a capitalist economy is a macro-level feature of the relation between classes: 'the working class is vulnerable to the capitalist class'.[95] To say that the working-class is vulnerable to the capitalist class is to say that workers have 'no acceptable alternative'[96] but to work for a capitalist. Workers' 'condition of vulnerability' is a 'structural' point about 'the whole capitalist economy and the general or collective position of wage laborers in it'.[97] It is not negated by the fact that in some cases, 'rarer' than 'quite often', 'workers may have the option of borrowing money and going into business for themselves'.[98]

The structural nature of workers' vulnerability suggests a decisive objection to the use of (4) in a FEI-based argument against capitalism. A FEI-based argument against capitalism from vulnerability must elaborate the treatment that some people suffer in capitalism in terms of vulnerability. Yet if (4) refers to the

---

95   Wood 2014, p. 297.
96   Wood 1995b, p. 149.
97   Wood 2004, p. 254.
98   Ibid. Wood here endorses G.A. Cohen's notion of 'collective unfreedom' (Cohen 1988, pp. 255–85).

capitalist's playing on the worker's vulnerability, (4) need not describe the act and end of the capitalist in hiring a worker. All the capitalist has to do in hiring a worker is invite the worker to act on the piece of reasoning: 'if I agree to work for this firm, I will be paid x in return for work y'. This simple piece of reasoning does not bear in mind the worker's vulnerability, for it does not bear in mind any collective position of workers vis-à-vis the capitalist class.

A proponent of the argument from vulnerability might respond: although this simple piece of reasoning does not refer to vulnerability, it does bear in mind an amount of money, x, which is determined by what the capitalist believes about the collective position of workers vis-à-vis the capitalist class. It is offered in the knowledge that a worker will take it, due to the latter's vulnerability. This proponent says: as this simple piece of reasoning rests on an assumption about workers' vulnerability, the capitalist plays on the worker's vulnerability by inviting the worker to act on it.

It may be conceded that an agent can use a background assumption in pursuing an end without referring to it. A person intent on murder who appears at the door and asks where little Johnny is, may assume that you will answer in the belief that you are helping them to reunite with their lost child. They use their assumption that you will be motivated to respond in this way, even if a description of their act and end need not refer to this assumption.[99] This concession cannot save the argument from vulnerability, however. It is neither necessary nor sufficient for the capitalist to believe that the worker they wish to hire is vulnerable, in order to determine what amount of money to offer.

To maximise profit, a capitalist has a reason to offer the lowest legally permissible wage that is consistent with its being the best pay option for the offeree. To this end, the capitalist must know (or make an assumption about) the next best pay option of the person they wish to hire. To obtain this knowledge (or make this assumption), it is not sufficient or necessary to know (or assume) that this person is a member of a class that is vulnerable to the capitalist class. It is not sufficient, because vulnerability, as a structural fact, reveals nothing about the salaries that rival capitalist firms may be willing to pay this person. It is not necessary, because the source of income in the next best pay option – a salary from a rival firm or from self-employment, profits from a start-up business or welfare benefits – as well as the rarity of this potential income source for workers, is irrelevant. Although capitalists can be said to use any knowledge presupposed by the simple piece of reasoning they invite

---

99   Compare Korsgaard 1996, p. 155.

workers to act on, no knowledge of workers' vulnerability is presupposed by this simple piece of reasoning. As the nature of the capitalist's conduct in the marketplace does not depend on the vulnerability of the workers they hire, the vulnerability argument does not show that FEI can condemn capitalism. It relies on a descriptive structural premise to which FEI cannot be applied.[100]

The Freedom in Production Argument

The freedom in production argument pursues strategies (3)–(4). It is presented as an argument against capitalist exploiters in the plural, however.[101] As only agents set ends, there are two ways forward.

Option *A* is to individualise the descriptive premise to which FEI is applied, in the freedom in production argument. This premise is then: the capitalist prevents the worker they hire from pursuing their own purposes with productive assets, to appropriate the product. This premise is not true as a description of capitalism, however. A worker is prevented from pursuing their own purposes with productive assets (other than their labour power; in other words, with means of production) if they are denied access to *all* productive assets other than their own labour power. No single capitalist firm taken in isolation acts to deny any worker it employs access to any productive assets beyond those it owns.

At most, each capitalist firm, by retaining its assets and reinvesting its profits, causally contributes to the continuation of a situation in which many workers remain without access to any productive assets, beyond their own labour power. Yet this consequence does not form part of a descriptive premise to which FEI can be applied. For it to feature in a descriptive premise as an *end* – this is option *B* – it is necessary to claim that each capitalist firm pursues the end of retaining its assets as part of a greater plan, in association with all other

---

100   The objection to the vulnerability argument has implications for a conception of exploitation that defines it as beneficial 'playing on some weakness or vulnerability' (Wood 1995b, p. 147). The objection to the vulnerability argument is that, if workers' vulnerability is structural in nature, then a capitalist need not play on a worker's vulnerability in order to hire them. But if a capitalist need not play on a worker's vulnerability to hire them, no capitalist need exploit any worker they hire, on this conception. To not exploit a worker they hire, the capitalist can invite the worker to act on the simple piece of reasoning described above. As no capitalist need ever play on any worker's vulnerability, Wood has no grounds to call the capitalist wage bargain inherently exploitative; yet the fact that it is 'virtually always' exploitative, Wood says, 'should be obvious' (Wood 1995b, p. 155).

101   See Schwartz 1995b, pp. 176–7.

capitalist firms, for all capitalist firms to retain their assets, or at least for all assets to be retained by capitalist firms. Yet this option is no more promising than the first. It is again untrue of really existing capitalism. No capitalist firm need belong to an association of capitalist firms committed to any such plan, provided that there is freedom of association. As the freedom in production argument suggests no true descriptive premise stating an act and end of a type of conduct to which it can be applied, it cannot show that FEI can condemn capitalism.

6   FEI and General Injustice

Thus far, we have been examining Kantian arguments for applying FEI to condemn capitalism that are *intrinsic* to the interpretation of FEI. That is to say, the normative premises of these arguments are provided solely by FEI, and by a contextualising premise that relates FEI directly to the act and end of a type of conduct. This is not the only way in which one might seek to apply FEI to condemn capitalism, however. A Kantian might seek to apply FEI to condemn capitalism with an argument that includes an additional normative premise that is *extrinsic* to the interpretation of FEI.

FEI's Never Merely as a Means principle imposes strict duties, and it is a strict duty not to violate another person's right. So, what FEI can condemn, on account of its Never Merely as a Means principle, will depend on what rights a person is considered to have. Even if *Kant* does not identify a right that is violated by a type of conduct essential to capitalism, if a Kantian principle of right can ground such a right, FEI's Never Merely as a Means principle can condemn capitalism, by condemning a type of conduct that violates a person's right. This kind of FEI-based argument against capitalism is extrinsic to FEI's interpretation in as much as the argumentative burden is to justify, on Kantian grounds, an application of a principle of right that condemns capitalism. If a Kantian principle of right can condemn capitalism, then FEI's Never Merely as a Means principle can also condemn capitalism, notwithstanding the inability of any intrinsically FEI-based arguments to condemn capitalism.[102]

---

102 A complementarity view that rests on an *extrinsically* FEI-based argument for condemn-
     ing capitalism remains subject to the objection regarding socialist strategy presented in
     Chapter 2. Indeed, in respect of socialist strategy, it faces an additional hurdle relating to
     the compatibility of a strategy of class struggle with Kant's grounding argument for the
     principle of right. Class-interest-pursuing, impartial-good-seeking actions by a working-
     class movement against a capitalist class may be precluded, if its use of coercion to abolish

In this chapter, we are asking whether FEI can sustain a *Kantian* condemnation of capitalism. Only a Kantian condemnation of capitalism can make the complementarity view plausible, at least in terms of the goal of abolishing capitalism. An extrinsically FEI-based argument can sustain a Kantian condemnation of capitalism only if a type of action essential to capitalism is found to violate a *Kantian* principle of right. A Kantian condemnation of capitalism need not be provided by conjoining FEI with just *any* principle of right. A Kantian condemnation of capitalism is not provided if, for instance, we affirm a version of the capability approach to justice that implies that the failure to promote the capability of everyone up to a certain level (subject to an efficiency constraint and a fairness constraint) is an injustice;[103] judge that this injustice is inherent to capitalism; and suggest that we may infer, from our conclusion that a lawmaker commits an injustice by maintaining capitalism, that the lawmaker also violates FEI's Never Merely as a Means principle. We would not have argued that our version of the capability approach to justice was a Kantian approach to justice. An extrinsically FEI-based argument against capitalism is only Kantian if it rests not just on a Kantian interpretation of FEI, but also on a Kantian principle of right.

If a Kantian accepts FEI, then we know what to expect from a Kantian principle of right. FEI commands us always to treat humanity in a person as an end, and never merely as a means. It presupposes an argument for why only humanity in a person has absolute worth. To affirm FEI is thus to be committed to respect the exclusive absolute worth of a person's humanity. It is to be committed to affirm only those principles of right that are consistent with this respect. Only principles of right consistent with the exclusive absolute worth of a person's humanity can be Kantian principles of right.

Principles of right (for us human beings) are distinct from objective categorical imperatives. Only the latter are addressed to all finite persons. However, the imperative expressed by FEI concerns the treatment of a person's humanity, and humanity and personality can be regarded as coextensive, at least as far as human beings are concerned. So, even if personality is bracketed in the formulation of principles of right, a fundamental principle of right will be consistent with FEI, and therefore applicable in an extrinsically FEI-based argument

---

a (by Kantian standards) unjust capitalist society is subject to the same constraints as uses of coercion in a (by Kantian standards) just society; namely, that however much coercion serves an end that conforms with morality, rightful coercion may not violate a Kantian principle of right.

103   Compare Sen 2009, p. 296.

against capitalism, only if it adequately expresses the value of human beings' humanity; in other words, the value of the non-moral part of our rational nature.

In *The Metaphysics of Morals*, Kant claims that there is only one principle of right that relates to our humanity:

> *Freedom* (independence from being constrained by another's choice), insofar as it can coexist with the freedom of every other in accordance with a universal law, is the only original right belonging to every man by virtue of his humanity.[104]

In Kant's view, the value of our humanity is adequately acknowledged in the sphere of right if we recognise one fundamental principle of right: a principle of freedom for all, in which freedom is 'independence from being constrained by another's choice'. An extrinsically FEI-based argument against capitalism is Kantian, therefore, only if it identifies a type of conduct essential to capitalism that violates FEI's Never Merely as a Means principle on account of violating the principle of 'independence from being constrained by another's choice'; or if it revises this principle of right, on the Kantian grounds that the revision expresses the value of humanity, and then argues that a type of conduct essential to capitalism violates FEI's Never Merely as a Means principle by violating this revised principle of right. This allows us to add one final strategy to the list of strategies, outlined in section 4, that a Kantian can employ, to use FEI to condemn conduct that Kant did not use FEI to condemn:

(1) Revise a value criterion in Kant's *a priori* argument for FEI as a categorical imperative, to strengthen the justification of FEI as a formula of a moral law whose principle is autonomy of the will.

(2) Revise Kant's statement of FEI, to better capture the value of rational nature.

(3) Affirm a contextualising premise that Kant did not affirm.

(4) Subsume under a contextualising premise a description of conduct that Kant did not consider.

(5) Revise Kant's statement of the principle of right, to express the value of humanity

In this section, we shall focus on an extrinsically FEI-based argument against capitalism that does *not* rely on strategy (5), but merely (3) and (4). Strategy (5) is seldom undertaken, if at all, explicitly, let alone in combination with an

---

104   *MS*, 6: 237.

explicit condemnation of capitalism. To illustrate this point, consider the revisions that would be required in order to present Rawlsian justice as fairness as a version of strategy (5) with which to condemn capitalism.

Two major revisions would be required, if Rawlsian justice as fairness was to be presented as an extrinsically FEI-based argument against capitalism. First, one would have to show that Rawls's view, in respect of the choice between a capitalist regime and a socialist regime, that 'the theory of justice does not by itself favour either form of regime',[105] does not reflect a true understanding of the method and principles of Rawlsian justice as fairness. Rather, Rawlsian justice as fairness would have to be shown to unambiguously condemn capitalism.[106] Second, however, one would have to argue that the value of our humanity, as it features (or should feature) in FEI, is expressed in the method and principles of Rawlsian justice as fairness. This hardly seems possible unless humanity is represented in the original position – Rawls's device for justifying principles of justice.[107] But humanity is not represented in Rawls's original position, and nor can it be.

Kant remarks in *Religion Within the Bounds of Bare Reason*:

> The predispositions to **humanity** can be brought under the general title of a no doubt physical but yet *comparing* self-love (for which reason is required): namely to judge oneself happy or unhappy only by comparison with others. From this self-love stems the inclination *to procure a worth for oneself in the opinion of others*, originally, to be sure, merely that of *equality*: to permit no one superiority over oneself, combined with a constant worry that others might strive for this, from which arises gradually an unjust desire to gain superiority over others.[108]

We may understand this statement by beginning with Kant's remark in *The Metaphysics of Morals* that '[t]he capacity to set oneself an end – any end whatsoever – is what characterizes humanity'.[109] If humanity is characterised by the capacity to set any end, it must also include any rational require-

---

105   Rawls 1971, p. 280.

106   Perhaps by arguing that, of the two options that Rawls seems to favour, property-owning democracy or liberal socialism, 'property-owning democracy ... offers little in the way of preventing those with concentrated ownership of capital from influencing legislation in their interests' (Shoikhedbrod 2019, p. 150).

107   See Rawls 1971.

108   *RGV*, 6: 27.

109   *MS*, 6: 392.

ment of setting ends. It must include the capacity to order ends rationally, and the capacity to select means to them rationally. This, Kant says, involves comparing our judgments with those of others, as an '*external* touchstone of truth'.[110] We are rationally required to compare our judgments with those of others not just in respect of our choice of means to an individual end, but in respect of our ordering of ends. As the rational aim of ordering ends is to bring them 'to harmony in a whole called happiness',[111] we judge ourselves 'happy or unhappy only by comparison with others' insofar as we compare our ordering of ends with others' orderings of ends. Further, if it is rational for us to affirm our judgments about means and the ordering of ends only after comparing our judgments with those of others, it is rational for us to want to believe that others would ultimately confirm our (revised) judgments. To want this is to want to believe that others *value* us (as we value them) as judgers. If all these non-moral capacities are rationally related in us, then, on Kant's account, our prudential reason is inseparable from a desire to see that others value us (as we value them) in respect of our capacity for judgment.

The part of humanity that involves a want to see oneself as an equal '*in the opinion of others*' finds no representation in Rawls's original position. From behind a veil of ignorance about anyone's place in society, or individual make-up, parties in the original position search for principles of justice that 'advance their system of ends as far as possible'.[112] The parties all 'accept the account of the good ... that they would prefer more primary social goods rather than less'.[113] But given the 'assumption of mutually disinterested rationality', each searches for principles that will provide them with 'as high an absolute'[114] amount of goods as possible, without considering how their own amount will then compare to the amount that others obtain, and so without considering how the respective amounts of each may bear on the possibility for each to see itself as valued by others. As the rationality of the parties in the original position is prudential *and yet* 'mutually disinterested', humanity as Kant conceives it is not fully represented in the original position. If Rawls's original position cannot adequately express the value of our humanity, no principle of right that is derived from Rawls's original position is sufficiently Kantian to qualify for use in a version of strategy (5).

---

110   *Log*, 9: 57; compare *Anth*, 7: 128–130. For comment, see ch. 8, sec. 3.
111   *RGV*, 6: 58.
112   Rawls 1971, p. 144.
113   Rawls 1971, p. 142.
114   Rawls 1971, p. 144.

In *Rescuing Justice and Equality*, G.A. Cohen elaborates an objection to Rawlsian justice as fairness that relates to its inadequate representation of humanity (as Kant conceives it) in the original position:

> the original position also excludes a concern for how much one person gets compared with somebody else: what I get by comparison with others finds no representation within that position, and believers in the claim to justice of relational equality should therefore be as wary of the original position, as a criterion of justice, as Nozick is. The original position gives no shrift to the motivating relational egalitarian thought that differences of fortune between people who are beyond their control represent the triumph of the "morally arbitrary". Since its denizens lack the very concept of justice, comparative rewards could matter within the original position only if those denizens were envious or spiteful, and so forth: being insensitive to justice, as such, they could care fundamentally about the fortunes of other people only from such lousy points of view. In fact, however, they are, *ex hypothesi*, mutually disinterested: nobody cares what others get, as such. The interpersonal-fairness aspect of justice, which motivated the whole enterprise, is thereby dropped at the front door, and there is no back door by which the equality favored by fairness might be reintroduced. What we have is a striking discrepancy between the motivating thought about justice that precedes recommendation of the original position and the character of that position. And because the denizens of the original position are entirely insensitive to inequality as such, they elect the difference principle in its canonical, lexical form, which permits increases in inequality that do not benefit the worst off (as long as they do not harm them), and which, as we have seen, gives no weight to equality at all.[115]

Either the rational desire to be valued by others as an equal is not represented in the original position, in which case Rawlsian justice cannot provide a version of strategy (5), because humanity is inadequately represented by its justificatory device; or the original position is modified to include it, in which case, the

---

115   Cohen 2008, pp. 158–60. Rawls says that parties in the original position do 'not ... try to gain relative to each other; they are not envious or vain ... nor do they seek to maximize or minimize the difference between their successes and those of others' (Rawls 1971, p. 144). Yet Rawls's 'mutually disinterested rationality' precludes not just envy and vanity but also the rational desire to see oneself valued by others as an equal, which, in Kant's view, is inseparable from prudential reason.

parties are motivated by a relational concern absent from the account of the good that Rawls ascribes to them, and they will not select Rawls's principles of justice as fairness. In particular, the parties will not select Rawls's difference principle. Either way, Rawlsian justice as fairness is unsuited to provide a version of strategy (5).[116]

Focusing, then, on extrinsically FEI-based arguments to condemn capitalism that do not rely on strategy (5), we need to consider what kinds of conduct are able to violate Kant's principle of right, as a principle of 'independence from being constrained by another's choice'. Kant's principle can be violated (i) by an unjust transaction between two actors, or (ii) by an unjust state of affairs, to which many separate acts of injustice contribute, and which a lawmaker is authorised to correct. The former is a case of transactional injustice, while the latter is a case of what Kant calls 'general injustice'. Kant distinguishes the two in a comment in *Lectures on Ethics*: '[o]ne may take a share in the general injustice, even though one does nobody any wrong by civil laws and practices'.[117] For a type of conduct essential to capitalism to violate Kant's principle of right, either a type of transaction that is essential to a capitalist economy must violate it, or a response by a capitalism-guaranteeing lawmaker to a state of affairs that is produced by many instances of unjust conduct essential to capitalism must violate it.

A number of factors make the prospects of a successful argument doubtful. Transactions involving workers and capitalist firms are concluded by individual workers (or a particular group of workers) and a particular firm (or firms in a particular branch of production), not between all workers taken together as one party and all capitalist firms taken together as the other party. This fact impacts on what Kant's principle of right can require. It is possible, in capital-

---

116   This raises the question: if a form of *post*-Rawlsian constructivism *were* to represent humanity in the original position, could *this* approach to selecting principles of justice require us to select principles that would condemn capitalism as unjust, and so sustain an extrinsically FEI-based condemnation of capitalism? A post-Rawlsian constructivism might select principles of justice that condemn coercion, as Wood (2017, p. 648) defines it, for reasons suggested by the vulnerability argument (see sec. 1 above). But as argued below against the morality of general injustice argument, to prohibit coercion (as Wood defines it) is not to prohibit capitalist wage labour.

117   *V-Mo/Collins*, 27: 416. The context is Kant's claim that, if we 'survey that worldly stage upon which nature has set us as guests ... everyone has a right to enjoy the good things of this world'. If I encounter a 'table laden with food in the forest', then 'I have obligations to limit my consumption' so that others can partake. If many of us each ignore our obligation, and take more than our share, we are each 'helping to take away' nature's goods from others who are left unable to enjoy their right 'through a general injustice' (*V-Mo/Collins*, 27: 414–16).

ism, to implement laws to ensure that each particular employer has no option but to hire on impartial criteria without deceit or threat, honour all terms of a contract, and refrain from interfering with its workers' rights to pursue other economic opportunities. If so, it seems possible for Kant's principle of right to be respected, in transactions involving workers and capitalist firms.

Second, although each market actor in capitalism, regardless of their class, is dependent on a price system that constraints them, this need not translate into a claim about a market actor in capitalism 'being constrained by another's choice'.[118] The circulation of commodities may require each separate market actor to seek to achieve their ends by adjusting to unpredictable movements in prices that result from 'nothing but the caprices of their customers and competitors'.[119] But a price system that aggregates caprice – that *results* from others' choices – is not itself a choice, or capacity for choice. Movements in prices do not have a volition of their own. As what each market actor depends on is not a human being with a capacity for choice, but a price system, this dependence does not appear to contradict Kant's principle of right. Kant's principle of right is not a normative standard that applies directly to systems any more than Kant's Formula of the End in Itself applies directly to systems.

More plausible, it might seem, is an extrinsically FEI-based argument against capitalism from general injustice. Vorländer suggests one argument of this kind, distinct from the community argument discussed above, although its suggestion represents something of a change of heart. In *Kant und der Sozialismus* (1900), Vorländer remarks:

> Kant's political ideal, as we noted above, remains shaped in the *first* instance by the thought of *freedom*. The *true* and *real* connection of socialism with critical philosophy is instead grounded in what is 'purely moral', in the consequences (not always practically drawn by Kant himself) of that simple, exquisite formula of the categorical imperative which teaches us to treat humanity in the person of each of our fellow human beings always and at the same time as an end in itself, and never merely as a means.[120]

---

118   Kant's phrase is: '*eines Anderen nöthigender Willkür*' (*MS*, 6: 237). '*Willkür*' can also denote 'volition' or 'caprice'. A system can be necessitating, but it is not the sort of thing that has '*Willkür*'. Kant's use of the singular, '*eines Anderen*', also discourages a view of what an individual is to have independence from on which the latter include the effects of systems that merely *result* from the choices of others.

119   Roberts 2017, p. 57.

120   Vorländer 1900, p. 13.

There is no suggestion here of the possibility of an extrinsically FEI-based argument against capitalism from general injustice. Consistent with his claim, earlier in the same text, that the defence of socialism rests on the concept of community,[121] Vorländer does not suggest that the concept of freedom underpinning Kant's principle of right has any relation to the defence of socialism. Any extrinsically FEI-based argument against capitalism from general injustice presupposes such a relation, however. Any such argument presupposes that Kant's principle of right can *also* be applied to condemn capitalism *independently* of FEI, on the grounds of general justice *alone*. No one who offers an extrinsically FEI-based argument against capitalism from general injustice can consistently claim that socialism's connection to Kant's philosophy is 'instead grounded in what is "purely moral"'.

Adopting a different tack, Vorländer offers a line of thought relating socialism to Kant's view of freedom in a later work, entitled *Kant, Fichte, Hegel und der Sozialismus* (1920):

> But it is a different question what consequences those of *us* living today ought to draw, for contemporary economic relations, from Kant's political ideal; whether – as Kant himself once said about Plato – we might not 'understand' him 'better than he understood himself'. At the point in *Critique of Pure Reason* just touched on – the crucial place that completes the transition from the doctrine of experience to the doctrine of ideas, and so to Kant's characteristic critical idealism – Kant characterises, as a 'necessary idea' that ought to lie behind any state constitution, indeed all laws, 'a constitution providing for the *greatest* human freedom according to laws that permit the freedom of *each* to exist together with that of *others*'. But where, today, is such freedom possible, except under socialist rule? The freedom of the individual is but an empty delusion as long as the rule of private capital in fact makes the individual a mere means of labour in the hands of the possessor, and for the latter's ends. Freedom only becomes a reality with the provision of a state of affairs [*Zustand*] in which it is also economically the case that no one is absolutely dependent on another. Only when the free development of all one's abilities is enabled not just in words, but by real, permanent institutions for *every* citizen, is Kant's supreme moral law fulfilled – that categorical imperative according to which no human being is a mere means, but is always at the same time an end in itself.[122]

---

121   Vorländer 1900, p. 7. Vorländer's community argument is discussed in sec. 1 and sec. 5.
122   Vorländer 1920, p. 45, citing Kant 1998, A 314/B 370 and A 316/B 373. A '*Zustand*' is a state

Vorländer now claims that the concept of freedom that underpins Kant's political philosophy is important to guarantee in and of itself; that this freedom cannot be guaranteed for all in the economic sphere if the latter is organised by private capital; and that capitalism is therefore to be condemned. (Indeed, rejecting his earlier suggestion that the concept of freedom in Kant's political philosophy and a defence of socialism are unconnected, Vorländer claims that, in the present historical conjuncture, the only feasible way for such freedom to be guaranteed to all is under socialism.)

As FEI condemns conduct, and as it is only the lawmaker who has the capacity, in capitalism, to modify or abolish a general economic state of affairs, an extrinsically FEI-based argument against capitalism from general injustice must be directed at conduct by the lawmaker. If we flesh out Vorländer's suggestion in this spirit, FEI can be applied to condemn capitalism if a lawmaker is under a strict moral duty to remove an unjust state of affairs in which some individuals (workers) are denied freedom (independence from another's constraining choice) by a capitalist economy. This is an extrinsically FEI-based argument against capitalism from general injustice, for it invokes FEI on the back of a judgment about the irreconcilability of a necessary state of affairs in capitalism with the concept of rightful freedom. The argument can be represented as follows:

(1) Never treat humanity in a person merely as a means.
(2) It treats humanity in a person merely as a means to violate a person's rights
      Therefore:
(3) It is a strict moral duty not to violate a person's rights
(4) A person's rights are determined by laws that reflect the concept of freedom as independence from being constrained by another's choice
(5) A state of affairs where workers lack independence from private capital is a state of affairs in which laws fail to reflect this concept of freedom
      Therefore:
(6) In the context of making laws, lawmakers violate workers' rights if they omit to pass laws to abolish a state of affairs where workers lack independence from private capital
      Therefore:
(7) It is a strict moral duty for a lawmaker to pass laws to abolish a state of affairs where workers lack independence from private capital

---

of affairs, as distinct from a transaction. For a similar appeal to Kant's principle of right to condemn capitalism, see Tugan-Baranowsky 1908, p. 12; Tugan-Baranowsky 1910, pp. 12–13.

Yet:

(8) In capitalism, the lawmaker omits to pass laws to abolish a state of affairs where workers lack independence from private capital, to avoid antagonising capitalist firms

Therefore:

(9) Insofar as lawmakers in all capitalisms omit to pass such laws, FEI condemns all capitalisms

We can call this argument from FEI the *morality of general justice* argument. From a Kantian perspective, the controversial normative premise is (5). To assess the argument, we must first determine what it is about producers' lack of independence from private capital that makes it an instance of being constrained by another's choice. Vorländer provides us with little more than a starting point. He claims that the worker in capitalism is 'absolutely dependent' on private capital, but he does not elaborate on this claim. The idea, presumably, is that, if the worker is to live, the worker has no option but to work for a capitalist firm.

Allen Wood has suggested a Kantian argument against capitalism from general injustice that incorporates this idea.[123] Wood identifies with the tradition of thinking about justice in which, 'as Kant puts it, freedom is independence of constraint by the will of another'.[124] Further, Wood suggests that under conditions of capitalism, workers are subject to a 'deprivation of freedom' that 'could be conceptualised in Kantian terms as a form of general injustice'.[125] If capitalism can be condemned as unjust by appeal to Kant's concept of rightful freedom, via the idea of general injustice, capitalism can also be condemned by appeal to FEI.

Wood's argument for why a Kantian can condemn capitalism as a form of general injustice rests on an analysis of coercion: 'to understand what freedom (freedom as non-domination) involves, we have also to become clearer about its opposite: *coercion*'.[126] Wood offers what he calls a 'simple' concept of coercion: 'you are coerced to do something if you either have no choice but to do

---

123   Wood 2017. I do not wish to imply that Wood is inspired by Vorländer, or that Wood seeks (like Vorländer) to offer an extrinsically FEI-based argument for condemning capitalism. Wood neither mentions Vorländer, nor infers the possibility of an extrinsically FEI-based argument against capitalism from the possibility of a Kantian argument against capitalism from general injustice. However, what Wood says in defence of the latter seems to me to be the kind of attempt at a defence of (5) that the morality of general justice argument requires.

124   Wood 2017, pp. 645–6.

125   Wood 2017, p. 656.

126   Wood 2017, p. 647.

it, or if all your other choices are *unacceptable*'.[127] *A* is coerced to *x* if *A*'s choice situation is one in which *A* has no choice but to *x*, or *A* has no acceptable alternative to *x*. Wood adds that, on this analysis of coercion: 'neither you nor anyone else may have put me in that position'.[128] Neither the beneficiary of *x*, nor any other person, need have causally contributed to *A*'s choice situation.

We apply this analysis of coercion to the situation of the worker in capitalism if *A* = a worker in capitalism, and *x* = take a job at a capitalist firm. A worker in capitalism is coerced to take a job at a capitalist firm if (a) the worker has no choice but to take a job at a capitalist firm, or if (b) the worker has no acceptable alternative to taking a job at a capitalist firm. If we say that a worker who takes a job when their only other option is to see their 'family starve' has an 'unacceptable option'[129] besides that of taking the job, (a) is impossible. The application of the concept of coercion to the worker's situation in capitalism reduces to (b). A worker in capitalism is coerced to take a job at a capitalist firm if they have no acceptable alternative to taking a job at a capitalist firm, and even if no one else, including any number of capitalist firms, has causally contributed to their choice situation.

By putting together (i) the Kantian normative premise that rights ought to protect freedom as independence from being constrained by another's choice, and (ii) the simple concept of coercion and its application to capitalism, Wood suggests that, by Kantian standards, the conditions of capitalist production can be judged to constitute an injustice:

> If I have no acceptable alternative to taking the job you offer me on your terms, then I am forced to take it, and do not have the freedom not to take it. If we determine that it belongs to a free mode of life, to my rightful freedom, that someone is not put in a position where they are coerced in this way, then the exploitation involves a violation of my rights, and constitutes an injustice.[130]

This passage offers no real argument for thinking that to be coerced in some respect is to be denied rightful freedom in that respect. On the one hand, if 'do not have the freedom not to take it' stands for: 'do not have any real option not to take it', then the clause is true, but redundantly repeats the previous clause. It gets us no closer to substantiating the argument. On the other hand, if 'do

---

127   Wood 2017, p. 648.
128   Ibid.
129   Ibid.
130   Wood 2017, pp. 650–1.

not have the freedom not to take it' stands for: 'cannot turn the job down while enjoying independence from being constrained by another's choice', then the claim is false. No other person need have put me in a position where, by turning down a job at a capitalist firm, I am only left with unacceptable options. As Wood says, 'neither you nor anyone else may have put me in that position'.[131] Nor can the second sentence provide the argument we are looking for. On account of its 'if ... then' structure, it just assumes what needs to be argued for.

Why should it belong to a person's rightful freedom that they not be subject to coercion, simply conceived? We require an argument for why coercion in some respect is a denial of rightful freedom in that respect, because coercion (on Wood's account) is not identical with a denial of rightful freedom. The simple concept of coercion does not require any agency that coerces. By contrast, a denial of rightful freedom, in Kant's view, requires an agency that constrains on account of its capacity for choice.

Relatedly, Wood's aforementioned claim that coercion is the 'opposite'[132] of Kant's concept of rightful freedom is false, on Wood's analysis of coercion. But it is this analysis of coercion that underpins Wood's claim that the worker in capitalism is deprived of freedom. As the freedom that a worker in capitalism is deprived of does not suffice for them to be deprived of (what Kant views as) rightful freedom, the worker's situation in capitalism is not a case of a general injustice, and so the application of Kant's doctrine of general injustice to the worker's situation does not result in its condemnation.

The main objection to the morality of general justice argument, then, is that no convincing argument has been supplied by Vorländer or Wood for premise (5). Wood's account of the coercion that workers face in capitalism implies that no such argument is available. Proponents of the morality of general justice argument must argue that the worker's situation in capitalism is an injustice because the worker's lack of independence from private capital violates their rightful freedom. If, however, capitalism merely deprives workers of acceptable alternatives to capitalist wage-labour, then that is not a violation of Kantian rightful freedom. On Kant's principle of right, it is not wrong for people to be coerced (on Wood's simple concept of coercion).

Even if we leave aside this objection, which is the main one, Wood vastly overstates the implication of any finding that workers in capitalism are deprived of rightful freedom (as Kant views it) by being coerced (as Wood views

---

131   Ibid.
132   Wood 2017, p. 647.

it). Even if the worker's coercion *were* to constitute a general injustice that the lawmaker was required to remove, the lawmaker would be required to remove the worker's lack of independence from capitalist firms. Establishing independence from something is not the same thing as abolishing it, however. In suggesting that the worker's situation in capitalism is an injustice in Kantian terms, Wood seems to confound the requirement for a lawmaker to enable a producer to be independent of capitalist wage labour with the much stronger requirement for a lawmaker to *prohibit* capitalist wage labour:

> The right to be *sui iuris* (one's own master) ... this thought might naturally be extended further than Kant actually extends it, and seen as prohibiting most forms of capitalist wage labour. All would have an absolute right to labour, all who are able would be required to work for their living, and no one's opportunity to work could be the private property of another. No one, not even the industrious ant, could deserve, or earn, ownership over the opportunity of another to labour. No one, not even the lazy grasshopper, ever deserves to have their conditions of life become the private property of someone else.[133]

An opportunity is the 'private property of another' if it is *monopolised* by *another*. In order to remove any monopoly that private capital enjoys over the worker's opportunity to work, it is sufficient to establish a mixed economy that includes some private capitalism and some not-for-profit public work schemes. Or, a lawmaker could enable profit maximising cooperatives to compete with hierarchically owned firms for custom on the market. On either scenario, or a combination of them, a producer need no longer be coerced (on Wood's view of coercion) to take a job at a capitalist firm. But capitalism has been reformed, not abolished. To ensure that an 'opportunity to work' is no longer 'the private property of another' is not to abolish differential private ownership in the means of production, or the accumulation of capital. To remove the general injustice in capitalism that Wood believes a Kantian can condemn, it is not necessary to condemn capitalism.

To be sure, one might believe, consistently with Wood's belief, that economic opportunities would in general be far *more* acceptable if capitalism was not just reformed but replaced. But even putting aside all of the above objections, no argument for this belief can be connected to Kant's principle of right to produce a condemnation of capitalism. Suppose, for argument's sake, that Kant's

---

133   Wood 2017, p. 652.

principle of right *did* require a lawmaker to correct a state of affairs whereby workers are coerced. To remove this coercion, it will be necessary for a lawmaker to offer alternative employment opportunities and/or to regulate the economy to ensure that wage-labour for private capital is no longer an option that anyone is coerced to take. The ultimate aim here is *not* to give workers acceptable options, however. It is to ensure that they are not coerced. Provided that a reformed capitalism prevents the coercion of workers, no proof that a post-capitalist society could provide them with better and/or more options than a reformed capitalism can enable Kant's principle of right to condemn capitalism.[134] The negative focus of Kant's principle of right, on removing a lack of independence, together with the idea that premise (8) need not be true of all capitalisms, by itself provides anti-capitalists with a reason to remain unsatisfied with the morality of general injustice argument.

The morality of general injustice argument thus faces two powerful independent objections. First, it implicitly requires us to revise Kant's principle of right, without offering any Kantian reason to do so. Second, even if we revise Kant's principle of right so as to make all coercion an injustice, this revised principle of right still cannot condemn all capitalisms.

7   Conclusion

The aim in this chapter was to assess the plausibility of the complementarity view from the side of the goal of condemning capitalism. As Marxists seek to condemn capitalism, it is only plausible to suggest that Kant's ethics provides the ethics that Marxists need if Kant's ethics can condemn capitalism. To this end, we outlined the form of argument required to apply FEI to condemn capitalism. If FEI is to condemn capitalism, a strict duty must be derived from its Never Merely as a Means principle that prohibits a type of conduct essential to capitalism, by means of one or more of five strategies. On this basis, we assessed the existing arguments for applying FEI to condemn capitalism. None of the arguments surveyed successfully derives a strict duty from the Never Merely as a Means principle that condemns capitalism. This is not, of course, to say that the criteria of uprooting the capitalist division of labour, vulnerability or capital accumulation, or of establishing institutional co-legislation, community, freedom or general justice, cannot serve in a non-Kantian argument against capitalism.

---

134   Compare Gilabert 2017, p. 562.

But by now one must wonder if FEI can offer a suitable framework for critics of capitalism to articulate what they perceive as its failings. Ferdinand Tönnies expressed this scepticism when, in response to Hermann Cohen, Tönnies claimed that a '*sociologically* grounded ethic' will be 'socialist not merely in its consequences but also in its premises'.[135] On one interpretation of this claim, FEI is unsuited to becoming a principle of a socialist ethics because a socialist ethics will be based on principles that apply to other descriptive premises, which do not merely describe the act and end of an agent (or of associated agents). As the objection to the capital accumulation argument shows, the claim that capital accumulation is contrary to the worth of x need not translate into a claim that anyone's end is contrary to the worth of x. As the objections to the vulnerability argument and to the freedom in production argument show, a macro-level fact about classes may be a condition of an end, without featuring in that end. Tönnies's judgment still seems correct: an ethics that is 'socialist in its premises' will have to be based on principles that (unlike FEI) apply to empirical premises that describe not an agent's act and end, but a system, defined by the generalised existence of certain types of interaction. This idea is taken up in Part III.

---

135   Tönnies 1909, p. 930. Staudinger's judgment was even harsher. For Staudinger, FEI 'is not an expression for the solidarity of will of a community relation, a realm of ends, but entirely an expression of that necessity of commerce in which the other must be recognised as a free contracting party if the commercial relation is not to be upset. It gives philosophical form to the phrase "live and let live" ' (Staudinger 1906, p. 89).

CHAPTER 4

Against the Incompatibility View

Marxists need an ethics that differs from Kant's; this is the finding of Chapters 1–3. But we may ask whether this ethics owes something, or nothing at all, to Kant. According to the incompatibility view, Marxists can take nothing at all from Kant's ethics. To show that those with an interest in Marxism have a reason to engage in a critique of Kant's ethics, we need to undermine the incompatibility view.

The incompatibility view can be undermined by considering the conditions that the arguments in Chapters 1–3 impose upon any ethics that Marxists offer. This ethics must be able to condemn capitalism as unjust and recommend socialism as just, so as not to preclude action necessary to achieve socialism. To avoid ideology, it must support at least one of the following two claims: (i) existing society ought to be revolutionised because the class oppression in it is in one way bad for everyone, or (ii) social arrangements that promote rational self-transparency ought to be adopted because false consciousness is in one way bad for everyone. To avoid a contradiction in socialist strategy, its grounding argument cannot be timeless, but must appeal to premises about capitalism. Finally, the ethics that Marxists need is one that can evaluate systems. The incompatibility view can be undermined if, by taking something from Kant, an ethics can meet one or more of these conditions.

Here we sketch one argument of this kind. Marxists need an ethics that justifies socialism, on a description of socialism that they can accept. The fundamental value, in Kant's ethics, is autonomy. One way to object to the incompatibility view, therefore, is to show that Marx's description of socialism is a description of a society that can be defended on ethical grounds by appeal to a conception of autonomy. If Marx's description of socialism can be defended by appeal to a conception of autonomy, and autonomy is the basic value of Kant's ethics, the ethics that Marxists offer can take something from Kant, namely, a concern with autonomy.

To make this argument is not to grant that autonomy is the *only* feature that a Marxist ethics has in common with Kant's. We shall argue later on (in Chapter 10) that a Marxist ethics can ground the value of autonomy by appeal to an antinomy in capitalism. Kant, of course, uses the argumentative figure of antinomy, both in the context of his theoretical philosophy[1] and in the context

---

1 Kant 1998, A 426–461/B 454–489.

of his moral philosophy.[2] So, if a Marxist ethics can appeal to an antinomy to ground an ultimate value, then, given Kant's use of this argumentative figure, a Marxist ethics has something in common with Kant's, in virtue of its argumentative strategy. It has *two* features in common with Kant's ethics: autonomy and antinomy. The focus in this chapter is on autonomy, rather than antinomy, because the incompatibility view is really a claim about the positive evaluative standards that Marxism offers (or needs). By focusing on autonomy, we meet the incompatibility view on its own ground.

To focus on how autonomy can justify socialism (on Marx's description of it) is also not to grant that autonomy does not underpin a Marxist condemnation of capitalism. The central condemnation of capitalism that Marxists offer is the condemnation of capitalist labour-exploitation. In Chapter 10, we argue that the condemnation of capitalist labour-exploitation rests on the same value of autonomy as the Marxist justification of socialism, insofar as it employs the system universalisability principle of justice.[3] The focus in this chapter is on the justification of socialism, not the condemnation of capitalism, because this is better evidence of a commitment to autonomy. That a thinker requires a value to affirm what they believe in is better evidence of their commitment to it than the fact that they require it to condemn what they do not believe in. One may condemn a society on account of its failure to realise a value held dear in that society without believing in the value. It is not possible, however, to affirm a society that one favours in terms of a value, and not believe in that value. If we presented evidence that Marx's condemnation of capitalism rests on the value of autonomy, we would still have to present evidence that Marx was committed to that value. But then we might as well just directly ask how socialism, on Marx's description, can be affirmed.

On Marx's descriptions, human freedom in a post-capitalist future includes two components: a development component and an awareness component. The relation between them commits Marx, we shall argue, to a rival conception of autonomy to Kant's. Indeed, there is also some direct evidence that Marx affirmed the value of the autonomy of a human community. The argument in this chapter is therefore more interpretive than the arguments in chapters 1–3. It needs to be shown, first of all, that Marx describes human freedom in a post-capitalist future in terms of development and awareness components.

---

2 *KpV*, 5: 113–14; *RGV*, 6: 116.

3 On exploitation, see also ch. 8 of Furner 2018.

1   Two Components of Human Freedom

We begin by outlining the components of human freedom that we wish to identify in Marx's descriptions of a post-capitalist future. To be free, on this view, is to exercise one's powers in meaningful activities, *and* to be aware that the promotion of this for all is a *principle* of society, that is, a publicly affirmed policy that is really being implemented. The exercise of an individual's powers in meaningful activities can be termed the *development* component of freedom. An individual can only develop by deliberately exercising their powers, in activities that they find meaningful. The awareness that the promotion of this for all is a principle of society can be termed the *awareness* component of freedom.

A view of human freedom that includes these two components is a view of human freedom as constitutively social, in virtue of its awareness component. If human freedom has not just a development component, but also an awareness component, human beings cannot be fully free just by virtue of their individual circumstances. To ask whether one individual is fully free is necessarily to ask whether individuals generally are free. Indeed, public institutions are constitutive of human freedom, on this view. Freedom requires an institutionalised awareness that the activities through which an individual develops are in harmony with, rather than at the expense of, those by which others develop; and an institutionalised awareness that this is of value.

Clearly, human freedom cannot include this awareness component without a development component. But its awareness component is irreducible to its development component. The awareness component of human freedom is not satisfied just by virtue of the satisfaction of its development component. To exercise one's powers in meaningful activities, it is sufficient to experience one's activities as stimulating, or as making a significant contribution to a meaningful life plan. But it is not necessary to be able to assume that others also exercise their powers in meaningful activities, even if in fact they do. Nor is it necessary to take an evaluative attitude to this.

As the awareness component of human freedom is not satisfied just by virtue of the satisfaction of its development component, human freedom involves a *relation* between *two* spheres: work, and decision-making.[4] Hence, on this view, human freedom cannot be reduced to individual self-realisation. Nor, on this

---

4   I am not arguing that development only occurs in work activities (understood in the broadest sense as activities that produce use-values, that is, items or services that can be used to satisfy human wants); development can also occur in consuming use-value. I am arguing against the idea that freedom concerns one sphere only (work).

view, can it be conceived in terms of capabilities to do or to be. Neither the exercise of one's powers in meaningful activity, nor the awareness of a principle, is a capability. Nor, on this view, can human freedom be conceived in terms of utility (conceived either as pleasure or desire-satisfaction). Human freedom has an evaluative component. If Marx's descriptions of socialism affirm this view of human freedom, then the typical evaluative spaces in consequentialist ethics are not best suited to answer a Marxist's need for an ethics.

Relatedly, this view of human freedom is not one that a proponent of the instrumental reasons argument for the irrelevance view can share. To be sure, it is consistent for this proponent to believe that, because human beings are deeply and equally sympathetic towards all members of their species, it is instrumentally rational for us to replace capitalism with a society that realises the development component of human freedom, and allows us to be aware that it is realised for all. The belief that a proponent of the instrumental reasons argument cannot share, however, is that to be free is (in part) to be aware that the promotion of development is a *principle* of society, because this would acknowledge the significance of our capacity for normative evaluation, as distinct from instrumental rationality.

2   Marx on Human Freedom

With this outline of the view that we are seeking to identify in mind, we may now examine some of Marx's statements on human freedom. We begin with a remark in *Capital* Volume I, because it is such clear evidence of this view. In the course of his analysis of capitalism in *Capital* Volume I, Marx expresses the hope for a 'higher form of society whose foundational principle is the full and free development of each'.[5] A society where the development of each is a foundational *principle*, rather than simply a *fact* about it, is a society in which people affirm its value, and are aware that it is implemented for all. A society is 'higher', or better from a normative point of view, if it exhibits the development and awareness components of human freedom than if it does not.

Moving on, secondly, to *On the Jewish Question* (1843), Marx concludes this text by saying:

> Only once the real individual human being reabsorbs in himself the abstract citizen, and, as an individual human being, has become a *spe-*

---

5   *MEW*, 23, p. 618; *MECW*, 35, p. 588; Marx 1976, p. 739.

cies – being in his empirical life, individual work, individual relations; only once man has cognised and organised his 'forces propres' as *social* powers, and therefore no longer separates social power from himself in the shape of *political* power, only then is human emancipation achieved.[6]

Marx's subject here is human freedom, and he highlights two quite different conditions for it, separated by a semi-colon. The first condition is that human freedom requires that (1) each individual is a *'species-being'* in its life activity. Using this term to characterise an *individual* seems to imply an alignment of individual and common interests. Work is both meaningful for the individual, and of benefit to the species, or directly social. It is no longer merely a means to an end, serving the purpose of private acquisition. The second condition is that (2) decision-making power is organised without being political. Some kind of collective decision-making power is presupposed, to coordinate individual activity to benefit the whole. But why does human freedom require that it is not *'political'*?

Political power is a form of social power that 'separates' social power from individuals. This suggests that social power becomes political if it is exercised by formally independent representatives. Political representatives are formally independent if they are not bound by a programme, petition or demand to speak or vote for or against any given law.[7] On account of this lack of mandate, a social power exercised by political representatives remains separated from individuals. By implication, an organised but non-political power is a decision-making power subject to direct mandate. One point in favour of this reading is that it allows (1) and (2) to enable each other. (1) enables (2) if a mandated power can be exercised *responsibly* only if the everyday life of members of a community is not overshadowed by the competitive pursuit of particular interests.[8] (2) enables (1) if real influence on or access to decision-making power enables individuals to acquire an *identity* that values the common good.

At issue, here, is just the extent to which Marx adopts a view of human freedom that has both development and awareness components. The above passage from *On the Jewish Question* affirms the development component of human freedom, insofar as work can only be referred to as 'individual work' if it is meaningful for those who perform it. It affirms the awareness component of human freedom, by treating the knowledge that work is organised to serve a

---

6   *MEW*, 1, p. 370; *MECW*, 3, p. 168, citing Rousseau 1790, p. 70; Rousseau 1997, p. 69.
7   Leibholz 1966, pp. 73–4.
8   Compare the considerations put forward for the community argument in ch. 3.

common good (a common good which must include the organisation of every-one's work as 'individual work') as an aspect of human freedom.

It has sadly escaped attention that Marx's view of human freedom in *On the Jewish Question* is in alignment with Marx and Engels's more famous charac-terisation of communism in *The Communist Manifesto* (1848). *The Communist Manifesto* characterises the future communist society to which it looks forward as an 'association, in which the free development of each is the condition for the free development of all'.[9] To appreciate the complexity of freedom in this characterisation, it is necessary to distinguish *two* aspects of freedom.

According to the *Manifesto*, the free development of each enables, or makes possible, the free development of all. This is implied by its use of the word 'condition'. The free development of all therefore cannot *consist in* the free development of each individual taken individually. For the claim would then amount to: the free development of each is a condition for the free develop-ment of each, which is nonsense. An enabling condition cannot be identical with what it enables. The 'free development of all' must refer to an aspect of freedom that is of 'all' rather than of 'each'. It must refer to an activity that is essentially all-inclusive rather than potentially individual. The *Manifesto*'s claim must be: the free development of each in their individual activities is a condition for the free development of all individuals as members of public decision-making institutions.

This still leaves the issue of how to account for the thought behind the con-ditioning relation between these two aspects of human freedom. Why is it that the exercise of decision-making power by all is conditional on each individual regarding their work as meaningful? This is the same sort of question as that raised by the above passage from *On the Jewish Question*. There we asked: why is it that a social power can cease to be '*political*' only once each individual is a '*species-being*' in their individual lives? *The Communist Manifesto* again prompts us to ask why an individual freedom is a condition of freedom in shar-ing the power of an association.

Again, one possible answer lies in an alignment of individual and common interests. If work that is organised so as to be of direct social benefit is mean-ingful for those who perform it, then production is less likely to create interests, contrary to the common good, in the personal avoidance of toil. People can be expected to deliberate from a general point of view only if they do not have to keep one eye on avoiding harsh burdens, such as prolonged toil, falling per-sonally on them. If individual work is meaningful, not just toil, this problem

---

9   *MEW*, 4, p. 482; *MECW*, 6, p. 506.

is alleviated. To the extent that work ceases to sustain strongly felt personal interests sharply diverging from the common good, general participation in public decision-making institutions need not be precluded by the disposition to seek and bend principles in one's own favour. Participation in decision-making is itself, moreover, an aspect of human freedom (*free* development of all) if it allows individuals to become aware that human development really is being treated as a principle.

Consider, by contrast, G.A. Cohen's account of *The Communist Manifesto*'s characterisation of communist association:

> In Marx's good society, productive resources are not privately (or, for that matter, jointly) owned, but the individual remains effectively sovereign over himself. He conducts himself 'just as he has a mind', developing himself freely not only without blocking the free development of others, but even as a 'condition' of the free development of others.[10]

Illustrating this claim, Cohen continues:

> One way of picturing life under communism, as Marx conceived it, is to imagine a jazz band each player in which seeks his own fulfilment as a musician. Though basically interested in his own fulfilment, and not in that of the band as a whole, or of his fellow musicians taken severally, he nevertheless fulfils himself only to the extent that each of the others also does so, and the same holds for each of them.[11]

The objection to this jazz band illustration is that it rewrites *The Communist Manifesto*. While the *Manifesto* uses 'each' and 'all', Cohen uses 'each' and 'others'. Cohen's first remark says that the free development of each is a condition for the free development *of others*. In the second remark, the free development of each jazz band player is a condition for the free development of 'the others', that is, every other member of the jazz band. Using the term 'others' after 'each' creates the impression that there is just *one* aspect to human freedom, that of fulfilment in individual work. This interpretation of the *Manifesto*

---

10   Cohen 1995, p. 16. The latter part of the claim is repeated at p. 122. Cohen had already reduced Marx's view of freedom to its development component at Cohen 1988, p. 136: Marx's 'philosophical anthropology says that humans are essentially creative beings ... man is an essentially creative being, most at home with himself when he is developing and exercising his talents and powers'.

11   Cohen 1995, p. 122; endorsed, among others, by Brudney 1998, p. 187.

is ruled out if its terms, 'each' and 'all', are retained. If the free development of each is the condition for the free development of 'all', free development of 'all' must be an aspect of human freedom distinct from the freedom that each can enjoy in individual activity. Cohen's claim that 'community is here a *means* to the independently specified goal of the development of each person's powers'[12] may be true of this jazz band. But it is not true of the view of community common to both *On the Jewish Question* and *The Communist Manifesto*. In these texts, human freedom has two components. Owing to its awareness component, human freedom is constitutively social. Human freedom is not fully realised, according to Marx, unless we enjoy an awareness of a publicly affirmed and implemented *principle* of development. As only a public power can provide this, human community is an end.

3   The True Realm of Freedom and the Realm of Necessity

We have seen how a view of human freedom in terms of development and awareness components unifies Marx's remarks on the future post-capitalist society in *On the Jewish Question*, *The Communist Manifesto*, and *Capital* Volume I. We shall now extend this interpretive claim to a famous passage from *Capital* Volume III. If this passage is correctly translated, it confirms that human freedom, in Marx's view, requires not only an awareness that the development component of human freedom is being generally promoted, but an awareness of this as *good*. The members of a free human community think of their policy of development as valid.

Marx writes:

> The realm of freedom in fact only begins where labour determined by necessity and external purpose has ceased; hence it lies, in the nature of the matter, beyond the sphere of material production proper. Just as a savage must wrestle with nature to satisfy his needs, to maintain and reproduce his life, so must a civilised being, and he must do so in all forms of society and in all possible modes of production. This realm of natural necessity expands with his development, because his needs do too; but the productive powers that satisfy them expand at the same time. Freedom in this sphere can only consist in the fact that socialised human beings, the associated producers, regulate their interchange with

---

12   Cohen 1995, p. 123.

nature rationally, bring it under their common control, instead of being dominated by it as by a blind power; perform it with the slightest application of power, and under conditions most worthy and adequate to their human nature. But it always remains a realm of necessity. Human development of power that is valid to itself as an end in itself [*die menschliche Kraftentwicklung, die sich als Selbstzweck gilt*], the true realm of freedom, begins beyond it, and can only bloom on the basis of that realm of necessity. The shortening of the working day is its fundamental condition.[13]

The 'true realm of freedom' is defined not simply by 'human development of power', but by human development of power that is 'valid to itself as an end in itself'. Part of what it is to be free is to value the human development that one's society is promoting. Its general promotion is regarded, after reflection, as an end in itself.

This interpretive position is made possible by my translation of the bracketed phrase. The translation of this phrase for *MECW* reads: 'development of human energy which is an end in itself'.[14] Similarly, the David Fernbach translation has: 'the development of human powers as an end in itself'.[15] The problem with both[16] translations is that they omit to translate the verb '*sich gelten*'. The verb '*gelten*' means: 'to be valid'. The effect of combining it with '*sich*', a reflexive pronoun that '*gelten*' need not take, is to make 'human development of power' that to which human development of power is valid (as an end in itself). Both the *MECW* and the Fernbach translation obscure Marx's claim that, in a true realm of freedom, human development of power is *valid to itself* as an end in itself. Use of 'valid (*gelten*)' implies that this freedom does not consist in the *mere pursuit* of human development of power as an end in itself. True freedom requires that its pursuit is judged valid as an end in itself; in other words, that it is affirmed as a fundamental principle. Adding 'to itself (*sich*)' implies that this value judgment is not *external* to 'human development of power'. The development of value judgment is part of the human development of power, and so constitutive of the true realm of freedom. If it is constitutive of human freedom that its development component is affirmed as a principle, human freedom has a development and an awareness component.

---

13   *MEW*, 25, p. 828; *MECW*, 37, p. 807; Marx 1981, pp. 958–9.

14   *MECW*, 37, p. 807. This phrase would translate: '*Entwicklung der menschlichen Energie, die Selbstzweck ist*'.

15   Marx 1981, p. 959. This phrase would translate: '*die Entwicklung der menschlichen Kräfte als Selbszweck*'.

16   And my earlier translation in Furner 2011, pp. 6–7.

A digression is in order. I have claimed that the official translations of the bracketed phrase are inaccurate; and, if corrected, the above passage from *Capital* Volume III can be seen to restate the view that Marx expresses elsewhere that human freedom has both a development and an awareness component. As this interpretation relies on offering a new translation, it may smooth its acceptance to show how it fits this passage's broader thesis, which concerns the relation between a 'realm of necessity' and a 'true realm of freedom'.

In the above passage, Marx offers an *irremovable basis* conception of the place of a realm of necessity in human society. An irremovable basis conception has two features. On the one hand, it says that a society with a realm of necessity also has something else, some 'external purpose' for which this realm is a basis. On the other hand, it says that the realm of necessity is irremovable. Even the freest human society has a realm of necessity. From this conception of the place of the realm of necessity in human society, it does not follow that a true realm of freedom exists just by virtue of the existence of a realm of necessity. The external purpose for which a realm of necessity is the basis may not qualify as a true realm of freedom. Indeed, the existence of a true realm of freedom requires a specifically freedom-enabling organisation of the realm of necessity.

A part of defending this conception of the place of a realm of necessity in human society is to defend a conception of the true realm of freedom. To conceptualise this realm, consider two premises. The first premise is: x is viewed as an end in itself if x would be valued even on the assumption that x does not serve as a means to anything beyond x. The second premise is: human development of power is a learning process, which requires conscious effort by the learner. It follows directly from this second premise that human development of power can only occur through the deliberate exercise of power. Conceptualising the true realm of freedom in light of these two premises, we may say: the true realm of freedom consists in exercises of power whose development can be valued even apart from any contribution it makes to anything beyond its own development. The true realm of freedom consists in the gaining and perfecting of proficiencies (including a proficiency in value judgment) that are valued for their own sake.

A development of power need not produce a product to belong to the true realm of freedom. The development of swimming proficiency can belong to the true realm of freedom, although swimming does not, just as such, produce a product. But what if a power is a productive power, that is, a power to produce a product that satisfies a need? In the case of an already proficient productive power, its development will often consist in an exercise of power that aims to produce a product satisfying a need. The development of a power to perform music from a proficient to a higher level will involve the performance of suitably challenging pieces of music before an audience. A performer must adopt an attitude to an audience as part of developing their proficiency, because the test of a successful performance is not audience-independent. So, in some cases at least, human development of power in the true realm of freedom involves the production of products that satisfy needs.[17] Even if we accept Marx's judgment in this passage that 'material production proper' belongs to the realm of necessity (more on which below), the true realm of freedom can include work, provided that work includes the 'free intellectual and social activity' that Marx, in *Capital* Volume I, distinguishes from 'material production'.[18]

What marks out human development of power that is valued as an end in itself is the impact of its development on its duration of exercise. Opportunities to exercise powers are always subject to external time constraints: the time required for doing other things, and to rest. But in the case of human development of power that is valued as an end in itself, the duration of its exercise will tend to be determined, within these constraints, by considerations about what befits its development. Its development is not a reason to shorten its future exercise. The duration of exercise of a power whose development is merely of *instrumental* value, by contrast, is determined solely by external constraints. Its development is valued for the time saved in using it to yield a given result. If the need for its products remains unchanged, the development of a power that is merely of instrumental value to develop *is* a reason to shorten its future exercise, to free up time for other things.

The true realm of freedom consists of activities that develop power, where this development, because it is valued for its own sake, is not itself a reason to shorten the power's exercise. The activity of the realm of necessity, by contrast, exercises powers whose development is valued on external grounds (whether

---

17 It is inaccurate to view Marx's true realm of freedom in terms of 'activity' that is 'savored for itself, not for what it may yield' (Booth 1989, p. 206). First, valuing *activity* for itself is not the same thing as valuing *human development of power* for itself. Activity, including activity savoured for itself (for example, a hot bath), may not bring about any development of power. It then cannot belong to the true realm of freedom. Second, an activity *is* valued 'for what it may yield' if the development of the power it develops is valued for itself. Third, if 'yield' is narrowed to denote produce, it may be necessary to value an activity's 'yield' if the power that it develops, and whose development is valued for itself, is a *productive* power.

18 *MEW*, 23, p. 552; *MECW*, 35, p. 530; Marx 1976, p. 667; see also *MEW*, 42, p. 512; *MECW*, 28, p. 530; Marx 1973, p. 611.

of efficiency, measured by the time freed up for other things; the promotion of humane working conditions; or the promotion of democratic control over productive resources). This general distinction is clear enough. Its acceptance does not presuppose complete agreement over which activities belong to which realm. The distinction is sound even if Marx errs in judging which particular activities belong to which realm.

There is a straightforward reason for why the realm of necessity is a *basis*, that is, defined by 'external purpose'. To value the development of power on external grounds like efficiency presupposes something not valued on external grounds, be it the enjoyment of rest, or other pleasures, or activities whose development of power is valued for its own sake. As activities may be performed purely for the external purpose of pleasure or desire-satisfaction, and as neither pleasure or desire-satisfaction suffice for a true realm of freedom, a realm of necessity is no guarantee of a true realm of freedom. Marx is not a utilitarian.

The reason for saying that the realm of necessity is an *irremovable* basis rests on a judgment about 'material production proper'; namely, that 'material production proper' is unavoidable, and always belongs to it. Material production services needs that must be satisfied within given time frames, with perishable items. This is obvious in the case of food and drink. But all material things have a certain average period of use, by which time a replacement must be produced if the need it satisfies is to continue to be satisfied. The same cannot be said for all objects of social and intellectual needs. A piece of music or scientific discovery is not created for a time frame after which point it cannot be heard or known. Materially imposed deadlines apply across the sphere of material production, but not across the production of *all* objects of social and intellectual needs. As such deadlines must inform rational decision-making as to what objects to produce as well as what means, methods and conditions of production to use, development of the powers used in 'material production proper' is always of instrumental value in reducing the total social time in which such deadlines determine the selection of the objects, means, methods and conditions of human activity. 'Material production proper' belongs, therefore, to the realm of necessity. As material production is a feature of 'all forms of society', even the freest human society includes a realm of necessity, or 'external purpose'.

For a true realm of freedom to exist, activities of 'external purpose' belonging to material production must be organised so as to promote the gaining and perfecting of proficiencies that are valued for their own sake. In Marx's view, social control, by 'socialised human beings', is required to ensure this means-end relation. This implies that 'human development of power' is affirmed as a principle in public deliberation. Human development of power is a principle of a social ethics, not merely a principle of private morality. In Marx's view, the good society is one in which this principle is affirmed by a public power, and guides public policy.

We can distinguish the characterisation of a principle as belonging to a social ethics from the more particular idea of its application to a sphere under the control of a public power. A principle can be affirmed by a public power and inform its policy even when it is not applied to a sphere under its control. A public power recognises a principle as properly bearing on its actions by recognising that its decisions ought to be guided by it. One way for a principle to guide the decisions of a public power is if the latter applies it in a sphere under its control. But a principle can also guide its decisions if it is affirmed as the basis for applying a distinct principle in a sphere under its control. Suppose that principle X can be applied in a sphere under A's control, and another principle, Y, can only be realised in a sphere outside of A's control. If A applies principle X on the basis that it promotes the realisation of principle Y, then there is a sense in which A adopts Y as a principle. Provided that A is a public power, Y is a principle of a social ethics.

This allows us to distinguish two ways in which the development and awareness components of human freedom are confirmed, in the above passage from *Capital* Volume III. One relates to the realm of necessity, and the other to the true realm of freedom. If a realm of necessity is composed of productive activities with materially imposed deadlines, development can occur in it through principles of democratic control and humane working conditions. Either or both of these principles can provide a reason for a producer to find the activities to which they are applied stimulating.[19] If they are applied, even a principle of time efficiency might provide part of a reason to affirm these activities' contribution to a valued life plan. If a public power organises the work of a realm of necessity to promote a true realm of freedom for all, a producer may take an other-regarding attitude to it, and value its performance for ensuring that others are not unfairly given a disproportionate amount. In these ways, the development component of human freedom can be realised in activities of a realm of necessity. It can also be known to be realised in it, and valued. This awareness is realised in respect of the realm of necessity by deliberation and

---

19   James 2017, pp. 12, 15–17. I concur with James Klagge that 'perfectly fulfilling unalienating activities' (Klagge 1986, p. 771) can belong to a realm of necessity. For Ali Rattansi, by contrast, 'Marx seems to argue that the day-to-day labour necessary for individual and social survival will always remain unrewarding' (Rattansi 1982, p. 52). I find no evidence for this claim in the text, however.

decision-making that values human development as the principle underlying the fair implementation of efficiency, democratic control, and humane working conditions.

In regard to the true realm of freedom, development remains the principle of a social ethics. A public power applies principles of efficiency, democratic control and humane working conditions to activities under its control on the basis that this will promote another principle – human development of power for its own sake – in activities not subject to its control. Human development of power is the principle of its social ethics just in virtue of that. An awareness of human development in the true realm of freedom rests on an awareness of the principles used to distribute the resources whose use is not subject to common control. In *Critique of the Gotha Programme*, Marx suggests that communism will at first give each able person a right to means of individual consumption proportional to productive contribution, and only later, as it matures, distribute means of individual consumption in proportion to need (where need includes the need for development), as part of a principle of solidarity.[20] The view of human freedom in terms of development and awareness components can therefore be extended to the distinction, in Marx's future post-capitalist society, between a realm of necessity, and the true realm of freedom.

4   The Link to Autonomy

On the evidence presented above, human freedom, according to Marx, has two components: a development component and an awareness component. As individual development occurs in individual activities, while the awareness of human development and of its value relies on a principle of a public power, human freedom depends on an awareness that activities generally are serving or exemplifying a publicly valued end. It rests on an awareness that human development of power is not merely announced by a public power as an end – public declarations can amount to empty aspirations, as a number of international human rights conventions attest – but that it is a *principle*, publicly affirmed *and* implemented.

To say that a principle of human development is implemented is to say that a process of human development forms out of all the various, mutually reinforcing activities of individual development. Thus, in virtue of its development

---

20   *MEW*, 19, pp. 20–21; *MECW*, 24, pp. 85–7.

and awareness components, human freedom rests on co-legislated principles that expressly recognise a harmonious social dynamic. But this is just what the autonomy of a human community consists in. We enjoy the autonomy of a human community if our social dynamics – which reflect the empirical fact that, as human beings, we are beings with capacities that we can develop – are expressly endorsed by us as principles of a public power, and are harmonious. For then, by developing ourselves in line with these social dynamics, we are obeying a self-given law.

5   Marx on the Autonomy of a Human Community

The form of argument so far has been to present evidence that Marx viewed human freedom in terms of development and awareness components, and to argue that their relation is best understood in terms of a conception of freedom as the autonomy of a human community. We now supplement this strategy with more direct evidence that Marx held this conception of freedom, leaving the clearest statement of autonomy to the end.

One piece of evidence is provided by a statement in *The German Ideology* (1845–6):

> Communism is distinguished from all previous movements in that it over-turns the foundation of all hitherto existing relations of production and intercourse, and treats all naturally emerging presuppositions for the first time, consciously, as creations of previous human beings, strips them of their naturalness, and subordinates them to the power of the united individuals.[21]

I want to focus on what Marx and Engels suggest about communism in the second part of this quote (after: 'and intercourse'). In communism, all existing states of affairs are to be regarded as historical outcomes of previous action *and inaction*. Omissions of collective responsibility – facts about society – are not to be misrepresented as facts about private individuals, or as facts about nature,

---

21   *MEJ*, 2003, p. 79; *MEW*, 3, p. 70; *MECW*, 5, p. 81. Relatedly, in *On the Jewish Question*, Marx says that 'the state allows private property, culture, occupation to *take effect* in *their* fashion, i.e. as private property, as culture, as occupation, and to assert their *particular* nature' (*MEW*, 1, p. 354; *MECW*, 3, p. 153); what a public power should be doing is '*revolutionising* these components themselves and subjecting them to critique' (*MEW*, 1, p. 369; *MECW*, 3, p. 167).

or as facts about human nature – with clear implications for the treatment of such issues as disability,[22] environmental pollution and gender. Such individualising or naturalising misrepresentations can be deprived of their raison d'être, Marx and Engels claim, once 'the united individuals' wield public power. There is then no longer any distinct ruling class that stands to benefit from the controlling effects of such misrepresentations.

Chief among the 'naturally emerging presuppositions' that a non-political form of public power is to take responsibility for revolutionising are any divisive dynamics that form within the law, without its express recognition. Some contemporary examples include: capital accumulation by capitalist billionaires;[23] environmental degradation;[24] a gendered distribution and devaluation of care work;[25] and the marginalisation of historically disadvantaged minority cultures.[26] These phenomena illustrate how social dynamics can define and divide our lives, without ever being set down as principles by a public power. Insofar as communism removes such dynamics, or else transforms them into harmo-

---

22   On the social interpretation of disability, see Furner 2020.

23   Samuel Stebbins and Gran Suneson report: '[t]he recession ushered in by the novel coronavirus has not meant economic catastrophe for everyone, however. In fact, in the months since the virus reached the United States, many of the nation's wealthiest citizens have actually profited handsomely. Over a roughly seven-month period starting in mid-March – a week after President Donald Trump declared a national emergency – America's 614 billionaires grew their net worth by a collective $931 billion' (Stebbins and Suneson 2020).

24   According to the Intergovernmental Panel on Climate Change Special Report of 2018, '[h]uman activities are estimated to have caused approximately 1.0°C of global warming', which is '*likely* to reach 1.5°C between 2030 and 2052' (IPCC 2018, p. 6). The Report notes: '[w]arming from anthropogenic emissions ... will continue to cause further long-term changes in the climate system, such as sea level rise', 'climate-related risks for natural and human systems are higher for global warming of 1.5°C than at present' and 'impacts on natural and human systems from global warming have already been observed' (IPCC 2018, p. 7).

25   '[C]are consumes a large part of our daily lives. Nevertheless, we do not pay systematic attention to this dimension of life' (Tronto 1993, p. 111); '[i]n modern industrial societies, these tasks of caring continue to be disproportionately carried out by the lowest ranks of society: by women, the working class, and in most of the West, by people of color. Because care is relatively disguised in our society, it is somewhat difficult to see this pattern' (Tronto 1993, p. 113). See also, more recently, Tronto 2015.

26   'The problem is not that traditional human rights doctrines give us the wrong answer to these questions [questions of culture – JF]. It is rather that they often give no answer at all ... These questions have been left to the usual process of majoritarian decision-making within each state. The result ... has been to render cultural minorities vulnerable to significant injustice at the hands of the majority, and to exacerbate ethnocultural conflict' (Kymlicka 1995, p. 5).

nious dynamics that a 'united' power can 'consciously' affirm, it exhibits the autonomy of a human community.

Communism would then succeed just where Marx takes capitalism to fail. Marx remarks in *On the Jewish Question*:

> The liberty [*Freiheit*] of the egoistic human being and the recognition of this liberty [as a human right – JF] is but the recognition of the *unbridled* movement of the intellectual and material elements which form the content of his life.[27]

If rights are the most basic features of law, then individuals' exercise of their capacities, in respect of what a right gives each individual a right to do, is subject only to negative limits: other individuals' rights, and public order. The concatenation of every individual's rightful exercise of their capacities may then produce a social dynamic without express recognition in law. The clearest example is private property law, and capital accumulation.

The law of capitalist society includes rights of private property. Typical ways of exercising private property rights are: using what exclusively belongs to you; making offers to others to acquire or part with what exclusively belongs to them or you; hiring and instructing others to use what exclusively belongs to you; and warning others not to interfere with what belongs exclusively to you. A law that recognises private property rights expressly recognises these ways of acting. But by their concept, none of these rights is necessarily a part of a process of capital accumulation. They are all used, for example, by collecting and swapping stamps, or cooperating with a neighbour to put up a garden fence. When these rights are treated as fundamental and generalised to all forms of resource, however, the combined effect of their exercise is to create processes of market competition, and capital accumulation. By enabling commodity production, they facilitate an ever smaller number of individuals gaining control of an ever greater proportion of the value of the total social product. Of this process of capital accumulation, it may be said, as the *Grundrisse* says of circulation, that

> it results from conscious individuals' effect on one another, but it neither lies in their consciousness, nor is it subsumed under them as a whole.

---

27   *MEW*, 1, p. 369; *MECW*, 3, p. 167; Marx 1975, p. 233; Marx 1994, p. 49. '*Freiheit*' is translated as 'liberty' (and not, as in Marx 1975 and Marx 1994, as 'freedom') because it is Marx's term for 'la *liberté*', as the latter appears in the French constitution of 1793. German, unlike English, does not have two distinct words, 'freedom' and 'liberty'.

Their own collisions with one another produce an *alien* social power standing over them; their interaction exists as a process and force independent of them.[28]

Whereas capitalism tolerates a difference between what the law expressly recognises and the real dynamics that it imposes on individuals, an autonomous human community treats any such '*alien* social power' as a 'naturally emerging presuppositio[n]' to be revolutionised.

A particular understanding of law underpins this view of human freedom. It requires us to see that law serves not just a guarantee function, but a recognition function as well. Laws serve a guarantee function, because, if they are clearly formulated, have adequate sanctions, and are reliably enforced, each individual can act on the expectation that, since no one will wish to incur the sanction, no one will obstruct them if their actions are permitted by law. But laws also serve a second, recognition function, in virtue of being publicly affirmed by a publicly recognised body. A principle that regulates how people are to behave and that is publicly affirmed by a publicly recognised body enjoys a standing above any individually held view to the contrary. It is in virtue of this recognition function of law that Marx argued that law is partly *constitutive* of freedom, writing in *Debates on Freedom of the Press* (1842) that 'laws' are 'positive, clear, general norms in which freedom has obtained an impersonal, theoretical existence independent of individual caprice'.[29] Although this is an early text, Marx continues to be committed to regarding constitutional principles as constitutive of freedom whenever he identifies an awareness component of human freedom (even if he does not use the language of 'law', perhaps out of the hope that a classless society will not rely on coercion).

While the affirmation of principles by a public power serves a recognition function, the same cannot be said for social dynamics. Social dynamics may be public knowledge. But unlike the publicly affirmed principles of a public power, social dynamics do not, just as such, enjoy an expressly acknowledged standing above any unfavourable view of them. Hence, where the law does not expressly recognise social dynamics, what the law publicly declares as having a standing above any individual view to the contrary is in reality a means for enabling a process without this standing. What society gives its stamp of approval to is a vehicle for guaranteeing something to which society does not give its stamp of approval. The public power of a human community is degraded.

---

28   *MEW*, 42, p. 127; *MECW*, 28, p. 132; Marx 1973, pp. 196–7.
29   *MEW*, 1, p. 58; *MECW*, 1, p. 162.

Human autonomy requires that social life truly and ultimately serves or exemplifies the co-legislated principles of a public power, and not something other than, or something bearing no resemblance to, these principles. Human autonomy requires that a public power exercised in the name of a community should not mislead its members as to its own priorities because the impression it is natural to have of these priorities on account of the law diverges from what social reality reveals them to be.

Insofar as Marx took it to be necessary to replace capitalism with communism to realise the autonomy of a human community, Marx's position can be expressed by saying that the state of capitalist society cannot be what Hegel claims the state ought to be. Hegel begins the section entitled 'The State' in paragraph 257 of *Elements of the Philosophy of Right*: '[t]he state is the actuality of the ethical Idea – the ethical spirit as substantial will, *manifest* and clear to itself'.[30] A state that realises the ethical idea is a state in which spirit, or 'the unity of the individual and the universal',[31] informs the decisions taken, and is clearly visible in its results. But spirit does not obtain a clearly visible existence in a state that does not expressly recognise what it gives effect to. Even if it foresees what it gives effect to, and to that extent makes informed decisions, what it gives effect to is not '*manifest*' from its laws.

This point connects to a final piece of evidence for thinking that Marx viewed freedom in terms of the autonomy of a human community, in an article published (in 1842) in the *Kölnische Zeitung*:

> Whereas earlier philosophical teachers of constitutional law construed the state from drives, whether of ambition or sociability, or even from reason – though not from the reason of society [*Vernunft der Gesellschaft*], but from the reason of the individual; the more ideal and rigorous view of the most recent philosophy construes it from the idea of the whole. It regards the state as the great organism in which legal, ethical and political freedom is to obtain its realization, and the individual citizen of the state obeys, in the laws of the state, only the laws of nature of his own reason, human reason.[32]

Freedom is realised, Marx says here, in a state in which the laws that each citizen obeys are 'only the laws of nature of his own reason, human reason'. This is a direct statement of freedom as autonomy, located at the level of a

---

30   Hegel 1986, § 257; Hegel 1991, § 257.

31   Hegel 1986, § 156; Hegel 1991, § 156.

32   *MEW*, 1, p. 104; *MECW*, 1, p. 202. The *MECW* translation of '*Vernunft der Gesellschaft*' as 'social

human community. In light of the evidence just presented, this statement does not express a view that Marx had to abandon, or in fact abandoned, when he later called for the abolition of private property and classes. The passages from *The German Ideology* and *Grundrisse* cited above suggest that the abolition of private property and classes are both aspects of overcoming the 'naturally emerging presuppositions' that stand in the way of autonomy. The value of the autonomy of a human community can also be used to criticise the state in capitalist society insofar as it fails, in one respect, to fulfil the idea of the state that Hegel outlines. So, even if Marx subsequently (after 1842) went on to criticise Hegel and capitalism, that is by itself no reason to think that Marx abandons the view of freedom as the autonomy of a human community.

In this passage, Marx implies that human beings are free qua autonomous if, in obeying the laws that they author as citizens, they merely obey laws of human reason. If, in *obeying* state laws, human beings are only obeying laws of human reason, these laws must be *known* by them as nothing other than laws of human reason. State laws can be known as laws of human reason only if they are known to meet certain general conditions. One condition is that they must be known to produce harmony, or reconcile, the projects of all human beings. No laws that lead to systematic divisions among human beings are laws of 'human reason', in the singular. A second condition is that each must know, from knowing state laws, the kind of whole that they are serving to reproduce by obeying them. No state laws that lead to social dynamics that they do not expressly recognise are laws of human reason, understood as the 'reason of society'. In sum: human beings are free, if they develop themselves in line with harmonious social dynamics that are expressly recognised in the co-legislated principles of a public power.

6   Marx's Commitment to a Critique of Kant's Ethics

If Marx has a conception of freedom as the autonomy of a human community, then Marx is committed to a critique of Kant's ethics. A conception of freedom as the autonomy of a human community is a *rival* conception of autonomy to that of Kant.

In the Introduction, we noted that the general concept of freedom as autonomy is the concept of freedom as obedience to a self-prescribed law. Kant's

---

reason' (which would be: '*soziale Vernunft*') is less literal than 'reason of society', and the latter ('of society' instead of 'social') links better with 'the idea of the whole'.

ethics revolves around a conception of autonomy on which the source of law is rational nature, and the morally free agent is a rational being with a will. For Kant, a rational being can think of itself as free insofar as it can think of itself as obeying a law that its will prescribes to itself. Autonomy, for Kant, lies in the possibility for a rational being to determine its will purely out of respect for the moral law.

Marx, we have argued, is committed to a different conception of autonomy, focused on a human community whose members co-author principles that expressly recognise a harmonious dynamic of development. This conception of autonomy differs from Kant's in that it reflects the empirical nature of human beings. As human beings are interdependent, needy beings with capacities that we can develop, no account of what we are required to obey can omit the fact of our social dynamics. As human beings can prescribe these dynamics to themselves only through a public power that adopts principles in the name of the community, human autonomy is located at the community level. This conception of 'self-legislative human community'[33] entails a critique of Kant's ethics, as Kant does not locate autonomy at the community level, or restrict it to human beings.

This suggests a different view of Marx's relation to Kant from the view outlined by Andrew Feenberg in an important book, *Lukács, Marx and the Sources of Critical Theory*. Feenberg, too, argues that Marx conceives of freedom as autonomy. On Feenberg's account, however, Marx did not locate autonomy at the level of a human community.

According to Feenberg, 'Marx assumes with Rousseau and Kant that freedom is not whim but "obedience to self-given law"'.[34] Elaborating on this, Feenberg remarks that, in Marx's view, 'the rational individual owes it to himself to maintain his autonomy from both his own needs and the power of other men'.[35] In this remark, Feenberg takes Marx to view autonomy as a quality of the 'rational individual'. This creates a tension, in Feenberg's interpretation of Marx, between the commitment to autonomy, and the justification of socialist revolution. When Feenberg considers Marx's 'concept of a social revolution', Feenberg characterises Marx's position by saying: '[c]ommunity can be realized at all levels of society, including the material level of the sphere of need, when the system of practice governing the pursuit of happiness in class society has been transformed'.[36] Class society is to be transformed in its 'system of practice'.

---

33   Furner 2018, p. 245.
34   Feenberg 1981, p. 32, citing Rousseau 1790, p. 31; Rousseau 1997, p. 54.
35   Feenberg 1981, p. 32.
36   Feenberg 1981, p. 39.

This implies that a direct condemnation of class society must condemn it as a 'system', by appeal to a principle that evaluates systems. To adopt a principle to evaluate systems is to be committed to a value conception that is located at the same level; a value conception of 'community', as Feenberg says. If Marx conceives of freedom as autonomy, this conception of autonomy is aligned to Marx's concept of social revolution, on Feenberg's own account of the latter, only if it is a conception of the autonomy of a human community. Yet this conception of autonomy differs from the one that Feenberg ascribes to Marx when Feenberg remarks that 'the rational individual owes it to himself to maintain his autonomy'.[37]

To reconcile the idea that Marx's approach is similar to that of Kant's in viewing freedom as autonomy, with the thought that Marx condemns capitalism at the system-level and in terms of community, Feenberg would have to reject the claim that Marx viewed autonomy as a quality of a 'rational individual', in favour of the idea of self-legislative human community. Marx's commitment to autonomy could then be thought to align with his concept of social revolution.

It is in this light that we may view Marx's declaration, in *Contribution to the Critique of Hegel's Philosophy of Right: Introduction* (1844), that

> The critique of religion culminates in the doctrine that *the human being is the supreme being for the human being*, and thus with the *categorical imperative to overthrow all relations* in which the human being is a debased, enslaved, abandoned, despicable being[38]

This is a remarkable declaration, in several respects.

First of all, it is remarkable that Marx invokes a concept coined by Kant, the '*categorical imperative*', in the introduction to a critique aimed at Hegel – aimed, indeed, at the very text in which Hegel describes Kant's ethics as an '*empty formalism*'.[39] This should give pause to the kind of hand-waiving that insists that Marxism cannot take anything from Kant's ethics because Marx regarded Hegel as having exposed its empty formalism.

Second, Marx's declaration is a rejection of parts of Kant's ethics, mischievously formulated in the language of Kant's ethics. On the one hand, Marx's declaration has a revolutionary, anti-religious and anthropological air that is opposed to Kant's philosophy. Kant denied any right to revolution;[40] took reli-

---

37   Feenberg 1981, p. 32.
38   *MEW*, 1, p. 385; *MECW*, 3, p. 182.
39   Hegel 1986, § 135; Hegel 1991, § 135.
40   *TP*, 8: 299.

gion, as the connection of the idea of freedom with immortality and God, to provide the postulates of practical reason;[41] and claimed that the categorical imperative is binding on all finite rational beings, not just on human beings.[42] Marx, by contrast, is declaring that there is a categorical imperative to '*overthrow*' relations, which sounds like a call to revolution. Marx's declaration also implies that practical reason does not require the support of religion, and, through repeated use of the term '*human being*', that autonomy is to be thought of as a specifically human quality.[43]

Third, Kant would object to the thought that there can be a categorical imperative to remove all defective '*relations*'. For Kant, the only end that can provide the basis of a categorical imperative is that of rational nature. The overthrow of defective relations, by contrast, would seem, for Kant, to be just a state of affairs to be brought about. A categorical imperative to bring this state of affairs about would entail that the rational nature of the agents it bound was merely of *instrumental* value for achieving this state of affairs. No finite rational agent could recognise such an imperative as categorical *and* take rational nature to have the dignity that grounds its autonomy. Thus, Marx's declaration seems to signal a move away not just from relating autonomy to the concept of a rational being (as distinct from the concept of a rational human being), but also a move away from relating autonomy to the concept of an individual being (as distinct from the concept of a community of human beings).

To declare that the removal of all defective relations is a categorical imperative is to suggest that the subject of autonomy is the kind of subject from which defective relations are expunged. It suggests that the subject of autonomy is a human community. If the subject of autonomy is a human community, the removal of defective relations is not a perfection of anything distinct from this subject (which would entail the thought of its instrumentalisation, and thus its inadequacy as a subject of autonomy). If so, Marx's declaration commits him to a post-Kantian conception of autonomy, on which the subject of autonomy is a subject from which defective relations can be thought of as expunged: a human community.

Fourth, insofar as Marx's declaration is a call to overcome existing defects, it requires the support of a non-timeless grounding argument that allows us to attribute necessity to a historical form of existence. If we attribute necessity to a historical form of existence, the removal of defects in this form of existence

---

41   *KU*, 5: 474; *KpV*, 5: 132.

42   *GMS*, 4: 410.

43   That Marx relates autonomy to 'human reason' is evident at *MEW*, 1, p. 104; *MECW*, 1, p. 202, cited above.

can inherit the necessity of this historical form. The imperative to remove its defects might be called 'categorical', in virtue of this necessity. But if so, Marx requires both an argument for the necessity of a historical form of existence, and an argument that identifies an irrationality in it that does not presuppose anything more than the concept of rationality itself. If these arguments can be put in place, we may ground the value of the autonomy of a human community by arguing that this value is presupposed by principles that we are committed to adopt in order to resolve a historically necessary irrationality. The grounding argument presupposed by Marx's declaration therefore differs in kind from the timeless grounding argument with which Kant seeks to ground the moral law.

In previous scholarship, Marx's declaration of a categorical imperative has been viewed in one of two ways: as a declaration to which 'not too much meaning should be given';[44] or as the statement of a Kantian ethics in which Marx uses 'self-consciously Kantian vocabulary' to 'encourage us to think of the individual as having a value'.[45] On the interpretation offered here, by contrast, Marx's declaration is significant in its suggestion of a post-Kantian ethics, in which autonomy is located at the level of a human community.

Marx's declaration suggests that a Marxist critique of Kant's ethics consists in two steps of argument. First, Kant's ethics must be shown to be mired in religion, and thus subject to a 'critique of religion'. In other words, it ought to be possible to show that our application of Kant's formulas of the categorical imperative relies on a belief in the existence of God, but that Kant offers us no good reason to believe in God's existence. Second, a non-timeless grounding argument for the value of the autonomy of a human community is to be offered. Ethical principles based on this value must be shown to be able to condemn what is wrong with capitalism and to recommend socialism, without relying on any unjustified religious belief.

7 Summary

Let us draw together the findings of the arguments against the irrelevance, complementarity and incompatibility views. Marxists need an ethics, and it is possible for Marxists to offer an ethics if this ethics

(1) condemns capitalism as unjust and recommends socialism as just

(2) does not preclude action necessary to achieve socialism

---

44   Van der Linden 1988, p. 337.
45   Leopold 2007, p. 155.

(3)   supports at least one of the following two claims: existing society ought to
      be revolutionised because the class oppression in it is in one way bad for
      everyone, or social arrangements that promote rational self-transparency
      ought to be adopted because false consciousness is in one way bad for
      everyone
(4)   is grounded by an argument that appeals to premises about capitalism
(5)   evaluates systems
(6)   rests on the value of the autonomy of a human community

(1)–(3) are upshots of the argument against the irrelevance view, (4)–(5) are
upshots of the argument against the complementarity view, and (6) is an
upshot of the argument against the incompatibility view. An ethics that satisfies these conditions is post-Kantian, on account of (6).[46]

A defence of the value of the autonomy of a human community may facilitate either of the forms of argument mentioned in (3). If a human community
exhibits autonomy, it exhibits a degree of rational self-transparency absent
from capitalism. If co-legislated principles expressly recognise social dynamics,
actors are provided with an awareness of the relation of their action to social
life as a whole by their knowledge of these principles. Moreover, if a human
community exhibits autonomy, it is distinguished from capitalism in being free
from class oppression. To say that social dynamics are harmonious is to posit
an end to competition between aggressive sub-groups who seek to place themselves above the community as a whole. In Part III, a system universalisability
principle of justice is shown to offer a way to press this charge against capitalism.

---

46   As we argue in ch. 10, sec. 4, an ethics that satisfies these conditions may also be post-
     Kantian insofar as it grounds autonomy by appeal to the need to resolve an antinomy in
     the social world.

PART II

A Critique of Kant's Ethics

∴

Introduction to Part II

In Part I, we sought to undermine three typical views of Marxism's relation to Kant's ethics. Having rejected these views, the rest of the book defends a different view of this relation: the critique view. There are two parts to the critique view, a negative part and a positive part. The negative part consists in an argument *against* Kant's ethics of the autonomy of the will. The positive part consists in an argument *for* an ethics of the autonomy of a human community. The aim in Part II is simply to defend the negative part of the critique view.

The main argument in Part II is that Kant fails to show that we ought to adopt the categorical imperative. The formulas that we are to use commit us to a belief in the existence of God, and Kant offers no good argument for why we should believe that God exists. This objection does not rest on the premise that it is self-evidently true that God does not exist. We simply argue that the use of these formulas commits us to a belief for which Kant offers no good argument. If we can only adopt the categorical imperative by employing the formulas that Kant offers, and these formulas commit us to a belief in the existence of God for which Kant provides no good argument, Kant has given us insufficient reason to adopt the categorical imperative. If this objection holds, it allows us to turn away from Kant's ethics. It gives us a reason to look elsewhere, if we are to ground autonomy.

To defend this objection, the following chapters (Chapters 5–8) begin by focusing on two of Kant's formulas of the categorical imperative in *Groundwork of the Metaphysics of Morals*: the Formula of the Law of Nature (FLN), and the Formula of the End in Itself (FEI). Our use of either formula is shown to rest on a premise that presupposes a belief in the existence of God. Our application of FLN presupposes a belief in the existence of God because it rests on a principle of natural teleology, the principle of suitability, that only a belief in the existence of God gives us a reason to accept. FEI presupposes a belief in the existence of God because any argument for FEI requires us to hold that there cannot be a species of being with humanity but without personality, and the only way that Kant allows us to hold this is to believe that God could have no purpose in creating such a species.

These arguments aim to show that our use of FLN or FEI rests on a belief in the existence of God. They are then followed (in Chapter 9) by objections to the arguments that Kant offers for why we should believe in God's existence. Two arguments are examined: the argument from the highest good, and the physicoteleological argument. The objection to the argument from the highest good is an objection from moral happiness. This objection says that it is self-contradictory to postulate the existence of God to think of Kant's concept of the highest good as possible. Postulating the existence of God deprives us of this thought, for it deprives us of moral happiness, which is part of the concept of happiness belonging to Kant's concept of the highest good. The objection to the physicoteleological argument is an objection from evolutionary theory. We can explain the existence of organisms in nature without the hypothesis of an intelligent world cause.

The upshot of this critique is that Kant gives us no good reason to adopt these formulas of the categorical imperative. Insofar as we must adopt them, to apply the categorical imperative, Kant provides us with no good reason to abide by the categorical imperative. If we have no good reason to abide by the categorical imperative, we are not committed to the value of autonomy that it expresses.

Indeed, and in addition to the main argument just outlined, if the objection from moral happiness succeeds, the concept of the highest good, as Kant conceives it, cannot be thought of as possible. On Kant's view of the relation between the moral law and the concept of the highest good, the moral law is only valid if we can think of the concept of the highest good as possible. If the objection from moral happiness reveals that Kant's concept of the highest good cannot be thought of as possible, it implies that, on Kant's premises, the moral law is not valid. This completes the argument presented in Chapters 5–9 for the negative part of the critique view.

Before embarking on this argument, we reply to three potential objections, all of which seek to question its sufficiency. We may frame these objections with reference to Kant's summary, in the *Groundwork*, of the formulas of the categorical imperative. Kant argues that he has provided *three* types of formula of the categorical imperative:

> The above three ways of representing the principle of morality are fundamentally only so many formulae of the selfsame law ... For all maxims have
>
> 1) a *form*, which consists in universality, and then the formula of the moral imperative is expressed as follows: that maxims must be chosen as if they were to hold as universal laws of nature;
>
> 2) a *matter*, namely an end, and then the formula says: that a rational being, as an end according to its nature, and hence as an end in itself, must serve for every maxim as the limiting condition of all merely relative and arbitrary ends;
>
> 3) *a complete determination* of all maxims by that formula, namely: that all maxims from one's own legislation ought to harmonize into a possible realm [*Reich*] of ends as a realm of nature.[1]

---

1 *GMS*, 4: 436. Translations of '*Reich*' as 'kingdom' have been altered to 'realm', both because the

Under 1) and 2), Kant refers, respectively, to FLN and FEI, both of which the *Groundwork* has already formulated.[2] Under 3), Kant offers the first[3] imperative statement of what is known as the Formula of the Realm of Ends (FRE). FRE is a formula of the categorical imperative, and yet the strategy just advertised for defending the negative part of the critique view did not refer to it. So, this strategy seems subject to the objection that it cannot suffice to show that Kant fails to justify our use of the categorical imperative. Insofar as no attempt is made to argue that Kant provides us with insufficient reason to adopt FRE, as distinct from FLN and FEI, the strategy cannot show that Kant fails to justify even just one of the formulas of the categorical imperative. If the validity of the moral law can be detached from Kant's concept of the highest good, and if the use of FRE does not rely on a belief in the existence of God, Kant may yet provide us with a basis for abiding by the categorical imperative, so this objection goes.

One reply (not the main one) is to deny that the validity of the moral law can be detached from Kant's concept of the highest good. For Kant, the concept of the highest good is the concept of virtue and happiness proportional to virtue as necessarily combined. In Kant's view, the moral law is valid only if we can think of this concept of the highest good as possible.[4] A Kantian might seek to detach the validity of the moral law from Kant's concept of the highest good by supposing that, although the validity of the moral law depends on the thought of the concept of the highest good as possible, and although virtue must be thought to belong to this concept, the latter does not include happiness. With this alteration to the concept of the highest good, the objection from moral happiness cannot impugn the validity of the moral law on account of any problem it poses for Kant's concept of the highest good. This is not a plausible way to detach the validity of the moral law from Kant's concept of the highest good, however. It leaves us with a conception of the highest good that a finite rational being who acknowledges the categorical imperative cannot accept. A finite rational being who acknowledges the categorical imperative must think of virtue without happiness as an offence to impartial reason. But no rational being can think of a good that contains an offence to impartial reason as 'the

---

latter is more literal ('kingdom' could be: '*Königreich*'), and to match the name by which the corresponding formula of the categorical imperative is more commonly known, the Formula of the Realm of Ends.

2 At *GMS*, 4: 421 and 4: 429, respectively.

3 There are two subsequent statements of FRE in the *Groundwork*, at *GMS*, 4: 438 and 439.

4 For discussion, see ch. 9.

whole and complete good'.[5] Hence, no finite rational being who acknowledges the categorical imperative can think of the concept of the highest good to consist solely of virtue. If the validity of the moral law can only be saved from the implications of the objection from moral happiness by revising Kant's concept of the highest good so that it does not include happiness, the validity of the moral law cannot be saved from these implications.

The main, more direct reply is that the Formula of the Realm of Ends relies on the concept of a realm of ends, which presupposes the concept of God. The dependence of our adoption of FRE on a belief in the existence of God is so manifest that no effort of the kind required in the case of FLN or FEI is even necessary to prove it.

The *Groundwork* is *explicit* that a realm of ends is to be thought of as including a 'supreme head [*Oberhaupt*]'.[6] There is no other way to think of this 'supreme head' than as a perfect moral creator; that is, as God. In elaboration of the concept of a realm of ends, Kant says:

> By a *realm*, however, I understand the systematic union of several rational beings through common laws ... A rational being, however, belongs to the realm of ends as a *member* if it is universally legislating in it, but also itself subject to these laws. It belongs to it *as its supreme head* [Oberhaupt] if as legislating it is not subject to the will of another.[7]

In further characterisation of this '*supreme head*', Kant says:

> A rational being must always consider itself as legislating in a realm of ends possible through freedom of the will, whether as a member, or as its supreme head [*Oberhaupt*]. It cannot, however, occupy the position of the latter merely by the maxims of its will, but only if it is a completely independent being, without need or limitation of its capacities adequate to the will.[8]

A rational being 'without need or limitation of its capacities adequate to the will' is not a finite being, but a perfectly moral being. Its will is a '*holy*, absolutely

5   *KpV*, 5: 110.

6   GMS, 4: 433, 434 and 439. Throughout Part II, I render '*Oberhaupt*' literally as 'supreme head'. Translators have used 'head' (Kant 2009, Kant 2011) (literally: '*Haupt*'), or 'sovereign' (literally: '*Souverän*') (Kant 1987, Kant 2009), or (in a political context) 'head of state' (which might be: '*Staatsoberhaupt*') (Kant 1996b).

7   GMS, 4: 433.

8   GMS, 4: 434.

good will' rather than a will that requires 'moral necessitation'.[9] Kant adds that, in the thought of a possible realm of ends, 'the natural realm as well as the realm of ends' is 'thought as united under one supreme head' as its 'sole limitless legislator'.[10] The supreme head of a realm of ends is thus a perfect, moral creator, or God.[11] If the concept of God belongs to the concept of a realm of ends, then any finite rational agent who adopts FRE ('all maxims from one's own legislation ought to harmonize into a possible realm of ends as a realm of nature')[12] is committed to a belief in existence of God. In the absence of an argument for why we should believe in the existence of God, there is manifestly no reason for us to adopt FRE.

Considerable argument, pieced together from the implications of what Kant says, must be provided for the view that our use of formulas reflecting the first two ways of representing the moral law (by the form or the matter of a maxim) presupposes a belief in the existence of God. By contrast, no extended argument is required to connect the third way of representing the moral law to this belief. To deny that the use of FRE presupposes a belief in the existence of God is to overlook what the *Groundwork* explicitly says in a relatively continuous passage of text. As the argument in the case of FLN and FEI is more complex, the strategy is to focus on them. If the argument across Chapters 5–8 holds, there is at least one point of consistency across the use of formulas reflecting all three ways of representing Kant's moral law. The use of formulas reflecting all three modes of its representation presupposes a belief in the existence of God.

To be sure, evidence is not explanation. It is one thing to bring forth evidence for the fact that Kant includes a 'supreme head' with the attributes of God in the concept of a realm of ends, and another to explain this fact. But an explanation can be offered. The first part of the explanation is to show that the inclusion of a supreme head with the attributes of God in the concept of a realm of ends involves no contradiction. The second part of the explanation is to show that its inclusion is necessary.

In respect of the first part of the explanation, Kant says that a '*realm*' is a 'systematic union of several rational beings through common laws'.[13] If a realm is a union of rational beings, then a realm of ends can be thought to include, besides rational beings whose will does not necessarily accord with practical

---

9   *GMS*, 4: 439.

10   Ibid.

11   See, also, *KU*, 5: 444.

12   *GMS*, 4: 436.

13   *GMS*, 4: 433.

reason, a rational being whose will necessarily accords with practical reason. More specifically, both the will of God and the wills of finite rational beings (insofar as they are thought to conform to practical reason) can be thought to belong to a union 'through common laws'. The will of God can be thought of as consistent with and supportive of all the maxims of all rational beings, once they are thought of as laws of a realm of ends, conforming to practical reason. Thus, we can think of the concept of God as included in the concept of a realm of ends.

It is possible to miss this part of the explanation by describing the realm of ends incorrectly. It is incorrect to describe the '"realm of ends" as a union under moral laws'.[14] The realm of ends is a union 'through [*durch*]'[15] common laws. The realm of ends is not defined by the fact that it relates all rational beings as obligated beings, as 'under' implies. It is defined by the fact that it relates all rational beings as 'legislating' beings. The realm of ends is a union insofar as the laws that define it and that are thought of as legislated by all rational beings are consistent with one another, and mutually supportive. As a realm of ends is a union of legislating beings, not a union of beings *under* moral laws, it is a union to which it is possible to suppose a 'supreme head' with the attributes of God can belong.

As to why Kant's concept of a realm of ends requires a 'supreme head', the *Groundwork* gives no immediate answer. As Herbert Paton notes: 'the doctrine of a supreme head is here introduced without any argument or defence'.[16] But it is possible to supply an answer on Kant's behalf, which makes sense of what the *Groundwork* argues after it has introduced the concept of a 'supreme head'. If a realm is a 'systematic union of several rational beings through common laws',[17] a realm of ends may be thought to require a 'supreme head' with the attributes of God both on account of the 'systematic' union of its ends, and on account of the 'common' laws through which this union is thought of as possible.

The *systematic* nature of the union in a realm of ends provides a reason to think of the latter to include God, for the thought of a supreme head as uniting 'the natural realm as well as the realm of ends'[18] strengthens the unity that can be thought to define it. If nature in a realm of ends is thought of as caused by the same intelligent world cause that is supreme head of the realm of ends,

---

14   Wood 1999, p. 166.

15   *GMS*, 4: 433. The preposition '*durch*' must be translated as 'through'; 'under' would be: '*unter*'.

16   Paton 1953, p. 188.

17   *GMS*, 4: 433.

18   *GMS*, 4: 439.

the law of cause and effect in a realm of ends can be thought of as *'directed to rational beings as its end'*.[19] This thought strengthens the unity that a realm of ends is thought to represent, because moral motivation alone cannot be thought to guarantee a systematic harmony of ends in a realm that includes finite rational beings, owing to our finite knowledge about how to coordinate our actions, and the effects of the use of our capacities. To think of all the universally binding laws formed from all the maxims of all the members of a realm of ends as making up a harmonious union, we must think of this realm of ends as one whose causal laws have been devised by a moral creator to ensure that our moral actions succeed.[20]

The *common* nature of the laws through which rational beings are thought of as united in a realm also provides a reason to think of a realm of ends to include God. But we must first accept the premise that it must be possible for the agents who belong to an ethical community to regard its common laws as the commands of a common legislator. To be sure, Kant does not state this premise in the *Groundwork*. But he does expound it in a later work, and it explains something that Kant does say in the *Groundwork*. In *Religion Within the Bounds of Bare Reason*, Kant remarks that, 'if an ethical community is to come about ... all laws that obligate them [its members – JF] must be capable of being regarded as commands of a common legislator'.[21] This legislator, Kant says, is a legislator in respect of whom the duties of the members of the community

> must *simultaneously* be conceived as his commands, who must thus also be one who knows the heart, in order to be able to see even through the innermost [core] of the attitudes of everyone and, as it must be in any community, to let everyone have whatever his deeds are worth. This, however, is the concept of God as a moral ruler of the world.[22]

The inclusion of God in the concept of a realm of ends strengthens our thought of its laws as 'common' laws, by allowing us to think of the ends of all its members as being judged from a single point of view. Thus, both the thought of the systematic nature of this union, as well as the thought of its laws as common laws, are strengthened, once we think of God as included in the concept of a realm of ends.

---

19   Paton 1953, p. 191.
20   Compare Paton 1953, p. 192.
21   *RGV*, 6: 98.
22   *RGV*, 6: 99.

If we accept this explanation, we can account for a passage in the *Ground-work* in which we read:

> a realm of ends would actually come about through maxims the rule of which the categorical imperative prescribes to all rational beings *if they were universally followed.* But even though a rational being that itself were to follow this maxim punctiliously cannot, because of that, count on every other to be true to it as well, or likewise that the realm of nature and its purposive order harmonize with him, as a fitting member, into a realm of ends possible through himself, i.e. that his expectation of happiness be favoured; nevertheless that law ... remains in its full force ... Even if the natural realm as well as the realm of ends were thought as united under one supreme head [*Oberhaupt*], and by this the latter would no longer remain a mere idea but obtain true reality, it would thereby no doubt gain the supplement of a strong incentive, but never any increase in its inner worth; for regardless of this, even this sole limitless legislator would still have to be represented as judging the worth of rational beings only by their disinterested conduct, prescribed to them directly, merely from that idea.[23]

In Kant's view, we *must* conceive of a realm of ends to include a supreme head with the attributes of God, because we thereby conceive of this realm's causal laws to accord with its members' moral efforts; and we thereby conceive of its members as being judged fairly by their moral efforts, so that it is truly just; and because both of these thoughts are necessary, in order to think of a realm of ends as a systematic union through common laws.

We now appreciate *why* a finite rational agent who adopts FRE is committed to a belief in the existence of God. The full explanation for this is not manifestly apparent in the *Groundwork*, as the reason why Kant includes a 'supreme head' with the attributes of God in its concept of a realm of ends is not immediately apparent. However, the *fact* that Kant includes God in it *is* apparent. The following chapters focus on FLN and FEI because, in their case, not even the fact of the matter is so apparent. Moreover, FLN and FEI are the two formulas that receive the most attention in Kant scholarship, and that those sympathetic to Kant most often seek to apply. So, this focus also tracks the distribution of interest among Kant's various formulas. (Perhaps this distribution of interest is partly explained by the fact that the connection

---

23   *GMS*, 4: 438–9.

of FLN or FEI to a belief in the existence of God is not as readily apparent as in the case of FRE.)

There are two further objections to the strategy to consider. One of these is to object that there is a formula of the categorical imperative, distinct from FRE, that reflects Kant's mode of representing the moral law as '*a complete determination* of all maxims',[24] and that avoids presupposing a belief in the existence of God: the Formula of Autonomy (FA). Like FRE, FA is based on 'the idea of the will of every rational being, as a *universally legislating will*'.[25] But FA does not refer to a possible realm of ends. FA simply commands: 'do everything from the maxim of one's will as one that could at the same time have as its object itself as universally legislating'.[26] Nothing said thus far, or proposed as part of the strategy to follow, denies that Kant gives us sufficient reason to adopt FA, so the objection runs.

There are two specific replies.[27] The first relates to Kant's claim that the concept of a realm of ends is 'attached' to the concept that underpins FA, 'the concept of every rational being that must consider itself as universally legislating through all the maxims of its will'.[28] If the former concept is attached to the latter in the sense that a realm of ends is the only way for us to think of 'the relation of rational beings', as universally legislating, 'to one another',[29] then FA commits to FRE. But if FA commits to FRE, and the adoption of FRE presupposes a belief in the existence of God, then anyone required to adopt FA is owed a reason to hold this belief. If Kant's arguments for the existence of God are rejected, then, just by virtue of FA's relation to FRE and the fact that FRE presupposes a belief in the existence of God, Kant does not give us sufficient reason to adopt FA.

The second reply relates to Kant's repeated claim in the *Groundwork* that FA 'follows' from the thought expressed in FEI, that every rational being is an end in itself.[30] In Chapter 8, we argue that the success of any argument for FEI rests on us supposing that there cannot be a species of being with humanity but without personality; and that the only way for Kant to allow us to suppose

---

24	GMS, 4: 436.
25	GMS, 4: 432.
26	Ibid.
27	One general reply is that, if the validity of the moral law rests on our being able to think of Kant's concept of the highest good as possible, and the objection from moral happiness shows that we cannot think of this concept as possible, then the moral law is not valid, and none of Kant's formulas are binding.
28	GMS, 4: 433.
29	GMS, 4: 434.
30	GMS, 4: 431 and 438.

this is through a belief in the existence of God. If this is correct, then the argument for why we are required to treat humanity in a person always as an end, as FEI commands, rests on a belief in God's existence. Hence if, as Kant says, FA follows from the thought expressed in FEI, then, in light of the fact that the derivation of FEI rests on a belief in the existence of God, FA commits us to this belief. If Kant's arguments for the existence of God are rejected, then, just by virtue of the relation of FA to FEI, and the dependence of FEI on a belief in the existence of God, Kant has not offered us a sufficient reason to adopt FA.

Indeed, there is a close relation between the value conceptions that underpin FEI and FA. In light of this relation, it is very hard to reject Kant's claim that FA follows from the thought expressed in FEI, and equally hard to avoid the conclusion that the adoption of FA commits us to a belief in the existence of God if the argument for FEI does.

The value conception that Kant uses to determine what there can be a categorical imperative to treat always as an end (and thus FEI) is: that which exists with 'absolute worth'.[31] Worth that is absolute contrasts with worth that is merely relative. Further, to ground a categorical imperative, Kant has to show that there can only be *one* candidate for the role of existence with absolute worth. Before we know (by consulting Kant's statement of FEI) that humanity in a person is what we are to treat always as an end, we know that, if Kant is to represent the moral law in terms of the matter of a maxim, he will have to argue that exclusively one type of entity exists with absolute worth.

We may offer an analysis of what worth a type of entity would have, if it were the only type of entity with absolute worth. To say that only one type of entity exists with absolute worth is to say that it has both non-derivative and transcendent worth. Y has non-derivative worth if Y does not owe its worth to an external source (which would make its worth dependent on that source). Y has transcendent worth if no amount of anything that is not Y can have a value equal to Y or exceeding that of Y (which would allow it to be treated purely instrumentally for a certain amount of some other thing).

From this analysis, it neither follows, nor is excluded, that the type of entity that alone exists with absolute worth is either a single particular or many particulars. If one or more particulars have absolute worth, this particular (or particulars) will have 'incomparable worth', that is, 'a worth that it is never legitimate to exchange'.[32] But as it does not follow just from this analysis of exclusive absolute worth as transcendent and non-derivative worth that what has absolute

---

31   *GMS*, 4: 428; see ch. 8.
32   Kerstein 2013, p. 125.

worth is a particular (or particulars), it does not follow just from this analysis that some particular (or particulars) with absolute worth is also of incomparable worth. For all this analysis reveals, the only type of entity existing with absolute worth may be an entire species of being considered as a whole. It would not then follow, just from an analysis of exclusive absolute worth, and a judgment about this species, that no particular member of it could be traded off, even for a large number of other members of its species.

Now, the value conception that underpins FA (and FRE) is the dignity of a rational being: 'this dignity (prerogative) it has above all merely natural beings brings with it that it must always take its maxims from the point of view of itself, but also at the same time of every other rational being as legislating'.[33] In elaboration of dignity, Kant says:

> In the realm of ends everything has either a PRICE, or a DIGNITY. What has a price can be replaced with something else, as its *equivalent*; whereas what is elevated above any price, and hence allows of no equivalent, has a dignity.[34]

For Kant, a being with dignity has a value that means that it cannot be traded off for anything else, including any aggregate number of entities of its own species, for it 'allows of no equivalent'. A being with dignity is a *particular* being with incomparable worth. But if a type of entity has incomparable worth, it will have exclusive absolute worth. Firstly, it will have transcendent worth, for if something that is not Y has a value equal to or more than Y, it is false that Y allows of no equivalent. Secondly, it will have non-derivative worth. If Y owes its worth to an external source, Z, then, if Z is cut off, Y may continue to exist, just not with its former worth; and if Y exists without its former worth, it may allow of an equivalent. As the concept of incomparable worth implies transcendent worth and non-derivative worth, it implies exclusive absolute worth. So, any particular being that has dignity, has exclusive absolute worth. The value conception that underpins FA (and FRE), namely, the dignity of a particular being, implies the value conception that underpins Kant's argument for FEI, namely, exclusively exists with absolute worth. But it also contains something more: that a *particular* being (or beings) exclusively exist with absolute worth.

---

33   *GMS*, 4: 438; see, also, *GMS*, 4: 434. The concept of dignity plays no role in Kant's argument for FEI.

34   *GMS*, 4: 434.

This is one reason for Kant to say that FA follows from the thought expressed in FEI. FEI commands: '[s]o act that you use humanity, in your own person as well as in the person of any other, always at the same time as an end, never merely as a means'.[35] This command implies that each rational being (each person with humanity) exists with incomparable worth. If humanity in a person is to be treated 'never merely as a means', humanity in one person is never to be treated merely as a means for anything other than humanity in a person, or merely as a means for humanity in any other person, or merely as a means for humanity in any number of other persons. No particular person's humanity allows of an equivalent. While the value conception: exclusively exists with absolute worth, does not imply any particular with incomparable worth, and so does not imply the value conception of the dignity of a particular being underlying FA, the statement of FEI does imply this value conception. The difference stems from the fact that Kant's statement of FEI comes after Kant's argument for why only humanity in a person can exist with absolute worth, and persons are particular agents. The value conception that Kant uses to *argue for* FEI, exclusively exists with absolute worth, does not imply a species of being each particular member of which has incomparable worth. But the value judgment *expressed in* FEI, which comes after Kant's argument for FEI, does imply the dignity of any particular rational being.

On this reading, Kant has a reason to say that FA follows from the thought expressed in FEI. The value conception underpinning FA is at bottom the same as that expressed in FEI. But if the value conception of FA follows from the thought expressed in FEI, as distinct from the value conception that Kant uses to arrive at FEI, it rests on Kant's argument for FEI. If Kant's argument for FEI rests on a belief in the existence of God, then the fact that FA follows from the thought expressed in FEI leaves those who adopt FA committed to this belief. If Kant's arguments for the existence of God are rejected, Kant has not offered us a sufficient reason to adopt FA, just in virtue of its relation to FEI.

A final objection to the strategy pursued in chapters 5–8 is to object that it is insufficient because it raises no opposition to our use of the Formula of Universal Law. The Formula of Universal Law (FUL), like the Formula of the Law of Nature (FLN), is a formula of the categorical imperative relating to the '*form*'[36] of a moral maxim. However, unlike FLN, FUL does not appeal to the concept of a universal law of nature. Whereas FLN commands: '*so act as if the maxim of your action were to become by your will a* UNIVERSAL LAW OF NATURE';[37] FUL

---

35   GMS, 4: 429.
36   GMS, 4: 436.
37   GMS, 4: 421.

simply commands: '*act only according to that maxim through which you can at the same time will that it become a universal law*'.[38] The argument presented in the following chapters for why our application of FLN presupposes a belief in the existence of God rests on the idea that Kant's concept of a universal law of nature reflects the principle of suitability. As FUL does not contain the concept of a universal law of nature, it does not seem possible to extend this argument to our use of FUL.

The reply to this objection is similar to the reply to the previous one. Just as FA commits to a belief in the existence of God simply by virtue of its relation to FRE, and also simply by virtue of its relation to FEI, FUL commits to this belief simply by virtue of its relation to FLN. Insofar as we apply a formula of the categorical imperative relating to the form of a moral maxim, we apply FLN, not FUL.

Kant implies that it is necessary for us to apply FLN, at least as distinct from FUL, to judge a maxim's permissibility, when he comments in *Critique of Practical Reason* that 'reason is entitled and also required to use nature (in terms of nature's pure form of understanding) as the type of the power of judgment'.[39] Even if FUL is an alternative formula for representing the moral law in relation to a maxim's form, it is necessary for us to apply FLN rather than FUL on account of a difficulty encountered by our power of judgment. This difficulty, Kant says, is 'due to [the fact] that a law of freedom is to be applied to actions as events that occur in the world of sense and thus, to this extent, belong to nature'.[40]

A formula of the categorical imperative is supposed to guide the conduct of finite rational beings, whose wills are not necessarily good, on account of the possibility for an incentive, related to their sensible nature, to provide their motivation for acting. To this end, the formula must be used to assess conduct that such agents conceive to be possible in the world of sense. In conceiving of an action as possible in the world of sense, an agent must represent it as part of nature, as falling under causal laws. So, any test of the permissibility of a maxim in respect of the universality of its form is a judgment about action as it is represented as falling under causal laws.

Now, '*law*', Kant writes in the *Groundwork*, 'carries with it the concept of an *unconditional* and indeed objective and hence universally valid *necessity*'.[41] On this view, a maxim can be thought to become a universal law in the world of sense only if it can be thought to govern the action of all finite rational agents

---

38   Ibid.
39   *KpV*, 5: 70.
40   *KpV*, 5: 68.
41   GMS, 4: 416.

unconditionally and necessarily. To carry this thought experiment out for any given maxim, it must be possible to conceive of an unconditional and necessary law as part of a world of sense. Otherwise, there can be no universal-law-based test of action belonging to the world of sense. This raises a problem. How are we to conceive of an unconditional, necessary law as belonging to a world of sense if we represent any action belonging to the world of sense as subject to causality, and, consequently, we cannot be sure of any such action that it is performed on purely moral grounds?

If we are to conceive of a universal law in the world of sense, we have to conceive of it as not subject to conditions and as holding with necessity. If we were to imagine a world of purely rational beings, we could imagine a maxim holding in it as a universal law in virtue of all of them treating it as intrinsically morally worthy to perform. In other words, a universal law of freedom would hold unconditionally and necessarily in a world of purely rational beings. But this is of no help to us, because the world in which we are to think of a law as unconditional and necessary is the world of sense, a world of merely finitely rational beings. We must find a way of representing a maxim as a universal law that does not depend on moral motivation for its representation as unconditional and necessary.

We can do this, Kant argues, only by representing it as a universal law *of nature*. Kant says in *Critique of Practical Reason* that in regard to 'merely the *form of lawfulness* as such ... to this extent laws, as such, are the same, no matter from where they take their determining bases'.[42] If a universal law of freedom is not 'a law that can be exhibited *in concreto* in objects of the senses', because we can never be sure that an action in the world of sense is performed on purely moral grounds, we may – and *must* – represent a universal law in the world of sense as a 'law of nature'.[43] To conceive of a maxim as a universal law, we must conceive of it as a universal law of nature. That is, we must conceive of it as a universal law against which it is causally impossible for all those in a certain type of situation to act. We can then conceive of it as unconditional and necessary, and as part of the world of sense.

In short, 'reason is entitled and also required'[44] to represent a universal law as a universal law of nature. It is entitled to do so, because 'it takes from sensible nature nothing more than what pure reason can also think on its own, i.e., lawfulness'.[45] If it were to take *more* than this, that is, specific empirical features

---

42   *KpV*, 5: 70.
43   *KpV*, 5: 69.
44   *KpV*, 5: 70.
45   *KpV*, 5: 71.

of a particular arrangement of nature distinct from the general concept of lawfulness, it could no longer serve as a test of pure practical reason.[46] Reason is required to represent a universal law as a universal law of nature, moreover, because 'without having something available that it could make an example in a case of experience, it could not provide to the law of a pure practical reason its use in application'.[47] Our power of judgment cannot apply the concept of a universal law to assess the permissibility of a maxim in respect of its form except by representing it as a universal law of nature. The only formula of a categorical imperative relating to the form of a moral maxim that we are to apply is FLN. We cannot apply FUL except in the form of FLN.

Due to the relation of FUL to FLN, FUL commits to any belief that is presupposed by the application of FLN. If the application of FLN presupposes a belief in the existence of God, FUL commits to this belief. For if we cannot apply the notion of a universal law, common to FUL and FLN, to judge a maxim's permissibility in respect of the universality of its form, other than by representing it as a universal law of nature, it is futile to affirm FUL without affirming FLN. To affirm FUL but not FLN is to have no means to judge the permissibility of maxims in respect of the universality of their form. Thus, FUL commits to FLN. But if FUL commits to FLN, and FLN rests on the principle of suitability, which presupposes a belief in the existence of God, to affirm FUL is to be committed to a belief in the existence of God. If Kant's arguments for the existence of God are rejected, then, by virtue of the relation of FUL to FLN, Kant has not offered us a sufficient reason to affirm FUL.

Bolstered by these replies, the strategy pursued in chapters 5–9 may, if the argument is sound, represent a sufficient critique of Kant's ethics, notwithstanding its focus on FLN and FEI. Chapters 5–7 examine FLN, while Chapter 8 examines FEI. Chapter 9 examines Kant's two arguments for why we should believe in the existence of God, and suggests why the principle of suitability presupposes this belief.

---

46   Interpretations of FLN often ignore this restriction; see chs 5–7.
47   *KpV*, 5: 70.

CHAPTER 5

Kant's Contradiction in Conception Test

The Formula of the Law of Nature is one of the formulas of the categorical imperative that Kant presents in the *Groundwork of the Metaphysics of Morals*. In asking an agent to consider whether they could will their maxim as a universal law of nature, the formula poses two tests: the contradiction in conception test (CC test) and the contradiction in the will test (CW test). The CC test, on which this chapter focuses, has been interpreted in three different ways: as a test of a teleological contradiction (TCI), a practical contradiction (PCI), or a logical contradiction (LCI). One indication that existing interpretations of the CC test need not be exhaustive, however, is that the established view of the *Groundwork*'s two applications of the CC test is a hybrid view. On the one hand, neither LCI nor PCI is thought to account for the *Groundwork*'s application of the CC test to a maxim of suicide. The established view of this application is that Kant appeals to a premise about the purpose of the instinct of self-love, and that the argument is unconvincing even on its own terms.[1] On the other hand, the *Groundwork*'s application of the CC test to a maxim of false promising, which is generally regarded as more of a success, is usually interpreted along the model of PCI[2] or, less often, LCI.[3] Thus, in respect of the *Groundwork*'s two applications of the CC test, the established view is a hybrid view. The *Groundwork*'s arguments are taken to differ in kind.

This chapter offers an alternative to this hybrid view, by defending a new, causal-teleological version of LCI. The distinctive feature of the causal-teleological version of LCI is that it holds that our conception of a hypothetical world in which a maxim is a universal law of nature is informed by a principle of natural teleology. If the thought of a universal law of nature is understood to have causal and teleological implications, it is possible to offer a unified account of the *Groundwork*'s arguments for why a maxim of suicide and a maxim of false promising fail the CC test. Relatedly, a causal-teleological version of LCI provides a solution to the problem of how the CC test can confirm the impermissibility of a self-directed maxim.

---

1 Allison 2011, p. 186; Aune 1979, p. 55, p. 60; Galvin 1991, pp. 393–4; Guyer 2007, p. 116; Korsgaard 1996, pp. 88–90; Paton 1953, p. 154; Wood 1999, pp. 85–6.

2 Allison 2011, pp. 186–7; Aune 1979, p. 54; Dietrichson 1964, p. 158; Guyer 2007, p. 93; Korsgaard 1996, pp. 92–3; O'Neill 2013, pp. 172–3; Timmermann 2007, pp. 82–3.

3 Galvin 1991, p. 397; Kemp 1958, p. 67; Wood 1972, pp. 618–19; Wood 1999, pp. 87–8.

As a version of LCI, the view defended here is that the CC test is a test of a logical contradiction (*p* and *not-p*) in the thought of a hypothetical world in which a maxim is a universal law of nature. The view defended here is a *causal-teleological* version of LCI as it holds that the thought of a universal law of nature has causal and teleological implications. On this view, to imagine a maxim as a universal law of nature is to imagine a hypothetical world in which (1) everyone who satisfies its condition cannot but adopt its means and achieve its end ('causal'); and in which (2) everyone regards the maxim as an indispensable part of their moral life, and regards their endowments as suiting them to lead a moral life that includes it ('teleological'). By conceiving of a hypothetical world in which a maxim has universal causal necessity and is an indispensable part of hypothetical agents' moral life, we moral theorists are to test whether, in our world, that maxim is permissible.

1   The Basic Features of the Causal-Teleological Version of LCI

The *Groundwork* expresses the Formula of the Law of Nature (FLN) as follows: '*so act as if the maxim of your action were to become by your will a* UNIVERSAL LAW OF NATURE'.[4] It distinguishes two respects in which FLN tests maxims, now termed the contradiction in conception test and contradiction in the will test:

> Some actions are such that their maxim [for example, the suicide maxim or the false promising maxim – JF] cannot even be *thought* without contradiction as a universal law of nature; let alone that one could *will* that it *should* become such. In the case of others that inner impossibility is indeed not to be found, but it is still impossible to *will* that their maxim be elevated to the universality of a law of nature, because such a will would contradict itself.[5]

The *Groundwork* remarks that 'a *maxim* is the subjective principle of willing',[6] or that 'a maxim is the subjective principle for acting'.[7] A maxim is a practical *principle* because it is a *type*-based course of proposed action. No individuating reference to a particular is included in its description. A maxim is a *subjective*

---

4   *GMS*, 4: 421.
5   *GMS*, 4: 424.
6   *GMS*, 4: 401.
7   *GMS*, 4: 420.

practical principle because it is a principle of a *particular* finite agent, with a particular biography and particular inclinations. On one widely expressed view, the form of a maxim is: 'I am to do X in circumstances C in order to bring about Y'.[8]

Kant's treatment of maxims raises a number of issues, such as the 'problem of relevance',[9] that is, the problem of determining which of the principles that apply to a given act it is relevant to assess. All that matters for defending a unified account of the *Groundwork*'s applications of the CC test, however, is that it is not unfaithful to state the suicide maxim and the false promising maxim in condition-means-end form.

Just before Kant makes his argument for why the suicide maxim fails the CC test, he states it as: 'from self-love I make it my principle to shorten my life if, when protracted any longer, it threatens more ill than it promises agreeableness'.[10] 'From self-love' is later cashed out as: 'preserving a bearable condition up to the end of life'.[11] Similarly, just before Kant makes his argument for why the false promising maxim fails the CC test, he states it as: 'when I believe myself to be in need of money I shall borrow money, and promise to repay it, even though I know that it will never happen'.[12] Restating both maxims in the order of a type of condition, a type of means and a type of end, we have:

> when living any longer threatens more ill than it promises agreeableness, I will end my life, to make my life bearable up until its end (the *suicide* maxim)

> when I am in need of money, I will make a false promise, to obtain a loan (the *false promising* maxim)

The *Groundwork* says that *law* is objective: it is independent of a particular subject.[13] But it also allows law to denote a relation of cause and effect.[14] Following these indications, a law in respect of acting on a maxim has the form: if, in a certain type of condition, a type of means is adopted to achieve a type of end,

8   Rawls 1989, p. 83; see also Allison 2011, p. 198; Herman 1993, p. 64; McNair 2000, p. 27; O'Neill 2013, p. 102; Pogge 1998, p. 189.

9   O'Neill 2013, p. 39.

10   *GMS*, 4: 422.

11   *GMS*, 4: 429.

12   *GMS*, 4: 422.

13   *GMS*, 4: 416.

14   *GMS*, 4: 421.

the end is achieved. For example: if somebody in need of money makes a false promise to obtain a loan, they obtain a loan.

A *universal* law, as distinct from a probabilistic law, is a law that holds for all the entities that satisfy its condition. It admits no exception. For example: *everyone* in need of money makes a false promise to obtain a loan, and they *all* obtain a loan.

It is a widely held view that a universal law *of nature* is a law whose universality holds 'by causal necessity'.[15] This is in line with Kant's characterisation, just prior to formulating FLN, of '*nature* in the most general sense' as 'the universality of the law according to which effects happen'.[16] To imagine a maxim as a universal law of nature, one supposes, in a counterfactual thought experiment, that it is causally impossible for anyone who satisfies a certain type of condition not to perform a type of action and thereby not to achieve a type of end. For example: everyone in need of money *cannot but* make a false promise to obtain a loan, and everyone *cannot but* thereby obtain a loan.

Further, any counterfactual thought experiment in which a maxim is a universal causal law rests on the thought of a hypothetical nature whose other features are consistent with it. Such a hypothetical nature must accord with the features of any possible system of nature. In other words, everything that is thought to be able to occur in it must be thought to have a cause in space and time (that is, no miracles are thought to occur; if, for example, loans are not repaid, it may not be imagined that God can repay them); and whatever is thought to have a causal effect in one case, is thought to have a similar causal effect in similar cases (that is, no exceptional flukes occur). To imagine a maxim as a universal causal law is to imagine it as one universal causal law in a hypothetical system of causal laws.

Finally – and this is what distinguishes the causal-teleological version of LCI from previous interpretations of the CC test – to conceive of a maxim as a universal law of nature is to conceive it to belong to a hypothetical system of nature whose agents we conceive in light of a teleological principle. This idea is inspired by the *Groundwork*'s remark:

---

15 Dietrichson 1964, p. 152; see also Allison 2011, p. 183; Herman 1993, p. 47; McNair 2000, p. 26; O'Neill 2013, p. 23; Rawls 2000, p. 168; Wolff 1973, p. 160; Wood 1999, p. 80.

16 *GMS*, 4: 421. Likewise, Kant refers to a 'universal law ... placed in us by natural instinct' (*GMS*, 4: 423); and he comments that what is 'generally similar to a *natural order*' in what FLN asks us to imagine is 'the lawfulness of actions [*Gesetzmäßigkeit der Handlungen*]' (*GMS*, 4: 431, translation modified). '*Gesetzmäßigkeit*' here means: happening in accordance with law. Thomas Pogge's dissenting view of universal laws of nature as maxims that 'everyone feels (morally) free to – and those so inclined ("by nature") actually do – adopt' (Pogge 1998, p. 190) is too subjective to fit these statements.

In the natural endowments of an organized being, i.e. one arranged purposively for life, we assume as a principle that no instrument will be found in it for any end which is not also the most fitting for that end and the most suitable for it.[17]

In this remark, the *Groundwork* advances a claim about an assumption that 'we' finite rational beings make in thinking about organised beings. We are said to assume, as a regulative principle to guide inquiry,[18] that the natural endowments of entities we identify as organised beings could not be bettered in respect of enabling them to pursue their ends. Christoph Horn terms this teleological principle 'the principle of suitability'.[19]

As we identify *ourselves* as organised beings, the *Groundwork* implies that we assume, as a regulative principle, that the capacities with which we human beings are endowed could not be bettered in respect of enabling us to pursue the ends we are to pursue. The *Groundwork* immediately goes on to say that human beings do not just possess 'reason and a will', but 'reason as a practical faculty', whose 'function must be to produce a *will that is good*'.[20] The *Groundwork*'s more specific claim, therefore, is that we assume that we are endowed with the best capacities we could have for cultivating a good will, which is to say, for leading a moral life. In other words, what we are guided by in our anthropological inquiry, according to Kant, is an assumption that our arrangements are such as to make us as well equipped as we could be for leading a moral life. In the *Critique of Judgment*, Kant offers a defence of this principle.[21]

---

17   GMS, 4: 395. Translation modified. I have altered the Kant 2011 translation of '*Naturanlagen*' from 'natural predispositions' to 'natural endowments' because an 'instrument (*Werkzeug*)' (GMS, 4: 395) is not a kind of predisposition (compare Mikkelsen 2013, pp. 38–9). I have also made small changes so that it is natural to read both uses of 'it' to refer to 'organized being'.

18   See Wood 1999, pp. 219–21.

19   Horn 2006, p. 46.

20   GMS, 4: 395–6.

21   All that matters for the causal-teleological version of LCI is that Kant should hold that we are necessarily led to adopt the principle of suitability in respect of *rational* organised beings.

Consider the following principles of teleology, listed in increasing order of stringency:

(1)   An organised being is fit for purpose

(2)   Everything about an organised being contributes to its fitness for purpose (the principle of the purposiveness of all parts, or nothing in vain)

(3)   Nothing about an organised being could be bettered in respect of its fitness for purpose (the principle of suitability)

The principle of suitability is relevant in the context of the CC test, because FLN requires us to conceive of a hypothetical system of nature that includes hypothetical agents. The question that arises in this context is: when, in performing the CC test, we conceive of a hypothetical system of nature, how must the principle of suitability guide our conception of its hypothetical agents?

The *Groundwork* claims that we finite rational beings are guided by the principle of suitability in thinking about our endowments. That is only so because we view our organisation as the result of a causal sequence of events beyond our doing, as part of nature. By contrast, we do not view the uses we make of our endowments to pursue our ends as results of external causes. We necessarily think of our ends, and hence those uses, as ends and uses we have chosen.[22] Hence, we are not guided by the principle of suitability to look for the endow-

---

In the *Critique of Judgment*, Kant argues that we are necessarily led to adopt (2), the principle of the purposiveness of all parts, to guide our study of organised beings. From Kant's argument, it follows that we are necessarily led to adopt (3), the principle of suitability, in respect of rational organised beings.

In the *Critique of Judgment*, Kant claims that we are necessarily led to think of organised beings 'as if' they have come about through 'a causality that only reason can have' (*KU*, 5: 370). If that is so, however, then 'the purpose [the idea] of nature has to be extended to *everything* that is in this product of nature' (*KU*, 5: 377). Further, 'this concept of a natural purpose leads us necessarily to the idea of all of nature as a system in terms of the rule of purposes' (*KU*, 5: 379). Reason, which seeks the unconditioned (*KU*, 5: 401), must then suppose that the *final* purpose of the creation of this system lies in a species with a 'supersensible ability (freedom)' (*KU*, 5: 431, 435), human beings. If, however, we are led to view the world, including the species with the capacity for morality, as if it has come about through an intelligent cause, then we must 'also' think of any such intelligence 'as the legislating supreme head in a moral realm of ends' (*KU*, 5: 444, amending the translation of '*Oberhaupt*' from 'sovereign' to 'supreme head' and of '*Reich der Zwecke*' from 'kingdom of purposes' to 'realm of ends'). In virtue of this, Kant argues, we must think of this intelligence as '*omniscient*', '*omnipotent*' and so on, in other words, perfect (*KU*, 5: 444). Now, if, as Kant held, our moral purpose is one that we can always strive to fulfil to a greater degree; and if we are led to think of our species as if it has come about as the final purpose of a perfect intelligence (*KU*, 5: 445); then we must assume, as a regulative principle, that nothing about us could be bettered in respect of making us fit for our moral purpose. For if an intelligent world cause is perfect, its creation must be perfectly suited to its purpose; and while an imperfection in a type of entity that is not the final purpose of this world need not hinder a species of being for which it serves as a means from serving its purpose perfectly, and hence need not imply that the world to which it belongs is imperfectly suited to its purpose; a world *is* imperfectly suited to its purpose if there is an imperfection in the species of being that is the final purpose of its creation.

The *Critique of Judgment* shows that Kant had a reason to hold the teleological principle of suitability expressed in the *Groundwork*, at least if the *Groundwork*'s remark is taken as a claim about our study of rational organised beings.

22 *GMS*, 4: 447–8.

ments that would best suit a member of our species for any of the ends we pursue merely because we pursue them. Nor are we guided by the principle of suitability to regard the ends we pursue as ones that belong to our purpose of leading a moral life merely because we pursue them.

This alters, however, when we conceive of a hypothetical system of nature in which a maxim is a universal causal law. Here *we do* think of action on this maxim as determined by a causal law. This gives a twist to our application of the principle of suitability. If we extend the principle of suitability to think about hypothetical agents who (like us) have practical reason but who also (unlike us) all adopt a specific maxim by causal necessity, we cannot simply assume that they (like us) are endowed with the best capacities they could have for leading a moral life. We must assume that the maxim they adopt by causal necessity is an indispensable part of their moral life. *Otherwise, we could not reconcile our assumption that they could not be better suited to the purpose of leading a moral life with the causality we conceive them to be subject to.* In sum, we assume that hypothetical agents' endowments are the best they could have for leading a hypothetical moral life that includes the maxim they adopt by causal necessity. On the causal-teleological version of LCI, the CC test is a test of whether the thought of *such* a hypothetical system of nature contains a logical contradiction.

Take, for example, the false promising maxim. On a causal-teleological view of a universal law of nature, to imagine the false promising maxim as a universal law of nature is to imagine a hypothetical system of nature in which: (1) everyone in need of money cannot but make a false promise to obtain a loan, and cannot but thereby obtain a loan; (2) false promising to obtain a loan when in need of money is an indispensable part of a moral life, and agents' capacities (for example, for communication) are the best they could have for leading such a life. The false promising maxim is impermissible if, in a hypothetical system of nature defined by (1) and (2), at least one agent who satisfies the condition of being in need of money is unable to make a false promise to obtain a loan.

To construct a test in which hypothetical agents regard a maxim as an indispensable part of their moral life is not, of course, to imply that we real world agents display that attitude to our maxims (no more than we adopt maxims with causal necessity). Further, the constituents of a test are not to be confused with what a test is used to decide. One constituent of the CC test, on the causal-teleological version of LCI, is a hypothetical system of nature in which a maxim is an indispensable part of a moral life. What this test is used to decide is the permissibility of that maxim for us. There is no inconsistency or erasure of the difference between the obligatory and the permissible in conceiving a *hypothet-*

ical system of nature in which a maxim is *obligatory* in order to test whether or not it is *permissible* for *us* to adopt it.

2   Further Features of a Causal-Teleological Version of LCI

Section 1 expounded the basic features of the causal-teleological version of LCI. This section outlines two further features of the causal-teleological version of LCI that is proposed here. Those who doubt them may still affirm a causal-teleological version of LCI as an account of why the suicide maxim and the false promising maxim fail the CC test. The interpretation of the *Groundwork*'s applications of the CC test to these maxims in sections 3–4 could still be upheld, with only minor alterations.

The first further feature of the causal-teleological version of LCI proposed here is that a maxim only fails the CC test if a logical contradiction is produced in *every* hypothetical system of nature to which its counterpart universal law of nature could consistently belong.

Ted McNair implies that this requirement makes for a CC test that is too lax:

> it is not sufficient to imagine that my universalized maxim *might be able to hold* by a fortunate happenstance under a certain set of favorable conditions that I have no good reason to believe must obtain ... if we take the universality test to be a test of the reasoning behind our conduct, its endorsement of that reasoning should not depend upon the accidental fulfilment of a certain set of conditions that our reasoning did not take into account.[23]

McNair objects to the idea that the hypothetical system of nature that FLN asks us to imagine may include features that a particular agent would have no good reason to believe must obtain in the real world. Consider the maxim, adapted from Jon Elster: when my view of a lecture is impaired, I will stand up, to get a better view.[24] Its counterpart universal law of nature is: everyone whose view of a lecture is impaired cannot but stand up, and cannot but thereby get a better view. As applied to this maxim, McNair's objection is that one may not argue

---

23   McNair 2000, pp. 34–5. Here McNair claims both that (i) a fortunate happenstance under unrealistic conditions may not bear on whether a universality test finds a maxim permissible; and that (ii) unrealistic (and in that sense accidental) conditions may not bear on whether a universality test finds a maxim permissible. Only (ii) is denied.

24   See Elster 1978, p. 110.

from the possibility of a hypothetical system of nature in which the long-legged always sit behind the short-legged that this maxim passes the CC test, if the particular agent who adopts it has no good reason to believe that the long-legged are likely to sit behind the short-legged. If a hypothetical system of nature in which a maxim is a universal law of nature can only be thought without logical contradiction if it includes a causal law which the particular agent who adopts the maxim would regard as unrealistic, that cannot allow it to pass the CC test, runs the objection.

McNair's objection commits to a view of the hypothetical system of nature that FLN asks us to imagine that is too subjective and empirical, however, to capture the spirit of the *Groundwork*. It commits to an overly subjective view of that hypothetical system of nature, for it can only contingently be the case that what one agent has good reason to believe must obtain in the real world is what every agent has good reason to believe must obtain. The reason one agent would have to refrain from adopting a maxim could only contingently rest on a logical contradiction in the same hypothetical system of nature as that conceived by any other agent to ascertain if they should refrain. The reason to refrain need not be provided by 'grounds that are valid for every rational being',[25] irrespective of biography. The objection also commits to an overly empirical view of the hypothetical system of nature which FLN asks us to imagine, for a hypothetical system of nature is no less a system of nature if its causal laws are not in sync with the probabilistic laws that can be expected to hold in the real world. Even if it is improbable that, for example, long-legged lecture attenders sit behind the short-legged, it is conceivable for there to be a system of nature in which long-legged lecture attenders sit behind the short-legged. As it is only contingently the case that long-legged lecture attenders do not sit behind the short-legged, it could only contingently be the case that this maxim of standing at a lecture failed the CC test; that is, it would fail the CC test only for as long as it was unlikely that long-legged lecture attenders sit behind the short-legged.

To insist that a logical contradiction be contained in the thought of *every* hypothetical system of nature to which a given universal law of nature could consistently belong better fits Kant's aim of offering an objective, *a priori* moral theory.[26] As argued below, it also fits the *Groundwork*'s arguments for why the suicide maxim and the false promising maxim fail the CC test.

---

25   *GMS*, 4: 413.

26   Kant writes in *Critique of Practical Reason* that, in aiding our power of judgment, reason 'takes from sensible nature nothing more than what pure reason can also think on its own, i.e., lawfulness' (*KpV*, 5: 71).

The second further feature of the causal-teleological version of LCI proposed here is that a logical contradiction can be identified on one of either
two counts. On the Logical Contradiction Interpretation, the CC test renders a
maxim impermissible if and only if submitting it to the CC test yields a logical
contradiction (*p* and *not-p*). While this may seem obvious, 'logical contradiction' and 'logical impossibility (of an action)' are sometimes used as if they
were interchangeable.[27] They are not interchangeable. Only one of two possible logical contradictions in the thought of a hypothetical system of nature
rests on an action's logical impossibility.

The thought of a hypothetical system of nature that includes a universal law
of nature will contain a logical contradiction *either* if it is both (1) the thought
of everyone who satisfies a certain type of condition unfailingly performing a
type of action and thereby achieving a type of end (as part of the moral life they
are to lead), and the thought of at least one agent who satisfies that type of condition as unable to perform that type of action (as part of the moral life they
are to lead); *or* if it is both (2) the thought of everyone who satisfies a certain
type of condition unfailingly performing a type of action and thereby achieving a type of end (as part of the moral life they are to lead), and the thought of
at least one agent who satisfies that type of condition and who performs that
type of action as not achieving that type of end (as part of the moral life they
are to lead).

I maintain that a unified account of the *Groundwork*'s examples of suicide and false promising can be offered on the basis of a causal-teleological
version of LCI *even if* one were to insist on a more restrictive view of it, on
which a maxim is only rendered impermissible if the thought of every hypothetical system of nature to which its counterpart universal law of nature
could consistently belong contains (1). But I also believe that no such restriction is necessary for it to count as a version of LCI, for the following reasons.

First, (2) *is* the thought of a logical contradiction (*p* and *not-p*). Hence, the
reason to insist on a more restrictive view of the causal-teleological version of
LCI cannot be that, if (2) sufficed to render a maxim impermissible, it would
not be rendered impermissible by a logical contradiction. It *would* be rendered
impermissible by a logical contradiction.

Second, it is false that, if, on LCI, (2) suffices to render a maxim impermissible, LCI can no longer be properly distinguished from another interpretation
of the CC test, PCI. The causal-teleological version of LCI, and PCI, can be

---

27   Galvin 1991, p. 387.

adequately distinguished even if, on a causal-teleological version of LCI, (2) suffices to render a maxim impermissible.

To confirm this point, consider how PCI's proponents have described and applied PCI. Onora O'Neill writes: 'the contradiction in conception test is itself a test of coherent intentions'.[28] Barbara Herman says: 'there is a contradiction in our willing the original maxim *and* its universal form'.[29] On PCI, a maxim fails the CC test, Christine Korsgaard argues, if 'in willing the World of the Universalized Maxim the agent undercuts the causal law behind the hypothetical imperative from which his own maxim is derived'.[30] To will a maxim is to adopt all necessary and some sufficient means to achieve it when those means are available, and, by implication, not to bring about a state of affairs that makes it impossible to achieve. It is incoherent, therefore, for one and the same agent to will a maxim and to will a world in which its universal adoption makes it impossible for that agent to achieve their end. On PCI, this is what the CC test is a test of.

Take O'Neill's application of PCI to the false promising maxim. In a world where everyone in need of money makes a false promise to obtain a loan, 'public confidence' in promises of repayment 'would diminish and eventually vanish'.[31] To will that world, proponents of PCI argue, is to will a set of consequences that would undercut the possibility for an agent who makes a false promise to achieve their end of obtaining a loan.

On this evidence, it is not necessary to adopt a more restrictive view of the causal-teleological version of LCI to distinguish it from PCI. An unrestricted causal-teleological version of LCI interprets the CC test as a test of a logical contradiction, whereas PCI interprets the CC test as a test of coherence between two acts of willing by a particular agent, which Korsgaard refers to as 'a specifically practical sense of "contradiction"'.[32]

3   The Suicide Maxim

One problem raised by FLN is how the CC test can confirm the impermissibility of a self-directed maxim, such as the suicide maxim, which does not presuppose action by anyone other than the agent whose maxim it is. If the notion

---

28   O'Neill 2013, pp. 173–4.
29   Herman 1993, p. 137.
30   Korsgaard 1997, p. xx; compare Korsgaard 1996, p. 94.
31   O'Neill 2013, p. 167; see also O'Neill 2013, p. 24.
32   Korsgaard 1996, p. 93.

of a universal law of nature is reduced to the universal adoption of a maxim by causal necessity, it can make no contribution to the argument. There is no number of people in virtue of which a causal necessity to adopt a self-directed maxim can hinder anyone else who satisfies its condition from adopting its means or achieving its end. No matter how many people commit suicide to make their life bearable until the end, it remains possible for any further individual to commit suicide to make their life bearable until the end. If the two-fold classification of duties as duties to oneself/others and as perfect/imperfect is 'absolutely vital'[33] to the structure of Kant's ethical theory, it is a problem if the notion of a universal law of nature can in principle make no contribution to the argument against *any* self-directed maxim. As all previous versions of LCI and PCI reduce the notion of a universal law of nature to a maxim's universal adoption by causal necessity, or to its universal availability,[34] the problem of the impermissibility of a self-directed maxim has proven intractable.

On the causal-teleological version of LCI, the notion of a universal law of nature has causal *and* teleological implications. A causal-teleological version of LCI solves the problem of the impermissibility of a self-directed maxim, because the principle of suitability informs our conception of the agents of a hypothetical system of nature in which a maxim is a universal law of nature *no matter how many hypothetical agents satisfy the conditions of this law*. Imagine, for argument's sake, a hypothetical system of nature in which a maxim, as a universal causal law, has only one instance, for example, a hypothetical system of nature in which the suicide maxim is a universal causal law, and living any longer only threatens more ill than it promises agreeableness for one agent. In conceiving of this hypothetical system of nature, we are guided by the principle of suitability just as we would be in conceiving of any other hypothetical system of nature in which a maxim is a universal law of nature. On account of this principle, we assume that the moral life any agent in this hypothetical system of nature is to lead has a certain content: the maxim that its agents adopt by causal necessity (here: the suicide maxim) is conceived of as an indispensable part of their moral life. In light of this content, an incongruity may arise between a moral obligation of a hypothetical agent in this hypothetical system of nature, and what this agent has to do to adopt the maxim. The incongruity arises just the same even if no other hypothetical agent satisfies the conditions of the law. Hence, even if a perfectly executable maxim has only one instance, it remains possible for that maxim to fail the CC test.

---

33   Wood 1999, p. 98.
34   See footnotes 16 and 46 to this chapter.

The suicide maxim, formulated as a universal law of nature, is:

> everyone for whom living any longer threatens more ill than it promises agreeableness cannot but end their life, and cannot but thereby make their life bearable until its end.

The *Groundwork* argues:

> But then one soon sees that a nature whose law it were to destroy life itself by means of the same sensation the function of which it is to impel towards the advancement of life, would contradict itself and would thus not subsist as a nature, hence that that maxim could not possibly take the place of a universal law of nature, and consequently conflicts entirely with the supreme principle of all duty.[35]

On the causal-teleological version of LCI, 'nature' is understood in causal and teleological terms. A 'nature' with the suicide maxim as a 'law' is a hypothetical system of nature in which the suicide maxim is a universal causal law, and an indispensable part of hypothetical agents' moral life. If a maxim is an indispensable part of a moral life, it follows from the hypothetical imperative that an agent must adopt all necessary means available to them to preserve their capacity to act on it. An agent can only act on a maxim if they can identify themselves as satisfying its condition. So a hypothetical rational agent who regards the suicide maxim as an indispensable part of their moral life must believe that they ought to use the means within their control to preserve their capacity for 'sensation', which records pleasures and pains, and so allows them to judge when it is necessary to end their life to make it bearable until the end.[36]

---

35 *GMS*, 4: 422.
36 One reviewer asked: how could anyone think that the capacity for sensation is obligatory to maintain for any Kantian? In fact, Kant did think it obligatory not to extirpate natural inclinations: '[n]atural inclinations, *considered in themselves*, are *good*, i.e., irreprehensible; and not only is it futile, but it would also be harmful and censurable, to want to eradicate them' (*RGV*, 6: 58). But Kant's (or a Kantian's) response to this question is not at issue here. The causal-teleological version of LCI is an interpretation of the CC test, that is, an interpretation of how to perform this test. To perform the CC test, an agent must imagine a *hypothetical* system of nature. As stressed at the end of section 1, a claim about how hypothetical agents are thought by us to adopt their maxims or to regard their obligations does not imply or support a matching claim about how we real world agents adopt our maxims or are to conceive of our obligations. On the causal-teleological version of LCI, an agent who tests the suicide maxim must imagine a hypothetical system of nature

Indeed, a hypothetical rational agent who regards the suicide maxim as an indispensable part of their moral life must believe that they are morally obliged to preserve their capacity for sensation even after asking themselves, at any given point in time, whether or not they satisfy its condition. They must believe that they remain under the obligation to preserve their capacity for sensation in any period between identifying themselves as satisfying the maxim's condition (the moment at which they judge that their life threatens more ill than it promises agreeableness), and the moment in which their life ends. The reason for this is that the relative agreeableness of living longer includes any agreeableness in avoiding the anticipation of death and the actual pain brought about by a suicidal course of action. That their avoidance may be agreeable is confirmed by depictions of suicidal persons in literature and film who, although initially convinced that they can no longer endure the pain of living, embark on a reversible suicidal course of action (for example, stepping onto a window ledge) only to discover that the prospect of death is so horrifying that they abort the attempt. If a person who embarks on a suicidal course of action experiences such overwhelming horror, they would no longer be acting on the suicide maxim if they continued with it. Thus, in a hypothetical system of nature in which the suicide maxim is an indispensable part of a moral life, even those agents who ascertain that they satisfy its condition and proceed to embark on a suicidal course of action are obliged to preserve their capacity for sensation until the end of their life.

What this reveals is that, in every hypothetical system of nature that includes the suicide maxim as a universal law of nature, an agent has two moral obligations during the time period between identifying themselves as satisfying the condition of the suicide maxim, and the moment in which their life ends. They must both end their life (in order to act on the morally indispensable suicide maxim), and preserve their capacity for sensation (in order to act on their moral obligation to preserve their capacity for sensation for every situation in which they are required to determine if they satisfy the condition of the suicide maxim). It is impossible for an agent to act on both of these moral obligations, however. In ending one's life, one destroys all one's capacities, including one's capacity for sensation; and it is impossible for one and the same agent simultaneously both to destroy and to preserve one and the same capacity.

Thus, on the causal-teleological version of LCI, the suicide maxim fails the CC test. In every hypothetical system of nature in which the suicide maxim is a

---

in which it is obligatory to maintain the capacity for sensation. But a proponent of this interpretation is not *thereby* committed to the claim that Kant held that it is obligatory for *us* to maintain our capacity for sensation.

universal law of nature, every hypothetical agent must believe that it is a moral obligation to preserve their capacity for sensation until the end of their life. Yet it is logically contradictory to imagine a hypothetical system of nature in which everyone observes this moral obligation, and even one agent who satisfies the condition of the suicide maxim acts on it to end their life. It is impossible even to conceive of the suicide maxim as a universal law of nature without contradiction.

Two textual points support this interpretation. One is that the *Groundwork* ties the problem in conceiving of a nature that includes the suicide maxim as a law to the fact that 'sensation' then serves both 'to destroy life' and 'to impel towards the advancement of life'. On the causal-teleological version of LCI, sensation is a means 'to destroy life' as it records pleasures and pains, and so allows hypothetical agents to ascertain whether they are obliged to end their life by acting on the suicide maxim. But for the same reason, sensation also impels 'towards the advancement of life'. It enables hypothetical agents to adopt a maxim (the suicide maxim) that forms an indispensable part of their moral life.

Second, the *Groundwork* locates a contradiction in 'a nature'. Only 'a nature' can 'contradict itself'. On the causal-teleological version of LCI, every hypothetical system of nature in which the suicide maxim is a universal law of nature is a nature that contradicts itself, as an implication of the fact that both of the above functions of sensation belong to it.

Compare, by contrast, Paton's widely followed interpretation of the suicide maxim.

On TCI, the CC test is supposed to be a test of a contradiction between a maxim as a universal causal law, and a 'complete harmony of ends both within the race and within the individual'.[37] A complete harmony of human ends is a moral community in which all ends pursued by members of the human race enable or promote one another. On TCI, a maxim fails the CC test if its universal adoption 'would destroy such a systematic harmony'.[38] On TCI, one would expect the suicide maxim to fail the CC test for the reason that any individual's suicide would destroy their end-setting capacity, and so destroy the possibility of harmony between their ends.

However, Paton says that when Kant turns to self-directed maxims, 'he does not test maxims by their fitness to produce a systematic harmony of purposes'.[39] In the case of the suicide maxim, Paton holds that Kant introduces

---

37   Paton 1953, p. 150.
38   Ibid.
39   Paton 1953, p. 154.

a premise about the 'purpose' of 'self-love';[40] namely, that the instinct of self-love, that is, the instinct to seek pleasure and avoid pain, is 'exactly adapted'[41] to the purpose of self-preservation. The suicide maxim then fails the CC test because it is contradictory to suppose both that the instinct of self-love always serves the purpose of self-preservation, and that that instinct sometimes leads agents to decide to stop living.[42]

On Paton's interpretation of the suicide maxim, the CC test tests for coherence across *two* natures. The premise about the purpose of self-love is a premise about us. It is in *our* life that sensation is held to be exactly adapted to the purpose of self-preservation. For the absence of the suicide maxim as a law of nature is a condition for supposing that the capacity for sensation is exactly adapted to *this* purpose. The 'life' that sensation destroys, by contrast, is life in a *hypothetical* system of nature that includes the suicide maxim as a law of nature. There is no contradiction in 'a nature', no nature that would 'contradict itself', if in one nature, the nature of humankind, endowment X is exactly adapted to function Y; but in another nature, a hypothetical system of nature in which the suicide maxim is a law, endowment X is not exactly adapted to function Y (but instead exactly adapted to function Z).[43] Judged by the criterion of whether it identifies a nature that contradicts itself, Paton's interpretation of the suicide maxim is not plausible.[44]

4   The False Promising Maxim

On the causal-teleological version of LCI, the reason why an other-directed maxim can fail the CC test is similar to why a self-directed maxim can fail it. An other-directed maxim may presuppose action to the performer of the maxim

---

40   Ibid.

41   Paton 1953, p. 150.

42   Paton 1953, p. 154.

43   In conceiving of the latter hypothetical system of nature, our teleological judgment will frame a different function for which the self-love of its hypothetical agents is exactly adapted (compare Wood 1999, p. 221).

44   Paton argues: 'If I conceive myself as having created man and given him self-love with this end in view, can I will, or even conceive, it to be a law of nature that this self-love should in certain circumstances aim at producing death? Kant's answer is "No"' (Paton 1953, p. 154). But to conceive the suicide maxim as a law of nature, a creator must conceive themselves to create a *new* nature, different from the existing world of 'man'. The law of nature this creator conceives is then not a law concerning 'this self-love', that is, the self-love given to 'man'.

that cannot go to plan in virtue of how the content of the moral life hypothetical agents are to lead shapes their interpretation of action. Kant writes:

> the universality of a law that everyone, once he believes himself to be in need, could promise whatever he fancies with the intention not to keep it, would make the promise and the end one may pursue with it itself impossible, as no one would believe he was being promised anything, but would laugh about any such utterance, as a vain pretense.[45]

On the causal-teleological version of LCI, to conceive of the false promising maxim as a universal law of nature, we must conceive of a hypothetical system of nature in which it is an indispensable part of a moral life. If hypothetical agents regard the false promising maxim as an indispensable part of their moral life, it is proper for them to interpret behaviour in light of its morality. It is proper for them (rather than a sign of unwarranted mistrust) to believe, of any needy agent inquiring after a loan, that the latter may have no intention to keep to what they say. The latter's utterance could retain the force of an invitation to donate. But it could not have the force of a repayment promise. If money changed hands, that could not be in light of the giver's belief that they were entitled to have it repaid.

If the false promising maxim is a universal law against which it is causally impossible to act, those in need of money must inquire after loans with utterances aimed at convincing another that they undertake to repay them, without having any such intention. Their utterances can only produce a 'laugh', however, as everyone believes, on account of their belief that the false promising maxim is an indispensable part of a moral life, that those in need of money may properly have no intention to keep to what they say about repaying it. The false promising maxim fails the CC test, therefore, for it is logically contradictory to imagine a hypothetical system of nature in which everyone in need of money makes a false promise and obtains a loan, *and* in which no one in need of money is understood as requesting a loan and so no one who inquires receives a loan.[46]

---

45   *GMS*, 4: 422.

46   Pogge reads Kant's use of the modal verb 'could (*könne*)' in the afore-cited passage at *GMS*, 4: 424 as support for his 'universal availability' interpretation, on which the formulation of the false promising maxim as a universal law of nature allows everyone to be 'permitted' to adopt it (Pogge 1998, p. 190). While Kant's verb is consistent with a universal availability interpretation, it is also consistent with other interpretations. To say that everyone in certain conditions is permitted to promise 'whatever he fancies' (*GMS*, 4: 424) to obtain a

One point in favour of this interpretation is that it directly accounts for the *Groundwork's* claim that, if the false promising maxim is a universal law of nature, 'no one' would believe he was being promised anything. The inability of any utterance by an agent in need of money to have the force of a repayment promise is intrinsic to how we must conceive of every hypothetical system of nature that includes the false promising maxim as a universal law of nature. It is not subject to any time delay. The response of those with money to spare is to laugh even at the first instance of this universal law.

Compare, by contrast, Korsgaard's (PCI) interpretation of the *Groundwork's* argument:

> There would be no such thing as a promise (or anyway a repayment promise) in the world of the universalized maxim. The practice of offering and accepting promises would have died out under stress of too many violations.[47]

If, as the *Groundwork* claims, 'no one' would believe he was being promised anything, its argument *cannot* be that the practice of repayment promising dies out under stress of too many violations. For a practice of repayment promising to die out, the first people to act on the false promising maxim must succeed in obtaining money by virtue of the practice of promising. Only then could those with money to spare review others' past behaviour and decline to lend owing to the risk of not being repaid. But in that case, at least *some* people who gave money to those in need of it who asked for a loan must have believed that they were promised it back.

It might be argued that this point is mitigated if PCI can incorporate an additional 'perpetuity condition'.[48] The perpetuity condition says that the CC test is whether an agent can achieve their purpose once the 'new order of nature' that results from adjoining a universal law of nature to the 'existing laws' of human

---

loan is consistent with everyone in such conditions *having* to make a false promise *of some kind* to obtain a loan. Kant's verb is not a decisive reason to favour one interpretation over another.

    Galvin (2013, pp. 352–3) offers some criticisms of the universal availability interpretation as an argument against the false promising maxim. The relevant drawback to note here is that the universal availability interpretation is designed *solely* to fit Kant's application of the CC test to the false promising maxim. It cannot unify both of the *Groundwork's* applications of the CC test. That is one main advantage of the causal-teleological version of LCI.

47   Korsgaard 1996, p. 82.
48   Rawls 2000, p. 171.

behaviour by which we understand our world 'has a settled equilibrium state'.[49] The violations of the practice of repayment promising occur in the process of its establishment. Of this settled state itself, it could still be maintained that no one would believe that they were being promised anything.

The perpetuity condition raises a problem of its own, however. In illustrating the Formula of Universal Law, the *Groundwork* claims that the false promising maxim must destroy itself 'as soon as it were made a universal law'.[50] It is unclear what reason we can have to suppose that FLN is to prove anything different. At the very least, the causal-teleological version of LCI is more direct in its preservation of the *Groundwork*'s claim that 'no one' would believe they were being promised anything.

Second, the *Groundwork* says that, if the false promising maxim is a universal law of nature, 'the promise and the end one may pursue with it' are both 'impossible'. On the causal-teleological version of LCI proposed here, either one of these counts is sufficient to generate a logical contradiction. Kant mentions both, on a par with one another, because each is equal evidence of a logical contradiction. On PCI, by contrast, one would expect the *Groundwork* to claim that if the false promising maxim is a universal law of nature, the promise, *and therefore* its end, is impossible; or else to omit all reference to the impossibility of the promise, and simply to state that its end is impossible.[51]

5   Summary

The aim of this chapter was to outline and defend a new, causal-teleological version of the logical contradiction interpretation. The causal-teleological version of LCI restores unity to the *Groundwork*'s applications of the CC test, in the spirit of that text. Relatedly, it solves the problem of how the CC test can confirm the impermissibility of a self-directed maxim. It can no longer be maintained that 'one of the few truly non-contentious claims in Kant scholarship and interpretation' is that the *Groundwork*'s application of the CC test to the suicide maxim 'is unsuccessful'.[52]

---

49   Rawls 2000, p. 169. For an argument that such an 'order of nature' is too empirical to capture the spirit of the *Groundwork*, see sec. 2.

50   *GMS*, 4: 403.

51   On a restricted version of LCI (see sec. 3), one would expect the *Groundwork* simply to claim that the promise is rendered impossible, and to omit reference to the impossibility of the end.

52   Allison 2011, p. 184.

In sections 3–4, the causal-teleological version of LCI was defended as a better interpretation of Kant's application of the CC test to the suicide maxim than Paton's interpretation, and as a better interpretation of Kant's application of the CC test to the false promising maxim than PCI. Neither claim is strictly necessary, however, in order to argue that the causal-teleological version of LCI improves on existing interpretations of the CC test. It is sufficient to argue that it offers a *plausible* interpretation of *both* applications. As Paton's interpretation of the suicide maxim suggests no analogous argument against the false promising maxim, while neither PCI nor previous versions of LCI suggest an analogous argument against the suicide maxim, a causal-teleological version of LCI improves on the established hybrid view already by virtue of the fact that it alone unifies Kant's applications of the CC test.

CHAPTER 6

Kant's Contradiction in the Will Test

In asking an agent to consider whether they could will their maxim as a universal law of nature, the Formula of the Law of Nature poses two tests: the contradiction in conception test (CC test) and the contradiction in the will test (CW test). The CW test, on which this chapter focuses, has generally received less attention than the CC test and its famous example of the false promising maxim. It is standardly interpreted as a test of whether a purpose of a human agent would be thwarted if their maxim was universally adopted. On this 'practical contradiction' approach, the difference between the CC and CW tests is that the former is a test of whether the universal adoption of a maxim would thwart a purpose of the agent lying '*in the maxim itself*', while the latter is a test of whether a maxim's universal adoption would thwart a purpose of the agent 'not ... in the maxim, but one that is essential to the will'.[1]

In the recent literature, three main ideas have been used to interpret this notion of a purpose essential to an agent's will: a principle of 'Rational Intending',[2] the concept of 'true needs'[3] and a veil of ignorance.[4] One indication that the interpretive options offered by these ideas need not be the last word on the CW test, however, is that proponents of the practical contradiction approach concede that it bases the CW test on external premises about empirical ends; and that its conception of a universal law of nature as a maxim's universal adoption (by causal necessity) adds nothing to the argument for why a self-directed maxim such as the maxim of neglecting natural gifts fails the CW test.[5] It is worth asking, therefore, if an alternative interpretation might be developed.

This chapter takes up this challenge by offering a new interpretation of the CW test, called the *extravagant imperfect nature* interpretation. The extravagant imperfect nature interpretation does not belong to the practical contradiction

1 Korsgaard 1996, p. 97.
2 O'Neill 1989, pp. 98–100; see also Dietrichson 1964, p. 156; Guyer 2007, p. 86; Kemp 1958, p. 69; Johnson 2011, pp. 55–64; O'Neill 2013, pp. 182–5; Timmermann 2007, p. 84; Wood 1999, pp. 90–6.
3 Allison 2011, p. 189; Herman 1993, p. 55; Rawls 1989, p. 85; Rawls 2000, p. 173; Reath 2006, p. 218.
4 Rawls 1989, p. 86; Herman 1993, pp. 50–1; Rawls 2000, pp. 162–80. Herman (1993, p. 50, p. 55) reports that Rawls's use of a veil of ignorance and the concept of true needs to interpret Kant's ethics dates from lectures given in 1977.
5 O'Neill 2013, pp. 182–4; Wood 1999, pp. 90–6.

approach. It interprets the CW test as a test of a contradiction not in the will of a rational human agent, but in the will of a hypothetical creator. On the extravagant imperfect nature interpretation, a maxim fails the CW test if a hypothetical creator who wills it as a universal law of nature would will an extravagant or an imperfect nature, that is, a nature in which hypothetical agents possess more than sufficient capacities to pursue their ends, or sub-optimal capacities to pursue their ends. There is then a contradiction in the will, for (according to Kant) we must assume that a hypothetical creator wills a non-extravagant perfect nature. The extravagant imperfect nature interpretation of the CW test is defended both as a plausible interpretation of the spirit and letter of the *Groundwork*, and as a better fit, on these scores, than the practical contradiction approach and other interpretations.[6]

The aim in this chapter is strictly interpretive. It seeks to show that the extravagant imperfect nature interpretation of the CW test accords with the spirit of the *Groundwork*, and the letter of its applications. An interpretation of the CW test preserves the *Groundwork*'s spirit, it is argued, if the notion of willing that a maxim become a universal law of nature is central to identifying a contradiction in the will; and this contradiction in will can be identified without relying on premises about empirical ends external to the maxim that is being tested. An interpretation of the CW test accords with the letter of the *Groundwork*'s applications if it fits its arguments for why a maxim of neglecting natural gifts and a maxim of refusing to help fail the CW test.

Section 1 extracts, from the *Groundwork*, four conditions that an interpretation of the CW test ought to satisfy. Section 2 argues that no existing interpretation satisfies all of these conditions. Section 3 then outlines the extravagant imperfect nature interpretation, and indicates how it may satisfy them. Section 4 formulates the two maxims to which the *Groundwork* applies the CW test. Finally, sections 5–6 defend the extravagant imperfect nature interpretation as a reading of the *Groundwork*'s applications of the CW test to these maxims.

1   Assessment Criteria

To count as a faithful interpretation of the *Groundwork*, an interpretation of the CW test must satisfy four conditions. Three conditions are apparent from the *Groundwork*'s formulation of the Formula of the Law of Nature, and how it distinguishes the CW test from the CC test:

---

6   See Paton 1953, pp. 150–5; Engstrom 2009, pp. 194–231.

so act as if the maxim of your action were to become by your will a UNIVER-
SAL LAW OF NATURE[7] (the Formula of the Law of Nature (FLN))

Some actions are such that their maxim cannot even be *thought* without
contradiction as a universal law of nature; let alone that one could *will*
that it *should* become such. In the case of others that inner impossibility is indeed not to be found, but it is still impossible to *will* that their
maxim be elevated to the universality of a law of nature, because such a
will would contradict itself.[8]

These statements suggest that the CW test confirms a maxim to be impermissible on account of
(1)   two contradictory acts of willing
(2)   belonging to the same will
(3)   that wills a maxim become a universal law of nature
Consider each condition in turn.

(1) requires that *p* and *not-p* are each objects of will. Unless both *p* and *not-p* are willed, there is no 'contradiction' in a 'will'. If, when a maxim fails the CW
test, 'inner impossibility' in its counterpart 'universal law of nature' is 'not to be
found', a contradiction must be identified between *two* acts of willing.

(2) requires that *p* and *not-p* are willed by the *same* will. If *p* was willed by
one agent while *not-p* was willed by another agent, no will would 'contradict
itself'.

(3) requires a contradiction to be identified in a will that wills a maxim
become a universal law of nature. It does not suffice that *p* and *not-p* are objects
of two individual maxims of the same will. A contradiction must be identified
in 'such a will' that wills a maxim 'be elevated to the universality of a law of
nature'.

An additional fourth condition relates to the status of FLN as a formula of
the categorical imperative. The *Groundwork* says:

there is one imperative that – without presupposing as its condition any
other purpose to be attained by a certain course of conduct – commands
this conduct immediately. This imperative is CATEGORICAL[9]

---

7   *GMS*, 4: 421.
8   *GMS*, 4: 424.
9   *GMS*, 4: 416; see also *GMS*, 4: 389.

If a course of conduct is commanded by the categorical imperative, it is not commanded for the sake of a further end beyond observance of that imperative. The categorical imperative commands 'immediately'. Moreover, if a course of conduct is commanded by the categorical imperative, the applicability of that command does not depend on an agent having 'any other purpose'. The categorical imperative commands unconditionally. Its 'necessity cannot rely on any presupposition'.[10]

FLN, as a formula of the categorical imperative, must confirm a maxim to be impermissible without appeal to criteria that would compromise either the immediate or the unconditional nature of the command to refrain to adopt it. Hence, as part of FLN, the CW test confirms a maxim to be impermissible on account of

(1) two contradictory acts of willing
(2) belonging to the same will
(3) that wills a maxim become a universal law of nature
(4) while eschewing external premises about empirical ends

Condition (4) requires a contradiction in the will to be identified without appeal to empirical ends that are not given in the maxim that is being tested. This is not to imply that no empirical facts are required for an agent to know whether they satisfy the conditions of a maxim that FLN commands them to refrain from adopting, or that no empirical facts are required for an agent to know *how* to observe any such command. Nor is it to imply that Kant's subsequent derivations of positive duties in *The Metaphysics of Morals* eschew premises about empirical ends when applying formulas of the categorical imperative that can yield positive duties. At issue here is simply the CW test. Its aim is more modest. The CW test (like the CC test) tests a maxim's permissibility only.

Consider two arguments, in the spirit of the *Groundwork*, for condition (4).

Firstly, if the categorical imperative necessitates the will immediately and unconditionally, no end can condition its force or applicability. Thus, not even an end that any rational human agent must will can condition its force or applicability. FLN is a formula of the categorical imperative. Hence, the tests that FLN provides for determining the permissibility of a maxim cannot rest on premises about empirical ends external to the maxim that is being tested. Only then is it possible for an agent, in applying FLN over all empirical grounds, to think of themselves as free.

Secondly, if a contradiction in the will can be identified without an external premise about an empirical end, it will be impossible to conceive of a fictional

---

10   *GMS*, 4: 419.

species of finite rational beings with a different empirical nature to ours, for whom an application of the CW test could give a different result. Every rational agent, and not just every rational human agent, may then be given a reason to refrain from adopting a maxim. The reason to refrain may be 'valid for every rational being'.[11]

Condition (4) is not uncontroversial.[12] But condition (4) might be controversial because no interpretation of the CW test has yet to satisfy it. Nor is condition (4) wholly lacking acknowledgement from advocates of the practical contradiction approach. Allen Wood, for example, claims that Kant seeks to show that the ground for following the Formula of Universal Law, and thus FLN, is 'an a priori necessary ground for all rational beings'.[13] Hence, if Kant's applications of the CW test were not to satisfy condition (4), there would be, for Wood, a mismatch between FLN's derivation, and these applications. That is enough to justify condition (4) to anyone who endorses Wood's claim, for anyone who endorses it is committed to the view that an interpretation of the CW test that avoids this mismatch by satisfying condition (4) is in one way more faithful than an interpretation that does not.

Finally, a sceptic of condition (4) might still be persuaded that the extravagant imperfect nature interpretation improves on the practical contradiction approach, if, as argued below, the latter *also* fails to satisfy conditions (2) and (3).

2   Assessing the Existing Interpretations

Consider, first, how the practical contradiction approach fares by the four conditions just outlined. We then ask whether the best known rival to this approach, Paton's interpretation, fares sufficiently better.[14]

---

11   *GMS*, 4: 413.

12   See Herman 1990, p. 242; Herman 1993, p. 59.

13   Wood 1990, p. 162. Wood defends the practical contradiction approach to the CW test in Wood 1999, pp. 90–7.

14   A more recent reconstruction of FLN outside the practical contradiction approach is offered by Engstrom 2009, pp. 184–239. On Engstrom's reconstruction, we are to consider 'whether it is possible for every person, or subject capable of practical knowledge, to share the practical judgement asserting the goodness of every person's acting according to the maxim in question' (Engstrom 2009, p. 194). Engstrom's reconstruction is not discussed further, as it tests for a contradiction between *judgments* rather than a contradiction in the will (see condition (1) in sec. 1).

On the practical contradiction approach, the CW test is a test of whether a purpose essential to the will of a human agent would be thwarted in a system of nature in which their maxim was universally adopted. The practical contradiction approach therefore satisfies condition (1). It can identify two contradictory acts of willing. Condition (2), the requirement to identify two contradictory acts of willing *by the same will*, poses more of a challenge.

On the practical contradiction approach, a contradiction is to be identified in the will of a rational human agent. The problem it faces, however, is that FLN asks an agent to imagine an act of will that cannot be ascribed to a rational human agent.

FLN asks you to imagine that your maxim '*become by your will a* UNIVERSAL LAW OF NATURE'.[15] There would be an omission in saying that FLN asks you to conduct a thought experiment in which you imagine a world in which your maxim *is* a universal law of nature. FLN asks you to imagine that such a world *comes about* in a certain way. (Hence the verb '*become*' in FLN's formulation, and in the passage from GMS, 4: 424 cited alongside FLN at the start of section 1). FLN does not ask you to imagine that such a world comes about independently of you, or as a 'quirk'[16] of something you do, but '*by your will*'. The *Groundwork* says: 'the will is thought as a capacity to determine itself to action'.[17] It adds that all action is oriented to an '*end*'.[18] What FLN asks you to imagine, therefore, is that a world in which your maxim is a universal law of nature comes about by you adopting its existence as your end.

It is irrational for you to adopt an end unless you believe that its necessary means are or could become available to you. If you believe you will never regain the power to move your arms, it is irrational for you to adopt the end of becoming a professional boxer. Clearly, no finite rational being can believe that they can ever acquire the power to make a maxim become a universal law of nature, as that would require a power to create a new system of nature. So, in asking you to imagine that your maxim '*become by your will a* UNIVERSAL LAW OF NATURE', FLN asks you to imagine that you will something that you could only will if you believed you could have a power you know you cannot have. FLN not only *expressly* asks you to imagine that your maxim become by your *will* a universal law of nature. FLN *tacitly* asks you to imagine that you have a *power* to make a maxim become a universal law of nature. In other words, FLN asks you to imagine yourself in the shoes of a creator of a hypothetical system of nature.

---

15   GMS, 4: 421.
16   Harrison 1957, p. 56.
17   GMS, 4: 427.
18   Ibid.

The act of willing that FLN asks you to imagine could only be willed by a creator, because it is only rational to adopt the end of bringing about a universal law of nature if one believes one has the power of a creator. As a rational human agent cannot believe that they can have the power of a creator, they cannot will a maxim become a universal law of nature. Hence, the act of willing a maxim become a universal law of nature, and the act of willing a purpose essential to the will of a human agent, cannot be conceived as acts of the same will. A contradiction between them is not a contradiction in a will.

The practical contradiction approach also fails to satisfy condition (3). Condition (3) requires a contradiction to be identified in a will that wills a maxim become a universal law of nature. As just argued, the only will that can will a maxim become a universal law of nature is the will of a creator. To identify a contradiction in the will of a hypothetical creator, it is necessary to argue that there is something a hypothetical creator must will, whenever they will a maxim become a universal law of nature. The practical contradiction approach does not offer any such argument.

Finally, the practical contradiction approach fails to satisfy condition (4), the requirement to eschew external premises about empirical ends. On the practical contradiction approach, a contradiction in the will is produced by appeal to a purpose that a *human* agent cannot rationally abandon, and which is not given in the maxim that is being tested.

The best known rival to the practical contradiction approach is Paton's *systematic harmony of human ends* interpretation. Paton interprets FLN in the belief that 'laws of nature' are 'teleological'.[19] What this suggests is that to conceive of a maxim as a universal law of nature is to suppose that its universal adoption is part of a systematic harmony of ends, that is, a moral community in which all ends enable or promote one another. What Paton actually takes FLN to ask, however, is more specific, namely: 'whether any proposed maxim, if it were made a law of nature, would fit into' a 'complete harmony of ends both within the race and within the individual'.[20] In other words, Paton takes FLN to ask whether the universal adoption of a maxim could belong to a systematic harmony of ends in *our species*: 'we are asking whether a will which aimed at a systematic harmony of purposes in human nature could consistently will this particular maxim as a law of human nature'.[21]

A will that aims at a systematic harmony of human ends is one way to conceive of the will of a creator. Thus, for Paton, a contradiction is to be identified

---

19   Paton 1953, p. 149.

20   Paton 1953, p. 150.

21   Paton 1953, p. 151.

in the will of someone who imagines themselves 'in the position of the Creator'.[22] A creator wills a 'complete' or 'systematic' harmony of human ends by creating a nature in which *every end* pursued by us human creatures forms part of this harmony, that is, by creating a nature in which no end of ours is destructive or redundant in this respect. On Paton's interpretation, if a creator would 'fail to foster' such a harmony by willing a maxim as a universal law of human nature, the maxim fails the CW test.[23] For Paton, a maxim of neglecting natural gifts fails the CW test because the non-development of talent makes no positive contribution to a harmony of ends within the individual human agent; and a maxim of refusing to help fails the CW test because refusing to help others makes no positive contribution to a harmony of ends among our species.

Paton's interpretation fulfils condition (1), as it is contradictory to suppose that a hypothetical creator who wills a *systematic* harmony of human ends also wills that human agents pursue an end that makes no contribution to that harmony. It fulfils condition (2), as it ascribes both the act of willing a systematic harmony of human ends *and* the act of willing a specific maxim as a universal law of human nature to the same will: that of a creator. It also, therefore, fulfils condition (3).

Paton's interpretation fails to satisfy condition (4), however. For Paton, the CW test tests whether a maxim can be willed as part of a systematic harmony of human ends. Paton infers: 'clearly we cannot do this [perform the test – JF] without empirical knowledge of the needs, desires, and powers of men'.[24] A will that aims at a systematic harmony of human ends must will the means by which every end pursued by human agents can contribute to a moral harmony. We cannot say what these means are without a claim about the human condition, that is, an empirical premise about what an individual human agent must do to be able to pursue ends in moral harmony, or how human agents must relate to one another if all of them are to be able to pursue ends in moral harmony. A maxim of neglecting natural gifts can only be deemed to fail the CW test given the empirical premise that a human agent must develop their capacities if they are to be able to act morally.[25] Similarly, the maxim of refusing to help only fails the CW test, on Paton's interpretation, given 'the fact that human beings are in need of mutual help' if they are to live in moral harmony.[26] On

---

22   Paton 1953, p. 146.
23   Paton 1953, p. 150.
24   Paton 1953, p. 151.
25   Paton 1953, p. 155.
26   Paton 1953, p. 152.

Paton's interpretation, therefore, the cw test can only give all *human* agents an *empirically grounded* reason to refrain from adopting a maxim.

3   The Extravagant Imperfect Nature Interpretation

The extravagant imperfect nature interpretation has two defining features. First, it interprets the cw test as a test of a contradiction in the will of a hypothetical creator. Second, it rests on the premise that (according to Kant) we assume that a hypothetical creator wills a non-extravagant perfect nature. The first defining feature distinguishes the extravagant imperfect nature interpretation from the practical contradiction approach, while the second also distinguishes it from Paton's interpretation. This last point requires elaboration.[27]

On Paton's interpretation, there is a contradiction in the will of a creator if, by willing a maxim as a universal law of nature, they fail to foster a systematic harmony of ends. It does not suffice for this that they will a universal law of nature that creates an extravagant nature. A nature is extravagant if its agents are endowed with a *capacity* that is harmless but redundant in respect of their ends (that is, with something akin to how the human appendix has been viewed).[28] An endowment with no impact on ends cannot lead agents to pursue an *end* that is redundant or destructive in respect of a harmony of ends. Nor, on Paton's interpretation, would it suffice to generate a contradiction in the will if a creator wills a universal law of nature that creates an imperfect nature. An imperfect nature does not guarantee that agents pursue an end that fails to foster a harmony of ends. An imperfect nature might simply make it harder to refrain from pursuing such an end. Thus, Paton's interpretation does not rest on the premise that we assume that a hypothetical creator wills a (human) nature that is either non-extravagant or perfect.

The claim that the cw test tests for a contradiction in the will of a hypothetical creator was defended in section 2. A contradiction is to be identified in a will that wills a maxim '*become* ... *a* UNIVERSAL LAW OF NATURE'.[29] Only a creator can be conceived to have such a will.

---

27   The next paragraph puts Paton's focus on *human* ends (noted above) aside, in order to emphasise that the extravagant imperfect nature interpretation's second defining feature distinguishes it from Paton's interpretation independently of that focus (which represents a further difference between the two interpretations).

28   Or a species of jellyfish whose venom is far more poisonous than necessary to catch its prey.

29   *GMS*, 4: 421.

The premise that (according to Kant) we assume that a hypothetical creator wills a non-extravagant perfect nature is inspired by the *Groundwork*'s remark that

> In the natural endowments of an organized being, i.e. one arranged purposively for life, we assume as a principle that no instrument will be found in it for any end which is not also the most fitting for that end and the most suitable for it.[30]

In this remark, Kant claims that 'we' finite rational beings make two assumptions in thinking about living beings. We are said to assume, as regulative principles to guide inquiry, that, firstly, living beings are 'arranged purposively for life', that is, that nothing in them is in vain;[31] and, secondly, that their natural endowments could not be bettered in respect of enabling them to pursue the ends they are to pursue. The former principle can be termed the regulative principle of the purposiveness of all parts; the latter, the regulative 'principle of suitability'.[32] Kant's *Critique of Judgment* attempts to ground these principles *a priori*, based on its (pre-Darwinian) claim that we are necessarily led to think of organised beings 'as if' they have come about through 'a causality that only reason can have'.[33]

We apply these two regulative principles, the principle of the purposiveness of all parts and the principle of suitability, in the thought experiment FLN asks us to perform, because FLN asks us to imagine a hypothetical system of nature that includes hypothetical agents. The question here is: what do these two principles lead us to assume about (a) the hypothetical agents of this hypothetical system of nature; and thus about (b) the will of their hypothetical creator?

Part of the answer to (a) can be formulated in the words of Kant's *Idea for a Universal History with a Cosmopolitan Purpose*, published the year before the *Groundwork*. We assume that the 'nature' of such hypothetical agents 'is not extravagant in the means employed to reach its ends';[34] and that it could not be bettered in respect of the ends they are to pursue. Hence, in answer to (b),

---

30 *GMS*, 4: 395. On the translation of this passage, see ch. 5, sec. 1.

31 'The concept of an organized being is the concept of a material being possible only through the relation of *all* that which is contained in it existing reciprocally as end and means' (*ÜGTP*, 8: 181, emphasis added).

32 Horn 2006, p. 46.

33 *KU*, 5: 370. See ch. 5, footnote 21.

34 *IaG*, 8: 19; Kant 1991a, p. 43.

we assume that their hypothetical creator only wills into existence hypothetical agents with a non-extravagant and perfectly suited nature.

Accordingly, the will of a hypothetical creator would contradict itself if, by willing a maxim become a universal law of nature, it creates a species of hypothetical agent whose nature is extravagant or imperfect. The nature of hypothetical agents is extravagant if it includes a capacity that need not be exercised or even developed for them to pursue the ends they are to pursue. It is imperfect if it includes a capacity sub-optimal for these ends.

From the foregoing, it is clear how the extravagant imperfect nature interpretation can satisfy conditions (1)–(3). If we assume that a hypothetical creator wills a non-extravagant perfect nature, there is a contradiction in the will if we also suppose that a hypothetical creator wills a universal law of nature that creates an extravagant or an imperfect nature. Moreover, condition (4), the requirement to eschew external premises about empirical ends, can also be satisfied. If a maxim's means or end precludes the development or exercise of a capacity referred to in its conditions, or precludes the satisfaction of a need of another agent referred to in its conditions, it may be possible to judge that a hypothetical system of nature in which that maxim is a universal law of nature is extravagant or imperfect without appeal to any further end.

4   Formulating the *Groundwork*'s Two Maxims

Kant's treatment of maxims raises a number of issues, such as the 'problem of relevance'.[35] At issue here, however, is not the interpretation of an act in the world around us, but the interpretation of a text. To defend a unified account of the *Groundwork*'s applications of the CW test, it suffices to formulate the two maxims it discusses, by specifying types of conditions, means, and end.[36]

The first is the 'maxim of neglecting natural gifts'.[37] This is the maxim of someone who

> finds in himself a talent that by means of some cultivation could make him a useful human being in all sorts of respects. However, he sees himself in comfortable circumstances and prefers to give himself up to gratifica-

---

35   O'Neill 2013, p. 39.

36   The view that the statement of a maxim specifies a type (or types) of condition, a type of means, and a type of end is expressed, among others, by Rawls 1989, p. 83; Allison 2011, p. 198; Herman 1993, p. 64; O'Neill 2013, p. 102.

37   *GMS*, 4: 423.

tion rather than to make the effort to expand and improve his fortunate natural endowments.[38]

Two conditions are mentioned. First, the agent has a 'talent'. We are not confronted with the case of someone who could not possibly make themselves useful. Second, the agent is in 'comfortable circumstances'. They can meet their needs even if they do not develop their talent. The agent's means and end are: by not developing their talent, they gratify themselves, or as the *Groundwork* proceeds to say, live a life of 'idleness, amusement, procreation, in a word ... enjoyment'.[39] Restating the maxim in conditions-means-end form, we have:

> when my circumstances are comfortable and I have a talent, I will neglect to develop it, to lead a life of enjoyment (the maxim of *neglecting natural gifts*)

The second maxim is given no name. Kant simply implies that it is found in the following way of thinking:

> Yet a *fourth*, who is prospering while he sees that others have to struggle with great hardships (whom he could just as well help), thinks: what's it to me? May everyone be as happy as heaven wills, or as he can make himself, I shall take nothing away from him, not even envy him; I just do not feel like contributing anything to his well-being, or his assistance in need![40]

Again, two conditions are mentioned. First, the agent is able to help another. Consider, for comparison, a remark in Kant's *Lectures on Ethics* (1784–5), delivered shortly before the *Groundwork*'s publication:

> If I now observe such a man sitting in distress, and see that I have no way of altering it, and cannot come to his aid in any fashion, I may turn away coldly and say, with the Stoic: What is it to me?[41]

Second, the agent is 'prospering'. Again, consider, for comparison, Kant's *Lectures on Ethics*:

---

38   Ibid. The Kant 2011 translation of '*Naturanlagen*' as 'natural predispositions' has been altered to 'natural endowments'; see above.
39   Ibid.
40   Ibid.
41   *V-Mo/Collins*, 27: 421.

I am obliged to care for my needs and for my comfort in life; if I cannot now care for the other's happiness, except by giving up my own needs and comfort, then nobody can oblige me, in that case, to care for the other's happiness.[42]

As regards the agent's means and end: by not helping another, the agent makes themselves as happy as they can. Restating the maxim in conditions-means-end form, we have:

> when I am prospering and I know that I could help another, I shall not do so, to maximise my own happiness (the maxim of *refusing to help*)

As the extravagant imperfect nature interpretation leads one to expect, the conditions of these maxims refer to an agent's ability (their talent) or another agent's need (for help), whose cultivation or satisfaction is precluded by the maxim's means. What remains to be seen is whether the *Groundwork*'s arguments for their impermissibility refer, explicitly or implicitly, to a contradiction in the will of a hypothetical creator; that is, to their willing a non-extravagant perfect nature, and their willing an extravagant or an imperfect nature.

5   The Maxim of Neglecting Natural Gifts

The maxim of neglecting natural gifts, formulated as a universal law of nature, is:

> everyone, when their circumstances are comfortable and they have a talent, will neglect to develop it, to lead a life of enjoyment

Kant argues:

> a nature could indeed still subsist according to such a universal law ... but he cannot possibly WILL that this become a universal law of nature, or as such be placed in us by natural instinct. For as a rational being he necessarily wills that all capacities in him be developed, because they serve him and are given to him for all sorts of possible purposes.[43]

---

42   *V-Mo/Collins*, 27: 424.

43   *GMS*, 4: 422–3.

On the extravagant imperfect nature interpretation, the CW test asks us to conceive of beings in two types of position: the position of (1) a *hypothetical creator*; (2) *hypothetical agents* in a system of nature created by a hypothetical creator. Both are distinct from (3) *us real world* agents. This dictates caution when interpreting such phrases as 'rational being', 'he', 'him', 'us', etc. These phrases may refer to beings in one of *three* types of position.

One piece of evidence that Kant's argument here appeals to the will of a hypothetical creator is the phrase 'all capacities ... given to him'. Neither a real world agent nor a hypothetical agent gives yet-to-be-developed capacities to itself, and to give is an act of will. The only possible giver is a hypothetical creator. Although ordinarily no giver like you and me can will something in respect of what we give to another, as we know we then lack power over it; we can imagine a hypothetical omnipotent creator who gives hypothetical agents certain capacities to will their development in those to whom they give them.

In the phrase '[a]s a rational being he necessarily wills', the 'he' denotes a real world agent who is considering adopting the maxim of neglecting his natural gifts. 'As a rational being' qualifies the respect in which 'he' wills. To will as a rational being can mean: to conform one's will to practical reason. FLN is a criterion of what practical reason requires. So, in the context of illustrating FLN, 'a rational being' is a real world agent who conforms their will to what FLN requires. To do so, they must ask themselves whether they can will their maxim become a universal law of nature. In asking this, they assume the position of a hypothetical creator. The phrase 'as a rational being he necessarily wills' should therefore be read as: *in the position of a hypothetical creator* he necessarily wills.

A hypothetical creator 'necessarily' wills that in a system of nature they create, a hypothetical agent develops 'all' their capacities, because a hypothetical creator wills a non-extravagant perfect nature. Accordingly, a hypothetical creator 'cannot possibly WILL' that the maxim of neglecting natural gifts become a universal law of nature, for such a creator would then will an extravagant nature. If the nature of hypothetical agents is not to be extravagant, the system of nature to which they belong cannot be made such that, in certain conditions, they neglect a capacity of theirs that they must develop in order to use. Yet that is what a hypothetical creator would will by willing that the maxim of neglecting natural gifts become a universal law of nature. The maxim of neglecting natural gifts fails the CW test, therefore, because there is a contradiction in the will of a hypothetical creator who wills its counterpart universal law of nature.

Suppose that Kant's phrase 'as a rational being he necessarily wills' were instead read as the practical contradiction approach requires: as a *particular* rational *human* being he necessarily wills. This reading attributes to Kant the view that a particular rational human agent must will to develop 'all' the capacities that they could develop. However, as the practical contradiction approach relies on rational intending – that is, a hypothetical imperative – to generate contradictions in the will, it cannot account for the claim it attributes to Kant. What it is prudent for a human agent to will, whether behind a veil of ignorance or not, and what a human agent must will to meet their true needs, can only be to develop *some* of the capacities they could develop.[44] A proponent of the practical contradiction approach *must* hold that Kant overstated matters: that Kant should have written 'some', not 'all'. On the extravagant imperfect nature interpretation, by contrast, the application relies on what the *Groundwork* says, and it does not appeal to an external premise about an empirical end.[45]

6   The Maxim of Refusing to Help

The maxim of refusing to help, formulated as a universal law of nature, is:

> Everyone, when they are prospering and they know that they could help another, shall not do so, to maximise their own happiness.

Kant argues:

> But even though it is possible that a universal law of nature could very well subsist according to that maxim, it is still impossible to WILL that such a principle hold everywhere as a law of nature. For a will that resolved upon this would conflict with itself, as many cases can yet come to pass in which one needs the love and compassion of others, and in which, by such a law of nature sprung from his own will he would rob himself of all hope of the assistance he wishes for himself.[46]

The will, Kant argues, that 'would conflict with itself', is the will that 'resolved' to make the maxim of refusing to help a universal 'law of nature'. Only a creator can be conceived to have such a will.

---

44   As Rawls himself argues: see Rawls 1971, p. 523.

45   Such as the premise (relied on by the practical contradiction approach) that 'we often have and may always will ends and purposes to which our present capacities/talents are inadequate' (Herman 1990, p. 240).

46   *GMS*, 4: 423.

A hypothetical system of nature in which refusing to help is a universal law of nature permits cases to 'come to pass in which one needs the love and compassion of others'. For any hypothetical agent who satisfies the conditions of this law knows that they could help another, and so it must be possible for another hypothetical agent to stand in need of help. But if hypothetical agents in a hypothetical system of nature may stand in need of help, it cannot be denied *a priori* that the kind of support which must be offered voluntarily, 'love and compassion', may sometimes be indispensable for them to pursue the ends they are to pursue. If this cannot be denied *a priori*, however, then the nature of these hypothetical agents is sub-optimal for the ends they are to pursue. To create a perfect nature populated by hypothetical agents who are prevented by a universal law of nature from providing one another with voluntary support when doing so would not plunge themselves in distress, their creator would have to create them never to need voluntary support, and so not to be adversely affected by the absence of 'hope' for it. The *mere possibility* that hypothetical agents may need help, combined with its *certain refusal* (or else its provision at the cost of bringing about distress in the helper), means that a hypothetical creator who wills such a system of nature wills an imperfect nature. As a hypothetical creator must be thought to will a non-extravagant perfect nature, there is a contradiction in the will of a hypothetical creator who wills the maxim of refusing to help as a universal law of nature.

The practical contradiction approach, by contrast, is confounded by Kant's argument. Kant mentions no act of *willing* of which a human agent is capable. Kant refers to a hypothetical agent's 'needs', 'hope' and 'wishes'. But I can need, wish and hope for something I do not will (for example, sunlight). Thus, no act of willing of which a human agent is capable is even implied.

Interpreting Kant's application of the cw test to the maxim of refusing to help along the lines of the practical contradiction approach, both Rawls and Pogge object that Kant's argument proves too much and is self-defeating, for 'an analogous argument would defeat any maxim of helping others in distress: Once again, many a situation might arise in which I would urgently want not to have to help'.[47] On the extravagant imperfect nature interpretation, Kant's argument is not subject to this objection. No analogous argument confirms a maxim of helping others in distress to be impermissible. If a hypothetical creator wills that a maxim of helping others in distress become a universal law of nature, they need not be taken to will either an extravagant or an imperfect nature. They can be taken to create a species of hypothetical agent whose

---

47   Pogge 1998, p. 196; see also Rawls 1989, p. 85.

members may find themselves in distress and cannot but help those in distress as the best way to draw forth their moral dispositions.

7   Summary

The aim in this chapter was to outline the extravagant imperfect nature interpretation of the CW test, and to defend it as an interpretation of the *Groundwork*. The extravagant imperfect nature interpretation is a plausible alternative interpretation to the practical contradiction approach, and improves on it in three general respects, corresponding to conditions (2)–(4). It identifies a will that contradicts itself; it locates this contradiction in the will of a hypothetical creator; and it eschews external premises about empirical ends. The extravagant imperfect nature interpretation also fits both of the *Groundwork*'s arguments in applying the CW test, and better explains what they do or do not mention.

One final point is worthy of note. The extravagant imperfect nature interpretation makes the notion of a universal law of nature central to why the CW test can confirm a duty *to oneself*. On the practical contradiction approach, to conceive of a maxim as a universal law of nature is to conceive of its universal adoption by causal necessity. But consider, then, an agent in a one-agent world. On the practical contradiction approach, this agent performs the CW test by imagining a one-agent hypothetical system of nature whose agent adopts the maxim by causal necessity. No self-directed maxim will fail this test unless, simply as an individual maxim, it *already* contradicts a purpose essential to the agent's will. On the extravagant imperfect nature interpretation, by contrast, the question is: is it contradictory for a hypothetical creator to will a self-directed maxim as a universal law of nature (even in a one agent world) and to will a non-extravagant perfect (one agent) world? A positive answer to this question does not presuppose that there is already a contradiction between the maxims or purposes of the individual agent. On the extravagant imperfect nature interpretation, the notion of a universal law of nature does the work in producing the contradiction in the will.

CHAPTER 7

The Principle of Suitability Interpretation of Kant's Formula of the Law of Nature

The arguments presented in Chapters 5–6 offer a solution to an old problem in Kant's account of the categorical imperative: to find a unitary interpretation of all four of the *Groundwork*'s applications of the Formula of the Law of Nature (FLN). FLN commands: '*so act as if the maxim of your action were to become by your will a* UNIVERSAL LAW OF NATURE'.[1] FLN requires us to refrain from adopting a maxim if a hypothetical system of nature in which it is a universal law of nature is contradictory in conception (the CC test), or if willing such a hypothetical system of nature would produce a contradiction in the will (the CW test).

In the last two chapters, I examined these tests separately, giving a different name to each interpretation.[2] But both chapters argued, in respect of the test examined, that we can only account for Kant's applications of FLN in the *Groundwork* by interpreting its notion of a universal law of nature in light of a regulative principle of natural teleology that is known as the principle of suitability.[3] Accordingly, taking FLN as a whole, these interpretations offer a principle of suitability interpretation of FLN. As Samuel Kahn notes in reply to the journal articles in which these interpretations were first advanced,[4] people now regard any such principle of natural teleology with 'suspicion'.[5] So, even if this solution may appeal from a history of philosophy perspective, it is likely to irritate Kant enthusiasts who wish to use FLN to ground moral duties.

The principle of suitability interpretation of FLN is offered as according with the spirit of the *Groundwork*, and the letter of its applications of FLN. The *Groundwork* seeks to provide an objective, a priori moral theory. If FLN is to belong to such a theory, it must be possible for finite rational agents, in applying FLN over all empirical grounds, to think of themselves as free. The principle

---

1 *GMS*, 4: 421.
2 I called my interpretation of the CC test a causal-teleological version of the logical contradiction interpretation, and my interpretation of the CW test an extravagant imperfect nature interpretation, abbreviated by Kahn in quotes cited below as CTCLI and EINI, respectively.
3 Horn 2006, p. 46.
4 Furner 2017a and Furner 2017b.
5 Kahn 2019, p. 98, endnote 22.

of suitability interpretation of FLN accords with the spirit as well as the letter of the *Groundwork* because it allows the CC/CW tests to confirm the impermissibility of all four of the maxims it discusses while eschewing external premises about empirical ends. It also shows how a self-directed maxim and an other-directed maxim can fail each test. Alternative interpretations of the CC/CW tests are inadequate in these respects.

Kahn, however, has suggested that there is 'prima facie disunity'[6] between my accounts of the CC and CW tests. Let me begin, therefore, by bringing out their unity. For this, we may recall the *Groundwork*'s remark:

> In the natural endowments of an organized being, i.e., one arranged purposively for life, we assume as a principle that no instrument will be found in it for any end which is not also the most fitting for that end and the most suitable for it.[7]

The *Groundwork* says that we assume, as a regulative principle to guide inquiry, that the natural endowments of entities that we regard as organised beings (that is, as material beings in which all parts are purposive)[8] could not be bettered in respect of enabling them to pursue their ends. Thus, for Kant, our use of the principle of suitability also involves another regulative principle of natural teleology, the principle of the purposiveness of all parts, or nothing in vain. These principles guide us in the thought experiment FLN asks us to perform, because FLN asks us to imagine a hypothetical system of nature that includes hypothetical agents.

The principle of suitability impacts on the CC test, because the *Groundwork* adds that human beings possess 'reason as a practical faculty', whose 'function must be to produce a will that is good'.[9] Accordingly, we assume that we are endowed with the best capacities we could have for cultivating a good will, which is to say, for leading a moral life. But then, as argued in chapter 5, section 1:

> if we extend the principle of suitability to think about hypothetical agents who (like us) have practical reason but who also (unlike us) all adopt a specific maxim by causal necessity, we ... must assume that the maxim they adopt by causal necessity is an indispensable part of their moral life.

---

6   Kahn 2019, p. 100, endnote 29.
7   *GMS*, 4: 395, reproducing the translation defended in chs 5–6.
8   See *ÜGTP*, 8: 181, cited in ch. 6, sec. 3.
9   *GMS*, 4: 395–6.

Otherwise, we could not reconcile our assumption that they could not be better suited to the purpose of leading a moral life with the causality we conceive them to be subject to.

On the principle of suitability interpretation, the CC test tests for a contradiction in the conception of a hypothetical system of nature in which the endowments of its hypothetical agents are assumed to be the best they could have for leading a hypothetical moral life that includes the maxim they adopt by causal necessity.

The principle of suitability also impacts on the CW test, for the latter tests for a contradiction in the will that wills a maxim become a universal law of nature. As it is only rational to will something (= adopt it as an end) if you believe that its necessary means are or could become available to you, FLN asks you to imagine yourself in the shoes of a creator of a hypothetical system of nature. This raises the question: what does our regulative use of the principle of suitability (which involves the principle of the purposiveness of all parts) in thinking about hypothetical agents in a hypothetical system of nature lead us to presuppose about the will of its creator? It leads us to presuppose that this creator wills a non-extravagant, perfect nature. This is something that we are led to presuppose in the bare thought of a hypothetical system of nature that contains hypothetical agents as having an intelligent cause, prior to any more determinate thought about the specific universal laws of nature it contains. A contradiction in the will is produced if, to think of a hypothetical creator as creating a hypothetical system of nature that includes some specific maxim as a universal law of nature, we would have to think of them as willing either an extravagant or an imperfect nature.

Kahn raises two main objections: (1) the principle of suitability interpretation of FLN fails to produce a contradiction for three of the maxims discussed in the *Groundwork* (the maxims of suicide, neglecting natural gifts, and refusing to help); and (2) the traditional interpretations fare significantly better than has been suggested, even if they cannot unify the *Groundwork*'s applications, given the 'philosophical differences manifest in *Kant*'s accounts'.[10] If these objections are sustained, then, even if the *Groundwork*'s application of FLN to the suicide maxim cannot be saved, it may yet be possible to defend a version of Kant's ethics incorporating the thoughts behind its other applications of FLN. If these objections can be overcome, however, this possibility seems to be excluded, given the suspicion with which the principle of suitability is viewed.

---

10   Kahn 2019, p. 87.

1   The Contradiction in Conception Test

One initial point is that, on the account presented in Chapter 5, the CC test tests for a logical contradiction (p and *not-p*) in the conception of a hypothetical system of nature. I called this account of the CC test a causal-teleological version of the logical contradiction interpretation (LCI), because it tests for a logical contradiction. I did not call it a version of the practical contradiction interpretation (PCI), because it does not test for a practical contradiction (an agent wills p, and wills not-p).

Kahn claims that this account of the CC test is really a version of PCI.[11] This is because Kahn does not accept the straightforward meanings of the terms logical contradiction and practical contradiction bracketed above. By logical contradiction, Kahn understands that 'action is impossible', and by practical contradiction, that a 'purpose ... is impossible'.[12] But this is to distort the meanings of these terms. The concept of logical contradiction is far broader than the different concept of the logical impossibility of an action.

The only reason suggested by Kahn *not* to use the meanings bracketed above to determine whether an account of the CC test is a version of LCI or PCI is that they are said to focus on something inessential. According to Kahn, whether the idea of an agent's purpose being impossible in a hypothetical world 'is explicated in terms of a logical contradiction in the conception of such a world[13] or whether this idea is explicated in terms of an incoherence in the agent's willing his/her maxim and its UTC [Universalised Typified Counterpart – JF] is inessential'.[14] But it is not inessential. The latter explication is a non-starter, because a finite rational agent *cannot* will the UTC of their maxim.[15] Kahn concedes this: 'it is perhaps true that no (non-delusional) finite rational agent genuinely can will the UTC of a maxim'.[16] This concession undermines PCI, as described by Korsgaard.[17] If replacing the straightforward meanings of logical and prac-

---

11   Kahn 2019, p. 98, endnote 19.

12   Ibid.

13   That is, explicated as 'the thought of everyone who satisfies a certain type of condition unfailingly performing a type of action and thereby achieving a type of end (as part of the moral life they are to lead), and the thought of at least one agent who satisfies that type of condition and who performs that type of action as not achieving that type of end (as part of the moral life they are to lead)'; see ch. 5, sec. 2.

14   Kahn 2019, p. 98, endnote 19.

15   And maxims are specific to finite rational agents; compare *KpV*, 5: 79.

16   Kahn 2019, p. 89.

17   As when Korsgaard claims: 'the sort of contradiction implied by the analyticity of hypothetical imperatives ... [is] the sort of contradiction employed in the categorical imper-

tical contradiction bracketed above with Kahn's understandings of these terms leads us to treat the avoidance of acknowledged untruth as inessential, that is a good reason not to replace them.

The *Groundwork*'s application of FLN to the suicide maxim is the most important to consider, given the difficulty it poses both for all previous versions of LCI and PCI, and for Paton's Teleological Contradiction Interpretation (TCI). Contrary to Kahn's claim that 'Furner fails to notice that Paton's TCI *is* able to give a unified account of these two cases [suicide and false promising – JF]',[18] I draw attention to what Paton openly says: that, to reject the suicide maxim, Kant appeals to a 'purpose' of 'self-love' rather than making the argument that, for Paton's TCI, 'would be more plausible'.[19]

The suicide maxim's counterpart universal law of nature is:

> everyone for whom living any longer threatens more ill than it promises agreeableness cannot but end their life, and cannot but thereby make their life bearable until its end.

To reject the principle of suitability interpretation of FLN in respect of the suicide maxim, Kahn needs to show that it cannot identify a logical contradiction in the conception of a hypothetical system of nature that includes this universal law of nature. Kahn argues:

> the contradiction alleged ... is illusory. The necessary means to acting on the suicide maxim do not include the unconditional preservation of the capacity for pleasure and pain. If the maxim is 'to reduce suffering by cutting life short,' then the necessary (and sufficient) means are a peaceful, relatively painless death. There are plenty of straightforward ways to achieve that, and there is no CTLCI contradiction that will arise from their adoption in a world in which the UTC of this maxim holds, at least not on Furner's argument. So Furner's argument ... fails.[20]

---

ative tests ... at the same time that [an agent] employs this hypothetical imperative in constructing his maxim, he wills its falsification, by willing a state of affairs (the world of the universalized maxim) in which it will be false ... Kant, therefore, not only has a specifically practical sense of "contradiction", but should be seen as employing it in his contradiction tests' (Korsgaard 1996, p. 94). PCI, on this description, is fundamentally incoherent, because no finite rational agent can be thought to 'will ... the world of the universalized maxim'.

18   Kahn 2019, p. 87.
19   Paton 1953, p. 154; compare ch. 5, sec. 3.
20   Kahn 2019, pp. 85–6.

Kahn fails to address the argument presented in chapter 5. First, the suicide maxim is not well described as: 'to reduce suffering by cutting life short'. This phrase (of Kahn's) is inadequate as a *suicide* maxim, for it leaves both the subject of suffering and the subject of the shortened life unspecified. A *murderer* may claim to act on it. It is also misleading to say that a suicide maxim's 'necessary (and sufficient) means' is 'a peaceful, relatively painless death'. This phrase describes an *event*, not the means of a maxim. A person might describe something that simply happens them, or to someone else, as 'a peaceful, relatively painless death'. A maxim, by contrast, is a subjective principle of *action*. The means of the suicide maxim is that *I end my life*.

This leads on to the crucial point. For a hypothetical agent in a hypothetical system of nature to know that she is acting in accordance with the universal law of nature formed from the suicide maxim that the *Groundwork* is examining – ending her life to make it bearable until its end – she must be able to consult her capacity for sensation throughout any suicidal course of action. Otherwise, she does not know that her suicide is a means to make her life bearable until its end. But this is something she is required to know. If her suicide were not a means to this end, she would have to refrain from it, to refrain from destroying her means to act on (what, in that hypothetical system of nature, is) the morally indispensable suicide maxim. Thus, she must seek to preserve her capacity for sensation throughout any suicidal course of action. As this contradicts her moral obligation to act on the morally indispensable suicide maxim by ending her life, it is impossible to conceive of the suicide maxim as a universal law of nature without contradiction.

Regarding the false promising maxim, Kahn does not deny that the interpretation offered in Chapter 5 identifies a contradiction in conception. Rather, Kahn claims that its interpretation of these two applications (suicide and false promising) is 'relevantly different' not to count as 'unified': 'the first relies on teleological assumptions about nature, the second relies on the fact that promising depends on a convention'.[21] Yet I refer not to convention but to 'interpretation of action'.[22] The false promising maxim fails the CC test because, as a universal law of nature, it presupposes 'action to the performer of the maxim that cannot go to plan in virtue of how the content of the moral life hypothetical agents are to lead shapes their interpretation of action'.[23] The interpretation of these two applications in Chapter 5 is unified, because the change in agents' interpretation of action is explained by the same causal-teleological notion of

---

21   Kahn 2019, p. 87.

22   See ch. 5, sec. 4.

23   Ibid.

a universal law of nature that explains why the suicide maxim fails the CC test. As to why 'an interpretation of the CC test *should* give a unified account of these cases',[24] the reason is simple: it is one test and not two.

2   The Contradiction in the Will Test

On PCI, the CW test tests whether a maxim's universal adoption would thwart a purpose of the agent 'not … in the maxim, but one that is essential to the will'.[25] This essential purpose of an agent (for example, to develop one's talents) is explicated without reference to any hypothetical system of nature. Kahn misunderstands my account of the CW test, which, unlike PCI, locates the contradiction in the will of a hypothetical creator, because he thinks of it as analogous to PCI. Kahn thinks that it tests whether a hypothetical creator who wills a universal law of nature would thwart a purpose essential to their will that is explicated without reference to a hypothetical system of nature.[26] In fact, on the account presented in Chapter 6, the CW test tests whether the will that we are led to presuppose a hypothetical creator to have in the bare thought of them as intelligently creating a hypothetical system of nature that contains hypothetical agents (a will that wills a non-extravagant, perfect nature) is in contradiction with the will to create a hypothetical system of nature that includes some specific universal law of nature formed from the maxim that is being tested. Both these acts of willing are explicated by reference to the same hypothetical system of nature.

Kahn's argument for why my account fails to produce a contradiction in the will for the *Groundwork*'s examples collapses. Kahn claims that 'no possible contradiction can arise' on my account if a universal law of nature (of neglecting natural gifts or of refusing to help) is 'vacuously satisfied';[27] that is, if no one satisfies its conditions, and so no one adopts its means to seek its end. But consider: a non-extravagant nature is a nature in which all parts are purposive. A universal law of nature of a hypothetical system of nature is a part of that nature. Thus, a hypothetical system of nature that includes a universal law of nature that has no purpose in it is extravagant. A vacuously satisfied universal law of nature has no such purpose. So, to will a hypothetical system of nature that contains a vacuously satisfied universal law of nature is to will an

---

24   Kahn 2019, p. 87.
25   Korsgaard 1996, p. 97.
26   Kahn 2019, p. 89.
27   Kahn 2019, p. 92.

extravagant nature. Hence, if a universal law of nature is such that a hypothetical system of nature to which it belongs is extravagant or imperfect if 'even a single rational being'[28] satisfies its conditions, as Kahn concedes, then it cannot be denied that willing it produces a contradiction in the will of a hypothetical creator who wills a non-extravagant perfect nature. Kahn therefore cannot deny that my account produces a contradiction in the will for the *Groundwork*'s examples.[29]

Kahn also misrepresents my claim that the CW test 'confirms a maxim to be impermissible ... while eschewing external premises about empirical ends'.[30] In Chapter 6, I distinguish this claim from other claims that Kahn proceeds to confuse. In particular, Kahn foists on me the idea that an account of the CW test should not imply that a different species to us 'would not have the same duties'[31] (in terms of *activities*) when all I say is that an account of the CW test should not imply that its application to a *given maxim* 'could give a different result'[32] for a different species. As there are many ways of acting on a maxim, a species of finite rational beings with 'vastly different abilities'[33] to ours would be able to perform activities on a given maxim that we cannot perform on that maxim. Suppose that FLN prohibits a maxim of doing nothing to end world suffering. What this prohibition imposes on a species with the ability to end world suffering by snapping its fingers, will differ from what it imposes on us. But this illustrates what I *already acknowledge* when I say (in Chapter 6, section 1) that the claim that

> a contradiction in the will [is] to be identified without appeal to empirical ends that are not given in the maxim that is being tested [does] not ... imply that no empirical facts are required for an agent to know whether they satisfy the conditions of a maxim that FLN commands them to refrain from adopting, or that no empirical facts are required for an agent to know how to observe any such command.

---

28   Ibid.

29   To say that Kahn's argument collapses does not commit to what Kahn simply asserts, that 'a world in which even a single rational being could live a life of comfort without developing his/her talents would be extravagant' or that 'a world in which any rational being genuinely needs help would be imperfect' (Kahn 2019, p. 92); compare the final sentence of ch. 6, sec. 6.

30   See ch. 6, sec. 1.

31   Kahn 2019, p. 90.

32   See ch. 6, sec. 1.

33   Kahn 2019, p. 91.

Kahn also raises a textual objection concerning FLN. Kahn claims that I fail to note that FLN says that 'the maxim is to become a universal law of nature through "*your*" will: it is the will of the agent at which FLN is directed, not the will of a hypothetical creator'.[34] To be sure, FLN is 'directed at' or binds a finite rational agent's will, not the will of a hypothetical creator. But, I maintain, the position of hypothetical creator is assumed in order to identify what maxims FLN binds finite rational agents not to adopt. An elaboration of FLN by hypothetical thought experiment is required by FLN's '*as if*'. As the phrase '*by your will*' comes after this '*as if*', it merely precludes an interpretation of FLN on which FLN asks agents to imagine someone other than themselves in a hypothetical position. It is Kahn who misrepresents FLN by replacing its notion that a maxim '*become by your will*' a universal law of nature with the different notion that a maxim 'is a universal law of nature';[35] something I sufficiently warned against.[36]

One final remark on the CW test. Kahn objects that a phrase I cite in my account of the neglecting natural gifts maxim ('all capacities ... given to him')[37] to support the idea that Kant appeals to the will of a hypothetical creator in fact 'refer[s] to an actual creator, not a hypothetical one'.[38] This suggestion (for which Kahn offers no argument) does not seem reconcilable with the context, which is Kant's attempt to exemplify a *counterfactual* thought experiment. But it should trouble a defender of any of the traditional interpretations of FLN, like Kahn, who claims that while my account of the CW test appeals to the will of a hypothetical creator, 'this distinguishes the EINI from the PCI, LCI and TCI, all of which take the contradiction to be in the will of the agent proposing to act on the maxim being tested'.[39] This is to concede that no traditional interpretation of FLN can fully explain Kant's reasoning in the case of the neglecting natural gifts maxim.

The aim in Chapters 5–6 was strictly interpretive, and not to substantively defend either test. But it is unwarranted to infer from this that 'Furner's project' is 'strictly textual' as distinct from 'philosophical'.[40] An argument with an interpretive aim can form part of a philosophical project. An argument for a plausible interpretation of the spirit and letter of the *Groundwork* is philosoph-

---

34 Kahn 2019, p. 89.
35 Ibid.
36 See ch. 6, sec. 2.
37 *GMS*, 4: 423.
38 Kahn 2019, p. 92.
39 Kahn 2019, p. 88.
40 Kahn 2019, p. 100, endnote 32.

ical, wherever its results lead. One need not defend Kant, to do philosophy by writing about Kant. The finding that, on the best interpretation of FLN, FLN is unattractive, would be a philosophical finding. It would imply that we should either give up on autonomy, or set about extricating it from FLN. If the principle of suitability interpretation alone unifies Kant's applications of FLN in the spirit of the *Groundwork*, then that is a reason to consider rescuing autonomy from Kant.

CHAPTER 8

Kant's Argument for the Formula of the End in Itself

This chapter offers a *logical pluralism* interpretation of Kant's argument for the Formula of the End in Itself (FEI), the most popular of his formulas of the categorical imperative:

> *So act that you use humanity, in your own person as well as in the person of any other, always at the same time as an end, never merely as a means.*[1]

For present purposes, FEI can be shortened to:

Always treat humanity in a person as an end

The logical pluralism interpretation is offered as an argument that Kant could give for FEI, even if it cannot be shown to be the argument that Kant had in mind. As Henry Allison notes, 'given the cryptic nature of Kant's argument, *any* interpretation is bound to be somewhat conjectural'.[2] After presenting the logical pluralism interpretation, I argue further that, on any plausible interpretation, Kant's argument for FEI rests on the premise that there cannot be a species of being with humanity but without personality. The only way that Kant allows us to accept this premise, however, is by believing that there could be no moral purpose in creating such a species. Thus, whether or not the logical pluralism interpretation avoids some of the disadvantages of existing versions of Kant's argument for FEI, Kant's argument for FEI presupposes a belief in the existence of God.

The logical pluralism interpretation shares two features of the approach developed by Christine Korsgaard and Allen Wood. It holds that Kant's argument for FEI (1) includes a *regressive* argument which (2) rests on a *non-moral* view of humanity or rational nature. A '"regressive"' argument, Korsgaard says, 'is an argument in which something is taken as given or actual and the condition of its possibility are explored'.[3] Humanity or rational nature, on this

---

1   *GMS*, 4: 429.
2   Allison 2011, p. 225.
3   Korsgaard 1986, p. 192, citing *P*, 4: 276.

approach, is a set of capacities that are not specifically moral. Most fundamentally, it is the general capacity for setting ends, whether or not the choice is subservient to incentives.[4] What the logical pluralism interpretation takes from the approach of Korsgaard and Wood, therefore, is the view that Kant grounds FEI as a possible categorical imperative with the help of an argument that reflects on the conditions of setting an end.

The logical pluralism[5] version of Kant's regressive argument has two characteristic features. One concerns how value enters the argument. The logical pluralism version says: if a rational agent sets an end, they must select means to that end, and ascribe goodness to them. The second concerns the source of this goodness. The logical pluralism version says: the source of this goodness is the adoption of the plural standpoint, which is self-affirming.

By virtue of these features, the logical pluralism version of Kant's regressive argument avoids three drawbacks of Korsgaard's and Wood's versions. On their versions, value enters the argument through the objectionable claim that a rational agent must take their end to be objectively good. The logical pluralism version avoids this claim. Second, Korsgaard's and Wood's versions attempt to ground the claim that a rational agent is committed to valuing everyone's rational nature by *first* showing that they must value that capacity in themselves, and *then* arguing that, if they value that capacity in themselves, they are committed to valuing it in others too. No such version of the regressive argument can avoid a 'self-regarding fallacy',[6] that is, the fallacy that if an agent values their own rational nature, then they must also value rational nature in others. By identifying, as the source of goodness, something that each rational agent only does as part of thinking of all rational agents as doing it with them, the logical pluralism version avoids this fallacy. Third, Korsgaard's and Wood's versions rely on the objectionable claim that *any* source of value must itself be of unconditional value. The logical pluralism version of Kant's regressive argument merely relies on the claim that a *self-affirming* source of value must itself be of absolute value.

Section 1 represents the structure of Kant's argument for FEI in four steps. Section 2 offers a brief account of steps 1–3. The focus then turns to step 4. Section 3 motivates interpreting this step as a regressive argument, and presents a logical pluralism version of this regressive argument. Section 4 presses the advantages of the logical pluralism version of Kant's regressive argument over

---

4 Korsgaard 1986, p. 186; Korsgaard 1990, p. 196; Korsgaard 2011, p. 2; Wood 1995a, p. 306; Wood 1999, pp. 118–20; Wood 2008, p. 88; see Kant, *RGV*, 6: 27; *MS*, 6: 392.

5 The name is inspired by a remark of Kant's discussed in sec. 3.

6 Cureton 2013, p. 371.

Korsgaard's and Wood's versions. Finally, section 5 argues that the logical pluralism version of the regressive part of Kant's argument for FEI remains as reliant as any other version on a belief in the existence of God.

1   The Structure of Kant's Argument for FEI

As Korsgaard says, the second section of the *Groundwork* contains 'three arguments that have the form: if there were a categorical imperative, this is what it
would have to be like'.[7] Kant's argument for FEI is one of them. Its structure can
be represented in four steps:

Step 1:   if there is a categorical imperative, it is explicable in terms of an oblig-
          atory end
Step 2:   an obligatory end is an end with characteristics X and Y
Step 3:   nothing that is not humanity in a person can be an obligatory end
Step 4:   humanity in a person can be an obligatory end, shown by a regressive
          argument
          Conclusion: 'Always treat humanity in a person as an end' is a possible
          categorical imperative

Steps 1–2 say that, if there is a categorical imperative, it can be formulated in
terms of an obligatory end, and exhibit the characteristics an obligatory end
must have. Steps 3 and 4 presuppose step 2 as well as step 1, for step 2 establishes
the criteria by which all items bar humanity in a person are rejected, in step 3,
as possible obligatory ends, and by which humanity in a person is affirmed, in
step 4, as a possible obligatory end.

The elaboration of step 2 proposed in this chapter (and defended as plausible in section 2) is:

> *Step 2*: an obligatory end is an end that all finite rational beings are
> required to adopt as an end in itself, whose object exists with absolute
> worth

Using these characteristics of an obligatory end as criteria, step 3 rejects all but
one item for the status of an obligatory end. Step 3 is not an argument by elimin-
ation, however, that is, an argument whose conclusion is the one uneliminated
item. Steps 1–3 do not show that there must be an item with the required characteristics. For all steps 1–3 show, no item may possess them. To complete the

---

7   Korsgaard 1986, p. 183.

argument for FEI, an additional step is required: step 4. Step 3 is nonetheless indispensable, however. To conclude that 'always treat humanity in a person as an end' is a possible categorical imperative, it is necessary to foreclose the objection that there are *multiple* possible obligatory ends.

On the elaboration of step 2 proposed here, step 3 becomes:

> *Step 3*: nothing that is not humanity in a person can be the object of what all finite rational beings are required to adopt as an end in itself, and exist with absolute worth

Step 4 supplies the positive argument that humanity in a person can be an obligatory end:

> *Step 4*: humanity in a person can be the object of what all finite rational beings are required to adopt as an end in itself and exist with absolute worth, as shown by a regressive argument

Step 4 presents the most difficulty.

2   Steps 1–3

Step 1 says: if there is a categorical imperative, it is explicable in terms of an obligatory end. Consider Kant's argument for step 1. A categorical imperative commands unconditionally and immediately.[8] Its command is not conditional on empirical facts, and it does not command for the sake of something beyond itself. To necessitate the will unconditionally and immediately, it must provide 'grounds that are valid for every rational being',[9] that is, a sufficient reason for any finite rational being to act. But 'what serves the will as the objective ground of its self-determination is the *end*',[10] that is, a sufficient reason to act that is represented by the agent as the reason they choose to act on. If a categorical imperative is to necessitate the will unconditionally and immediately, it must be explicable in terms of an obligatory end, that is, an end that is obligatory for all finite rational beings.

---

8   '[T]here is one imperative that – without presupposing as its condition any other purpose to be attained by a certain course of conduct – commands this conduct immediately. This imperative is CATEGORICAL' (*GMS*, 4: 416).

9   *GMS*, 4: 413.

10   *GMS*, 4: 427.

Step 2 is more complex. The aim here is simply to outline a case for conceiving an obligatory end as an end that all finite rational beings are required to adopt as an end in itself, whose object exists with absolute worth. This conception of an obligatory end is consistent with the *Groundwork*'s statement:

> But suppose there were something *the existence of which in itself* has an absolute worth, that, as an *end in itself*, could be a ground of determinate laws, then the ground of a possible categorical imperative, i.e. of a practical law, would lie in it, and only in it alone.[11]

The two-part argument for step 2 is: (i) an obligatory end (that is, an end that is obligatory for all finite rational beings) is an end that all finite rational beings are required to adopt as an *end in itself*; (ii) the object of such an end in itself must *exist*, with *absolute* worth.

Consider (i). An '*end in itself*' is a sufficient reason to act that is represented by the agent as a reason they choose to act on *independently of any other end*. For example: to qualify as a doctor is a sufficient reason to study medicine; the end of qualifying as a doctor may be the end of someone who studies medicine; but this end is not their end in itself unless they decide to qualify as a doctor independently of any of their other ends, including finding employment, etc. An end in itself can ground a possible categorical imperative because an end in itself is of immediate value; that is, it is valued for its own sake. An end in itself may necessitate the will unconditionally as well as immediately if all finite rational beings are required to adopt it as an end in itself.

Consider (ii). Kant says that the object of the end in itself that grounds a possible categorical imperative has '*existence*', and, as something existent, has '*absolute worth*'. Now, it does not follow just from the concept of an end in itself that its object exists. If a student of medicine sets, as an end in itself: qualifying as a doctor, its object does not exist. It is an outstanding qualification. It is conceivable for all agents to adopt a perfection of a kind that they could only ever strive after as an end in itself; for example, an unrealistic body shape. That the object of an obligatory end in itself has '*existence*' is a further claim. Here is one argument for it, and for the claim that, as something existent, it has absolute worth.

A categorical imperative, as an *imperative* form of the moral law, is only possible, if it is possible for there to be a kind of *finite* being capable of acting on it. So, suppose it is inconsistent with the thought of any kind of finite being

---

11   *GMS*, 4: 428.

capable of acting on a categorical imperative that there be nothing about such a being that is the object of an obligatory end in itself. If that be true, then, if there is a categorical imperative, and hence (given (i)) an obligatory end in itself, its object exists whenever beings capable of acting on it exist. A statement of this categorical imperative addressed to beings capable of acting on it (such as Kant's statement of FEI) would have to refer to something existent.

Further, *if* the object of this obligatory end in itself exists, then, as it is the object of an end that every agent is required to adopt independently of any other end, it must exist with absolute worth. As every agent is required to adopt an obligatory end in itself independently of any other end, every agent is required to adopt it no matter what other ends it is possible to adopt rationally in the circumstances. But if so, every agent is required to adopt it no matter what objects have to be possible for any other end to be adopted rationally in the circumstances. The worth of the object of an obligatory end in itself therefore cannot depend on any other object. Its worth must be non-relative or absolute.[12] *If* the object of what all finite rational beings are required to adopt as an end in itself exists, it exists with absolute worth. If there is just one existent thing with absolute worth, it will be the object of the only end that all finite rational beings are required to adopt as an end in itself.

Now, it *is* inconsistent with the thought of any kind of finite being capable of acting on the categorical imperative that nothing about it is the object of an obligatory end in itself. A categorical imperative is an imperative form of a moral law whose principle is freedom as *autonomy* of the will. A finite being can only regard themselves as free *qua* autonomous in being bound to adopt an end for its own sake if what grounds this obligatory reason for acting is some valued part of them. If what grounds this obligatory reason for acting is the value of something else, a categorical imperative to honour its value by treating it as an end in itself would imply that any agent bound by this imperative was merely of instrumental value. No such agent could recognise this imperative as categorical *and* regard themselves as free *qua* autonomous. So, if there is an obligatory end in itself, the object that provides this obligatory reason for acting must be taken to exist, with absolute worth.

We can now turn to step 3. Step 3 says: nothing that is not humanity in a person can be the object of what all finite rational beings are required to adopt as an end in itself, and exist with absolute worth. To foreclose the objection that there can be, *besides* humanity in a person, an object of an end in itself that

---

12   Kant leads us to believe that absolute worth contrasts with relative worth, for at GMS, 4: 427, Kant describes ends to be effected as 'relative' because 'merely their relation' to a faculty of desire gives them their worth.

all finite rational beings are required to adopt, and therefore *multiple* possible obligatory ends, Kant rejects three other items: (a) 'objects of inclinations'; (b) 'inclinations themselves'; and (c) *'things'*.[13]

Regarding objects of inclination, Kant argues that their value is relative rather than absolute, insofar as it is contingent on the existence of inclinations. For any object of inclination, we can identify an inclination on the part of the agent, and say that if the agent did not have that inclination, the object of inclination would lack value. Kant then moves on to our inclinations themselves: 'inclinations themselves ... are so far from having an absolute worth ... that to be entirely free from them must rather be the universal wish [*Wunsch*] of every rational being'.[14] Kant suggests in *Critique of Practical Reason* that

> inclinations vary, grow with the indulgence that one allows them, and always leave behind an even greater void than one had meant to fill. Hence to a rational being they are always *burdensome*, and even if the being cannot easily shed them, they nonetheless force from him the wish [*Wunsch*] to be rid of them.[15]

Our inclinations are inconstant and so they cannot always be planned for; they must also be repeatedly satisfied, and may expand with satisfaction. Given this, Kant reasons, we must, as rational beings, wish to be the kind of beings who could cultivate virtue without having to satisfy any inclinations, even as we also

---

13   *GMS*, 4: 428.

14   Ibid. Compare the use of '*Wunsch* (wish)' in the next citation.

15   *KpV*, 5: 118. In *Religion Within the Boundaries of Mere Reason*, Kant suggests that, 'natural inclinations, *considered in themselves*, are *good*, i.e. irreprehensible; and not only is it futile, but it would also be harmful and censurable, to want [*wollen*] to eradicate them' (*RGV*, 6: 58). Both Korsgaard and Wood cite this passage from *Religion* as evidence that Kant 'goes back on' his view that 'a rational being should prefer to be altogether free' of inclinations (Korsgaard 1990, p. 259; compare Wood 2008, p. 90). Yet it clearly does *not* show this. We may not overlook the difference between 'to will (*wollen*)' and 'to wish (*wünschen*)'. I can wish for something that I do not, and cannot, will; sunlight, for example. The claim that a rational being must wish to be free of *X* does not imply the claim that a rational being must will to be free of *X*, for a rational being may be aware that the means to free themselves rationally of *X* will never be available, and it is irrational for an agent to will an end unless they believe that means to pursue it rationally are or could become available. That is the case here: a finite rational being is aware that they can never rid themselves of their inclinations without destroying their rational nature. This ensures that a rational being does not will what they are said to wish for. However much of an inconvenient truth it may be, the view that Kant expresses in the above passages from the *Groundwork* and *Critique of Practical Reason* is not rejected in *Religion Within the Boundaries of Mere Reason*.

assume (adopting regulative principles of natural teleology) that our inclinations are a part of nature's plan to get us to become as moral as we can be. Insofar as a rational being has this wish, a rational being acknowledges that any value that their inclinations have is merely relative to their finitude, not absolute.

Finally, the worth of nonrational beings is 'only a relative worth'.[16] As nonrational beings lack the capacity for setting ends, no such being can be the object of an end in itself for itself. It can only be the object of an end in itself for another. But if so, its worth would depend on something other than itself: the moral cultivation of rational beings. So, no nonrational being can be the object of an end that all finite rational beings are required to adopt as an end in itself, and exist with absolute worth.

3   Step 4: The Logical Pluralism Version of Kant's Regressive
        Argument

We can now turn to step 4. Step 4 says: humanity in a person can be the object of what all finite rational beings are required to adopt as an end in itself and exist with absolute worth, as shown by a regressive argument. Kant writes:

> The ground of this principle [the supreme practical principle – JF] is: *rational nature* [die vernünftige Natur] *exists as an end in itself*. The human being necessarily represents his own existence in this way; so far it is thus a *subjective* principle of human actions. But every other rational being also represents his existence in this way consequent on just the same rational ground that also holds for me;* thus it is at the same time an *objective* principle from which, as a supreme practical ground, it must be possible to derive all laws of the will. The practical imperative will therefore be the following: *So act that you use humanity, whether in your own person or in the person of any other, always at the same time as an end, never merely as a means.*

> * Here I put this proposition forward as a postulate. The grounds for it will be found in the last Section.[17]

---

16   *GMS*, 4: 428.
17   *GMS*, 4: 429. Here I use the Gregor translation (Kant 1997a) rather than the Gregor/Timmermann translation (Kant 2011). In Kant 1997a, '*die vernünftige Natur*' is translated as 'rational nature'. By contrast, in Kant 2011 it is translated as 'a rational nature'. If Kant had

The main reason to view step 4 to require a regressive argument relates to Kant's use of the word 'necessarily' in his claim that 'the human being necessarily represents his own existence' as the existence of '*rational nature … as an end in itself*'. A claim about what is 'necessarily' the case, which is not immediately certain, can be supported by reflecting on the necessary conditions of something that we *can* take as given.

An additional point in favour of interpreting Kant's claim as based on a regressive argument is that this claim is only consistent with the rest of the passage if its defence avoids appeal to an already established moral duty. Only if this claim is defended without appeal to an already established moral duty may it be 'possible to derive all laws of the will' from FEI. If a step in the argument for FEI had to be defended by appeal to an already established moral duty,[18] then at least one law of the will, namely this moral duty, could not be derived from FEI, as FEI would then be derived from it. By its nature, a regressive argument avoids appeal to an already established moral duty. An argument that is truly regressive is bound not to introduce premises that do not follow from whatever initial fact it takes as given.

If there is reason to take Kant's claim to rest on a regressive argument, the first issue is to identify the indubitable premise that might serve as its starting point. One such starting point is suggested by the *Groundwork*'s remark: 'rational nature is distinguished from the others by this, that it sets itself an end'.[19] As we are to start from an indubitable premise about a human being, the starting premise this suggests is: a rational human being, A, sets an end.

The next move draws on Kant's account of the good. Something can be called good, the *Groundwork* says, if it is what 'reason, independently of inclination, recognizes as practically necessary'.[20] An agent can call something they choose good, therefore, if they know that its choice is a result of rational deliberation.

---

wanted to say 'a rational nature', to denote any one of a number of rational natures, he would have used an *indefinite* article: '*eine vernünftige Natur*'. While Timmermann reports that 'Natur' *could* be used in Kant's time 'as a count-noun' (Timmermann 2006, p. 71), this is unlikely if accompanied by a *definite* article in the *singular*. The Grimm dictionary to which Timmermann refers offers examples of the use of 'Natur' as a count-noun in the *plural*, or with an *indefinite* article, as does Timmermann (Timmermann 2006, p. 87). On the logical pluralism version of Kant's regressive argument, Kant does not first argue that an agent must represent itself as 'a rational nature' that is an end in itself, and only then argue that they must also represent others' rational nature in this way; see below.

18 As, for example, at Cureton 2013, p. 365.

19 *GMS*, 4: 437. Translation modified. '*Die vernünftige Natur*' is rendered as 'rational nature' (not as 'a rational nature' as in Kant 2011) because Kant uses a definite article; see footnote 19.

20 *GMS*, 4: 412.

Kant's *Critique of Practical Reason* suggests how goodness can enter a regressive argument that begins from the premise that a rational human being sets an end. It says that a maxim may have its determining ground in an object of pleasure or displeasure, and, if that is so,

> the purpose itself, the gratification that we seek, is ... not a *good* but a
> *well-being*, not a rational concept but an empirical concept of an object
> of sensation; however, the use of the means to it, i.e., the action, is non-
> etheless called good (because rational deliberation is required for it)[21]

An action is a result of rational deliberation if it is chosen for possessing all necessary and some sufficient means to bring the agent's end about.[22] So, any agent may call an action good in respect of their end, whatever end they set, if they know that they have chosen it (as rationally required) on the basis that it possesses all necessary and some sufficient means to bring about that end, however much or little they desire to perform it. An agent endorses it as good in respect of their end just by choosing it on this basis.

The *Groundwork* says that adopting means to an end is part of what it is for a rational being to set an end.[23] Goodness can therefore enter Kant's regressive argument as follows: in setting an end, *A* is rationally required to choose an action to which *A* ascribes goodness as a means.

The next question is: on what condition is it rational for *A* to choose a given action as an action possessing all necessary and some sufficient means to bring about their end, and so to ascribe goodness to it?

To answer this question, consider Kant's remark in *Anthropology from a Pragmatic Point of View*:

> The *logical egoist* considers it unnecessary to test his judgment also by the
> understanding of others; as if he had no need at all for this touchstone
> (*criterium veritatis externum*). But it is so certain that we cannot dispense
> with this means of assuring ourselves of the truth of our judgment ...

---

21   *KpV*, 5: 62.

22   See O'Neill 1989, p. 91.

23   'Whoever wills the end also wills (in so far as reason has decisive influence on his actions)
        the indispensably necessary means to it that is in his control. As far as willing is concerned,
        this proposition is analytic; for in the willing of an object, as my effect, my causality is
        already thought, as an acting cause, i.e. the use of means, and the imperative already
        extracts the concept of actions necessary to this end from the concept of a willing of this
        end' (*GMS*, 4: 417).

The opposite of egoism can only be *pluralism*, that is, the way of thinking in which one is not concerned with oneself as the whole world[24]

Relatedly, Kant remarks in his *Lectures on Logic*:

An *external* mark or an *external* touchstone of truth is the comparison of our own judgments with those of others, because what is subjective will not be present in all others in the same way, so that illusion can thereby be cleared up. The *incompatibility* of the judgments of others with our own is thus an external mark of error, and to be regarded as a cue that we should examine our procedure in judgment, but not for that reason to reject it at once.[25]

These remarks suggest the following: A's choice of a type of action, x, as a means to a type of end, y, is a rational choice, and hence it is rational for A to ascribe goodness to x, only if A compares their judgment with that of others, and, in light of this comparison, and any further examination by A it may prompt, A reaffirms their choice of x. In other words, A's choice of x and ascription of goodness to x is rational if A adopts a plural standpoint in A's deliberation. Adopting the plural standpoint is a rational requirement of choosing action and ascribing goodness to it, for any finite rational agent has a particular biography on account of which they are to some extent prone to error or ignorance.

A adopts the plural standpoint in choosing x and ascribing goodness to x in one of three ways. A may: (i) conclude that all others (who A thinks of as comparing their judgments) should agree with A that, in such and such a type of situation, x possesses all necessary and some sufficient means to bring about y; or A may (ii)(a) conclude that all others (who A thinks of as comparing their judgments) should agree with A that it is only relevant for A to compare their judgment with *some* others, and then (b) conclude that *these* others (who A also thinks of as comparing their judgments) should agree with A that, in such and such a type of situation, x possesses all necessary and some sufficient means to bring about y; or A may (iii) conclude that all or, after (ii)(a), some others (who A thinks of as comparing their judgments) should agree with A that in such and such a type of situation, no comparison of judgments about

---

24   *Anth*, 7: 128–30. Deligiorgi 2002 first drew my attention to this passage, and the following one.

25   *Log*, 9: 57; see also *KU*, 5: 295.

x need be made. For *A*'s choice of action and ascription of goodness to it to be rational, *A* must adopt the plural standpoint by doing (i), (ii) or (iii), if only implicitly.

Next: if *A* is rationally required to adopt the plural standpoint in choosing means to any end they set, *A* is rationally required to adopt this plural standpoint from the plural standpoint. For it, too, is a means that *A* – refusing the irrationality of logical egoism – chooses: a means of setting *any* end rationally. Just as *A*'s choice of action is only rational if *A* compares their judgment with that of others (who *A* thinks of as comparing their judgments), this very choice of the plural standpoint is only rational if *A* compares their judgment on adopting it to choose action with others' judgment on adopting it to choose action (who *A* thinks of as comparing their judgments). If *A*'s ascription of goodness to their action is only rational if *A* adopts the plural standpoint in choosing it, *A*'s ascription of goodness to this plural standpoint, on which the rationality of *A*'s ascription of goodness to their action rests, is itself only rational if *A* chooses it from the plural standpoint. If *A* is rationally required to adopt the plural standpoint from the plural standpoint, *A* must suppose that the plural standpoint that *A* is rationally required to adopt, in setting an end, is self-affirming; and that, as self-affirming, it is the source of the goodness of their action.

Now, if something is taken to be self-affirming, it is taken to have a worth that is independent of the worth of anything beyond itself.[26] As *A*, by setting an end, is rationally required to adopt a self-affirming standpoint, *A* presupposes that its worth is independent of its relation to anything beyond itself. That is, *A* presupposes that its worth is absolute. Thus, *A* presupposes that the rational nature of all those whose judgments *A* is required to think of as belonging, with *A*'s, to the plural standpoint – which is to say, the rational nature of everyone capable of adopting it – has absolute worth. If something exists with absolute worth, then (per step 2) it will be the object of what all finite rational beings are required to adopt as an end in itself.[27] As the appropriate response to something presupposed to have absolute worth is to regard it as an end in itself, *A* is committed to regarding the rational nature of everyone capable of adopting the plural standpoint as an end in itself.

---

26 Not all self-affirming standpoints are justified, of course. A weird contrarian might believe that an action is good as a means if only they think it is good, and believe that that is a good decision procedure because only they think it is good. The logical pluralism interpretation does not hold that any self-affirming standpoint is justified. It holds that any self-affirming standpoint that is a *rational requirement* of setting an end is justified.

27 See xx in the summary below.

To summarise the argument for step 4 thus far, let us make the following stipulations. One activity is *rationally required* by another if an agent cannot rationally perform the latter unless they perform the former. A belief is a *presupposition* of an activity if it is irrational for its performer to deny it.[28] A belief about the value of something *commits* an agent who has that belief to take an appropriate attitude to its value. Given these stipulations, the logical pluralism version of the regressive argument may be summarised as follows:

I.   A rational human being, *A*, sets an end
II.   In setting an end, *A* must choose an action as a means
III.   *A* is rationally required to choose such an action on the basis that it possesses all necessary and some sufficient means to this end
IV.   In so choosing it, *A* ascribes goodness to it as a means
V.   The action so chosen is chosen rationally by *A* only by *A* adopting the plural standpoint
VI.   Therefore, *A* must adopt the plural standpoint for *A*'s ascription of goodness to their action to be rational
VII.   But it also follows, from II and V, that the plural standpoint is a means of rationally setting any end
VIII.   As such a means, *A* is rationally required to choose it rationally
IX.   The plural standpoint is chosen rationally by *A* only by *A* adopting the plural standpoint
X.   Therefore, *A* is rationally required to choose the plural standpoint by adopting the plural standpoint
XI.   In so choosing the plural standpoint, *A*'s ascription of goodness to it is rational
XII.   *A*'s ascription of goodness to their action, which is chosen by adopting the plural standpoint, is then also rational
XIII.   Therefore, the plural standpoint is the self-affirming source of the goodness that *A* ascribes to their action
XIV.   Something has absolute worth if its worth is not relative to something else
XV.   If something is taken to be self-affirming, it is taken to have absolute worth
XVI.   Therefore, *A* presupposes that the capacity to adopt the plural standpoint has absolute worth
XVII.   Therefore, *A* presupposes that the rational nature of everyone capable of adopting the plural standpoint has absolute worth

---

28   McFarland 1970, p. 86.

XVIII.   It follows from I–V that every rational human being is capable of adopting the plural standpoint

XIX.   Therefore, *A* presupposes that the rational nature of every human being has absolute worth

XX.   Something that exists with absolute worth will be the object of an obligatory end in itself

XXI.   Therefore, *A* is committed to regarding the rational nature of every human being as an end in itself

The conclusion of this regressive argument is that a rational human being is committed to regarding the rational nature of every human being as an end in itself. As a rational human being is also committed (per step 3) to regarding any other possible object of an end, besides rational nature, to lack absolute worth, they are committed to regarding the rational nature of every human being as the only end in itself.

One outstanding issue is Kant's footnote,[29] cited above. Kant appends the footnote to a clause advancing a claim about how 'every other rational being' necessarily represents its existence, and not to the preceding sentence, which advances a parallel claim about 'human' actions. This suggests that the footnote refers to a passage in the third section of the *Groundwork* that licenses us to think about how any finite rational being must regard its existence along the model of how we human beings must regard our existence.[30] If so, the passage could license an extension of the argument just summarised. It would justify the removal of the qualifier 'human' from I, XVIII, XIX and XXI. Together with step 3, the conclusion of the argument is then: a rational being is committed to regarding the rational nature of every rational being as the only end in itself.

One backdrop to Kant's argument in the final section of the *Groundwork* is his description of the will in its second section. 'The will', Kant says shortly before his argument for FEI, 'is thought as a capacity to determine itself to action *in conformity with the representation of certain laws*'.[31] The will is a capacity to commit to or withdraw from a type of action in light of an anticipation of the form: if type of action *x*, then type of effect *y*.

In the third section of the *Groundwork*, Kant adds that it is impossible for a rational being to attribute a judgment to perform an action it performs to an external cause:

---

29   *GMS*, 4: 429.
30   See Herman 2011, p. 109.
31   *GMS*, 4: 427.

It is not enough that, on whatever grounds, we attribute freedom to our will if we do not have grounds sufficient to attribute it to all *rational beings* as well ... Now I say: every being that cannot act otherwise than *under the idea of freedom* is actually free, in a practical respect, precisely because of that ... Now I assert: that we must necessarily lend to every rational being that has a will also the idea of freedom, under which alone it acts. For in such a being we conceive a reason that is practical, i.e. has causality with regard to its objects. Now, one cannot possibly think of a reason that would self-consciously receive guidance from any other quarter with regard to its judgments, since the subject would not then attribute the determination of judgment to his reason, but to an impulse.[32]

If a rational being were to conceive of its action as determined by something other than it, it would have to think of it as determined in light of an anticipation of the form: if type of action x, then type of effect y, of which not it, but something other than it, was aware. If so, it would not know what action it was performing, or even whether it was acting at all. It is contradictory to suppose that a rational being conceives of its action as determined by something other than it, and does not know if it is acting. So, a rational being must attribute a judgment to perform any action it takes itself to perform to itself. As anyone who takes themselves to perform an action must conceive of themselves as choosing it, any being we think of as a rational being is a being we think of as acting '*under the idea of freedom*'. But if we suppose that a rational being is free from a practical point of view, then, for the reasons outlined in the case of a rational human agent, we must suppose that any finite rational being that sets an end is rationally required to adopt the plural standpoint in choosing an action as a means. If so, the logical pluralism version of the regressive argument reveals how the status of end in itself must be represented to hold by every rational being for each rational being, as a possible '*objective* principle'[33] requires.

If the logical pluralism version of the regressive argument is plausible, we can only think of practical reason as existing in agents who are committed to regarding the rational nature of all rational beings as an end in itself. An agent committed to regarding everyone's rational nature as an end in itself is an agent who can recognise everyone's rational nature as an end in itself. One feature of a person is a capacity to recognise the categorical imperative. Hence, according

---

32   *GMS*, 4: 447–8.
33   *GMS*, 4: 429.

to the logical pluralism version of the regressive argument, we can only think of rational nature as existing in agents with this feature of a person. Whether this is sufficient to ground FEI, as a formula that commands: always treat humanity in a person as an end, is considered in section 5. Beforehand, we may press some advantages of the logical pluralism version of Kant's regressive argument over Korsgaard's and Wood's versions.

4   **Advantages of the Logical Pluralism Version of Kant's Regressive Argument**

A logical pluralism version of Kant's regressive argument has three advantages over Korsgaard's and Wood's versions.

(i)   *The Logical Pluralism Version Avoids the Claim That a Rational Agent Must Take Their End to Be Objectively Good*
Both Korsgaard and Wood claim that 'setting an end for ourselves involves ascribing *objective* goodness to it'.[34] The logical pluralism version does not advance this claim. Consider two reasons not to advance it.

First, the textual evidence offered for the claim is problematic. Korsgaard cites a statement in the Beck translation of *Critique of Practical Reason*: '"we desire nothing, under the direction of reason, except in so far as we hold it to be good or bad"'.[35] However, Kant's statement begins: '*wir wollen*'.[36] '*Wir wollen*' does *not* mean 'we desire' (which could, for example, translate: '*wir begehren*'), but: '*we will*'.[37] *If* Kant had said that we value any desire that our reason directs us to act on as good, it might be argued that he was of the view that we ascribe objective goodness to any end that we set. But it does not follow from what Kant says, that we ascribe objective goodness to any end that we set. Although 'human choice ... can ... be determined to actions by pure will',[38] it need not be. It may instead be determined to action by the endorsement of an inclination. In that case, Kant says in *Critique of Practical Reason*, 'the purpose itself ... is ... not a *good* but a *well-being*'.[39]

---

34   Wood 1999, p. 127; see also Korsgaard 1986, p. 195; Korsgaard 1996, p. 122; Wood 2008, p. 91.
35   Korsgaard 1986, p. 190, citing Kant 1956; compare Wood 1999, p. 128.
36   *KpV*, 5: 60.
37   The statement cited by Korsgaard is translated by Pluhar as follows: 'according to reason's instruction we will nothing except insofar as we consider it to be good or evil' (*KpV*, 5: 60).
38   *MS*, 6: 213.
39   *KpV*, 5: 62; see sec. 3 above for the longer quote.

Second, the substantive argument offered for the claim is unconvincing. Korsgaard states: 'a thing, then, can be said to be objectively good, either if it is unconditionally good or if it is conditionally good and the condition under which it is good is met'.[40] This statement is to be read in conjunction with the further statement that there is only '*one* end' that 'dependent beings' necessarily have: their '*happiness*'.[41] If, in light of these two statements, setting an end is to involve ascribing objective goodness to it, it must be the case that, when we set an end, we take it to be objectively good either simply because we take it to contribute to our happiness, which we take to be unconditionally good, or else because we take it to contribute to our happiness *and* we take ourselves to be worthy of happiness. To do the former is to be afflicted by 'self-conceit', which Korsgaard characterises as 'the tendency to suppose that the objects of our inclinations are good just because they contribute to our happiness'.[42] Yet it is *possible* for a rational agent, A, in setting an end, not to take themselves to be worthy of happiness, *and* not to be self-conceited, that is, not to assume that all others are at least required to refrain from interfering with A's pursuit of their end because it contributes to A's happiness. A may set an end that A does not regard as of moral merit, *and* rationally choose means, such as concealment, which imply, on A's part, no belief that others may not stop A from pursuing the end, or may not condemn or punish A for pursuing it, should they find out. Given this possibility, ascribing objective goodness to an end is not a rational requirement of setting it. Even if A takes any end that A sets to be a type of end good for anyone with the same conception of happiness as A, A need not take it 'as having a rational claim on the will of every rational being'.[43]

If there is no reason to suppose that a rational agent must take their end to be objectively good, it is an advantage of the logical pluralism version of Kant's regressive argument that goodness enters the argument by other means.

(ii)   *The Logical Pluralism Version Avoids the Self-Regarding Fallacy*
The self-regarding fallacy, Adam Cureton writes,

> is to erroneously claim that if someone values a feature of themselves then they must value that same feature in others, for someone may value

---

40   Korsgaard 1986, p. 193.

41   *GMS*, 4: 415.

42   Korsgaard 1990, p. 207; compare Kant, *KpV*, 5: 74.

43   Wood 1995a, p. 309; see also Wood 1999, p. 127.

a personal characteristic on grounds that include an ineliminable back-reference to that agent.[44]

Suppose that I value my height, and I know that others are of exactly the same height. I am not committed just by virtue of these facts to value others' height, for I may value my height on the 'grounds' that it is *mine*. From the fact that the same characteristic is found in several agents, it does not follow that an agent who values that characteristic in themselves cannot do so on grounds that avoid committing them to valuing it in the others. If *A* values their rational nature, and *A* knows that others also possess rational nature, *A* is not committed just by virtue of these facts to valuing others' rational nature. *A* may value their rational nature on the grounds that it is *theirs*. It is simply the case that *A* then has little basis to complain if others likewise value only their rational nature.

The fact that an agent can have an agent-relative reason for valuing their rational nature poses a challenge for a regressive argument to the conclusion that a rational agent is committed to regarding the rational nature of all rational beings as an end in itself. A regressive argument is not supposed to introduce external premises; in other words, premises that are not rational requirements, presuppositions, commitments or implications of its given starting point. No moral premises may be introduced just because they are true. The premise that it is morally irrelevant to the value of a type of characteristic that it belongs to a particular agent, may not be introduced, just because it is true (if it is true). It may not be claimed, as part of a regressive argument, that, if *A* values their rational nature, *A* cannot value it for an agent-relative reason, because agent-relative reasons are morally unsound. If the only barrier preventing *A* from valuing others' rational nature is the agent-relative form of *A*'s reason for valuing *A*'s rational nature, which appears morally arbitrary to us, a regressive argument cannot remove that barrier just because it appears morally arbitrary to us.

As a regressive argument in support of FEI cannot introduce external *moral* reasoning to bar the end-setting agent from which it begins from having agent-relative reasons for what they value, it can only avoid the self-regarding fallacy (and support its intended conclusion) by virtue of how it *describes* the self-affirming source of the goodness that the agent ascribes to their action. It can avoid the self-regarding fallacy only if this self-affirming source of goodness is thought to include the rational nature of all. If the self-affirming source of

---

44   Cureton 2013, pp. 371–2.

goodness is the rational nature of all, any given agent is committed to valuing rational nature in itself only insofar as it is committed to valuing rational nature in all.

The logical pluralism version of the regressive argument can avoid the self-regarding fallacy. What it identifies as the self-affirming source of goodness that each agent ascribes to their action is a *plural* standpoint. To adopt the plural standpoint, A compares their judgment with that of others (*B, C, D*, etc.), each of whose judgments are conceived by A as formed in light of B's, C's, D's, etc., adoption of the plural standpoint. When A adopts the plural standpoint, *A must imagine all others as themselves adopting it with A*.[45] The capacity of one agent to adopt the plural standpoint cannot be described without implicitly referring to the capacity of every other agent to adopt it. The self-regarding fallacy is excluded, on the logical pluralism interpretation, because each rational agent views everyone's rational nature taken together as the self-affirming source of goodness.

Suppose, by contrast, that a version of Kant's regressive argument *first* seeks to show that an agent must value rational nature in itself and *then* argues, in a *further* move, that, if an agent values that capacity in itself, it is committed to valuing it in others too. If so, it will be unable to avoid the self-regarding fallacy. To believe that it is possible to reach these conclusions in separate moves is to suppose both that the source of the goodness that one agent ascribes to their action is their own rational nature considered separately from that of others, and that no agent-relative reason for valuing it can stand in the way of their valuing every rational nature. Both Korsgaard's[46] and Wood's[47] versions of the regressive argument are arguments of this kind. If the source of the goodness that each rational agent ascribes to their action is not the rational nature of all, any attempt to show that a rational agent must value others' rational nature will either (i) commit the self-regarding fallacy, or else (ii) rely on an external moral premise, and so cease to be a regressive argument.[48]

---

45   Hence the bracketed phrase 'who A thinks of as comparing their judgments' in sec. 3 to describe A's adoption of the plural standpoint.

46   'If you view yourself as having a value-conferring status in virtue of your power of rational choice, you must view anyone who has the power of rational choice as having, in virtue of that power, a value-conferring status' (Korsgaard 1986, p. 196).

47   'The next step in Kant's argument is to claim ... not only my rational nature, but the rational nature in every person, is an end in itself' (Wood 2008, p. 92; see also Wood 1999, p. 125, pp. 130–1).

48   An example of the latter is Martin (2006, p. 118): 'It is a matter of showing the individual

(iii)   *The Logical Pluralism Version Avoids the Claim That Any Source of*
         Value Must Itself Be of Unconditional Value

A source of goodness is that which has the power to confer goodness (by virtue of a procedure employing certain standards), and is not lent this power by
something else. Now, it is false that, for any x taken by A to be good and to owe
its goodness to a source, that source must itself be taken by A to be (unconditionally) good. A law may be taken by A to be good and to owe its goodness to
the sovereign decision-making body that passed it, although that body is not
itself taken by A to be (unconditionally) good; for instance, because A believes
that it only accidentally followed the procedure that it followed for passing that
law. But a narrower claim is true: for any x taken by A to be good and to owe its
goodness to a source that confers the same value on itself as it does on x, that
source must be taken by A to be absolutely good. This is the claim on which the
logical pluralism version of the regressive argument rests. On the logical pluralism version of the argument, the source of an action's goodness (the plural
standpoint) is a *self-affirming source* of goodness. As it is the source of its own
goodness, the worth of rational nature is absolute. The logical pluralism version therefore does not rely on the more general claim that any source of value
(and hence even a non-self-affirming source of value) must itself be of unconditional value.

On Korsgaard's and Wood's versions of the regressive argument, by contrast,
the argument does involve an inference that the source of value must itself be
of unconditional value. Korsgaard supposes that 'the power of rational choice',
because it is 'the unconditioned condition of the goodness of anything', 'must
itself be something of unconditional value'.[49] Likewise, Wood holds that Kant's
inference 'from the *objective* goodness of the end to the *unconditional* objective
goodness of the capacity to set the end' is based on the fact that this capacity
is 'the *source* of the objective value of the end'.[50] One advantage of the logical
pluralism version of the regressive argument is that it does not suggest any such
inference.

---

that the thing she values as an end in itself and her justification for the valuing are
arbitrary in a specific way: the valued thing is not something only she possesses, and
its value does not come from the fact that it is hers'. Confronting an individual with the
moral arbitrariness of their justification is not a strategy belonging to a regressive argument.

49   Korsgaard 1986, p. 197.
50   Wood 1999, p. 127.

5   Humanity, Personality and a Belief in the Existence of God

The logical pluralism interpretation of Kant's argument for FEI is a plausible interpretation that, in regard to Kant's regressive argument (step 4), avoids three problems in the versions offered by Korsgaard and Wood. It introduces goodness into the regressive argument less objectionably; it avoids the self-regarding fallacy; and it does not claim that any source of value must itself be of unconditional value. On the logical pluralism interpretation, these problems do not prevent a derivation of FEI from including a regressive argument for why we are committed to valuing everyone's rational nature absolutely.

One remaining question, however, left hanging at the end of section 3, is whether this is sufficient for step 4. Step 4 is to show that humanity *in a person* can be an obligatory end. Step 4 carries this burden, because FEI commands an agent to '*use humanity, in your own person as well as in the person of any other*'[51] always as an end. FEI does not command us to cherish humanity unconditionally. Here we depart from Korsgaard's view that 'it is the capacity for the rational determination of ends in general ... that the Formula of Humanity orders us to cherish unconditionally'.[52] FEI does not command us to cherish humanity unconditionally, because it does not command us to cherish humanity whether or not it is in a person. This is in line with Kant's remark in the *Groundwork*: 'morality [a capacity for moral action – JF] is the condition under which alone a rational being can be an end in itself'.[53] Korsgaard draws a distinction between acting on maxims of one's choosing, where 'in choosing the maxim one also chooses an end', and 'morally worthy actions', where 'the end is chosen because of the necessity of the principle embodied in the maxim'.[54] FEI requires us to cherish a capacity for the former only in beings with a capacity for the latter.

That an argument for FEI is required to show that humanity in a person can be an obligatory end adheres not just to Kant's formulation of FEI, but to the principle of autonomy of the will. That is, there is a reason, relating to autonomy of the will, why any interpretation of FEI has to allow us to conclude that we are always to treat humanity *in a person* as an end, where a person is someone who can subject their proposed conduct to moral criteria, and *act for the sake of duty*. A person does not merely have capacities to set ends in general, and to identify the moral status of ends (whether impermissible, permissible

---

51   *GMS*, 4: 429.
52   Korsgaard 1986, p. 187.
53   *GMS*, 4: 435.
54   Korsgaard 1986, p. 187.

or obligatory). A person also has the capacity (not implied by the former capacities) to make the obligatory status of an end serve as a sufficient determination of their will.

Suppose that a formula of a categorical imperative whose principle is freedom as autonomy of the will is to command that something (call it 'S') is always to be treated in a certain way (= 'as W'). Any formula of this kind must command every finite rational being capable of treating S as W to treat S as W. Otherwise, the imperative is not categorical, because it is not binding unconditionally. Further, any finite rational being capable of treating S as W must be able to act on this imperative for its own sake. Otherwise, the imperative is not categorical, because it is not binding immediately. Indeed, those and only those who can strive to obey this imperative for its own sake can strive to obey *themselves*, and so can think of themselves as positively free. To suppose that there could be a being capable of treating S as W and thus bound to treat S as W that could not treat S as W for its own sake, would be to concede that the formula does not express a principle of freedom as autonomy for all finite rational beings. Besides the fact that FEI, as Kant formulates it, commands us to always treat humanity in a person as an end, a formula of its kind (treat S as W) presupposes that we can think of any being with humanity as a person. So, on any plausible interpretation of FEI, its derivation must include an argument to the effect that we are committed to treat humanity *in a person* always as an end.

Indeed, on any account of Kant's derivation of FEI, as a formula of an *objective* principle, we require a reason to suppose that humanity and personality are coextensive. For if FEI is to bind *all* finite rational beings, we must think of every finite rational being as negatively free, and for this, we must think of every such being as a person. Kant's argument for saying that FEI is an objective principle, represented to hold by and for every finite rational being, rests on his claim, in the third section of the *Groundwork*, that 'we must necessarily lend to every rational being that has a will also the idea of freedom, under which alone it acts'.[55] In Kant's view, we can think of actions of a finite rational being as negatively free, or as uncaused in their causing, only insofar as we think of it as having the capacity to act for the sake of duty. Kant expresses this view in *Religion Within the Bounds of Bare Reason*, which distinguishes three predispositions in a human being:

1. The predisposition to the *animality* of the human being as a *living* being
2. To the *humanity* of him as a living and at the same time *rational* being

---

55   *GMS*, 4: 448.

3. To his *personality* as that of a being who is rational and at the same time
    capable of imputation [of actions to him][56]

Kant appends the following note to his description of the third predisposition:

> One cannot treat this predisposition as already contained in the concept
> of the preceding one, but must necessarily regard it as a special predispos-
> ition. For from [the fact] that a being has reason it does not at all follow –
> at least as far as we can see – that this reason contains an ability to determ-
> ine the power of choice unconditionally through the mere presentation
> of the qualification of its maxims for universal legislation, and thus to be
> practical on its own. The most rational of all beings of the world might yet
> always need certain incentives, coming to him from objects of inclination,
> in order to determine his power of choice, but might apply to this the most
> rational deliberation as regards finding the greatest sum of incentives as
> well as the means for attaining the purpose determined by them, without
> suspecting so much as the possibility of such a thing as the moral, abso-
> lutely commanding law, which proclaims that it is itself an incentive, and
> moreover the highest one. If this law were not given within us, no reason
> would ever enable us to excogitate it as a law, or to talk the power of choice
> into it; and yet this law is the only thing that makes us conscious of the
> independence of our power of choice from determination by any other
> incentives (conscious of our freedom) and thereby at the same time of
> the imputability of all actions.[57]

According to Kant, we are aware of ourselves as acting under the idea of freedom (under the idea of acting as uncaused in our causing) only insofar as we are
aware of a moral law that allows us to think of ourselves as morally responsible;
that is, as able to determine our will by the moral law. Relatedly, if, as Kant says,
we must think of every rational agent as acting under the idea of freedom, then
we must think of every rational agent as a person. As the argument for FEI as an
objective principle rests on the thought of every rational being as acting under
the idea of freedom, it rests on the thought of every rational being as a person.

Kant's statement of FEI, the nature of FEI as an obligatory-end-based imperative formula of a moral law whose principle is autonomy of the will, and Kant's
argument for FEI as an objective principle, all require that it is humanity in a
person that is to be treated always as an end.

---

56   *RGV*, 6: 26.
57   *RGV*, 6: 26.

With this in mind, let us reconsider whether the logical pluralism version of Kant's regressive argument is sufficient for step 4. If this argument is accepted, we can only think of rational nature as existing in agents committed to regarding the rational nature of every rational being as an end in itself. An agent committed to regarding everyone's rational nature as an end in itself is an agent who can recognise everyone's rational nature as an end in itself. But this is *not* to say that such an agent can make the worth that they identify rational nature to have into an unconditional and solely sufficient determination of their will.[58] Hence, it is not to say that this agent is a person. But if so, a logical pluralism version of Kant's regressive argument does not allow us to conclude that humanity in a person can be an obligatory end. Together with steps 1–3, it does not suffice to ground FEI as a possible categorical imperative.

The same insufficiency will characterise *any* version of Kant's regressive argument for why humanity in a person can be an obligatory end. Any such argument proceeds from a given fact about humanity – that a rational human being sets an end – and examines its conditions. Such arguments can at most reveal a value commitment on the part of every rational being. They cannot reveal a capacity to act for the sake of duty on the part of every rational being. At most, they can show that every rational being is committed to regarding rational nature as an end in itself. But what they cannot show is that every rational being is committed to regarding rational nature in a person as an end in itself. Yet this is just what a regressive argument has to show, if (along with other steps of argument) it is to ground FEI as a formula of the categorical imperative.

To this problem, Kant could have thought that he had a response. The response is to make it a premise of Kant's derivation of FEI that we cannot suppose that a perfect moral creator (God) could have a purpose in creating a species of beings with humanity but without personality. This supposition is implied by Kant's afore-cited statement in *Religion* that the predisposition

---

58   Wood claims: 'it would seem that personality is always found where humanity is found, because the rational capacity to set ends involves the capacity to recognize humanity as an end, and hence both the capacity to give oneself the moral law and to obey that law out of the motive of respect for the worth of humanity' (Wood 1999, p. 364). A capacity to 'recognize humanity as an end' (and a regressive argument may reveal a commitment to 'recognize humanity as an end' on the part of a rational agent, if to 'recognize' an end is to identify its worth) does *not* imply a capacity to make its worth one's unconditional and solely sufficient 'motive' for acting. It is unclear, however, if Wood intends for us to take this claim seriously, as Wood concludes: '[f]or practical purposes, then, Kant must assume that personality is found wherever humanity is found' (Wood 1999, p. 366). A claim that is assumed for 'practical purposes' is not a claim that *can* be proven (or disproven) theoretically.

to personality is not included in the predisposition to humanity 'at least as far as we can see'.[59] Even if we cannot have knowledge of why personality is coextensive with humanity, we may still be unable to think it possible that a perfect moral creator could have a purpose in creating a species of beings with humanity but without personality. If we cannot think it possible for a perfect moral creator to have a purpose in creating such a species,[60] and if we have an a priori reason to believe in the existence of God, then we can believe, on a priori grounds, that personality is coextensive with humanity. No regressive argument can allow us to conclude that humanity in a person can be an obligatory end. But we could support this step of argument if we were also to believe that humanity and personality are coextensive. That humanity and personality are coextensive is not something that we can know, according to Kant. But it is something that we can suppose, on a priori grounds, if we can suppose, on a priori grounds, that there is a perfect moral creator.

Imagine a being, B, who can set any end whatsoever, and therefore has humanity, but who cannot act for duty's sake.[61] If personality is a capacity to subject one's actions to the moral law *and* to act for duty's sake, B has humanity but not personality. B may act with '*legality*', that is, adhere to the '*letter*' of the moral law; but B's acts cannot exhibit its '*spirit*'.[62] Faced with the claim that we can conceive of a species of B as belonging to the world, Kant has two options. If Kant admits this, Kant concedes that the moral law is not a principle of autonomy for every rational being, and is deprived of an argument for FEI. But if Kant denies it, on the basis that we not only cannot know of a B by experience, but that we must also assume that there could be no moral purpose in creating a species of B, Kant can avoid this concession, and retain an argument for FEI, if he can offer an a priori argument for us to believe in a perfect moral creator.

If, as Kant claims, we 'necessarily lend' the idea of freedom to every being with practical reason, and this is only possible if we also attribute personality to

---

59   *RGV*, 6: 26.

60   For quotes that support attributing this view to Kant, see the opening of ch. 9.

61   This being differs from 'a being who could select among a variety of ends, and yet such that all of these ends are bad' (Ameriks 2003, p. 200). To have humanity, one must be able to set 'any end whatsoever' (*MS*, 6: 392). If ends can be specified that a being cannot adopt, it lacks humanity. If Ameriks's being's ends are 'always wrong' (Ameriks 2003, p. 200), two classes of ends are specified as ends it cannot adopt: ends that conform to what morality requires, and morally neutral ends. As Ameriks's being lacks humanity, Kant need not argue that such a being can recognise FEI, and nor does FEI command us to treat it always as an end.

62   *KpV*, 5: 71.

it, then we require a reason to attribute personality to every such rational being necessarily, in spite of the fact (as Kant sees it) that we 'cannot treat' personality 'as already contained in the concept'[63] of humanity. An a priori argument for the existence of God, and for the incompatibility of the thought of a nature created by a perfect moral creator with the thought of it as containing a species of being with humanity but without personality, would provide this reason.

Kant can believe that he has an argument for FEI, on the logical pluralism interpretation, if he can believe that there is a philosophical reason for us to believe in the existence of God. As we will see in the next chapter, Kant does argue that we have such a reason to believe in the existence of God. On the logical pluralism interpretation, we can therefore account for why Kant affirmed FEI. But to say this is not to be committed to affirm FEI, provided that we may reject Kant's arguments for why we must believe in the existence of God.

---

63   Ibid.

CHAPTER 9

Kant's Arguments for a Belief in the Existence of God

In Chapters 5–8, we examined two of Kant's formulas of the categorical imperative: the Formula of the Law of Nature (FLN), and the Formula of the End in Itself (FEI). We found that their use or derivation (and therefore also their use) presupposes certain assumptions of natural teleology. On the one hand, our application of FLN presupposes the principle of suitability, at least in respect of rational organised beings. It presupposes that we assume, as a regulative principle, that nothing about a rational organised being can be bettered in respect of its fitness for purpose. On the other hand, the derivation of FEI presupposes a belief that humanity and personality are coextensive. We have also suggested that, on account of these assumptions, Kant needs to argue that we have an a priori reason to believe in the existence of God if he is to give us sufficient reason to abide by the categorical imperative.

Consider, firstly, the connection between the principle of suitability, and a belief in the existence of God. If we believe in the existence of God – a perfect moral creator – then we must assume that the nature created by this creator is perfectly suited to its purpose, of promoting finite rational beings' cultivation of a moral disposition. A belief in the existence of God gives us a reason to adopt the regulative principle of suitability, at least in respect of rational beings. If we believe in the existence of God, then we must believe that nature is perfectly suited to its moral purpose. If so, we must believe that nothing about a rational organised being with a capacity for morality can be bettered in respect of its fitness for its moral purpose.

If, however, we do not believe in the existence of God, then reason alone cannot provide us with grounds to adopt the principle of suitability, even just in respect of rational organised beings. Our reason may aim to unify our empirical knowledge of the world. But the aim of unifying this knowledge cannot provide grounds to adopt the principle of suitability if our knowledge disconfirms this principle. This is the case in respect of our knowledge of living organisms, in the form of the theory of natural selection. The theory of natural selection leads us 'to expect organisms that evolve in one environment, with a corresponding survival strategy, might have to find new ways of surviving under quite different circumstances'.[1] The news ways that organisms find to ensure their survival

---

1 Wood 1999, p. 223.

in different circumstances, 'jury-rigged from a limited set of available components',[2] may offer a workable solution, but fall short of optimal design. As the
theory of natural selection leads us to expect the organisation of organisms
to disconfirm the principle of suitability, reason alone cannot provide us with
grounds to adopt it. Only a belief in the existence of a perfect moral creator
could encourage us to adopt it.

There is also a connection between the belief that humanity and personality
are coextensive, and a belief in the existence of God. If we believe that there is
a perfect moral creator, we must assume that nature is perfectly suited to its
purpose of promoting finite rational beings' cultivation of a moral disposition.
This purpose cannot be served by creating a species of being with humanity
but without personality. It cannot be served by creating, as the *only* species of
finite rational being, a species of being with humanity but without personality.
For then there are *no* finite rational beings in nature who are able to cultivate a
moral disposition. So, we cannot suppose, consistently with a belief in the existence of God, that the only finite rational beings in nature are members of such
a species. A belief in the existence of God must lead us to suppose that nature
contains a species of rational being with personality, whatever else nature contains.

The only remaining way to suppose that nature contains a species of being
with humanity but without personality is to suppose that nature contains (at
least) *two* species of finite being: (at least) one species with humanity and personality, and (at least) one species with humanity but without personality. Yet
this would be doubly contrary to the principle of suitability to which a belief in
the existence of God leads us. The existence of a species of being with humanity but without personality would not promote, but *hinder*, a moral disposition
in the species with personality. Its members would be left in doubt as to which
species of being a given individual belonged to. This would leave them in doubt
as to how to do their duty, if, as FEI commands, they are only to treat humanity
in a person always as an end.

A species of being with humanity but without personality is also, for Kant,
imperfect. If a finite rational being lacks personality, then, Kant remarks in
Critique of Practical Reason, 'reason is to serve him only for the sake of what
instinct accomplishes in animals; reason would in that case be only a particular manner that nature had employed in order to equip' a rational being 'for the
same purpose to which it has destined animals'.[3] However, Kant observes in the

---

2   Gould 1982, p. 20, where Gould cites as examples orchids, or the sesamoid thumb of pandas.
3   *KpV*, 5: 61.

Groundwork, 'in a being that has reason and a will, if the actual end of nature were its *preservation*, its *prosperity*, in a word its *happiness*, then she would have made very bad arrangements for this in appointing the creature's reason as the accomplisher of this purpose' because this purpose 'would be marked out for it far more accurately by instinct'.[4] A belief in the existence of God, together with the principle of suitability that this belief supports, require us to assume that humanity and personality are coextensive.

If, however, we do not believe in the existence of God, then reason alone cannot provide us with grounds to assume that there cannot be a species of being with humanity but without personality. First of all, it is *logically* possible for us to conceive of such a species of being, because humanity and personality are distinct concepts. Kant says that we 'cannot' treat the concept of personality as 'already contained' in the concept of humanity.[5] Second, Kant must deny that we can have knowledge of any conditions that would make it *causally* impossible for a species of beings with humanity but without personality to exist. This is because Kant holds that we can have no knowledge of how the capacity for morality possessed by a species of finite rational beings is caused. In *Religion Within the Bounds of Bare Reason*, Kant argues:

> it is absolutely incomprehensible to our reason how beings could be *created* for the free employment of their powers; for according to the principle of causality we can attribute to a being, assumed to have been produced, no other intrinsic basis for its actions except the one put into it by the producing cause; but then every action of this being would also be determined through this basis (and hence through an external cause), and hence this being itself would not be free[6]

If we can have no knowledge of how personality is caused, we can have no knowledge of any conditions that would make it causally impossible for a species of being with humanity but without personality to exist. If we must think of such a species of being as logically possible, and we cannot think of it as causally impossible, reason alone provides no grounds to believe that humanity and personality are coextensive. Only a belief in the existence of a perfect moral creator can support a belief that humanity and personality are coextensive.

---

4   *GMS*, 4: 395.
5   *RGV*, 6: 26, cited in ch. 8, sec. 5.
6   *RGV*, 6: 142.

In short, there are no belief-in-God-independent grounds to apply FLN or FEI. A belief in the existence of God (a perfect moral creator) is a tacit presupposition in both cases, as it then is for FUL and FA; as well as an explicit presupposition of FRE.[7] To ground these formulas, Kant needs to provide an a priori argument for why we should believe that God exists. Unless this argument is provided, we lack sufficient reason to adopt these formulas, as formulas of a categorically binding imperative.

Kant does indeed argue that we have a compelling reason to believe in the existence of God, however. So, taken by itself, the line of argument pursued thus far does not yet constitute a fatal objection to Kant's ethics. If, however, Kant's arguments for why we must believe in the existence of God are unsuccessful, Kant's ethics is subject to a fatal objection. We would have no good reason to abide by the categorical imperative. There would be no good reason for us to adopt any of Kant's formulas of the categorical imperative, and no other way for us to abide by it.

The aim in this chapter is to undermine Kant's arguments for why we should believe in the existence of God. By pursuing this aim, we grant that Kant may rely on the premise that we have a reason to believe in the existence of God to ground or state or apply a formula of the categorical imperative, provided that this reason is a priori. A formula of the categorical imperative is grounded, if an a priori argument can be offered for it. So, if Kant can show, by a priori reasoning, that we must believe in the existence of God, then a formula's grounding or statement or application may rely on this premise. For if the belief is based in pure reason, its use in grounding or stating or applying a categorical imperative need not prevent the latter from providing an imperative form of the principle of autonomy of the will. It would be contrary to this principle to claim that a formula's grounding or statement or application rests on a non-rational faith in God, and/or to claim that to act from duty is to act to satisfy God's will. But neither view is attributed to Kant, simply by granting that, in grounding or stating or applying a categorical imperative, Kant may rely on the premise that we must believe in the existence of God, provided that Kant can show that there are rational grounds for this belief.

Kant offers two arguments for why we must believe in the existence of a perfect moral creator. One argument, presented in *Critique of Practical Reason* (1788),[8] and later relied on in *Religion Within the Bounds of Bare Reason* (first

---

7   See the Introduction to Part II.

8   *KpV*, 5: 124–5. Kant also suggests this argument in *Lectures on Philosophical Theology* (Kant 1830, pp. 159–60; Kant 1978, pp. 122–3), which are thought to have been delivered in the Winter of 1783/84 (Wood 1978, p. 15), but (unlike *KpV* and *RGV*) were not written for publication.

published as a whole in 1793),[9] is that the existence of God is a postulate of pure practical reason. According to this argument, the existence of God is a proposition that we are required to assume from a practical point of view, to think of the concept of the highest good as possible. We shall call this argument for why we should believe in the existence of God, the *argument from the highest good*.

A second argument, advanced in *Critique of Judgment* (1790),[10] and implied by the 'Fragment of a Moral Catechism'[11] in *The Metaphysics of Morals* (1797), relates to a premise about our experience of organised beings in nature. According to this argument, it is only possible for us to account for the existence of organised beings in nature by supposing that they are created by an intelligent world cause; and, if our system of nature includes moral agents, then we must think of this intelligent world cause more particularly as a perfect moral creator, or God. We shall call this argument for why we should believe in the existence of God, the *physicoteleological argument*.

If either of these arguments is successful, Kant can claim to have supported the teleological view of nature that the *Groundwork*'s discussion of the categorical imperative relies on. Only the argument from the highest good rests on the concept of the highest good, while only the physicoteleological argument rests on a premise about how we account for organised beings in nature. To the extent that these arguments rest on different premises, *both* must be rejected, before we can conclude that Kant fails to show that we must believe in the existence of God. We may begin with the argument from the highest good.

1   Kant's Concept of the Highest Good

Kant summarises the argument from the highest good in *Religion Within the Bounds of Bare Reason* (hereafter: *Religion*): 'the idea of a highest good in the world, for the possibility of which we must assume a higher, moral, holiest, and all-powerful being that alone can unite the two elements of this good'.[12]

To understand the argument from the highest good, three features of Kant's thinking about the highest good must be explained. We need to explain the moral importance, for Kant, of the concept of the highest good; why the concept of the highest good has two elements; and how these elements must be

---

9   *RGV*, 6: 5; see also *RGV*, 6: 139.
10   *KU*, 5: 370, 377, 379, 401, 431, 435, 444.
11   *MS*, 6: 480–4.
12   *RGV*, 6: 5.

thought to be connected. Only then can we consider (in the next section) Kant's argument for why the thought of the concept of the highest good as possible gives us a reason to believe in the existence of God.

To explain these issues, we may begin by considering Kant's concept of a postulate. The argument from the highest good is that the existence of God is a postulate of pure practical reason. A '**postulate** of pure practical reason', Kant states in *Critique of Practical Reason*, is 'a *theoretical* proposition, though one not provable as such, insofar as it attaches inseparably to a *practical* law that holds a priori [and] unconditionally'.[13] Even if a proposition cannot be proven to the satisfaction of theoretical reason, it may produce no conflict with any proposition that can be proven to its satisfaction. If a theoretically unproven proposition cannot contradict anything that theoretical reason can prove, we have an a priori reason to postulate it, Kant says, if its postulation is required for practical purposes; that is, if it 'attaches inseparably to a *practical* law that holds a priori [and] unconditionally'. As theoretical reason cannot prove or disprove the existence of God,[14] we may have a reason to postulate the existence of God. We have a reason to postulate the existence of God, if a belief in the existence of God is required for practical purposes.

We already know that the way in which a proposition about God 'attaches inseparably' to a practical law cannot concern our awareness that we are under a duty to obey the moral law, or our motive to act morally. According to Kant, we recognise the moral law as a command of reason. Also, to act morally, we need not seek to please God. It would be contrary to Kant's principle of autonomy of the will if an agent had to believe in the existence of God, to have a motive to bring their will into conformity with the moral law. In claiming that a proposition about God is inseparably attached to a practical law, Kant is not claiming that we must believe in the existence of God to establish the possibility of the moral law, or of moral motivation.

This may leave us wondering how the postulation of God could be inseparably attached to a practical law at all. But there is a further possibility. A proposition is inseparably attached to a practical law if the latter is inseparably attached to something, *X*, and if, to think of *X* as possible, it is necessary to postulate the proposition. The argument from the highest good in *Critique of Practical Reason* is an argument of this kind, where *X* stands for our thought of the concept of the highest good as possible. The thought of the concept of the

---

13   *KpV*, 5: 122.

14   *KpV*, 5: 4–5; see also *KpV*, 5: 120.

highest good as possible is inseparably attached to the moral law, and, to think of this concept as possible, it is necessary for us to postulate the existence of God; or so Kant argues.

To act morally is to act solely out of respect for the moral law. But the morality of action can also be expressed in terms of an end. To act morally is to strive to be virtuous, to seek to cultivate a virtuous disposition. A proposition can be inseparably attached to a practical law, therefore, by being inseparably attached to something distinct from, but necessarily linked to, the striving for virtue. This 'something' is the thought of the concept of the highest good as possible. We must think of virtue as the first but not the only element of the concept of the highest good. Its other element is happiness in proportion to virtue. 'The concept of the highest good', Kant says, is 'that of a whole in which the greatest happiness is presented as linked in the most exact proportion with the greatest degree of moral perfection (possible in creatures)'.[15] The highest good is the combination of the greatest virtue with the happiness that is proportionate to this greatest virtue. As the moral law implies that virtue must be the first element of the concept of the highest good, if Kant can show that happiness proportional to virtue must also be included in this concept, and that the connection in it between virtue and happiness proportional to virtue can be thought as possible only on the assumption of the existence of God, Kant will have shown that a belief in the existence of God is inseparably (even if indirectly) attached to an a priori practical law.

Why is happiness proportional to virtue included in the concept of the highest good? Its inclusion cannot be a direct consequence of the fact that the maxims of finite rational beings inevitably reflect our inclinations as to our choice of goals, because that would be to present a statement of value as directly derived from a statement of fact. Happiness can only be a part of the concept of the highest good if it is of value. If, however, there is a moral law, then the cultivation of a virtuous disposition is of unconditional value. So, happiness can only be of value and thus a part of the concept of the highest good, if it has a value conditional on a virtuous disposition; that is, if our striving to be virtuous makes us worthy of happiness.

In *Critique of Practical Reason*, Kant argues:

> The same law [the moral law – JF] must also lead to the possibility of the second element of the highest good, viz., to the **happiness** commensurate

---

15   *KpV*, 5: 129.

to that morality, and must do so with just as little self-interest as before, solely from impartial reason.[16]

If there is a moral law, and thus an obligation to strive to be virtuous by making conformity to it the sole ground of the adoption of all our maxims, then, Kant suggests, for the same impartial reason that we ought to strive to be virtuous, we must also think it morally just if finite rational beings, who have inclinations by nature, are happy in proportion as they are virtuous. Earlier in *Critique of Practical Reason*, Kant remarks:

> that virtue ... is ... the *supreme* good has been proved ... But virtue is not yet, on that account, the whole and complete good ... For, in order to be that, *happiness* too is required in addition [to virtue], and this not merely in the partial eyes of a person who makes himself a purpose but even in the judgment of an impartial reason, which regards a person as such in the world as a purpose in itself. For, to be in need of happiness, and also worthy of it, but nonetheless not to partake of it is not at all consistent with the perfect volition of a rational being that also had all power, even if we only think such a being by way of experiment.[17]

If the concept of the highest good includes all that is good in respect of finite rational beings; and if happiness in proportion to virtue is a good; then happiness in proportion to virtue must be included in the concept of the highest good. Happiness in proportion to virtue is a good in respect of finite rational beings because our concept of good must extend to anything for which we can make ourselves worthy by striving to be virtuous. By striving to be virtuous, finite rational beings make themselves worthy of any end whose pursuit they cannot reject. This applies to our pursuit of happiness:

> the human being insofar as he belongs to the world of sense is a needy being, and to this extent his reason does indeed have a mandate from the side of sensibility which he cannot reject, to attend to its interest and to frame practical maxims also with a view to happiness in this life and, if possible, in a future life as well.[18]

---

16   *KpV*, 5: 124.
17   *KpV*, 5: 110.
18   *KpV*, 5: 61.

We must seek to tame our inclinations, by bringing them into a harmony called happiness, 'so that they do not themselves wear one another out',[19] which might hold back our striving for virtue. As happiness is an end that finite rational beings cannot dispense with, it is an end that finite rational beings can make themselves worthy of, by striving to be virtuous. As happiness is an end that finite rational beings can make themselves worthy of by striving to be virtuous, happiness in proportional to virtue belongs to the concept of the highest good.

If happiness is of some value, conditional on virtue, a concept of the good does not include all goodness if it does not include, besides virtue, a happiness for which finite rational beings can make themselves worthy. That is, happiness in proportion to virtue must also be included in the concept of the highest good. The two elements of the concept of the highest good are virtue, and happiness in proportion to virtue. Virtue is merely the unconditioned element of the concept of the highest good. In the concept of the highest good, happiness is proportional to virtue, while virtue is not proportional to anything. Virtue is 'the *supreme* good', while virtue combined with happiness proportional to virtue is 'the complete good'.[20]

Some objections have been raised to Kant's concept of the highest good that bear on Kant's argument from the highest good. While the aim in this chapter is to reject and not to defend Kant's argument from the highest good, it does not repeat or rely on these objections. So, it may be thought appropriate to say something about them.

In *Kantian Ethics and Socialism*, Harry van der Linden raises two main objections to Kant's concept of the highest good. Firstly, Kant is said to 'confus[e] the demands of morality with those of desire in holding that practical reason thinks of virtue and happiness as necessarily combined within the highest good'.[21] Van der Linden claims: 'the ground that is provided for this good is that it accords with the desires of the disinterested observer, i.e., the judgment of an impartial reason, and that an omnipotent rational being would bring it about'.[22] In van der Linden's view, this is not well-reasoned, both because the demands of desire are not demands of morality, and because 'it does not follow that the failure to realize this object of desire is a deontic failing', for '"ought implies can"'.[23] Secondly, van der Linden claims that a world in which 'everyone

---

19   *RGV*, 6: 58.

20   *KpV*, 5: 110.

21   Van der Linden 1988, p. 69.

22   Van der Linden 1988, p. 77.

23   Van der Linden 1988, p. 76.

will obey the moral law and will cooperate to promote universal happiness' is a 'morally (deontologically) perfect world',[24] regardless of whether everyone succeeds in realising universal happiness. As a moral duty to cooperate to promote universal happiness is already a duty under the moral law, Kant has no reason, according to van der Linden, to additionally include happiness proportional to virtue in the concept of the highest good. As Kant fails to ground his concept of the highest good, van der Linden concludes that 'there is no antinomy of practical reason, and, hence, no need to postulate God'.[25]

We may begin with a reply to the first objection.

First of all, the inclusion of happiness in proportion to virtue in the concept of the highest good is not, as van der Linden suggests, a confused concession to a 'desire' that is distinct from 'moral reason'.[26] Van der Linden offers no evidence for this. Van der Linden cites no passage in which Kant refers to 'the demands … of desire' or 'the desires of the disinterested observer'. In both of the two penultimate indented quotes from *Critique of Practical Reason* reproduced above, 'impartial reason'[27] is the basis of the judgment that the concept of the highest good includes happiness in proportion to virtue. Considerations of what finite rational beings make themselves worthy of, which belong to impartial reason, motivate the inclusion of happiness in proportion to virtue in Kant's concept of the highest good.

Provided that we think of ourselves, on account of doing x, as *worthy* of y, we have to judge a world in which we do x, but lack y, as less than completely good. To judge this world as less than completely good, we do not require, in addition, a *desire* to enjoy y, or a *desire* to enjoy y in the knowledge that we are worthy of y. Nor, to judge this world as less than completely good, need we posit a desire, on the part of another being, that we enjoy y. So, the inclusion of happiness in proportion to virtue in Kant's concept of the highest good is not a confused concession to a desire as distinct from moral reason. To be sure, what y, in this case, consists in – happiness – is an idea that an agent forms in virtue of having a faculty of desire that is affected by objects; and the content

---

24   Ibid.
25   Van der Linden 1988, p. 81. If there is no antinomy of practical reason, Kant cannot show that a belief in the existence of God is inseparably tied to the moral law by the need to think of virtue and happiness proportional to virtue as necessarily connected in the concept of the highest good. This would be fatal for the argument from the highest good (and bad news for Kant's ethics, insofar as the formulas of the categorical imperative all rely on a belief in the existence of God). But I do not find this way of objecting to Kant's argument from the highest good convincing, for the reasons given in reply.
26   Van der Linden 1988, p. 76.
27   *KpV*, 5: 124 and 110.

of an agent's happiness will vary with their desires. But to say that *what* we are worthy of depends on desire is not to imply that *that* the virtuous are worthy of it depends on a desire.

Further, van der Linden's claim that a failure to realise universal happiness is not a moral failing depends on a question-begging appeal to Kant's principle that 'ought implies can'. Kant's principle of 'ought implies can' must be interpreted in the light of Kant's doctrine of the primacy of pure practical reason. The doctrine of the primacy of pure practical reason says that if a proposition that speculative reason cannot either prove or disprove is inseparably tied to our practical moral interest, we are justified in believing it. If speculative reason can neither prove nor disprove that God exists, and a belief in the existence of God is inseparably tied to our practical interest, then, by the doctrine of the primacy of pure practical reason, we are justified in believing in the existence of God. This doctrine of the primacy of pure practical reason conditions Kant's principle of 'ought implies can', for it implies that we may only appeal to the principle of 'ought implies can' to conclude that we have no duty to *x after* considering any proposition that cannot be disproven and that is inseparably tied to our practical interest. The doctrine implies that we can only conclude that there is no duty to realise the highest good because the highest good *cannot* be realised *after* considering what we may justifiably believe God may cooperate with us in doing, or else complete. As such, it is presumptuous to use Kant's principle of 'ought implies can' to object to Kant's concept of the highest good on the grounds that we have no duty to realise the highest good because we finite rational beings alone cannot realise it. Insofar as van der Linden's objection rests on interpreting the principle of 'ought implies can' as it would have to be interpreted only if God was not a practical postulate, and this objection is aimed at a concept with which Kant argues for God as a practical postulate, the objection assumes what it is supposed to prove.

Turning to van der Linden's second objection, we find that it rests on a false inference. Kant can grant that the inclusion of happiness in proportion to virtue in the concept of the highest good does not impose on us a duty to do anything in respect of happiness beyond what the moral law already requires of us, namely, promote others' permissible ends. All that Kant need deny is the suggested implication that there is then no reason to include happiness in proportion to virtue in the concept of the highest good that we are to think of as possible. Kant can deny this suggested implication by replying that a world in which we are worthy of happiness, and lack happiness, is less than completely good. To promote others' permissible ends may be to do all that is in our power, in respect of others, to realise happiness in proportion to virtue. But, if we include happiness in proportion to virtue in the concept of the highest good, we may think of our promotion of others' permissible ends as potentially contributing to the possibility of this concept. This, for Kant, is a view of our efforts that we have an impartial reason to want to be able to take. Reason's search for 'the unconditioned totality of the *object* of pure practical reason'[28] is satisfied, while the moral law remains the sole determining ground of the will.

Having rejected van der Linden's objections to Kant's inclusion of happiness proportional to virtue in the concept of the highest good, we may consider the nature of their connection. Kant argues that the concept of the highest good is the concept of virtue as *necessarily* connected with happiness proportional to virtue. It is the concept of 'a necessary connection between morality and the happiness, proportionate thereto'.[29] To say that happiness proportional to virtue is thought of (in the concept of the highest good) as necessarily connected with virtue is to say that happiness proportional to virtue is thought of as coming about on account of how virtue comes about. Happiness proportional to virtue is thought to come about independently of anything that is unconnected to how virtue comes about. If happiness proportional to virtue were thought to come about on account of something unconnected to how virtue comes about, the proportionality of happiness to virtue would have to be thought of as contingent. But the thought of this proportionality as contingent cannot satisfy reason, if the unconditional value of a virtuous disposition is to be thought of (as befits its unconditional value) as the sole basis of the worthiness to be happy. The concept of the highest good is therefore not merely the concept of virtue and happiness proportional to virtue, but the concept of virtue and happiness proportional to virtue as necessarily connected.

2   The Argument from the Highest Good

The argument from the highest good is that it is necessary to postulate the existence of God in order to think of the concept of the highest good – virtue and happiness proportional to virtue as necessarily connected – as possible. Kant presents this argument as a response to what, in *Critique of Practical Reason*, Kant calls 'the antinomy of pure practical reason'.[30] The antinomy of pure practical reason is characterised as an 'antinomy in linking morality with happiness according to a universal law'.[31]

---

28   *KpV*, 5: 108.
29   *KpV*, 5: 124.
30   *KpV*, 5: 111.
31   *KpV*, 5: 115.

We have seen that the concept of the highest good has two elements, connected necessarily. Kant adds: 'two determinations *necessarily* linked in one concept must be connected as basis and consequence'.[32] This connection can either be analytic, or synthetic. It is not analytic, because there is no logical contradiction in thinking of an agent who is virtuous but not happy or happy but not virtuous. As the connection is not analytic, Kant concludes that it must be synthetic; that is, a connection 'according to the law of causality'.[33]

There are just two ways to think of virtue and happiness proportional to virtue as necessarily connected by a universal causal law. Either 'the striving for happiness produces a basis for a virtuous attitude', or 'a virtuous attitude necessarily produces happiness'.[34] An antinomy arises, for we are led to oscillate between the thought that one of these two propositions must be true (because the moral law, which Kant here takes as given, requires us to think of the concept of the highest good as possible); and that neither of them can be true, owing to the 'conflict between natural necessity and freedom in the causality of events in the world'.[35] One of two propositions must be true, although they both seem false.

The antinomy of pure practical reason is resolved, according to Kant, by arguing that the second proposition is false only conditionally:

> The first of the two propositions, that the striving for happiness produces a basis for a virtuous attitude, is *false absolutely*; but the second, that a virtuous attitude necessarily produces happiness, is false *not absolutely* but only insofar as this attitude is regarded as the form of causality in the world of sense, and hence only if I assume the existence in that world to be the only kind of existence of a rational being, and therefore is false only *conditionally*.[36]

Kant argues that the first proposition is false in the first book of *Critique of Practical Reason*. A virtuous attitude can be produced only by cultivating respect for the moral law, which is to say, only by taking up the moral law as the will's sole determining ground.[37] In determining itself by the moral law, the will gives no consideration to happiness. Accordingly, the ground of a virtuous attitude can-

---

32 *KpV*, 5: 111.
33 Ibid.
34 *KpV*, 5: 114.
35 Ibid.
36 Ibid.
37 *KpV*, 5: 32–3.

not be found in a will that gives consideration to happiness by striving for it. As the first proposition is false, this leaves only the second proposition, which is that a virtuous attitude necessarily produces happiness. Yet, viewed as 'the form of causality in the world of sense', a virtuous attitude does not necessarily produce happiness. It is not necessary, but contingent, in light of the limited nature of our knowledge and power, that, when we strive to be virtuous, by making the moral law our will's sole determining ground, we succeed in accomplishing any of our ends. If we fail to accomplish our ends, our actions may not produce happiness. Nor can we reshape nature to make the moral motivation of action a sufficient cause of its succeeding in producing happiness. As finite beings, we cannot rid ourselves of needs that rest on more than moral motivation for their satisfaction. The conditions for a moral disposition (the moral law is the sole ground of the will's determination) and the conditions for action to succeed in producing happiness, must remain permanently non-identical, and the former no guarantee of the latter. Hence, we cannot think of a virtuous attitude as necessarily producing happiness in 'the world of sense'.

To think of a virtuous attitude as necessarily producing happiness, we must think of a virtuous, happiness-producing attitude that is not in the world of sense. Our knowledge of causality, however, is restricted to the world of sense. As we cannot resolve the antinomy of pure practical reason by affirming the second of the above propositions unless we posit a causality related to the existence of a rational being that is not of the world of sense; and as we can have no knowledge of any causality that is not of the world of sense; we can only resolve the antinomy of pure practical reason with a practical postulate – that is, with a proposition that, although it cannot be proven, also cannot be disproven. We must resort to a practical postulate in order to think of the possibility of virtue and happiness proportional to virtue as necessarily connected in the concept of the highest good.

The first postulate that Kant introduces is not the postulate of the existence of God, but the postulate of 'the immortality of the soul'.[38] This is because the first, unconditional element of the concept of the highest good – virtue – is said to consist in a moral perfection of which 'no rational being in the world of sense is capable at any point of time in his existence'.[39] Virtue can therefore only be found in an infinite progression towards its perfection, which is practically possible for a finite rational being 'only on the presupposition of the immortality

---

38   The latter is introduced at *KpV*, 5: 122, the former at *KpV*, 5: 124.

39   *KpV*, 5: 122.

of the soul'.[40] While Kant adds that only an '*infinite*'[41] being can perceive our adequacy to the moral law in this infinite progression, Kant does not deduce the existence of God from this. Even if only an all-knowing being can regard our endless approximation to a perfect (or 'holy') will for such, it does not follow that this being must be a *perfect, moral* creator. To think of an all-knowing being who regards our endless approximation to a moral disposition for such, it is not necessary to think of the being who grants this equivalence as doing so from morality, because their nature is such that they cannot but act morally. Hence, it does not follow that, once we have postulated the immortality of the soul, we must also postulate the existence of *God*, just to postulate a being who can find in us the virtuous disposition to which we can only approximate in an infinite progression.

To be sure, only a being that is thought to be able to find in us a virtuous disposition can be thought to ensure that virtue and happiness in proportion to virtue are necessarily connected. We must think of a being as having a capacity to intuit a virtuous disposition in us if we are to think of them as containing the ground of a necessary connection between virtue, and happiness proportional to virtue. But while the postulation of a being with this capacity is a necessary condition of the postulation of God (a perfect moral creator), it is not a sufficient condition. The postulation of the existence of God involves three further steps of argument.

First, to think of happiness proportional to virtue as the necessary consequence of virtue, it is necessary to think of happiness proportional to virtue as linked with virtue by a universal causal law that could only be brought about by a being thought of as 'not ... dependent'[42] on nature, but nevertheless related to nature, as its cause. A being that was dependent on nature could not determine a universal causal law connecting happiness with virtue. In order to think of this being as related to nature, we must instead think of it as a creator of nature. So, to think of the possibility of the concept of the highest good, we must postulate a creator of nature.

Second, to exercise the power to create universal causal laws for the purpose of ensuring, to virtuous agents, a happiness proportional to virtue, is to exercise this power in accordance with the impartiality of morality. It is 'a causality conforming to the moral attitude'.[43]

---

40   Ibid.
41   *KpV*, 5: 123.
42   *KpV*, 5: 124.
43   *KpV*, 5: 125.

Third, if virtue and the happiness proportional to virtue are to be thought of as necessarily connected, then the fact that the power to create universal causal laws is used to ensure the happiness of virtuous agents must itself be thought of as a necessary fact about this causal power. This use is only thought of as a necessary fact about this causal power, however, if it is thought of as the use of a power by a creator who *necessarily* acts in accordance with morality. The thought of a creator who necessarily acts in accordance with morality is the thought of a perfect, moral creator, or God. To think of virtue and happiness proportional to virtue as necessarily connected in the concept of the highest good, we must postulate the existence of God. Only the thought of a being that necessarily exercises its power morally, and so necessarily exercises its power to apportion happiness to virtue, can be thought to contain the ground of a necessary connection between virtue, and happiness proportional to virtue.[44]

3   Wood's Version of the Argument from the Highest Good

Allen Wood draws attention[45] to a remark by Kant in *Lectures on Philosophical Theology* (1783–4) that serves to characterise the kind of argument that Kant offers in *Critique of Practical Reason* for why we should believe in the existence of God:

---

44   Van der Linden objects that 'in postulating God he [Kant – JF] assumes more than is strictly necessary to solve the antinomy. All we need to assume is that somehow nature can be brought into complete harmony with morality' (van der Linden 1988, p. 83). *If* 'we' view the concept of the highest good not as Kant presents it in *Critique of Practical Reason*, as linking two elements *necessarily*, but rather, with van der Linden, as 'a moral order of colegislators who enhance one another's ends', *then* no antinomy need arise. Perhaps all we need *then* believe, to believe in the possibility of this different concept of the highest good, is 'that nature will continue to be (to some degree) consonant' with this task (van der Linden 1988, p. 76). For this, it may suffice to view this continuity in nature as based in nothing more than 'the contingent character of nature' (van der Linden 1988, p. 82). But as a claim about what *Kant* assumed unnecessarily 'to solve the antinomy', the objection is misplaced, since van der Linden asserts that on his own concept of the highest good (virtue plus promotion of happiness), 'the antinomy dissolves' (1988, p. 69). That van der Linden's concept of the highest good produces no antinomy is not evidence that Kant assumed too much to resolve the antinomy arising from Kant's concept of the highest good (and, for the reasons given in replies above, van der Linden's objections to Kant's concept of the highest good are not convincing).

45   Wood 1970, pp. 28–9.

Our moral faith is a practical postulate, in that anyone who denies it is brought *ad absurdum practicum*. An *absurdum logicum* is an absurdity in judgments; but there is an *absurdum practicum* when it is shown that anyone who denies this or that would have to be a scoundrel. And this is the case with moral faith.[46]

The fundamental characteristic of an *absurdum practicum* argument is that, once a deep moral commitment is taken as given, it is irrational for an agent not to hold a belief that is a presupposition of this moral commitment. Not to hold the belief is to put oneself at odds with the deep moral commitment. The argument from the highest good is an *absurdum practicum* argument, if, once the moral law is taken as given, it is irrational for an agent not to believe in the existence of God, as a belief in God's existence is a presupposition of their deep moral commitment to the moral law, given that the thought of the concept of the highest good as possible is inseparably attached to the moral law.

On the interpretation offered in sections 1–2, the argument from the highest good is a type of *absurdum practicum* argument. For the purposes of the argument from the highest good, Kant takes the moral law as given. Kant then argues that a belief in the existence of God is a presupposition of our acknowledgment of the moral law, for the moral law requires us to think of the concept of the highest good as possible, and the only way to resolve the antinomy that this leads us into is to postulate the existence of God. The upshot of this argument, Kant says, is that 'it is morally necessary to assume the existence of God'.[47]

To reject Kant's argument from the highest good, it is not necessary to reject either the notion of an antinomy, or the notion of an *absurdum practicum* argument. It is sufficient to show that Kant's argument from the highest good fails as an *absurdum practicum* argument. This is what we shall argue. In this section, Wood's defence of the *absurdum practicum* argument from the highest good is shown to fail. In the following section, the interpretation of Kant's argument from the highest good outlined above (in sections 1–2) is represented in the form of an *absurdum practicum* argument, and it, too, is shown to fail.

We shall make some stipulations. Let us say that a belief is a *presupposition* of the pursuit of an end if it is irrational for its pursuer to deny it. A belief shall be said to *commit* an agent who has the belief to an appropriate course of action. We will also call conditions that are beyond an agent's power to bring about

---

46   Kant 1830, p. 160; Kant 1978, pp. 122–3.
47   *KpV*, 5: 125.

external conditions, in respect of that agent. With these stipulations, we may represent Wood's version[48] of Kant's argument from the highest good as follows:

(1) There is a valid moral law
(2) If the moral law is valid, I am bound to pursue the highest good as an end
(3) If I pursue an end, I presuppose that it is possible of attainment
(4) If the possibility of attaining an end rests on external conditions, then, by pursuing it, I presuppose that these conditions exist
(5) For the highest good to be possible of attainment, either the striving for happiness must produce a virtuous attitude, or a virtuous attitude must produce happiness
(6) It is impossible for the striving for happiness to produce a virtuous attitude
(7) It is possible for a virtuous attitude to produce happiness only if there is a God and a future life
(8) Therefore, if I deny that there is a God or a future life, I am committed not to pursue the highest good
(9) If I am committed not to pursue the highest good, I presuppose that the moral law is not valid
(10) If I deny the validity of the moral law, I am a scoundrel
(11) Therefore, I must either not deny that there is a God and a future life, or be a scoundrel
(12) As a moral agent, it is abhorrent for me to think of myself as a scoundrel
(13) Therefore, I must not deny that there is a God and a future life
(14) There is a difference between not denying something, and positively believing it
(15) However, I must not merely pursue the highest good, but do all in my power to pursue it
(16) If the possibility of attaining an end that I must do all in my power to pursue rests on external conditions, it is more rational to hold that they obtain than merely not to deny their possibility
(17) Therefore, it is more rational for me to believe in God and a future life than merely not to deny their possibility
(18) Therefore, I should believe in God and a future life

Wood's version of the argument from the highest good is an *absurdum practicum* argument. It takes the moral law as given, and as requiring us to pursue the highest good. It also has two parts: (1)–(13) form one part of the argument,

---

48 Compare Wood 1970, pp. 20–32.

and (14)–(18) the other. If the conclusion of the first part is that we may not deny the existence of God, because 'it has been the "denial" of the existence of God and a future life which has led us to an *absurdum practicum*', the conclusion at the end of the second part is that we may 'exclude religious "doubt" as well as "denial"'.[49] What is rationally commanded, by the end of the argument, is a 'positive *belief* in God and immortality'.[50] The practical absurdity of a morally committed agent having to regard itself as a scoundrel (an absurdity that is to motivate merely a refusal to deny a future life and the existence of God) is complemented by the practical absurdity of a morally committed agent having to regard itself as awkwardly aloof from its vital concern (an absurdity that is to motivate a positive belief in a future life and the existence of God).

One problem with Wood's version of the argument from the highest good is that its division into two parts is not sustainable, owing to what (4) implies. Wood treats (4) as a part of the argument in remarking:

> The importance of the relation between belief and action for Kant is that it is a *rational* relation. Kant's point is that a finite rational being acting purposively in a situation always "presupposes," "implies," or "commits himself to" certain beliefs about his situation which form the "ground for the employment of means" to the ends which he has set himself.[51]

The choice of an action as a means to an end is a rational choice, if it is chosen for possessing all necessary and some sufficient qualities for bringing the end about in the 'situation' in which the agent finds itself. The elements of this situation that are beyond the agent's power to bring about, but which enable their chosen action to serve as a means to their end, are thereby presupposed to exist. If I ask someone a question to find out the time, I presuppose that my addressee exists. I am acting irrationally if I ask my question while having no opinion as to whether anyone is there to answer, because I have never given the matter any thought.

Wood's division of Kant's *absurdum practicum* argument into two parts is not sustainable, because (4) (read together with the other steps of argument) implies a stronger claim than that stated in (8). It is only because (8), as stated above, is much weaker than what (4) supports, that a positive belief in God and a future life is not seen to be required as soon as an agent refuses to think of itself as a scoundrel. (8) says: therefore, if I deny that there is a God or a future

---

49   Wood 1970, p. 30.
50   Ibid.
51   Wood 1970, p. 20.

life, I am committed not to pursue the highest good. (8) would only draw out all the implications of the previous steps of argument if (4) were altered to: if the possibility of attaining an end rests on external conditions, then, by pursuing it, I presuppose that these conditions *are possible*. Yet (4) states: if the possibility of attaining an end rests on external conditions, then, by pursuing it, I presuppose that these conditions *exist*.

(4), *as presently stated*, is true. An agent who pursues an end whose attainment rests on external conditions is acting irrationally if they have no opinion as to whether these external conditions exist, because they have never given the matter any thought. Because (4), as presently stated, is true, we draw out all its implications (read together with the other steps of argument) only once we amend (8) to: therefore, *unless I believe in the existence of God and in a future life*, I am committed not to pursue the highest good. Once (8) is amended in this way, a positive belief in God and a future life is reached at (13). Only one practical absurdity is then relevant for Wood's version of the argument: the absurdity of a morally committed agent having to regard itself as a scoundrel, motivating a belief in the existence of God.

Now to the main objection, which concerns (2): if the moral law is valid, I am bound to pursue the highest good as an end. Wood treats (2) as part of the argument from the highest good in saying:

> Kant's philosophical thought about religion is founded on the relation between obedience to the moral law and the adoption of the highest good as an end. I cannot deny or seriously doubt that this object can be conceived possible without committing myself not to obey the moral law. Hence it is of crucial importance to Kant's *absurdum practicum* argument, and to his religious thought as a whole, that the highest good be viewed as an *end* to which any moral agent commits himself in obeying the moral law.[52]

(2) is a crucial step of Wood's version of the argument, due to what it implies taken together with (3), which Wood affirms in saying: '[w]e might say ... that a person who pursued an end E but did not believe E was possible of attainment was acting "irrationally", involving himself in a "practical contradiction" of some sort'.[53] Taken together, (2) and (3) imply that, by pursuing the highest good as an end, a moral agent presupposes that the highest good is possible of

---

52   Wood 1970, p. 95.
53   Wood 1970, p. 22.

attainment. The main objection to Wood's version of the argument from the highest good is that a moral agent is *not* committed to pursue 'the highest good … as an *end*'. Rather, we are committed to strive to be virtuous, as the moral law commands; and rationally required to *view* our striving for virtue, including our attempts to promote others' permissible ends, as potentially contributing to the possibility of the concept of the highest good.

Lewis White Beck remarks:

> For suppose I do all in my power – which is all any moral decree can demand of me – to promote the highest good, what am I to do? Simply act out of respect for the law, which I already knew. I can do absolutely nothing else toward apportioning happiness in accordance with desert – that is the task of a moral governor of the universe, not of a laborer in the vineyard. It is not *my* task[54]

The highest good is not an end to be pursued by us finite rational agents, because it is not something that we can intend to bring about. Intending to bring it about would require us to know something that we cannot know. To apportion happiness to virtue, it would be necessary to have knowledge of others' virtuous characters, as distinct from mere knowledge of the permissible or obligatory status of the end that they pursue in a given action. While we may make more or less accurate judgments about the latter, Kant insists that no agent can be sure of another's moral character.[55] As Kant remarks in *Religion*: a 'human judge cannot see through the inside of other human beings'.[56]

The thought of the concept of the highest good as possible satisfies impartial reason, and allows us to view our striving for virtue, including our striving to promote others' permissible ends, as potentially contributing to its possibility. It does not, however, constrain us to pursue any end that we were not already required to pursue. Wood's version of the argument from the highest good does not show how an end that a finite moral agent is truly committed to presupposes a belief in the existence of God.

On Wood's version of the argument, the highest good is presented as an end that a moral agent is to pursue. Relatedly, on Wood's version of the argument, we postulate the existence of God in order to postulate an agency that cooperates with our efforts in pursuing the highest good as an end. Wood says we 'must postulate in nature, then, a cooperating agency with the ability to give efficacy

---

54   Beck 1960, pp. 244–5; compare van der Linden 1988, p. 77.
55   *RGV*, 6: 20.
56   *RGV*, 6: 95.

to our moral efforts in a systematic way, a way not subject to human limitations'.[57] Or again: 'if we are to conceive the possibility of our final moral end, we must postulate the purposive cooperation of nature in aiding and giving efficacy to our moral intentions'.[58] Having rejected Wood's version of the argument on account of its claim that a finite rational agent is committed to pursue the highest good as an end, we may also question what it says about this 'cooperating agency'.

To put this into relief, imagine (putting aside Kant's view of its impossibility for humans, and of the limits to finite agents' virtue) a world in which hypothetical finite rational agents *could* know others' virtuous characters, and who pursued the highest good as an end, by striving for virtue and apportioning happiness to virtue. In such a world, the existence of God might (for all our objections to Wood's version of the argument show) be postulated to think of the end of the highest good as possible. Even if its hypothetical agents strain all their powers in pursuit of the highest good, they may not succeed. They may postulate the existence of God as a cooperating agency in realising the highest good as an end. They are committed to pursue the highest good as an end; and they postulate a cooperating agency, to be able to think of the intended outcome of their strivings as realised. The cooperation occurs in the hypothetical world of these agents. It is not thought to extend beyond it. The happiness that is proportional to virtue and necessarily connected to it in these hypothetical agents' concept of the highest good is located exclusively in the world in which they live.

Now recall the main objection to Wood's version of the argument from the highest good. The main objection is directed at (2), which says that a moral agent is bound to pursue the highest good as an end. If we reject the idea that a moral agent is bound to pursue the highest good as an end, then no causal agency postulated by a moral agent to think of the concept of the highest good as possible is postulated to think of the concept of the highest good as possible in this world alone. Nor, therefore, will an agency be postulated to think of the possibility of a concept of the highest good in which the happiness that is proportional to virtue is defined exclusively with reference to this world.

If, as Kant claims, we cannot know what we would have to know ('the inside of other human beings'), to pursue the highest good as an end, the pursuit of the highest good can never be an end of ours in this world. No agency, not even

57   Wood 1970, p. 115.
58   Wood 1970, p. 134.

an agency beyond this world of sense, can be thought to be 'cooperating' with us in respect of pursuing the highest good as an end. No agency can be thought to cooperate with us to achieve something we cannot know how to achieve. Any necessary connection between the elements of the highest good must be a matter for a future life, for which this one is just a preparation. The necessary connection between virtue and happiness proportional to virtue in Kant's concept of the highest good is not thought of as possible on account of the existence of an intelligent cause of *this* world only, *as distinct from a future life.* As Wood says: 'a systematic connection between worthiness and happiness ... must be postulated as existing – in part, at least – in the sensible world'.[59] If the connection between worthiness and happiness exists *only in part* in this world, it cannot exist just on account of nature in this world 'aiding and giving efficacy to our moral intentions'.[60]

This brings us to the happiness that is thought of as necessarily connected to virtue in Kant's concept of the highest good. Kant says in *Lectures on Philosophical Theology*:

> all earthly happiness is far outweighed by the thought that as morally good men we have made ourselves worthy of an uninterrupted future happiness. Of course, this inner pleasure in our own person can never compensate for the loss of an externally happy state. But it can still uplift us even in the most troubled life when it is combined with its future prospects.[61]

For Kant, two types of joy taken together outweigh (i) the joy of an 'externally happy state', even if they do not entirely compensate for its absence. They are: (ii) the joy of bettering one's virtuous disposition, and so of knowing that one is not unworthy of happiness; and (iii) the joy of anticipating an 'uninterrupted' future life in which one will have made oneself not unworthy of happiness. Together, (ii)–(iii) can 'uplift us' in this life even if we lack happy states that depend on external empirical conditions, and so lack (i). The necessary connection of virtue and happiness exists *only in part* in this world, therefore. If happiness in this world includes (i)–(iii), the happiness that is proportional to virtue, and that is to be thought of as necessarily connected with virtue in the concept of the highest good, must extend to happiness in a future life.

---

59 Wood 1970, p. 131.
60 Wood 1970, p. 134.
61 Kant 1830, p. 172; Kant 1978, p. 130.

By implication, we cannot think of happiness proportional to virtue as necessarily connected to virtue in Kant's concept of the highest good *purely* on account of any assurance that nature will give effect to our moral intentions in this world. To be sure, Kant remarks in *Critique of Practical Reason* that a necessary connection between a virtuous disposition and happiness can be thought of as possible 'by means of an intelligible originator of nature'.[62] Wood seems to interpret Kant to say that this connection is to be thought of as possible on account of the assurance, given by the thought of an 'intelligible originator of nature', that nature will give effect to our moral intentions. But there is an alternative way to interpret this phrase. We may postulate an 'intelligible originator of nature' to think of virtue and happiness in proportion to virtue as necessarily connected in the concept of the highest good, because an 'intelligible originator of nature' creates a sensible world with finite rational beings who are to strive to be virtuous, and who are to obtain virtue and happiness proportional to virtue only in a future life. This interpretation is given plausibility if, as Woods says, for Kant, 'the temporal progression of man within this life is to be thought of as "within" this eternal progression'.[63]

Virtue and happiness proportional to virtue are necessarily connected in Kant's concept of the highest good on account of the thought of a perfect moral creator who creates this world of sense as a preparation for a future life beyond it. The 'intelligible originator of nature' is the creator of a nature that contains beings who, by striving for virtue, bring about a condition for the concept of the highest good to be thought of as possible in reference to a future life. It is only if this world of sense is thought to have an intelligible originator that it can be thought of as part of an infinite progression that extends beyond this world.

This suggestion relates the thought of the possibility of virtue and happiness proportional to virtue as necessarily connected to the thought of a progression in which, according to Kant, *virtue is possible*. For Kant, it is *only* in a progression including a future life that virtue is possible. As Wood notes, for Kant 'the attainment of holiness of will is impossible for finite rational beings as we know them in the world of sense'.[64] Virtue, Kant comments, is a moral perfection that 'no rational being in the world of sense is capable at any point of time in his existence'.[65] Only in a world beyond our world of sense can virtue be identified in our infinite progression towards virtue. If so, the thought of the concept of

---

62   *KpV*, 5: 115.
63   Wood 1970, p. 123.
64   Wood 1970, p. 133.
65   *KpV*, 5: 122.

the highest good as possible must be located in a progression that includes a future life, on account of a creator of nature who creates nature as part of an infinite progression that extends beyond it.

4   The Objection from Moral Happiness

Any version of the argument from the highest good that rests on the premise that a moral agent is bound to pursue the highest good (as Kant conceives it) as an *end*, is subject to a fatal objection. A moral agent is not bound to pursue the highest good as an end. This need not be fatal for the argument from the highest good, however. The argument from the highest good need not rest on the premise that a moral agent pursues the highest good as an end. A version of the argument may instead appeal to the premise that we must think of Kant's concept of the highest good as possible (together with our moral commitment to strive to be virtuous). To undermine the argument from the highest good, we need to reject this alternative *absurdum practicum* argument for a belief in the existence of God.

In this section, we offer an objection to this version of the argument called the *objection from moral happiness*. Taking Kant's concept of the highest good as the concept of the greatest virtue necessarily connected with the greatest happiness,[66] the objection from moral happiness can be stated as follows:

> The *objection from moral happiness*: it is self-contradictory to postulate the existence of God to think of the concept of the highest good as possible. For if we postulate the existence of God to think of the concept of the highest good as possible, we deprive ourselves of moral happiness, which is part of happiness.

The objection from moral happiness is that, if we postulate the existence of God to think of the concept of the highest good as possible, the concept of the highest good cannot be thought as possible, for the thought of its possibility then rests on the thought of a causality that produces our agency, and this precludes moral happiness, which is part of the concept of the highest good. Representing the features of Kant's *absurdum practicum* argument from the highest good by (1)–(7), the objection from moral happiness is represented by (8)–(16):

---

66   *KpV*, 5: 129.

(1)   There is a moral law

(2)   If there is a moral law, I am bound to strive to be virtuous

(3)   If there is a moral law, I must be able to think of the concept of the highest good (the greatest virtue and the greatest happiness as necessarily connected) as possible

(4)   I can think of the concept of the highest good as possible only if I believe in the existence of God

(5)   Therefore, I must believe in the existence of God, or be a scoundrel

(6)   As a moral agent, it is abhorrent for me to think of myself as a scoundrel

(7)   Therefore, I must believe in the existence of God

(8)   The greatest happiness includes moral happiness (the awareness of being not unworthy of happiness)

(9)   Moral happiness involves an awareness of needing nothing in respect of the will's determination

(10) If, on account of (1)–(6), I must believe in the existence of God, then I am aware of needing something in respect of the will's determination (God as its producing cause)

(11) Therefore, if I must believe in the existence of God, I cannot enjoy moral happiness

(12) Therefore, if I must believe in the existence of God, I cannot enjoy the greatest happiness

(13) Therefore, if I must believe in the existence of God, I cannot think of the concept of the highest good as possible

(14) Therefore, if I must believe in the existence of God, I presuppose that there is no moral law

(15) Therefore, the moral law cannot give me a reason to believe in the existence of God

(16) As the condition under which the moral law is valid (a belief in the existence of God, supposedly allowing us to think of the concept of the highest good as possible) is a condition under which it is not valid, the moral law is not valid

We may begin by arguing for (8): the greatest happiness includes moral happiness, that is, the awareness of being not unworthy of happiness. To say that the greatest happiness includes moral happiness is not, of course, to say that moral happiness is the whole of happiness. That Kant rejects the claim that moral happiness is the whole of happiness – as in his criticism of the Stoics[67] –

---

67   *KpV*, 5: 111–12, 115–18.

does not show that Kant rejects (8). The objection from moral happiness does not require us to view moral happiness as more than a part of happiness. The concept of the highest good is the concept of a whole that includes 'the greatest happiness'.[68] The 'greatest happiness' is not lacking in even a part of happiness. It cannot lack moral happiness, if moral happiness is even just a part of happiness. It is an objection to postulating the existence of God to think of the concept of the highest good as possible, if a moral agent who postulates the existence of God is deprived of moral happiness.

Let us present some evidence for holding that Kant accepts (8).

In *Lectures on Philosophical Theology*, Kant remarks that 'the *consciousness of one's own worth* or self-contentment belongs to a perfect happiness'.[69] Kant adds: 'in fact all earthly happiness is far outweighed by the thought that as morally good men we have made ourselves worthy of an uninterrupted future happiness'.[70] The first of these remarks is a clear statement of the idea that moral happiness belongs to the greatest happiness. The second remark implies that moral happiness is a significant part of happiness as a whole. X can outweigh Y only if X and Y are qualitatively homogeneous. To say that the thought of having made oneself worthy of happiness outweighs earthly happiness is to imply that the thought of having made oneself worthy of happiness is a (significant) part of happiness.

In *Critique of Practical Reason*, Kant comments that 'a righteous person cannot think himself happy if he is not first conscious of his righteousness'.[71] It is a condition of happiness, on the part of a righteous person, that this person is aware of acting righteously. Kant also says that 'the possibility of the highest good' is something that 'reason marks out for all rational beings as the goal of all their moral wishes'.[72] As moral happiness is something that we can morally wish for, it seems that moral happiness must be thought of as included in the concept of the highest good.

Finally, in *Religion*, Kant refers to 'the satisfaction and moral happiness which consists in the consciousness of his progress in the good'.[73] Kant adds that this provides 'a glimpse into an *immense* but wished-for and happy future'.[74]

---

68   *KpV*, 5: 129.
69   Kant 1830, p. 171; Kant 1978, p. 129.
70   Kant 1830, p. 172; Kant 1978, p. 130.
71   *KpV*, 5: 116.
72   *KpV*, 5: 115.
73   *RGV*, 6: 75.
74   *RGV*, 6: 69.

Besides this direct evidence, it is consistent with Kant's concept of happiness that it should include moral happiness. Happiness, according to Kant, requires an arrangement of satisfactions into a harmonious whole. Kant remarks in *Religion*:

> Natural inclinations, *considered in themselves*, are good, i.e., irreprehensible; and not only is it futile, but it would also be harmful and censurable, to want to eradicate them. Rather, one must only tame them, so that they do not themselves wear one another out but instead can be brought to harmony in a whole called happiness. The reason, however, that accomplishes this is called *prudence*.[75]

It does not follow from Kant's description of the arranging of satisfactions into a harmonious whole as an activity of 'prudence' that happiness cannot include moral happiness, but can only consist in the satisfaction of natural inclinations. Van der Linden claims that 'Kant's idea of happiness as a harmony of ends is restricted to the latter kind of happiness, as is clear from his claim that the pursuit of happiness is a mere prudential task'.[76] We may distinguish (i) the task of assessing potential satisfactions by the criterion of whether they can be integrated into a whole, and (ii) the nature of the satisfactions that belong to this whole. Just because the task of integration is non-moral, it does not follow that the nature of what is integrated is non-moral.

The satisfaction of natural inclinations belongs to 'fortune ... in the physical state of life';[77] to physical happiness as distinct from moral happiness. But if happiness requires a 'harmony' between satisfactions, then that is no reason not to include moral happiness in the concept of happiness. Indeed, if, as Kant says, a righteous agent cannot think of themselves as happy unless they are aware of the righteousness of their conduct, moral agents will never enjoy the harmony of happiness without moral happiness. The beings whose happiness is relevant, in the context of an *absurdum practicum* argument, are rational agents, who acknowledge the moral law. As agents who acknowledge the moral law cannot achieve a harmonious whole of satisfactions without moral happiness, moral happiness must be thought of as included in the idea of the greatest happiness that belongs to the concept of the highest good.

Indeed, Kant's *Critique of Practical Reason* underscores the importance of moral happiness in its remark, in respect of the 'feeling of satisfaction with

---

75   *RGV*, 6: 58.
76   Van der Linden 1988, p. 71.
77   *KpV*, 5: 116.

oneself' that arises from 'repeated performance in conformity with' the moral law as its 'determining basis': 'to establish and cultivate this feeling, which – properly – alone deserves to be called moral feeling, itself belongs to duty'.[78] To be sure, an agent acts in a moral spirit by making respect for the moral law into the sole determining basis of their will. An agent does not act in a moral spirit if their motivation is to feel good about themselves as a moral agent. But moral happiness is a concomitant of acting morally. Insofar as an increase in the significance of moral happiness within an agent's happiness as a whole is a foreseeable result of acting morally, an agent can have a duty to strengthen the feeling that comprises their moral happiness.

To be sure, moral happiness is not the whole of happiness. On the one hand, Kant explicitly says in the above passage in *Religion* that the satisfaction of natural inclinations can belong to happiness, if their satisfaction is 'brought to harmony in a whole'.[79] On the other hand, it is of systematic importance that moral happiness is not the whole of happiness. There is an antinomy of pure practical reason only if we cannot find a necessary connection in the world of sense between virtue, and happiness proportional to virtue. This is a connection that we are not unable to find, from the side of happiness, if happiness is reduced moral happiness. For moral happiness, as an awareness of being not unworthy of happiness, is an immediate consequence of virtue. To resolve the antinomy of pure practical reason, Kant must show that it is not unconditionally false that 'virtue produces happiness as something distinct from the consciousness of virtue, as a cause produces an effect'.[80] But none of this counts against the present claim, which is that the greatest happiness includes moral happiness. The claim that the greatest happiness includes moral happiness is consistent with the view that happiness as a whole is 'something distinct from the consciousness of virtue', and consistent with Kant's account of the antinomy of pure practical reason.

Although there is one remark in *Critique of Practical Reason* that appears to contradict the claim that moral happiness is a part of happiness, this remark can be interpreted consistently with the above evidence. At one point, Kant remarks of moral happiness that 'this enjoyment cannot be called happiness, because it does not depend on the positive participation of a feeling'.[81] Kant does not explain the significance of this lack of positive participation of a feeling, however. The enjoyment provided by the awareness that the determination

---

78   *KpV*, 5: 38.
79   *RGV*, 6: 58.
80   *KpV*, 5: 111.
81   *KpV*, 5: 118.

of the will is independent of inclination is not part of 'fortune ... in the physical state of life',[82] but it is, as moral happiness, a part of happiness. Otherwise, Kant would have contradicted himself in the previous paragraph in claiming that there is a 'happiness that must necessarily accompany the consciousness of virtue'.[83] Kant's remark can be reconciled with the evidence presented above by saying: an enjoyment cannot be called *physical* happiness if it does not depend on the positive participation of an empirical feeling.

We now turn to (9), which says: moral happiness involves an awareness of needing nothing in respect of the will's determination. Kant remarks in *Critique of Practical Reason*:

> But do we not have a word that, without designating an enjoyment, as the word happiness does, indicates nonetheless a liking for one's existence, an analogue of the happiness that must necessarily accompany the consciousness of virtue? Yes! This word is *self-satisfaction*, which in its proper meaning always implies only a negative liking for one's existence, a liking in which one is conscious of needing nothing [*nichts zu bedürfen sich bewußt ist*]. Freedom, and the consciousness of it as a power to comply with the moral law with an overweighing attitude, is *independence from inclinations* – independence from them at least as motivating causes determining (even if not as *affecting*) our desire – and insofar as I am conscious of this freedom in complying with my moral maxims, it is the sole source of an unchangeable satisfaction linked necessarily with it and resting on no special feeling, and this satisfaction can be called intellectual.[84]

Self-satisfaction, Kant says, denotes a 'liking for one's existence' as an existence in which one is 'conscious of needing nothing'. Self-satisfaction is an 'analogue' of the happiness that accompanies the awareness of acting morally. In other words, while a finite rational being depends on nature for its existence, and cannot experience self-satisfaction, it can experience something analogous to self-satisfaction, on account of its practical reason. In thinking of itself as possibly acting solely out of respect for the moral law, a finite agent can experience moral happiness: an awareness that it thereby makes itself not unworthy of happiness. As moral happiness depends on moral conduct, in which an agent chooses their maxim independently of inclinations as motivating causes, moral

---

82   *KpV*, 5: 116.
83   *KpV*, 5: 117.
84   *KpV*, 5: 117. Compare Kant's use of '*Bedürfnis* (need)' in this passage with the cognate verb '*bedürfen* (to need)' in the next citations.

happiness involves an awareness of needing nothing in respect of the determination of the will. A moral agent is not unaware of their natural inclinations. But they have to be aware of the possibility that their adoption of their maxim does not reflect a determining influence on the part of anything external to their will, to enjoy moral happiness. Moral happiness is thus analogous to the kind of liking that a being with no needs can take in their existence just as such.

We may now turn to (10), which says: if, on account of (1)–(6) – that is, the steps of Kant's *absurdum practicum* argument from the highest good – I must believe in the existence of God, then I am aware of needing something in respect of the will's determination (God as its producing cause). We may begin by noting that Kant uses the terminology of 'need' on several occasions in *Critique of Practical Reason*. Kant refers to our assumption of the conditions of the possibility of the concept of the highest good as 'a need [*Bedürfnis*] of pure *practical* reason'.[85] Kant remarks more specifically:

> the highest good in the world is possible only insofar as one assumes a supreme cause of nature that has a causality conforming to the moral attitude. Now, a being capable of [performing] actions according to the presentation of laws is an *intelligence* (a rational being), and such a being's causality according to this presentation of laws is a *will* of this being. Therefore the supreme cause of nature, insofar as it must be presupposed for the highest good, is a being that is the cause of nature through *understanding* and *will* (and hence is its originator), i.e., **God** ... it is morally necessary to assume the existence of God.

> Now, it must be noted carefully here that this moral necessity is *subjective*, i.e., a need [*Bedürfnis*], and not *objective*, i.e., itself a duty; for there can be no duty whatever to assume the existence of a thing (because doing so concerns only the theoretical use of reason). I also do not mean by this that it is necessary to assume the existence of God *as a basis of all obligation as such* (for this basis rests, as has been proved sufficiently, solely on the autonomy of reason itself).[86]

According to Kant, our belief in the existence of God is a need because:
(a)   a belief in the existence of God is not presupposed by the concept of duty;
(b)   a moral agent is morally required to believe in the existence of God

---

85   *KpV*, 5: 142.
86   *KpV*, 5: 125; see also *KpV*, 5: 126.

According to Kant, a belief in the existence of God is not a belief that we require, to think of the concept of duty or the concept of the moral law. Kant remarks in *Religion*: 'the doctrine of virtue subsists through itself (even without the concept of God)'.[87] However, a belief in the existence of God is, for Kant, a moral requirement; this is what the argument from the highest good aims to show. A moral agent is required to believe in the existence of God, to conceive of the possibility of something that they are rationally required to conceive as possible; namely, the concept of the highest good.

Indeed, the 'causality' of God is central to why we can believe in God as the condition under which the two elements of the concept of the highest good can be thought of as *necessarily* connected. The thought of these elements as necessarily connected is the thought of their connection 'according to the law of causality'.[88] A belief in the existence of God can only allow us to think of these elements as necessarily connected, and so amount to a need of pure practical reason, insofar as it is a belief in an intelligent cause of nature.

A belief in an intelligent cause of nature is, however, a belief in a causality entirely independent of us that extends to our own creation. So, if a moral agent has a need to believe in the existence of God as an intelligent cause of nature, a moral agent has a need to believe in a causality that, in creating nature, causes its capacity for morality. But if a moral agent has a need to believe in such a causality, it cannot view itself as needing nothing in respect of the determination of its will. It must view itself as needing God as its producing cause, and hence view God as the determining basis of its action,

> for according to the principle of causality we can attribute to a being, assumed to have been produced, no other intrinsic basis for its actions except the one put into it by the producing cause; but then every action of this being would also be determined through this basis (and hence through an external cause), and hence this being itself would not be free[89]

If, in order to think of the possibility of the elements of Kant's concept of the highest good as necessarily connected, an agent must postulate an intelligent world cause, then an agent cannot think of their necessary connection without also thinking of its agency as produced by an external cause.

This leads to (11), which says: therefore, if I must believe in the existence of God, I cannot enjoy moral happiness. Moral happiness involves an awareness

---

87   *RGV*, 6: 183.
88   *KpV*, 5: 111.
89   *RGV*, 6: 142.

of needing nothing in respect of the will's determination. Unless I can believe that it is on my own account – on account of my will alone – that I am not unworthy of happiness, I cannot enjoy moral happiness. But if a belief in the existence of God is inseparably attached to the demands of practical reason, the demands of practical reason require me to believe in an independent causality that produces my being, and thereby determines my action. This belief in God as my producing cause bars me from the enjoyment of moral happiness.

So as not to be misunderstood, let us say what the objection from moral happiness is not. The objection from moral happiness is not that, if we postulate God, we will lack moral happiness because a belief in the existence of God will come to have a pathological effect on our choice of maxims. To be sure, Kant highlights the possibility for us to be led away from moral duty by inclinations that presuppose a belief in the existence of God.[90] But this is not the objection we are raising. The objection from moral happiness does not say that moral happiness is destroyed by a morally required belief in the existence of God because this belief must corrupt our action. The objection from moral happiness focuses on what a moral agent must believe to enjoy moral happiness, on a contradiction in its normative self-conception.

The moral law and the thought of the concept of the highest good as possible are treated by Kant as inseparable demands of reason, but they relate to the awareness involved in moral happiness in contradictory ways. Moral happiness rests on an awareness that one may act as a free cause, purely out of respect for the moral law. To enjoy moral happiness is to be aware of needing nothing, as far as the determination of one's will is concerned. As far as its will is concerned, a moral agent must assume that it determines itself independently of any external cause, to enjoy moral happiness. Yet this agent is also required to view the concept of the highest good as possible, for which they postulate God. In postulating God, an agent assumes the existence of a causality that is independent of itself and that, on account of producing the world, and thus of producing itself, determines its action. The view of itself as a free cause is a view of itself that a moral agent must have, to enjoy moral happiness, but that

---

90 In *Religion*, Kant says: '[b]y a pseudoservice (*cultus spurius*) is meant the persuasion that one is serving someone by actions that in fact undo the latter's intention. In a community, however, this occurs when something that has only the value of means, so as to satisfy the will of a superior, is passed off as, and put in the place of, what is to make us pleasing to him *directly*; as a result, then, the intention of the latter is foiled' (*RGV*, 6: 153). In *Critique of Practical Reason* Kant remarks that, if all action was done 'from fear' of God or 'from hope' of reward from God, 'a moral worth of actions ... would not exist at all. The conduct of human beings ... would thus be converted into a mere mechanism' (*KpV*, 5: 147).

it can no longer consistently hold, given the view of its agency as produced that is implied by its morally required belief in the existence of God.

As an agent who enjoys moral happiness must not only take itself to act out of respect for the moral law but *also* think of the concept of the highest good as possible, the moral happiness that it might otherwise enjoy (for all that the objection from moral happiness says) if the *only* rational requirement on it was to obey the moral law, is no longer available. But as a belief in the existence of God attached to our moral striving precludes moral happiness, it precludes a part of happiness. If a morally required belief in the existence of God precludes even just a part of happiness, it precludes the greatest happiness. But if a belief in the existence of God precludes the greatest happiness, it prevents us thinking of the concept of the highest good as possible. If a belief in the existence of God prevents us thinking of the concept of the highest good as possible, to hold this belief is to presuppose that there is no moral law. But this is just to say that the moral law, via the concept of the highest good, gives us no reason to believe in the existence of God. This destroys the argument from the highest good.

Indeed, as we cannot think of Kant's concept of the highest good as possible, the premises of Kant's argument from the highest good lead to the conclusion that the moral law is not valid. We cannot think of Kant's concept of the highest good as possible, because the condition for us to think of it as possible – a belief in the existence of God – bars us from thinking of it of possible. A belief in God's existence bars us from thinking of Kant's concept of the highest good as possible by precluding moral happiness. If we cannot think of Kant's concept of the highest good as possible, and if an agent cannot rationally strive to be virtuous unless they can think of this concept as possible, an agent cannot rationally strive to be virtuous. But if an agent cannot rationally strive to be virtuous, the moral law is not valid. The objection from moral happiness is therefore also an objection to the moral law.

5   The Physicoteleological Argument

The argument from the highest good is not the only argument that Kant offers for why we must believe in the existence of God. Kant also offers a physicoteleological argument. The physicoteleological argument is distinct from the argument from the highest good. The physicoteleological argument does not appeal to Kant's concept of the highest good. Nor is it an *absurdum practicum* argument. Rather, the physicoteleological argument appeals to a premise about our experience of organised beings in nature.

Kant writes in the 'Moral Catechism' in the *Metaphysics of Morals*:

> Teacher: But even if we are conscious of such a good and active will in us, by virtue of which we consider ourselves worthy (or at least not unworthy) of happiness, can we base on this a sure hope of sharing in happiness?
>
> Pupil: No, not on this alone. For it is not always within our power to provide ourselves with happiness, and the course of nature does not of itself conform with merit. Our good fortune in life (our welfare in general) depends, rather, on circumstances that are far from all being in man's control. So our happiness always remains a wish that cannot become a hope, unless some other power is added.
>
> Teacher: Has reason, in fact, any grounds of its own for assuming the existence of such a power, which apportions happiness in accordance with a man's merit or guilt, a power ordering the whole of nature and governing the world with supreme wisdom? that is, any grounds for believing in God?
>
> Pupil: Yes. For we see in the works of nature, which we can judge, a wisdom so widespread and profound that we can explain it to ourselves only by the inexpressibly great art of a creator of the world. And with regard to the moral order, which is the highest adornment of the world, we have reason to expect a no less wise regime, such that if we do not make ourselves *unworthy of happiness*, by violating our duty, we can also hope to *share* in happiness.[91]

The physicoteleological argument is *distinct* from the argument from the highest good, as can be seen from the fact that the final three clauses in this passage ('such that if we do not make ourselves *unworthy of happiness*, by violating our duty, we can also hope to *share* in happiness') play no role in its argument for why we must believe in the existence of God. Rather, the thought of the possibility of virtue combined with happiness proportional to virtue is suggested to *follow* from what we have 'reason' to believe about the existence of God. In the physicoteleological argument, the reason we are offered to believe in the existence of God proceeds from a claim about how we must view and explain 'works of nature'.

Indeed, the physicoteleological argument is *independent* of the argument from the highest good. It is possible to advance the physicoteleological argument, while rejecting the premise of the argument from the highest good that,

---

91   *MS*, 6: 482 (numbering omitted).

if there is a moral law, a moral agent must be able to think of the concept of the highest good as possible. To show that Kant offers us no good reason to believe in the existence of God, it is necessary to reject not just Kant's argument from the highest good, but also Kant's physicoteleological argument.

The physicoteleological argument can be represented as follows:
(1)   We must judge nature to contain organised beings[92]
(2)   We cannot explain the existence of organised beings in nature other than as caused by an intelligent world cause[93]
(3)   Everything in such beings must be taken to contribute to its fitness for purpose[94]
(4)   But if so, we must explain the entire system of nature by an intelligent world cause[95]
(5)   Reason seeks the unconditioned[96]
(6)   As reason seeks the unconditioned, we must suppose that the final purpose of the entire system of nature lies in a species with a supersensible ability, a capacity for morality[97]

---

92   '[O]rganized beings are the only beings in nature that, even when considered by themselves and apart from any relation to other things, must still be thought of as possible only as purposes of nature. It is these beings, therefore, which first give objective reality to the concept of a *purpose* that is a *purpose of nature* rather than a practical one, and which hence give natural science the basis for a teleology' (*KU*, 5: 375–6).

93   '[R]eason, even if it tries to gain insight only into the conditions attached to the production of a natural product, must always cognize not only the product's form but the form's necessity as well. And yet in that given form it cannot assume that necessity. Hence that very contingency of the thing's form is a basis for regarding the product as if it had come about through a causality that only reason can have. Such a causality would be the ability to act according to purposes (i.e., a will)' (*KU*, 5: 370).

94   '[T]he purpose [the idea] of nature has to be extended to everything that is in this product of nature' (*KU*, 5: 377).

95   '[T]his concept of a natural purpose leads us necessarily to the idea of all of nature as a system in terms of the rule of purposes' (*KU*, 5: 379).

96   'Reason is a power of principles, and its ultimate demand [for principles] aims at the unconditioned' (*KU*, 5: 401).

97   'Man is indeed the only being on earth that has understanding and hence an ability to set himself purposes of his own choice, and in this respect he holds the title of lord of nature; and if we regard nature as a teleological system, then it is man's vocation to be the ultimate purpose of nature, but always subject to a condition: he must have the understanding and the will to give both nature and himself reference to a purpose that can be independent of nature, self-sufficient, and a final purpose. The final purpose, however, we must not seek within nature at all' (*KU*, 5: 431). 'Man is the only natural being in whom we can nonetheless cognize, as part of his own constitution, a supersensible ability (*freedom*) ... Only in man, and even in him only as moral subject, do we find unconditioned legislation regard-

(7) If we must think of the entire system of nature, including this species, as caused by an intelligent world cause, we must think of this intelligence as the legislating supreme head in a moral realm of ends[98]

(8) Therefore, we must also think of this intelligence as perfect[99]

(9) The concept of a perfect, moral creator is the concept of God

(10) Therefore, we must believe in the existence of God

Represented in this form, the physicoteleological argument is consistent with what Kant denies in the following remark from *Critique of Practical Reason*:

> Since we can be acquainted with this world only in small part, still less can compare it with all possible worlds, we can indeed from its order, purposiveness, and magnitude infer a wise, benign, powerful, etc. originator of it, but not his omniscience, omnibenevolence, omnipotence, and so on ... Therefore on the empirical path (of physics) the concept of God remains always a concept – of the perfection of the primary being – not determined precisely [enough] to be considered adequate to the concept of a deity.[100]

Kant here denies that we can arrive at a sufficiently determinate concept of God so long as we conceive of an intelligent world cause *merely* in terms that can be inferred from how we must view the world of sense. However, there is

---

ing purposes. It is this legislation, therefore, which alone enables man to be a final purpose to which all of nature is teleologically subordinated' (*KU*, 5: 435–6).

98 '[I]t is only as a moral being that we acknowledge man to be the purpose of creation ... we now have *a principle* that allows us to conceive of the nature and properties of this first cause ... We shall have to think of this being not merely as an intelligence and as legislating to nature, but also as the legislating supreme head in a moral realm of ends' (*KU*, 5: 444). I have amended the translation of '*Oberhaupt*' from 'sovereign' to 'supreme head'; and of '*Reich der Zwecke*' from 'kingdom of purposes' to 'realm of ends'.

99 'In reference to the *highest good*–possible solely under the reign of this being – namely, the existence of rational beings under moral laws, we shall think of this original being as *omniscient*, so that even our inmost attitudes (in which the proper moral value of the acts of rational world beings consists) will not be hidden from it. We shall think of it as *omnipotent*, so that it can make all of nature accord with that highest purpose. We shall think of it as *omnibenevolent* as well as *just*, because these two properties (which together constitute *wisdom*) are the conditions under which a supreme cause of the world can be the cause of the world [taken] as the highest good under moral laws. And we shall similarly have to think of this being as having all the remaining transcendental properties (for goodness and justice are moral properties), such as *eternity*, *omnipresence*, etc., which [achieving] such a final purpose presupposes' (*KU*, 5: 444). Kant uses 'highest good' here in the sense of 'supreme good' (see *KpV*, 5: 110).

100 *KpV*, 5: 139, amending '*Reich der Zwecke*' from 'kingdom of purposes' to 'realm of ends'.

no inconsistency in denying this, and in offering an argument for why we must assume that a world that we take to be caused by an intelligent world cause *and* to include *moral* agents, is created by a perfect moral creator, or God. As Kant puts it in *Critique of Judgment*:

> it is only as a moral being that we acknowledge man to be the purpose of creation ... we now have *a principle* that allows us to conceive of the nature and properties of this first cause, i.e., the supreme basis of the realm of ends [*Reich der Zwecke*], and hence allows us to give determination to the concept of this cause. Physical teleology was unable to do this; all it could do was to give rise to concepts of this supreme basis that were indeterminate and on that very account were inadequate for both theoretical and practical use.[101]

'Physical teleology' alone does not give us a reason to believe in the existence of a perfect moral creator, Kant suggests, for it can only require us to assume that a system of nature is explained by an intelligent world cause of some kind. It can only justify premises (1)–(4) of the physicoteleological argument. These premises can contribute to supporting an argument for why we must believe in the existence of God if they are combined with further premises about what we must assume about an intelligent world cause once we are required to view the world it causes as containing *moral* agents.

The main objection to Kant's physicoteleological argument concerns premise (2). (2) says: we cannot explain the existence of organised beings in nature other than as caused by an intelligent world cause. We object to (2) by arguing that any 'order' or 'purposiveness' that we detect in nature does *not* require us to 'infer a wise, benign, powerful, etc. originator'. It is sufficient to reject (2), to reject the physicoteleological argument. For without this premise, it will not be possible to argue that a world that includes moral agents must be thought by us as created by a perfect moral creator. If we are not required to think of the world as caused by an intelligent cause to explain the existence of organised beings in nature, then we cannot be required to think of this intelligent world cause in any of the more determinate terms with which we would need to think of it, to think of it as God.

Before presenting this objection, we note a distinction drawn by Beck between two uses of the term 'hypothesis' in Kant:

---

101   *KU*, 5: 444.

Kant likewise discriminates between hypothesis and postulate. Given some X, whether merely actual or necessary, Y is postulated if Y is known a priori to be the only condition under which X is known to be even possible; or Y is hypothesized if it is merely assumed as an explanation for X. Sometimes Kant writes as if the difference lies in the nature of the purposes involved in the explanation of X. If X is necessary and Y is a priori essential to it, then Y is postulated; if knowledge of X is an arbitrary (theoretical) purpose, Y is hypothesized, even though it is necessary to it. This is Kant's meaning in saying that we must postulate, e.g., the existence of God because morality (the "X" of our schema) is necessary and God is necessary to it, while the existence of God is only hypothesized in natural theology or speculative metaphysics – not because the concept is any less essential there but because the purpose is arbitrary.[102]

Beck distinguishes between two uses of the term 'hypothesis' in Kant, which we shall call a revisable hypothesis, and a hypothesis for a theoretical purpose. The difference between a revisable hypothesis and a postulate is that acceptance of a revisable hypothesis does not presuppose a belief that it is impossible for us to discover a different empirical explanation, independent of the factors cited in the revisable hypothesis. To accept a revisable hypothesis that Y explains X does not presuppose a belief that it is impossible to find a Y-independent explanation of X. There is no contradiction between accepting a revisable hypothesis, and believing that new facts, requiring us to reject our assessment of the factors it cites as causes, may come to light. Insofar as a postulate contrasts with a revisable hypothesis, to postulate Y on the basis of X is to hold that it is impossible for us to think of X in the absence of Y. It is self-contradictory to assert that Y is a postulate of X, and to believe that new facts could come to light that would allow us to see that Y is not a condition of X.

By contrast, for the term: hypothesis for a theoretical purpose, to be used in contrast with that of a postulate, we need not say that a hypothesis for a theoretical purpose is revisable. For these terms to be used in contrast, it suffices that there is a difference between a hypothesis for a theoretical purpose and a postulate concerning the nature of the purpose for which each is made. If it is an unconditional practical requirement to hold X, the Y that makes X possible is a postulate. If there is no unconditional practical requirement to hold X, the Y that makes X possible is a hypothesis for a theoretical purpose.

---

102   Beck 1960, p. 252.

To be sure, a hypothesis can possess the qualities of a revisable hypothesis and a hypothesis for a theoretical purpose. The point to hold on to here, however, is that a hypothesis for a theoretical purpose need not be a revisable hypothesis. Kant treats the assumption of an intelligent world cause as an unrevisable hypothesis for the theoretical purpose of explaining organised beings in nature.

Kant claims that an intelligent world cause is an unrevisable hypothesis for this theoretical purpose in *Lectures on Philosophical Theology*:

> If one argues from the contingency of the world to a supreme author, then this is only a hypothesis, even if it is one which is necessary for us as an explanation, and hence something like a highly probable opinion. But such presuppositions, which flow from some absolutely necessary datum (as in morality and mathematics), are not mere opinions, but demand of us a firm belief.[103]

Likewise, when Kant writes, in *Critique of Judgment*, that we are led to think of organised beings 'as if' they have come about through 'a causality that only reason can have',[104] Kant is saying that the hypothesis of an intelligent world cause is an unrevisable hypothesis for us. The hypothesis of an intelligent world cause is something that we endorse after 'seeing ... that the thing's form could not have arisen according to mere natural laws'[105] rather than something that we endorse after not seeing how it could have arisen according to mere natural laws. For Kant, the hypothesis that organised beings are caused by an intelligent world cause is, as Beck says, similar to a postulate in that it is 'not subject either to supplementation or correction by new facts'.[106] It is not subject to correction or displacement by empirical study or theory construction.

Kant's hypothesis of an intelligent world cause must be rejected, therefore, if it is possible for us to explain the existence of organised beings in nature without any appeal to an intelligent world cause. It is possible to explain the existence of organised beings in nature without any such appeal, if 'design-without-designing'[107] is possible. As Wood notes, Charles Darwin's theory of natural selection 'makes intelligible how animals and plants have arisen purely through the operations of matter as we understand it in accordance with phys-

---

103   Kant 1830, pp. 160–1; Kant 1978, p. 123.
104   *KU*, 5: 370.
105   *KU*, 5: 369–70.
106   *KU*, 5: 370.
107   Deacon 2012, p. 111.

ical laws (as we now understand them), apart from any order imposed on them by any intention'.[108] Indeed, as Terrence Deacon explains Darwin's theory:

> all that is required to explain how organisms become suited to their particular environments is (1) reproduction, with offspring inheriting traits from parents; (2) some degree of spontaneous variation from strict inheritance; and (3) reproduction in excess of the potential support that can be supplied by the local environment. This limitation will inevitably result in reproductive inequality among variant individuals. Those lineages with individual variants that are better suited to utilize available resources in order to support reproduction will gradually replace those lineages that are less well suited ... Whereas previously it seemed natural to assume that the processes responsible for orderly function and adaptive design necessarily preceded their effects ... Darwin showed that ... [t]he process that generated variant forms could be completely uncorrelated with the process that determined which variant forms were functionally superior to the others in a given environment. So long as the options with favorable outcomes were preferentially reproduced or retained and re-expressed in future contexts, it did not matter why or how they were generated ... The mechanism responsible for the origin of a given trait would therefore be irrelevant, so long as that trait got successfully preserved in the future population. In the world of reproducing organisms, an effect could in this way be the explanation for the current existence of functional organization, even if that effect had no role in producing it ... Darwin could thus explain the presence of a living form bearing the marks of design, without invoking any hint of intelligence, representation, agency, or prescience.[109]

Further, the theory of natural selection can now be supported by a theory of the generation of 'a first spontaneous self-reproducing system', or (in Deacon's terms) a first 'autogen', whose component processes exhibit the reciprocal means-end relation by which Kant characterises the parts of an organism[110] and which explains the conditions for natural selection to operate.[111] Of an autogen's component morphodynamic processes, Deacon says:

---

108   Wood 1999, p. 222.

109   Deacon 2012, pp. 110–14.

110   'An organized product of nature is one in which everything is a purpose and reciprocally also a means' (*KU*, 5: 376; see also *ÜGTP*, 8: 181).

111   Deacon 2012, pp. 288–92, pp. 311–25.

Though each component process is self-undermining in isolation and co-dependent, together they are reciprocally self-limiting, so that their self-undermining features are reciprocally counteracted ... [A]lthough auto-gens are incredibly simple molecular systems, their self-reconstitution properties in favorable environments spontaneously bring into being the systemic conditions that are sufficient to initiate a persistent, if weak, form of natural selection. In molecularly complex environments, auto-gen lineage competition for resources will tend to lead to the evolution of variant lineages differentially "fitted" to their local environments. This satisfies all necessary and sufficient material and logical conditions for natural selection[112]

If a scientific theory (or combination of scientific theories) can explain the existence of natural organisms, for whose explanation we might otherwise have entertained the hypothesis of an intelligent world cause, the need to explain the existence of living organisms gives us no reason to postulate an intelligent world cause. Indeed, in light of these scientific theories, the existence of living organisms gives us no reason even to retain the assumption of an intelligent world cause. Retaining the assumption of an intelligent world cause merely on the basis that an intelligent world cause is *consistent* with (that is, not refuted by) the existence of living organisms is contrary to the scientific maxim to unify explanations under as few principles as possible.[113] The theories of natural selection and of the emergence of spontaneous self-reproducing systems on the one hand, and a belief in the existence of God on the other hand, are entirely heterogeneous points of view. But in any case, if we accept these scientific theories, the existence of organised beings in nature gives us no reason to assume an intelligent world cause as a hypothesis for a theoretical purpose. This undermines premise (2) of the physicoteleological argument. Kant's physicoteleological argument for a belief in the existence of God can therefore be rejected.

6   Conclusion

The aim in this chapter was to show that Kant's arguments for why we are required to believe in the existence of God do not succeed. The argument from

---

112   Deacon 2012, p. 308, p. 312.
113   See *KU*, 5: 182.

the highest good is subject to an objection from moral happiness, while the physicoteleological argument rests on a premise about the need to posit an intelligent world cause to explain the existence of organised beings that the development of evolutionary theory has supplanted. The rejection of these arguments has consequences for Kant's entire ethics, however, if our application of Kant's formulas of the categorical imperative rests on a belief in the existence of God. If our application of these formulas presupposes a belief in the existence of God, then rejecting Kant's arguments for why we must believe in the existence of God undermines our use of these formulas. In the absence of an alternative a priori argument for a belief in the existence of God that is consistent both with Kant's account of freedom of the will, and the development of evolutionary theory, we have no good reason to abide by the categorical imperative. Indeed, if the thought of the concept of the highest good as possible is inseparably attached to the moral law, then the objection from moral happiness implies that the moral law is not valid. The simplest way to avoid this conclusion while retaining as much of Kant's practical philosophy as possible is to reject Kant's concept of the highest good. To this end, a Kantian would have to argue that the moral law carries no commitment to the thought of the possibility of Kant's concept of the highest good. But this only underscores our main objection, which is that Kant's formulas of the categorical imperative rest on a belief in God's existence that Kant fails to justify.

PART III

Founding a Post-Kantian Ethics

∴

Introduction to Part III

Let us draw together the arguments of Parts I–II. In Part I, we took an interest in Marxism as given, and argued that, if you have an interest in Marxism, then you ought to have an interest in an ethics of autonomy distinct from Kant's. In Part II, we defended the negative part of the critique view. Kant gives us no good reason to abide by the categorical imperative, for to do so is to presuppose a belief in the existence of God that Kant fails to justify. We therefore have no reason to buy into Kant's ethics. Taken together, the arguments of Parts I–II say: if you have an interest in Marxism, then you ought to have an interest in an ethics of autonomy distinct from Kant's, and it is substantively sound not to affirm Kant's ethics. Or put the other way around: as we have no reason to buy into Kant's ethics, we are free to take an interest in Marxism, as Marxists are committed to a critique of Kant's ethics. The limits of Parts I–II are apparent, however. Parts I–II do not ground an alternative ethics of autonomy. For all that they argue, Marxists might need an ethics that is impossible to ground.

Part III presents the positive part of the critique view. This consists in a grounding argument for the autonomy of a human community. While we shall show that the form and content of the argument is outlined by Marx, the argument does not presuppose the truth of Marxism. A grounding argument may only take something relevantly *general* as given. The argument for the autonomy of a human community merely takes as given a belief that freedom, however it is to be conceived, is to be conceived as something that everyone is to enjoy; and that, once freedom is conceived as something that everyone is to enjoy, freedom must be conceived as something that cannot be enjoyed without at least some period of capitalism. To take these beliefs as given is not to take as given anything that defenders of capitalism object to. Nor is it to take as given any belief that socialists dispute. You have to be either radically anti-egalitarian or radically anti-modern to object to these beliefs. The grounding argument for the autonomy of a human community cannot engage these radical views. But its starting point remains sufficiently general, as capitalism tends not to nurture such views.

In its form, the argument is a distinctively social version of a foundational argument. It starts from a social fact independent of intuition: the basic structure of capitalism. It then uses a social theory to explain the acceptance of two premises that produce an antinomy in this basic structure. Given the beliefs that freedom is to be conceived as something that everyone is to enjoy, and that everyone can only enjoy after a period of capitalism, the rational requirement to resolve antinomies commits us to conceive of freedom in terms that include a principle with which resolve this antinomy. In the context of capitalism's basic structure, this principle commits us to other values and principles that end in a commitment to the value of the autonomy of a human community. Hence, we are committed to conceive of freedom as the autonomy of a human community.

This foundational argument for autonomy constitutes a challenge to two assumptions about the options in normative political philosophy. It shows that it is possible to ground a political philosophy by appeal to normative self-conceptions and conceptions of society without practising what Rawls calls the 'Kantian form of constructivism'.[1] It also shows that a political philosophy can employ impartial reasoning without treating what Amartya Sen refers to as equality in 'some particular aspect of a person'[2] as of fundamental value. It has escaped mainstream imagination that a normative political philosophy can be both *post*-Kantian and non-*liberal*-egalitarian.

The argument also contains a challenge for Marxists, because Marxists do not typically offer *any* grounding argument for the value that they use to condemn capitalism and recommend socialism. Studies of Marx's normative views or commitments tend to focus on just one side of things. They examine *what* value Marx adopts (or needs to adopt) to condemn capitalism and recommend socialism, and/or *to what extent* Marx adopts this value. They ask: does Marx use a positive conception of freedom, to recommend socialism and condemn capitalism? If so, how does Marx conceive of freedom? Does Marx think that capitalist exploitation is unjust? If so, by what standard? Is Marx an advocate or an opponent of the rule of law, and why? Does Marx appeal to the value of equality? To what extent are Marx's normative views consistent or plausible?

These are valid questions. But I say: even if they are all answered satisfactorily, at least one question remains – how can the value on which these views rely be *grounded*? Imagine if studies of Rawls's theory of justice were to expound Rawls's principles of justice and their implications, but did not examine Rawls's argument for the original position as a device for justifying principles of justice. Their one-sidedness would be apparent. Studies of Marx's normative commitments that are confined to expounding the value that informs Marx's normative judgments are also one-sided, even if this has not been as apparent. Such studies implicitly raise, but do not answer, the question of how this value is to be grounded. The grounding argument in Part III defends one approach to this question.

---

1   Rawls 1980, p. 516.
2   Sen 1992, p. 2.

A Marxist Argument for Autonomy

We concluded Part I by saying that a Marxist can offer an ethics if this ethics

(1) condemns capitalism as unjust and recommends socialism as just

(2) does not preclude action necessary to achieve socialism

(3) supports at least one of the following two claims: existing society ought to be revolutionised because the class oppression in it is in one way bad for everyone, or social arrangements that promote rational self-transparency ought to be adopted because false consciousness is in one way bad for everyone

(4) is grounded by an argument that appeals to premises about capitalism

(5) evaluates systems

(6) rests on the value of the autonomy of a human community

We now defend a grounding argument for an ethics that satisfies these conditions, that

(7) appeals to an antinomy to ground the value of the autonomy of a human community

The argument can be viewed in terms of a distinction between two types of argumentative strategy for grounding an ultimate value, which Wood calls the 'intuitional model' and the 'foundational model'.[1] The 'intuitional' strategy is exemplified by Henry Sidgwick's *The Method of Ethics* (1874). On this strategy, a fundamental value is grounded by showing how it 'sustains the general validity' of 'current moral judgments' by providing 'a method for binding the unconnected and occasionally conflicting principles of common moral reasoning into a complete and harmonious system'.[2] On the 'foundational' strategy, by contrast, the argument for grounding an ultimate value proceeds from a fundamental structure that is independent of intuition; that is, independent of our moral judgments. (This is not to say that it makes *no* appeal to intuition). On this strategy, a grounding argument aims to show that requirements arising from this fundamental structure commit us to acknowledging the value. Kant's use of a regressive argument in deriving the Formula of the End in Itself, examined in chapter 8, exemplifies this second type of argumentative strategy.

---

1 Wood 2008, p. 54.
2 Sidgwick 1962, p. 422.

One might suppose that Marxist versions of either argumentative strategy are possible. A Marxist version of the intuitional strategy could be supposed to defend the claim: an ethical approach is valid insofar as it provides a method for systematising the intuitions of members of a particular class (or classes). A Marxist version of the foundational strategy, on the other hand, could defend the claim: an ethical approach is valid if a commitment to it arises from the basic structure of a historically necessary form of society.

However, from Marx's perspective, a Marxist version of the intuitional strategy is unappealing. Marx's Preface to the First Edition of *Capital* Volume I refers scornfully to 'the prejudices of so-called public opinion, to which I have never made concessions'.[3] An insistence 'never' to make concessions to public opinion follows from Marx's project, an *'intransigent critique of all existence'*, if this project is 'intransigent in the sense that critique neither fears its results, nor conflict with the existing powers'.[4] Marx regards common moral opinions as, by and large, a depository of prejudices reflecting the unequal power relations in which they are formed. In the words of *The German Ideology*, 'the ideas of the dominant class are, in every epoch, the dominant ideas'.[5] If Marx is right on this point, then a method that controls its results by common moral opinions will result in an ethics marked by existing power relations. If so, no revolutionary ethics can hope to employ such a method. This counts against a Marxist take-up of the intuitional strategy, if by this strategy, as Sidgwick says, 'the truth of a philosopher's premises will always be tested by the acceptability of his conclusions: if in any important point he be found in flagrant conflict with common opinion, his method is likely to be declared invalid'.[6]

By contrast, a Marxist version of a foundational strategy appears more promising. Marx's later writings focus on the fundamental nature of capitalist production. If capitalism has some basic structure, then it can be taken to define a period in a theory of history. If capitalism has an indispensable place in the history of human freedom, that may give its basic structure a necessity to which a foundational argument can appeal, to ground a commitment to an ultimate value.

---

3   *MEW*, 23, p. 17; *MECW*, 35, p. 11; Marx 1976, p. 93.
4   *MEW*, 1, p. 344; *MECW*, 3, p. 142.
5   *MEJ*, 2003, p. 40; *MEW*, 3, p. 46; *MECW*, 5, p. 59.
6   Sidgwick 1962, p. 373.

1   Relativising Practical Reason

In Chapter 9, we examined Kant's arguments for why we must believe in the existence of God; that is, a perfect moral being as intelligent world cause. Kant's main argument, the argument from the highest good, faces an objection from moral happiness: if we postulate the existence of God to think of the concept of the highest good as possible, we deprive ourselves of moral happiness, which is part of happiness, and so part of the concept of the highest good. Kant's other argument for a belief in the existence of God, the physicoteleological argument, faces an objection from evolutionary theory: we may explain the existence of organisms in nature without the hypothesis of an intelligent world cause. In light of these objections, we concluded that Kant offers us no good reason to believe in the existence of God.

To the extent that we have no reason to believe in the existence of God, we have no reason to treat any demands of reason that may be binding on us as anything other than demands of *human* reason. We regard reason's demands as demands of and on human reason insofar as we regard them as demands of and on members of a species of rational being who are interdependent, needy and equipped with capacities open to development. The question of what it is moral for a non-social or non-needy or non-developing being to do, or of what it is moral for every conceivable rational being to do (whether interdependent or not, whether needy or not, whether existing as always already fully developed or not), are not recognised as questions that have any bearing on what we ought to do. As Marx writes in *Contribution to the Critique of Hegel's Philosophy of Right: Introduction*: '[t]he critique of religion culminates in the doctrine that *the human being is the supreme being for the human being*'.[7]

The demands of reason are not to be understood as related to the concept of a rational being per se. They are no longer to be understood as demands to which any finite rational being is required to adjust, prior to any consideration of how its characteristic activities can be organised. The demands of reason are relativized to human beings, that is, taken to operate only through and in relation to our characteristics. Our question is what members of a species of being who are interdependent, needy and with capacities open to development ought to do. We may treat the question of how we ought to organise the activities that express our interdependence, neediness and development – evolving cooperative activities of production and need satisfaction – as intrinsic to reason's demands.

---

7   *MEW*, 1, p. 385; *MECW*, 3, p. 182.

Consider Kant's Formula of the Law of Nature: '*so act as if the maxim of your action were to become by your will a* UNIVERSAL LAW OF NATURE'.[8] To apply this formula, it is necessary to imagine a world containing your maxim as a universal law of nature as coming about by you adopting its existence as your end. It tacitly asks you to imagine that you have a power to make a maxim become a universal law of nature. This is a position that no member(s) of the human species could ever be in. This kind of thought experiment is ruled out, once reason is relativised to human beings. To adopt it is to assume that our use of reason may be limited by a use of reason of which our characteristics make us incapable. If a principle involves a thought experiment, it can only ask us to conceive of ourselves in a position defined by powers that we human beings can have.[9]

Consider what this implies for a principle that involves a universalisability test. If a principle requires us to ask whether a type of conduct can be thought as a universal law, this universal law must be thought of as legislated *by* human agents in a way that human agents are *able* to legislate universal laws, *and* as effecting a universal law *of human* nature. As human beings are only able to legislate universal human conduct through a public power, the concept of a universal law, relativised to human nature, is the concept of the universal adoption of conduct on its being legislated by a public power. This carries implications for how we are to think of autonomy. Any position that a principle requires agents to conceive themselves in must be appropriate to the value underlying the principle. As human beings can only conceive of themselves as bringing about a universal law through a public power, a principle that incorporates a universalisability test must express a value that relates our use of reason to the exercise of public law-making power. Human beings can only exercise public law-making power in the name of a community. So, once practical reason is relativised to human beings, if we are bound by a principle that involves a universalisability test, this is as much as to say that we are committed to the value of a human community. We must think of autonomy as the autonomy of a human community.

Further, it is inconsistent with evolutionary theory to suppose that an interdependent and needy species of rational being could first appear in a form and under conditions precisely suited to its cooperation and need-satisfaction.

---

8   *GMS*, 4: 421.

9   It was therefore incorrect to claim that an 'anthropological system-level universalisability test' could ask us to imagine that 'hypothetical agents ... adopt a maxim by causal necessity' (Furner 2018, pp. 247–8), as we have no power to alter causal necessity.

If each type of species emerges from another by chance variation and sub-sequent adaption, then the characteristics of an emergent species and its environment are not created from scratch, or from a prior use of its own characteristic powers. It cannot be expected, therefore, that any species will first appear fully formed, or in external conditions that it cannot adapt to its needs by using its characteristic powers. Marx can write in the *Economic and Philosophic Manuscripts of 1844* that a species of being 'only stands on its own feet once it owes its *existence* to itself',[10] as an interdependent and needy species of rational being can only perfect itself through a historical process of development in which it produces the conditions of its own perfection.

As an evolved species of rational being that is interdependent and needy must have a history, to relativise the demands of reason to human beings is to relate them intrinsically to what our development demands. The demands of reason are demands to subject the development of social production and need satisfaction to reason. If, however, a principle is to articulate how the members of an interdependent, needy species are to subject their development to reason, then it must direct us to the kind of thing that *can* shape this development. Human conduct can only bear on our development if it is *systematic*. The dynamics of our development are set by generalised interactions that enable and constrain one another. So, our principles must submit systems to reason. As this applies to any principle, it applies to a principle that incorporates a universalisability test. If a principle incorporates a universalisability test, it must test the kind of thing that can bear on human development: systematic conduct. It must test a systematically reinforced end, rather than the maxim of a particular agent taken in isolation, even if no agent acts to reinforce its systematic character. If a principle incorporates a universalisability test, this test must be a system-level universalisability test.

Only a system-level test can hope to support Marx's claim, in *The Holy Family*, that the task of emancipation is 'to abolish the inhumanity of the present-day practice of life, which obtains its pinnacle in the *money system*';[11] or *The German Ideology*'s claim that 'the central relations of exploitation are determined independently of the will of individuals by production as a whole';[12] or Marx's adoption in *Value, Price and Profit* of 'the revolutionary watchword, "Abolition of the wages system!"'[13]

---

10   *MEW*, 40, p. 544; *MECW*, 3, p. 304.

11   *MEW*, 2, p. 116; *MECW*, 4, p. 110.

12   *MEW*, 3, p. 398; *MECW*, 5, p. 413.

13   *MECW*, 20, p. 149.

2   An Argumentative Strategy

In *Letters from the Deutsch-Französische Jahrbücher* (1843), Marx offers a statement of his approach to questions of value:

> everyone will have to admit to themselves that they have no exact view of what ought to become. But that is just the advantage of the new perspective, that we do not seek to anticipate the world dogmatically, but to find the new world only from a critique of the old. Previously, philosophers had the solution to all puzzles in their pulpit, and the stupid exoteric world had only to open its jaw for the roasted pigeons of absolute science to fly into its mouth. Philosophy has become worldly, and the most striking proof of this is that philosophical consciousness itself has been drawn into the torment of the struggle not merely externally, but intrinsically. If the construction of the future and conclusions for all time are not our concerns, then it is all the more certain what we currently have to accomplish: I mean the *intransigent critique of all existence*, intransigent in the sense that critique neither fears its results, nor conflict with the existing powers.
>
> ... Reason has always existed, just not always in rational form. The critic can therefore latch onto any form of theoretical and practical consciousness, and, from out of existing reality's *own* forms, develop true reality as its ought and ultimate end ...
>
> We do not, then, confront the world doctrinairely with a new principle: here is the truth, kneel down here! We develop new principles for the world out of the world's own principles. We do not say to it: stop your struggles, they are silly things; we want to tell you the true slogans of the struggle. We merely show the world why it is really struggling, and that consciousness is something it must acquire, even if it does not want to.[14]

Marx here claims that a basic value ('ultimate end') is to be grounded ('its ought') by appeal to the general and necessary features, or 'forms', of existing society that produce 'struggles'. These 'forms' are normatively relevant insofar as the struggles that they produce are informed by conflict-generating principles, and can be resolved only if their participants adopt new principles to

---

14   *MEW*, 1, pp. 344–5; *MECW*, 3, pp. 142–4.

replace the conflict-generating principles with which their conflict began. The implied test of normative principles is whether their application can remove the conflicts informed by principles produced by the forms of an existing society. Or as Marx claims in *Critique of Hegel's Doctrine of the State* from the same year: '[t]hat the rational is actual is proven by the contradiction of irrational reality'.[15] We recognise the validity of normative principles by their capacity to resolve contradictions produced by an existing social form. These claims sound amenable to reconstruction in the form of a foundational argument.

However, in 1843, when these two texts were composed, Marx had yet to begin his study of capitalist production. Marx had yet to identify the forms of consciousness that he would later describe, in *Capital* Volume I, as 'socially valid, hence objective thought-forms for the relations of production of this historically determined, social mode of production, commodity production'.[16] Thus, in 1843, Marx has little grasp of the social reality that he concedes, in 1843, he has to grasp, to ground a basic value. Marx's formulation of a strategy for grounding a value pre-dates his studies of the social relations on which any execution of this strategy rests. Once Marx embarks on a critique of political economy, however, other priorities take hold. Marx's studies of political economy take up decades of his life, and he never completes the critique of political economy as planned. As much as one may agree with the judgment, evident from how Marx chose to use his time, that it was more important for Marx to write a critique of political economy, a critique of political economy cannot replace a grounding argument for a basic value, which Marx never expounded.

To be sure, the above passage in Marx's *Letters from the Deutsch-Französische Jahrbücher* suggests that the role of normative principles is limited. But this should not be mistaken for a rejection of normative principles altogether. Marx says that he sees no need to offer an 'exact view' of the world that nevertheless 'ought' to take the place of the existing one. We can reconcile this limit with a foundational argument if we distinguish between a 'scientific' conception and a 'philosophical' conception of the role of normative principles.[17]

On the scientific conception of the role of normative principles, the aim of a normative theory is 'to settle all moral questions and make all moral decisions, as far as possible, by a rigorous derivation from precisely stated principles'.[18] By contrast, on the philosophical conception of the role of normative principles, the function of a fundamental principle is 'not to tell us what to do, but

---

15   *MEW*, 1, p. 266; *MECW*, 3, p. 63.
16   *MEW*, 23, p. 90; *MECW*, 35, p. 87; Marx 1976, p. 169.
17   The distinction is from Wood 2008, p. 54.
18   Wood 2008, p. 47.

instead to provide a basic framework, or value-oriented background, for justifying, modifying and applying the more particular rules or precepts of morality that do tell us this ... [which] they can do only to a limited extent'.[19] Marx's eschewal of an 'exact view' of the new 'principles' that 'ought' to be adopted signals a rejection of a scientific conception of normative principles for a philosophical conception. Even without an exact view of the world that is to be brought about, such as the scientific conception of normative principles would require, some basic value framework is presupposed, simply to justify Marx's claim that new principles 'ought' to replace the existing ones.

Thus, on this reading, when Marx writes that it is 'the advantage of the new perspective, that we do not seek to anticipate the world dogmatically, but to find the new world only from a critique of the old', Marx is not rejecting ethics, as Steinbüchel and Cohen believe.[20] Rather, Marx is suggesting a foundational strategy for grounding an ultimate value that appeals to a rational requirement to resolve a contradiction in an existing, conflict-ridden social form, and that reflects a philosophical conception of the role of a normative framework. Marx's *Letters from the Deutsch-Französische Jahrbücher* should encourage us to examine Marx's later critique of political economy for indications of such a foundational argument. If only we are prepared to look closely enough, we will find that *Capital* Volume I does not disappoint on this score. It highlights an antinomy in the antagonistic relation between capitalist and worker that requires a rational resolution.

3   The Need for a Duty to the Whole

Marx's preferred strategy for grounding a basic value, we have suggested, is to appeal to the need to resolve conflicts informed by principles that are socially cemented by the forms of an existing human society. A principle, along with the value underpinning it, is justified, if it can be adopted by participants in such struggles and implemented to resolve them.

On this understanding, a Marxist grounding argument will include a premise (or premises) that implies that an agency exists that can act on a principle embodying the value grounded by this argument. This seems essential. Unless there is an agency that can act on a principle because its interests can align with it, a grounding argument for the value it expresses is in vain. Without an

---

19   Wood 2008, p. 57.
20   See ch. 2, sec. 3.

agency to act on such a principle, the only practical effect of a grounding argument for its underlying value is to excuse, surreptitiously, something other than action on this value. To identify an agency that can act on such a principle is not to treat this agency as the extraneous vehicle of a normative theory, if the agency is acknowledged to have a goal independently of the value that is to be grounded. What the argument is to allow for is that an agency can achieve its independently identified goal by adopting a principle that rests on the value that the argument grounds.

Marx claims to identify this agency in *Contribution to a Critique of Hegel's Philosophy of Right. Introduction* (1844). What we are concerned with here, however, is not so much its class identity, but the character of the principle that Marx believes it can adopt:

> Where, therefore, is the *positive* possibility of German emancipation?
>
> *Answer*: in the formation of a class with *radical chains*, a class of bourgeois society that is no class of bourgeois society, an estate that is the dissolution of all estates, a sphere that possesses a universal character through its universal suffering, and lays claim to no *particular right* because no *particular wrong* is committed against it, but *wrong as such* [Unrecht schlechthin], which can no longer invoke a *historical* but only a *human* title, which stands not in a one-sided opposition to the consequences but in an all-round opposition to the premises of the German state; a sphere, finally, that cannot emancipate itself without emancipating itself from all other spheres of society, and thereby emancipating all other spheres of society; which, in short, is the *complete loss* of humanity, and so can only win itself through the *complete reclamation of humanity*. This dissolution of society as a particular estate is the *proletariat*.
>
> ... Philosophy cannot realise itself without the abolition of the proletariat, and the proletariat cannot abolish itself without the realisation of philosophy.[21]

One claim that this text adds, to the above passage from Marx's *Letters from the Deutsch-Französische Jahrbücher*, is that it claims to identify the agency that is to champion the new principle that is to resolve conflicts in existing society: 'the proletariat', or working-class. Of present concern, however, is the character

---

21   *MEW*, 1, pp. 390–1; *MECW*, 3, pp. 186–7. *MECW* translates 'das Unrecht schlechthin' as 'wrong generally' but that would be: '*das Unrecht im allgemeinen*'. I follow Forst 2017, p. 545, in translating 'schlechthin' as '*as such*'. Here, 'schlechthin' means 'without condition' (compare the note in Kant 2011, p. 163).

of the principle that this agency is to demand. Its character is implicit in Marx's contrast of *particular wrong* to *wrong as such*. The new principle for resolving existing conflicts is one that overcomes *wrong as such*, as distinct from *particular wrong*. If, as Marx says, a particular wrong is resisted in the name of a *particular right*, then *wrong as such* is resisted in the name of justice. To see why Marx suggests that the principle for resolving existing conflicts is a principle of justice that is not a principle of *particular right*, we need to explain how a wrong can consist in something other than a particular wrong, and how the correction of a wrong can consist in something other than the affirmation of a particular right.

Wood suggests that, for Marx, an agency suffers wrong as such if it does 'not suffer merely some contingent denial of a right, which might leave intact their dignity and their will to defend their rights generally'.[22] Yet this hardly seems plausible. The proletariat that suffers *wrong as such* is plainly a subject that Marx believes retains the will required to resist. Its chains are *'radical chains'*, chains that can lead to a radical response. Wood does not explain how resistance in defence of something other than a right could be prompted by being too downtrodden to resist in defence of a right.

Feenberg is on the right track when he says that Marx aims to identify a class with no interest 'opposed to that of society as a whole'.[23] The proletariat is said to have an interest in its own emancipation. But its emancipation consists not in winning a stake within existing society at the expense of other classes, but in the abolition of class society, which is 'emancipating' for 'all other spheres of society'. This raises the question as to what form of principle accords with a demand to abolish class society in the interests of all.

An act that is *wrong as such* is clearly a wrong. It is wrong *as such*, because we do not need to know anything further, to know that it is a wrong. We do not need to know that it violates another's right, to know that it is a wrong. It is not wrong only under the condition that it violates another's right. It is wrong immediately, or as such, because its nature as a wrong can be determined without reference to another's right. To suffer *wrong as such* is to be the object of an action that can be determined as a wrong without reference to a right, and thus as wrong without reference to any of one's own rights. As the suffering that results from *wrong as such* can be determined without reference to any of the sufferer's rights, it can be resisted without appeal to any particular right that the sufferer may have.

22   Wood 1993, p. 425.

23   Feenberg 1981, p. 41.

How can an act be wrong, even without violating a right? By violating a duty that has no correlative right; that is, no correlative unconditional advantage that a party can choose whether or not to waive. Examples can be found in environmental ethics: it may be wrong to hunt and kill the members of an endangered species of wild animal because it is a duty not to hunt and kill them, even if no one (living or in the future) has a waivable right over any of its members. This parallels Marx's claim, in *Capital* Volume III, that '[e]ven an entire society, a nation, or all co-existing societies taken together, are not own-ers of the earth', even though we still have a duty 'to bequeath it, improved, to succeeding generations'.[24] As a duty can be enforceable even if its enforce-ment does not protect a right, understood as an unconditional advantage that a party can choose whether or not to waive, principles of justice are irreducible to principles of particular right.

An act may violate a duty but no right if it disrespects the value of a human community. As a community is disrespected, no individual member may lift the duty, like an individual may waive a right. Nor is an individual guaranteed any particular advantage of their own if the duty is observed. A duty to admit people to a public gallery does not guarantee that *I* can gain admission, for it may already be full. I call this kind of duty, which has no correlative right, a duty to the whole: 'a duty to the whole is a duty underpinned by the value of a property of a group or society, which does not give any individual member an unconditional advantage'.[25]

If an act violates a duty to the whole, the act is '*wrong as such*'. To end the wrong is to enforce the duty. But as the duty's enforcement does not imply the enforcement of a right, the wrong need not be resisted in the name of a '*par-ticular right*'. It may be resisted in the name of upholding a principle of justice that expresses a duty to the whole.

Given Marx's aim in the passage above, it is no accident that Marx intro-duces the concept of '*wrong as such*'. If an agent is to ensure its own abolition, it must act in the name of a duty to the whole, rather than a right. No struggle that culminates in a principle that awards an agent a right can ensure that agent's abolition. The holder of a right can waive it, allowing things to carry on as before. The abolition of an existing state of affairs or agent can, however, be ensured by enforcing a duty to the whole that prohibits conduct essential to it. A struggle that culminates in a principle that expresses a duty to the whole

---

24   *MEW*, 25, p. 784; *MECW*, 37, p. 763; Marx 1981, p. 911.
25   Furner 2018, p. 109; compare Furner 2018, pp. 109–17, pp. 282–4. That duties need not have correlative rights is a basis for rejecting all three established positions in the debate on Marx and justice; see Furner 2018, pp. 11–13, pp. 270–88, pp. 482–3.

merely presupposes that the community whose value is thought of as respected by the duty's observance can exist at its end. Insofar as this valued community need not contain, as members, agents in the identity in which they struggled for the implementation of the duty, a struggle that culminates in its implementation may abolish the identity of the agents who struggled for it.

On this analysis, if there is to be a struggle for a classless society, it must be waged in the name of a duty-to-the-whole-based principle of justice. Marx's argumentative strategy for grounding a value, we have said, is to appeal to a principle that can resolve the conflicts of principle that are generated by the forms of existing society. Insofar as these conflicts are understood as conflicts inherent to the relations between the individual members of different classes, a principle is justified if it can be implemented to abolish classes. If the abolition of classes requires a duty-to-the-whole based principle of justice, Marx's argumentative strategy will consist in showing that it is a rational requirement for the member of different classes who are embroiled in conflict to affirm a duty-to-the-whole-based principle of justice, while allowing for this principle to be in at least some participants' class interests.

One option is a principle that incorporates a system-level universalisability test. A principle that incorporates a *system*-level universalisability test relativises the demands of practical reason to human beings. It also creates a duty with no correlative right. What it establishes is a prohibition on a certain type of system. It prohibits any systematically reinforced end that cannot be universalised. To enforce this prohibition is to set about removing the system that enables and constraints the end. This may yield advantages for particular individuals as a by-product. But that is not what the principle guarantees. Its enforcement protects no correlative right. If a principle of justice incorporating a system-level universalisability test prohibits a systematically reinforced end whose pursuit is a condition of existence of classes, a demand for a classless society can assume 'a universal character' by appealing to this principle.

4   The General Features of a Foundational Argument

A foundational argument appeals to a basic structure that is independent of intuition to explain the acceptance of one or more evaluative premises, and shows that an agent who accepts these premises is committed to an ultimate value. We now comment on the general nature of this strategy by highlighting some similarities between Kant's regressive argument for the Formula of the End in Itself (FEI), John Stuart Mill's proof of the general happiness principle, and a Marxist foundational argument.[26] Differences between the arguments offered by Mill and Kant on the one hand, and a Marxist foundational argument on the other, will be discussed in section 6.

First, to say that the starting point of a foundational argument is a basic structure independent of intuition is to say that the argument proceeds from an intuition-independent fact (or facts) that can be taken as given. An intuition-independent fact can be taken as given if it is relevantly necessary. If an intuition-independent fact is contingent rather than necessary, no actor can be bound by a value commitment arising out of it, for they could always deny the fact from which the commitment arose.

What sort of intuition-independent fact is relevantly necessary depends on what the argument is to achieve. As Kant aims to ground an imperative valid for all finite rational beings, Kant's regressive argument for FEI begins from what Kant views as a necessary feature of finite rational nature: 'rational nature is distinguished from the others by this, that it sets itself an end'.[27] As Mill aims to ground a principle of human morality, Mill's argument for the general happiness principle appeals to a desire for happiness viewed as a permanent fact of human psychology: 'to desire anything, except in proportion as the idea of it is pleasant, is a physical and metaphysical impossibility'.[28] Insofar as Marx provides an ethics to actors in capitalism, its grounding argument may begin from capitalism's basic structure, understood as a necessary feature of human history. Marx emphasises the absence of a capitalism-free route to human freedom in *Results of the Immediate Process of Production*:

> The capitalist's domination of the worker is thus the domination of the thing over the human being, of dead labour over living labour, of the product over the producer ... Viewed *historically*, this inversion appears as the necessary transit point [*notwendige Durchgangspunkt*] for enforcing, at the expense of the majority, the creation of wealth as such, i.e. of the relentless productive powers of social labour, which alone can form the material basis of a free human society.[29]

---

26   The similarities between Kant's argument for FEI, and Mill's proof of the principle of utility, are discussed in Haezrahi 1962, pp. 215–17; Paton 1953, p. 176; Sayre-McCord 2001; Wood 1995a, p. 308; and Wood 2008, pp. 43–65, pp. 88–90. The comparison is extended to Marx in Furner 2018, pp. 3–4.

27   GMS, 4: 437. For discussion, see ch. 8, sec. 3.

28   Mill 1962, p. 36.

29   MEGA II, 4.1, pp. 64–5; MECW, 34, pp. 398–9; Marx 1976, p. 990. MECW translates 'Durchgangspunkt' as 'point of entry' (which would be: 'Einreiseort'), but a 'Durchgangspunkt' is an intermediate point in a journey. Marx makes similar points using the same phrase ('not-

If a society in which human freedom is realised is only possible after a period of capitalism, a period of capitalism is historically 'necessary' in respect of realising human freedom. If we grant that a period of capitalism is necessary in this respect (which is not to grant the truth of Marxism, for we may believe, consistent with this, that human freedom can only be realised in mature capitalism), a grounding argument for an ultimate value can take capitalism's basic structure as given.

A second feature of a foundational argument is to show that the intuition-independent fact (or facts) from which it begins accounts for the acceptance of an evaluative premise (or premises) on the part of an agent relevantly related to this fact. An evaluative premise must be introduced, because evaluative conclusions – such as the conclusion that we are committed to an ultimate value – cannot be supported without one or more evaluative premises. An evaluative premise can be introduced on the back of the fact from which a foundational argument proceeds either as a rational requirement following on from it, or as a sociologically explained consequence. One step in Kant's argument for FEI is that a rational agent who sets an end must think of the action that they are rationally required to select as a means to it as good. One step in Mill's argument for the general happiness principle is that, given the impossibility of desiring anything except in proportion as the idea of it is pleasant (and a further principle of evidence), we must regard happiness as the only thing worthy of being desired.[30] One step in a Marxist foundational argument is to argue that actors in capitalism's basic structure accept the evaluative premise that commodity exchangers are to recognise one another as self-owners.

Third, any foundational argument has to show that a commitment to an ultimate value arises on account of the evaluative premise (or premises) that the intuition-independent fact (or facts) allows us to treat as accepted. A commitment arises, if the case for it is convincing from the perspective of the agent who accepts the evaluative premise. As we shall see in the next section, it is not clear that Mill's grounding argument for the general happiness principle satisfies this criterion. But in Kant's case, the strategy (on the interpretation defended in Chapter 8) is to argue that a rational agent's ascription of goodness (as a means) to the action that they are rationally required to select as a means to their end presupposes the adoption of a self-affirming plural standpoint; so, a categorical imperative that commands us to treat humanity in a person always as an end accords with the worth that agents already presuppose

---

wendige Durchgangspunkt') at *MEW*, 42, p. 422; *MECW*, 28, p. 439, and at *MEW*, 25, p. 453; *MECW*, 37, p. 434; Marx 1981, p. 568.

30   See sec. 5.

rational nature to have (if we also assume that humanity and personality are coextensive). In Marx's case, the strategy is to argue that actors in capitalism who recognise one another as self-owners assert rights vis-à-vis one another that form an antinomy; and that the rational requirements to remove, avoid and undermine this rights-antinomy ultimately commit to the value of the autonomy of a human community.[31]

On this elaboration, it is not accurate to describe the general nature of a grounding argument, on the foundational strategy (with an eye to Mill and Kant), by saying:

> the underlying strategy is to rely on the initial evaluative commitments people find themselves with and show that considerations of consistency based on the content of these commitments carry further, and perhaps unexpected, commitments in their wake.[32]

On the above elaboration of a foundational argument, 'evaluative commitments' are not 'initial'. Rather, they arise from something initial, an intuition-independent fact (or facts). If evaluative commitments were themselves initial, the grounding argument would not be of the foundational type. It would not proceed from an intuition-independent fact.

Indeed, this correction helps to reveal a *post*-Kantian option in political philosophy. Rawls characterises the Kantian constructivist approach to political philosophy as follows:

> What distinguishes the Kantian form of constructivism is essentially this: it specifies a particular conception of the person as an element in a reasonable procedure of construction, the outcome of which determines the content of the first principles of justice. Expressed another way: this kind of view sets up a certain procedure of construction which answers to certain reasonable requirements, and within this procedure persons characterized as rational agents of construction specify, through their agreements, the first principles of justice.[33]

Insofar as the Kantian constructivist approach proceeds from specifications of a person and of a rational consensus-seeking procedure that explicate, or are congenial to, our intuitions, the Kantian constructivist approach is not

---

31   A summary of the steps of argument is presented in section 13.
32   Sayre-McCord 2001, p. 355.
33   Rawls 1980, p. 516.

a kind of foundational argument. In a foundational argument, an intuition-independent fact (or facts) is initial. Moreover, as, in a foundational argument, evaluative commitments are shown to arise from this intuition-independent fact (or facts), Rawls's recommendation of the Kantian constructivist approach rests on an overly restrictive view of the options in political philosophy:

> The aim of political philosophy, when it presents itself in the public cul-ture of a democratic society, is to articulate and to make explicit those shared notions and principles thought to be already latent in common sense; or, as is often the case, if common sense is hesitant and uncertain, and doesn't know what to think, to propose to it certain conceptions and principles congenial to its most essential convictions and historical tradi-tions ... The search for reasonable grounds for reaching agreement rooted in our conception of ourselves and in our relation to society replaces the search for moral truth interpreted as fixed by a prior and independent order of objects and relations, whether natural or divine, an order apart and distinct from how we conceive of ourselves.[34]

What Rawls here overlooks is that a grounding argument for an ultimate value may be of the foundational kind: it may appeal to an intuition-independent fact *and related* normative self-conception. Such a grounding argument is distinct from both of the options mentioned by Rawls. It is distinct from Kantian con-structivism, if it begins from an *intuition-independent* fact. It is distinct from an argument from 'an order apart and distinct from how we conceive of ourselves', insofar as it appeals to a normative self-conception that it presents as *related to* an intuition-independent fact. Indeed, the intuition-independent fact that a foundational argument proceeds from need not be reducible to a conception of a person or a consensus-seeking procedure. It must simply be relevantly neces-sary, and give rise to a normative self-conception.

As the foundational strategy fails to register on Rawls's radar as a possible option in political philosophy, Rawls is bound to overlook the possibility of any *post*-Kantian option in political philosophy that offers a foundational argu-ment. A political philosophy is not post-Kantian just by virtue of its use of a foundational argument.[35] As we saw in Chapter 8, the regressive part of Kant's argument for FEI is a foundational argument. But a foundational argument *is* post-Kantian, if it proceeds from certain kinds of intuition-independent

---

34   Rawls 1980, pp. 518–19.
35   By implication, 'Kantian' constructivism is not the only Kantian approach to political philosophy.

facts and evaluative premises. According to Rawls, 'a Kantian doctrine joins the content of justice with a certain conception of the person'.[36] A foundational argument is Kantian, then, if it links the content of justice to a normative conception of a person that it relates to an intuition-independent fact (or facts). A foundational argument is *post*-Kantian, if it proceeds from intuition-independent facts – such as facts about capitalism's basic structure – that are *irreducible* to a conception of a person or a consensus-seeking procedure, and if it relates them to evaluative premises that are *irreducible* to a normative conception of a person or a consensus-seeking procedure; and the argument *nevertheless* owes something to Kant. The antinomy premise discussed below – antinomies in the social world ought to be resolved – is irreducible in either way. So, a foundational argument from capitalism's basic structure that appeals to an antinomy in it to ground an ultimate value is a kind of post-Kantian political philosophy, one whose possibility has been overlooked.

5   A Lesson from Mill's 'Proof'

It is useful, at this point, to highlight a problem in Mill's attempt to prove the principle of utility, or general happiness principle. Any foundational argument must negotiate it.

In *Utilitarianism* (1861), Mill sets out to defend a 'principle of utility' as the 'one fundamental principle or law, at the root of all morality'.[37] In Chapter IV, entitled 'Of what sort of proof the principle of utility is susceptible', Mill offers the following proof:

> The only proof capable of being given that an object is visible, is that people actually see it. The only proof that a sound is audible, is that people hear it: and so of the other sources of our experience. In like manner, I apprehend, the sole evidence it is possible to produce that anything is desirable, is that people actually desire it. If the end which the utilitarian doctrine proposes to itself were not, in theory and in practice, acknowledged to be an end, nothing could ever convince any person that it was so. No reason can be given why the general happiness is desirable, except that each person, so far as he believes it to be attainable, desires his own happiness. This, however, being a fact, we have not only all the proof

which the case admits of, but all which it is possible to require, that happiness is a good: that each person's happiness is a good to that person, and the general happiness, therefore, a good to the aggregate of all persons. Happiness has made out its title as *one* of the ends of conduct, and consequently one of the criteria of morality.[38]

Having then argued that we do not desire anything else besides happiness, Mill concludes:

If the opinion which I have now stated is psychologically true – if human nature is so constituted as to desire nothing which is not either a part of happiness or a means of happiness, we can have no other proof, and we require no other, that these are the only things desirable. If so, happiness is the sole end of human action, and the promotion of it the test by which to judge of all human conduct; from which it necessarily follows that it must be the criterion of morality[39]

Mill's advertised proof of the principle of utility can be represented in three steps. The first step is an argument by analogy for a principle of evidence which says: the only evidence that anything is worthy of being desired, and therefore worthy of being pursued as an end, is that it is desired. Mill then claims that, as a psychological fact, happiness is the only thing that we desire. Objects of desire that might be regarded as counterexamples to this claim are, Mill says, either desired as a part of happiness (virtue, for example), or as a means to it (money, power, even constancy of habit). Finally, Mill suggests that it follows from the principle of evidence and the psychological fact that each person desires only their own happiness, that everyone is committed to pursue the general happiness.[40]

Each of these steps of Mill's proof can be (and has been) disputed. However, we may focus on just two points. One is that Mill does not argue – as Mill's

---

38   Mill 1962, pp. 32–3.

39   Mill 1962, p. 36.

40   Wood claims that Kant and Mill attempt 'to provide a *philosophical interpretation of what we are committed to* simply in rationally desiring ends and willing actions toward them' (Wood 2008, p. 55). In respect of Mill's proof, this is less than accurate: Mill does not proceed 'simply' from (rational) desire. Mill does not *infer his principle of evidence* from a fact about what people (rationally) desire. Mill infers his principle of evidence from a *second* intuition-independent fact (an alleged analogy between the self as knower and the self as moral agent) distinct from the fact (concerning the desiring self) that happiness is the only thing that we desire.

stated principle of evidence might lead us to expect – that we are committed to pursue the general happiness as an end because *general* happiness is
the only thing that we desire. To argue for this commitment using a principle
of evidence related to what people desire, some of Mill's sympathisers revise
Mill's principle of evidence to the following, different principle: the only evidence that anything is worthy of being pursued as an end is that a commitment
to pursue it as an end arises from what is desired.[41] This is one way to make
out a form of argument for a general happiness principle using a principle of
evidence along with a psychological fact about each person only desiring their
own happiness. The most that this agent-relative fact leaves Mill in a position
to show is that a commitment to pursue the general happiness as an end *arises
from* what people desire.

The other point concerns the final step in a proof of the general happiness
principle: the step from an accepted principle of evidence and a psychological
fact that each person desires only their own happiness, to the conclusion that
everyone is committed to pursue the general happiness as an end. Even if we
accept all the previous steps of the argument, we still need to show how a commitment to pursue the end of general happiness can arise from what are, at
bottom, egoistic desires for one's own happiness. Henry Sidgwick identifies an
insuperable difficulty in this part of the argument:

> If the Egoist strictly confines himself to stating his conviction that he
> ought to take his own happiness or pleasure as his ultimate end, there
> seems no opening for any line of reasoning to lead him to Universal-
> istic Hedonism as a first principle; it cannot be proved that the difference
> between his own happiness and another's happiness is not *for him* all-
> important.[42]

Sidgwick presses against Mill the same objection that Cureton presses against
Wood's and Korsgaard's versions of Kant's argument for FEI.[43] As an agent
'may value a personal characteristic on grounds that include an ineliminable
back-reference to that agent', it is a fallacy, Cureton says, to suppose that, if an
agent 'values a feature of themselves then they must value that same feature
in others'.[44] This fallacy is to be avoided by any proof of the general happiness
principle as much as by any regressive argument for FEI. If *A* values their own

---

41   See Hall 1949, p. 9; Sayre-McCord 2001, p. 342, p. 345.

42   Sidgwick 1962, p. 420.

43   See ch. 8, sec. 4, (2).

44   Cureton 2013, pp. 371–2.

happiness because it is theirs, and *A* also knows that others may enjoy happiness, *A* is not thereby committed to value others' happiness. There appears to be no route from the agent-relative fact that Mill presents to Mill's conclusion, that each of us ought to pursue the *general* happiness as an end, that does not commit the self-regarding fallacy.

To be sure, those who accept that there is an impartial point of view may regard it as morally irrelevant to the value of happiness that it belongs to a particular agent. That is, agent-relative reasons for valuing one's own happiness may be irrelevant, from an impartial point of view. But this is of no support to a foundational argument for the general happiness principle. It presupposes acceptance of an impartial point of view. To introduce a principle endorsed from an impartial point of view – such as Sidgwick's principle of rational benevolence 'that each one is morally bound to regard the good of any other individual as much as his own'[45] – is to depart from the chain of reasoning internal to the perspective of the agent relevantly related to the intuition-independent facts from which Mill's proof is supposed to proceed (the fact that each person desires their own happiness, and a principle of evidence).

This excursus on Mill's 'proof' of the general happiness principle allows us to generalise a finding presented in Chapter 8. There, we suggested that any version of Kant's regressive argument that *first* seeks to show that an agent must value rational nature in itself and *then* argues, in a *further* move, that, if an agent values rational nature in itself, this agent is committed to valuing it in others, will either commit the self-regarding fallacy, or else rely on an external moral premise, and so cease to be a regressive argument. We may now express this point in more general terms.

Put negatively: it is impossible to get from a 'proprietary commitment' (that is, an agent-relative reason to value a personal characteristic) to the corresponding 'non-proprietary'[46] commitment (that is, an agent-neutral reason to value a personal characteristic) by premises internal to the perspective of the agent from which a foundational argument proceeds, *unless* it is in this agent's *self-interest* to affirm the agent-neutral principle. More positively: the agents who are relevantly related to the initial intuition-independent fact(s) of a foundational argument must accept evaluative premises that (dis)value something whose description relates everyone to what is (dis)valued. If each

---

45   Sidgwick 1962, p. 382.
46   Sayre-McCord 2001, p. 356. If 'Kant's argument, just like Mill's, supposes that a proprietary commitment must be grounded on a nonproprietary one' (ibid), then it would fail just for that reason.

is committed to (dis)valuing something common to all, each is committed to (dis)valuing the same thing. If so, all agents can be committed to the same principle or value.

6 The Distinctive Features of a Marxist Foundational Argument

A Marxist foundational argument has four distinctive features, at least when compared to Mill's proof of the greatest happiness principle, and Kant's regressive argument for FEI. A Marxist foundational argument: (i) starts from a social fact; (ii) moves from this social fact to an evaluative premise with the aid of a social theory; (iii) reveals a defect in what is valued; and (iv) relies on evaluative premises that are irreducible to normative conceptions of persons. Consider each in turn.

(i) The Starting-Point Is a Social Fact
The facts from which Kant and Mill proceed are non-social facts. As Kant can only claim that FEI gives expression to an a priori moral law by offering an argument for FEI that holds for *all* finite rational beings, Kant's argument for FEI must proceed from a fact about any finite rational being, social or non-social: the fact that a finite rational being sets an end.[47] Mill's proof of the general happiness principle proceeds from the psychological fact that the only thing that a human being desires is its own happiness. By suggesting that a denial of this fact involves the assertion of a 'physical and metaphysical impossibility',[48] Mill implies that this fact is independent of the social character of humankind, and is unalterable by social change. The starting-point of Kant's and Mill's foundational arguments is thus a basic aspect of experience that does not presuppose any kind of social relation. A Marxist foundational argument differs on this point: it proceeds from capitalism's basic structure. The description of capitalism's basic structure is the description of a social fact.

(ii) A Social Theory Explains the Acceptance of an Evaluative Premise
All foundational arguments for an ultimate value appeal to at least one evaluative premise, as evaluative conclusions require evaluative premises. But they differ in how they account for their acceptance. Kant accounts for an agent's ascription of goodness to an action rationally adopted as a means by an 'ana-

---

47   Compare Tönnies's comment at Tönnies 1909, p. 930, cited at the end of ch. 3.
48   Mill 1962, p. 36.

lytic'[49] proposition that the selection of means belongs to the setting of an end, and by a rational requirement to adopt a self-affirming plural standpoint in selecting this action as a means. Neither aspect of this account relies on a social theory.

To adopt a plural standpoint, an agent compares their judgment with that of others who are understood as comparing their judgments with those of others. An agent may apply aspects of a social theory in considering others' judgments and how others might revise these judgments if they compared them. At issue here, however, is not whether *agents* use a social theory *in* the plural standpoint, but whether *Kant* uses a social theory to explain *why* an agent is rationally required to adopt the plural standpoint. For Kant, the adoption of a plural standpoint is a rational requirement of ascribing goodness to the means of an end. As all finite rational beings adopt ends and select means to them, the adoption of a plural standpoint is a rational requirement on all finite rational beings. Nothing specifically social accounts for the rational requirement to adopt it. Accordingly, no social theory informs Kant's argument for why an agent is committed to a judgment about the absolute worth of rational nature.

No social theory is used to explain the acceptance of an evaluative premise in Mill's proof, either. Mill accounts for the acceptance of his principle of evidence by appeal to an analogy between the test of what is audible or visible, and the test of what is desirable. Mill does not appeal to a social theory to justify the proper test of what is audible or visible, or to justify the relevance of an analogy between these tests, and the test of what is desirable.

By contrast, a Marxist foundational argument uses a social theory to explain the acceptance of an evaluative premise. This is apparent from the argumentative strategy that Marx outlines in 1843. In *Letters from the Deutsch-Französische Jahrbücher*, Marx proposes to 'develop new principles for the world out of the world's own principles'.[50] The 'world's own principles' are principles that are exhibited in generalised social relations. Before we can argue that an irrationality in these principles commits actors to adopt new principles, we need to explain how actors come to accept them in the first place. To do this, we need to offer an account of how actors relate to the social world of which they are a part.

The use of a social theory to explain the acceptance of an evaluative premise offers a way to navigate the problem of self-regard that Sidgwick first drew attention to. The problem of self-regard, as we have seen, is that value judg-

---

49   *GMS*, 4: 417.
50   *MEW*, 1, p. 345; *MECW*, 3, p. 144.

ments that contain an ineliminable back-reference to a personal characteristic of an agent cannot directly ground a commitment to a general principle or value. Yet it cannot be denied that such value judgments may be sincerely held. People routinely act on the fact that a sum of money (or period of leisure, or power, or honour) is valuable because it is *theirs*.

A social theory can be used to explain the acceptance of an agent-neutral principle by actors in capitalism's basic structure if it identifies a social interest. A social interest is an interest that is common to a number of individuals (under some description), and that no one satisfies without everyone satisfying it *or* that each only tends to satisfy in conditions that promote its satisfaction for all. An interest satisfied by a law of general application is a social interest of the former kind, while public spaces may give rise to a social interest of the latter kind: an interest in a virus-free environment is a social interest, if each person living in a particular vicinity only tends to enjoy a virus-free environment if public places in that vicinity are virus-free. Social interests show that self-interest need not be a barrier to acceptance of an agent-neutral principle, for even self-interested actors have a reason to respond to a social interest by affirming an agent-neutral principle that upholds it. If capitalism's basic structure generates a social interest, it may explain the acceptance of an agent-neutral principle that can provide an evaluative premise of a Marxist foundational argument.

(iii) *A Defect Is Revealed in What Is Valued*
Wood claims that any foundational argument 'must begin with value judgments we already accept and then provide a convincing theoretical interpretation of these judgments that supports the pertinent philosophical claim about ultimate value'.[51] This makes it sound as if a foundational argument must *preserve* the value judgments that agents relevantly related to an intuition-independent fact first affirm. It makes it sound as if a foundational argument *must* say: if you maintain any value judgment that an intuition-independent fact reveals you to be committed to, as indeed you must, then you are also committed to endorsing a value as a condition of maintaining it.

To be sure, the regressive part of Kant's argument for FEI fits this pattern. Kant's regressive argument (on the logical pluralism version) says: if an agent sets an end, then it is rationally required to choose an action to which it ascribes goodness as a means; to do this rationally, it must adopt a plural standpoint, which is self-affirming; and to adopt such a standpoint is to presuppose that

---

51   Wood 1999, p. 125.

rational nature has absolute worth. In this argument, the first value judgment –
action rationally selected as a means to an end is good as a means – is pre-
served. But it cannot simply be assumed that this is a *necessary* feature of a
foundational argument. A foundational argument need not preserve all value
judgments that an intuition-independent fact first commits agents to. It is sufficient to offer a compelling chain of reasoning from premises that the agent
accepts, to the value that is grounded. This chain of reasoning can be compelling even if it requires an evaluative premise to be rejected.

The intuition-independent fact of a Marxist foundational argument is the
basic structure of a historically specific form of human society, capitalism. If a
social theory can appeal to this fact to explain the acceptance of an evaluative
premise, it may reveal this evaluative premise to be problematic by reference
to the same basic structure that explains its acceptance, by showing that it
informs conduct in this basic structure that exhibits an antinomy. Actors in capitalism may then be required to remove this conduct and to reject an evaluative
premise that they first accepted, in order to remove, avoid and undermine an
antinomy. If these requirements commit to a value, this commitment need not
preserve every evaluative premise that the intuition-independent fact allows us
to take as accepted. On a Marxist foundational argument, actors who reject an
evaluative premise that they first accepted do not thereby reject an aspect of
finite rational nature, or an aspect of human nature, but merely a belief that
is generated by and practised in a historically specific form of human society.

If the value commitment revealed by a foundational argument does not
preserve an evaluative judgment that agents first accepted, the argument may
justify social transformation. Feenberg suggests: 'Marx finally derives a wholly
new ground for revolution: the ultimate demand of reason is rationality; revolution alone can satisfy this demand by resolving the antinomies'.[52] We concur,
provided that we replace 'antinomies' with a more precise reference to the
rights-antinomy that Marx describes as such, in *Capital* Volume I.

(iv)   *The Evaluative Premises Are Not Exhausted by Normative Conceptions of Persons*

The evaluative premises in Kant's and Mill's foundational arguments evaluate
items that are particular aspects of persons. In Kant's case, the item is an action
that an agent is rationally required to select as a means to their end: an agent
ascribes goodness to this action. In Mill's case, the item is a person's desire: the

---

52   Feenberg 1981, p. 56.

desires of a person are treated as evidence of what it is worthy to pursue as an end. By contrast, while a Marxist foundational argument can include evaluative premises that evaluate a particular aspect of a person, its evaluative premises are not exhausted by such premises. A Marxist foundational argument also relies on the premise that antinomies in the social world ought to be resolved. In section 4, we noted that this premise qualifies a foundational argument as *post*-Kantian. Its other implication – that it qualifies a foundational argument as *non-liberal* – is discussed in conclusion (in section 15).

7   A Simple Account of Capitalism's Basic Structure

A foundational argument proceeds from a fact that is independent of intuition. This fact must exhibit necessity and universality. If all relevant actors are to be committed to a value, this commitment must arise non-contingently. Such a commitment can only arise from an intuition-independent fact that itself possesses necessity and universality.

Given the objections to Kant's arguments for why we should believe in the existence of God, we may conceive of reason's demands as demands of and on the members of a species of needy, interdependent beings who develop over time. A foundational argument can therefore proceed from a form of society conceived of as historically necessary for human freedom – where a 'form of society' is a type of society with generalised features that can reproduce themselves as part of a process of development. More specifically, a foundational argument can proceed from an account of capitalism's basic structure, if capitalism is historically necessary for human freedom, and possesses some general features by which it contributes to a process of development. To say that capitalism has some general features is just to say that it has features that pull everyone into their orbit, and that these features are able, for a time at least, to sustain the dynamics unleashed by their generalised existence. While this starting point is certainly consistent with a Marxist theory of history, it does not incorporate any very controversial claims. It contains no claims that defenders of capitalism need dispute.

If this starting point is accepted, then we may regard a value to which actors in capitalism are committed as an ultimate value. If we knew of a route to human freedom that did not require any period of capitalism, we would have to acknowledge that we had no way to adjudicate between any value to which we were committed, on account of capitalism's basic structure, and any value to which actors in a non-capitalist but human-freedom-facilitating society were committed. But as we know of no capitalism-free route to human freedom, we need not doubt that a commitment that we have to a value, on account of capitalism's basic structure, is a commitment to an ultimate value.

Most fundamentally, capitalism can be understood to combine generalised purchase and sale with generalised production with wage-labour for continuous money maximisation. As Marx writes in the draft of *A Contribution to a Critique of Political Economy* known as the *Urtext*, 'within the bourgeois mode of production, simple circulation itself only exists as a precondition of capital, and as presupposing capital'.[53] If exchange takes the form of an exchange of commodities for money, or purchase and sale, then each is enabled to sell any type of commodity that anyone with money wants to acquire, and to acquire any type of commodity that anyone wants to sell. If production is with wage-labour and for continuous money maximisation, then the volume of a firm's output rises as far as it profitable, in a context where every other firm requires inputs of a volume that allow it to raise its output as far as is profitable; and each firm produces the commodities it sells by employing voluntarily recruited paid producers with private autonomy.

The generalised existence of these two types of interaction is maintained by the facts that money possessors, who acquire whatever they want to acquire, do not turn down the offer of the same commodity at a cheaper price; money maximising firms can therefore out-compete other types of producing units that produce for the market; money maximising firms will seek to purchase any alienable resource that allows them to make more money, and thereby conquer any branch of market production; and wage-labourers are less likely than other types of capitalistically-employed producer to misuse the expensive, fragile technologies developed by capitalist firms, owing to their individual responsibility as persons.

8   Explaining the Premises

In virtue of its basic structure, capitalism tends to reproduce social division, *and* a context of narrow equality. Capitalism's basic structure, we said, combines generalised purchase and sale with generalised production with wage-labour for continuous money maximisation. It is therefore inherently competitive. Competition among money maximising units of production rewards reinvestment, as a means to outdo competitors in the future, and causes some firms to succeed only because others fail. As a result, the monetary wealth necessary

---

53   *MEGA*, II, 2, p. 91; *MECW*, 29, p. 505.

to purchase productive facilities and hire a sufficient number of wage-labourers to produce competitively remains under the control of a minority. This reproduces a social division between capitalists, who need not perform any wage-labour themselves, and the workers that they hire to perform wage-labour, who are not capitalists. The ends of these two types of actor can be represented as: hiring wage-labour to produce for continuous money maximisation, and: minimising labour performed at a given wage in order to live.

Nonetheless, despite this social division, capitalists and workers interact with each other in the market-place as independent persons in buying or selling the capacity to work, or labour power. In this market interaction, and in every other act of purchase and sale, each party asserts exclusive control over their respective commodity or sum of money while simultaneously leaving intact the exclusive control asserted by the other. In making offers and reaching an agreement on a deal, Marx writes in *Capital* Volume I,

> the commodity keepers must relate to one another as persons whose will resides in those things, such that it is only with the other's will, and thus by means of an act of will common to both, that each appropriates the alien commodity, by alienating their own commodity. They must therefore mutually recognise one another as private property owners.[54]

In purchase and sale, each party can assume that the other is aware that it is in their interest not to practice coercion or deception, to retain the reputation of someone with whom it is economically desirable to have future dealings. Each can assume that it is in the other's self-interest not to disrupt the exclusive control that they assert vis-à-vis the other. Although this stops short of genuine mutual recognition, generalised purchase and sale generates the belief that each must be able to attribute to the other, in order to regard this non-disruptive conduct as genuine mutual recognition.

Generalised purchase and sale generates this belief, by establishing a social interest in the security of private property ownership. Security of private property ownership is a social interest, for it is an interest that each actor, *qua* buyer or seller, only tends to satisfy in conditions that promote its satisfaction for all buyers and sellers. Each actor *qua* buyer or seller is advantaged by a general fall in coercive or deceptive disruptions to acts of purchase and sale, and disadvantaged by a general rise in such disruptions. Each is disadvantaged by a general rise, because money generates acquisitiveness, and is no less worth

---

54   *MEW*, 23, p. 99; *MECW*, 35, p. 95; Marx 1976, p. 178.

gaining from one person than from any other; and because those who acquire money by means of coercion or deception will be emboldened by their success. If there is a general fall in disruption to acts of purchase and sale, any given individual's acts of purchase and sale are less likely to be disrupted. The fear of disruption that each can reasonably claim to have to live with is also reduced. Insofar as any individual obtains these benefits only with a *general* fall in disruption to acts of purchase and sale, security of private property ownership is a social interest. Expressing scepticism that capitalism can sustain any more noble a social interest than a social interest in security, Marx remarks in *On the Jewish Question*: '[s]ecurity is the highest social concept of bourgeois society'.[55]

A social interest in the security of private property ownership is significant, because even self-interested actors have a reason to affirm a principle that upholds a social interest. Even buyers and sellers who are aware of their self-interest have a reason to affirm a principle with which to uphold acts of purchase and sale, and condemn disruptive uses of coercion or deception. Once such a principle is affirmed, each exchanger of commodities or money can assume that the other believes that they *ought* to leave intact the exclusive control asserted by the first in purchase and sale. In light of this assumption, actors in capitalism's basic structure can interpret one another's non-disruptive conduct in purchase and sale as the genuine mutual recognition of private property ownership.

This leads on to a relevant evaluative premise, for the genuine mutual recognition of private property ownership implies the genuine mutual recognition of self-ownership. As Marx writes in *Capital* Volume I, exchangers 'confront one another tacitly as private property owners of those alienable things, and thereby [*eben dadurch*] as independent persons [*Personen*]'.[56] It is only by willing to exercise one's parts and capacities that one can will to act in respect of a thing. To assert exclusive control over commodities or money, one must assert exclusive control over one's own parts and capacities. So, if private property ownership is recognised in purchase and sale, so is the principle of self-ownership; that is, the principle that each individual has enforceable rights over all their parts and capacities, and may not be forced by another to do something, or to part with the fruits of what they do, provided merely that oth-

---

55   *MEW*, 1, p. 365; *MECW*, 3, p. 163.
56   *MEW*, 23, p. 102; *MECW*, 35, p. 98; Marx 1976, p. 182. [1] The Marx 1976 translation of '*eben dadurch*' as 'precisely for that reason' (which would be: '*aus eben dem Grund*') is not literal. '*Dadurch*' means 'by means of that/in consequence of that'; '*eben*' is a particle emphasising simultaneity. [2] *MECW* translates '*Personen*' as 'individuals', but that would be: '*Individuen*'. Compare the reference to '*Personen*' in the next citation.

ers' rights over their parts and capacities are not infringed. The recognition of self-ownership is thus a principle that actors in capitalism affirm, and can see exhibited in its basic structure. As Marx remarks, '[t]he sphere of circulation' is 'a true Eden of the innate rights of man' in which parties enjoy the liberty of 'persons [*Personen*]'.[57] Capitalism's basic structure therefore allows us to treat as accepted the evaluative premise that commodity exchangers are to recognise one another as self-owners.

A premise about the recognition of self-ownership is not the only premise that capitalism's basic structure explains, however. The ends pursued by the capitalist and the worker are: hiring wage-labour for continuous money maximisation, and: minimising labour performed at a given wage in order to live. It is a presupposition of both ends that labour power can only be purchased for money sufficient to purchase its means of reproduction.

For the capitalist's part, we said that their end is *continuous* money maximisation. If so, the capitalist is aware that they must continuously hire wage-labour. Now, no capitalist plans to hire a new set of workers from each day to the next. Moreover, insofar as each capitalist imposes a full working day, each capitalist must assume that their workers receive no payment from any other capitalist enabling them to make any purchases. So, insofar as each capitalist imposes a full working day, each capitalist presupposes that *their* payment to a worker is to facilitate the worker's continued work for them, at least for some period. As such, this payment must enable the worker to purchase the means of reproducing their labour power, at least for some period. As the capitalist pursues continuous money maximisation, and the purchase of labour power for money sufficient to purchase the means of its reproduction is a necessary condition of this, the capitalist can be taken to accept the premise that they can only purchase labour power for money sufficient to purchase the means of its reproduction.

As far as a worker is concerned, the aim of selling their labour power and performing wage-labour is to obtain means of existence. Moreover, by virtue of wage-labour, workers cannot all obtain means to live without having to sell their labour power in the future. Even if the sale of labour-power allows a few workers to obtain means, that, combined with credit, allow them to start up as capitalists, they then have to hire workers themselves. As wage-labour cannot relieve more than a few workers from having to sell their labour power to live, the worker's aim, insofar as they do not regard themselves as an exception, is to obtain means of reproducing their labour power. The worker can therefore

---

57   *MEW*, 23, p. 190; *MECW*, 35, p. 186; Marx 1976, p. 280.

be taken to accept the premise that their labour power can only be purchased for a sum of money sufficient to purchase its means of reproduction, out of a need to work, and because they want to live.

Both arguments say that the capitalist or worker can be taken to accept a premise about the labour power that *they* purchase or sell. Both the capitalist and the worker can also be taken to be aware of the fact that each capitalist and each worker accepts this premise in respect of the labour power that they purchase or sell. But to identify an antinomy in capitalism's basic structure, we need not argue that capitalists and workers also accept an evaluative, agent-neutral premise that labour power ought to be purchased for money sufficient to purchase its means of reproduction. All we need is the factual premise.

Finally, we take as given the evaluative premise that antinomies in the social world ought to be resolved. This evaluative premise is not explained sociologically, by appeal to capitalism's basic structure. It is a rational requirement on any member of an interdependent species of rational being. This is because, firstly, it is a rational requirement to avoid logical contradiction (p and not-p). Secondly, an antinomy involves a logical contradiction. We saw this in respect of 'the antinomy of pure practical reason'[58] described by Kant in *Critique of Practical Reason*. There, the antinomy consisted of the fact that we are required to believe that one of two proposition is true, *and* that both propositions are false – at least insofar as we assume that a virtuous attitude is 'the form of causality in the world of sense'.[59] An antinomy involves a logical contradiction if we adopt the following definition: an antinomy consists of two incompatible assertions that leave no middle ground and appear to be valid, although both assertions rest on the same premises, one or more of which is false. As an antinomy, on this definition, involves a logical contradiction, it is a rational requirement to avoid antinomy. So, if, thirdly, our social world contains antinomy-exhibiting conduct, a rational requirement to avoid logical contradiction and a definition of antinomy as a kind of a logical contradiction entail that we are required to resolve this antinomy. Although the premise that antinomies in the social world ought to be resolved is not a premise that capitalism's basic structure itself explains, actors in capitalism's basic structure, like all rational human beings, are committed to it. This commitment is relevant, if actors in capitalism's basic structure act on principles that lead to an antinomy.

On this account, actors in capitalism's basic structure can be taken to accept the following premises:

---

58   *KpV*, 5: 111. For discussion, see ch. 9, sec. 2.
59   *KpV*, 5: 114.

(1)   Commodity exchangers are to recognise one another as self-owners (the *recognition of self-ownership premise*)
(2)   Labour power can only be purchased for money sufficient to purchase its means of reproduction (the *value premise*)
(3)   Antinomies in the social world ought to be resolved (the *antinomy premise*)

The recognition of self-ownership premise and the value premise are premises that actors in capitalism's basic structure are taken to accept on account of capitalism's basic structure. The antinomy premise is also a premise that actors in capitalism's basic structure are taken to accept, but they accept it just because they are rational human beings. The recognition of self-ownership premise and the antinomy premise are evaluative premises, or statements of value, while the value premise is a factual premise, or statement of fact. The recognition of self-ownership premise and the antinomy premise are also both agent-neutral premises. The explanation of the recognition of self-ownership premise avoids the self-regarding fallacy by appeal to a social interest. The explanation of the antinomy premise avoids the self-regarding fallacy because neither a logical contradiction nor the social world is an aspect of a person. The recognition of self-ownership premise and the antinomy premise are thus both premises that (dis)value something whose description relates everyone to what is (dis)valued. The recognition of self-ownership premise and the value premise lead to antinomy-exhibiting conduct, while the antinomy premise tells us that actors in capitalism are required to resolve any antinomy-exhibiting conduct.

9   The Rights-Antinomy

We now need to argue that conduct in line with the recognition of self-ownership premise and the value premise in capitalism's basic structure exhibits an antinomy.

In the *Economic Manuscripts of 1861–63*, Marx claims of capitalist production: 'an antinomy occurs here in the general relation itself'.[60] Marx sets out the basis of this claim in the chapter of *Capital* Volume I entitled 'The Working Day':

> The capitalist has purchased labour power at its daily value. Its use-value throughout a working day belongs to him ... But what is a working day?

---

60   *MEW*, 43, p. 172; *MECW*, 30, p. 184.

It is certainly shorter than a natural day. But by how much? The capitalist has his own view of this *ultima Thule* ... The time the labourer works is the time in which the capitalist consumes the labour power he purchased from him. If the labourer consumes his disposable time for himself, he steals it from the capitalist.

The capitalist thus appeals to the law of commodity exchange. Like every other buyer, he seeks to extract the greatest possible utility from the use-value of his commodity. But all of a sudden a labourer's voice pipes up ...

The use of my daily labour power therefore belongs to you. But by means of its sale price for the day, I must be able to reproduce it daily, and hence be able to sell it anew. Leaving aside natural deterioration with age, etc., I must be able to work with the same normal amount of strength, health and freshness tomorrow, as I do today ... Like a sensible, thrifty innkeeper, I shall be economical with my singular fortune, labour power, and abstain from wildly squandering it. Each day I will realise, set in motion, put to work, only so much of it as its normal duration and healthy development can bear ... The use of my labour power, and the deprivation of it, are entirely different things ... I demand the normal working day, because, like any other seller, I demand the value of my commodity.

... [T]he nature of commodity exchange itself provides no limit to the working day, hence no limit to surplus labour. The capitalist asserts his right as a purchaser when he tries to make the working day as long as possible, and, if possible, to turn one working day into two. On the other hand, the specific nature of the commodity sold includes a limit on its consumption by the purchaser, and the labourer asserts his right as a seller when he wills to limit the working day to a certain normal magnitude. An antinomy therefore arises, of right against right, both equally licenced by the law of commodity exchange. Between equal rights, force decides. Hence, in the history of capitalist production, the regulation of the working day presents itself as a struggle over the limits of the working day – a struggle between the collective capitalist, i.e. the class of capitalists, and the collective labourer, or working-class.[61]

---

61   *MEW*, 23, pp. 247–9; *MECW*, 35, pp. 241–3; Marx 1976, pp. 341–4.

Capitalism's basic structure generates an antinomy, on account of how the capitalist and the worker conduct themselves. Their conduct in capitalism's basic structure implicitly amounts to the assertion of rights that form an antinomy. The capitalist asserts a rights claim 'when he tries to make the working day as long as possible, and, if possible, to turn one working day into two', while the worker also asserts a rights claim 'when he wills to limit [*beschränken will*] the working day'. A right to an unlimited working day and a right to a limited working day are incompatible rights that leave no middle ground. If the same premises lie behind the implicit assertion of these rights, and the premises appear valid, the conduct exhibits an antinomy, and at least one of the premises must be false. If so, capitalism's basic structure contains an irrationality that defines a struggle over the use of time.

Before explaining this antinomy, we may note that the official translations of *Capital* Volume I make a complete mess of this bracketed phrase. In both, we read that the worker maintains his right as a seller 'when he wishes to reduce the working day'.[62] This is doubly mistaken. First, '*will*' is a conjugation of '*wollen* (to will, to want)', not '*wünschen* (to wish)'. A worker may possess means to limit their working day, by taking a sly break: '"snatching a few minutes"',[63] as the factory inspectors of Marx's day called it. As a worker may possess means to limit the working day, a limited working day is emphatically not something that the worker can only wish for. A worker implicitly asserts a right to a limited working day in their action; and only on this assumption can there be antinomy-exhibiting conduct in capitalism's basic structure. Second, '*beschränken* (to limit)' is not '*reduzieren* (to reduce)'. If one side asserts a right to reduce X, and another side asserts a right to increase X, each side may agree to a compromise that leaves the magnitude of X unaltered, proving the absence of antinomy.[64] An antinomy arises because the capitalist seeks an

---

62   *MECW*, 35, p. 243; Marx 1976, p. 344; 'wishes to reduce' would be: '*reduzieren wünscht*'.

63   *MEW*, 23, p. 257; *MECW*, 35, p. 250; Marx 1976, p. 352.

64   In a review of Furner 2018, Rory Gillis (Gillis 2020) reports: 'Furner ... highlights that there is in fact an antinomy present in the duelling rights claims between the worker and the capitalist. The worker claims that they have a right to a shorter working day because they need time to replenish their labour power. The capitalist claims that they have a right to make the labourer work for a longer period each day'. In fact, I argued that we should reject this view: 'no antinomy can arise between attempts to "prolong" and to "shorten" the working day, for that suggests the option of keeping the working day at its current length' (Furner 2018, p. 430). There is, rather, an antinomy between 'a right to an unlimited working day and a right to a limited working day' (Furner 2018, p. 429). Gillis's misrepresentation of my view stems from his claim (in the first clause of the following statement) that 'an antinomy involves a contradiction between two reasonable claims, though Furner

unlimited working day, while the worker seeks a limited working day, on the same premises, which leave no other option. To rely on the official translations of *Capital* Volume I is to have no chance of comprehending Marx's description of the rights-antinomy in capitalism's basic structure, which is one of the reasons why it is so under-theorised.[65]

Capitalism's basic structure exhibits an antinomy, because the recognition of self-ownership premise and the value premise that it leads actors to accept can both be taken in one of two different, contradictory ways. The recognition of self-ownership premise can either be taken to require the recognition of self-ownership in an act of purchase and sale, or across an entire series of such acts. The value premise can be taken to signify the purchase of labour power for money sufficient to purchase means of reproduction for the period of hire, or its purchase for money sufficient to purchase means of reproduction not just for the period of hire but also for any further period in which the worker is deprived of labour power as a result of labour in the hire period.

It might seem obvious that the capitalist's payment is to be sufficient to purchase means of reproduction only for the period of hire, as no one need pay for what they have yet to hire. But we have to consider the possibility of excessive labour. Excessive labour can be defined, non-normatively, as an amount of labour that, through exhaustion, injury or illness, reduces the total time for which a worker can sell their labour power to a capitalist for a living wage. Excessive labour deprives a worker of labour power to sell in a period beyond the hire period. It may seem that the capitalist's payment to the worker ought to cover the purchase of means of reproduction for any period of non-hire induced by excessive labour when hired. If not, the capitalist fails to compensate for not returning the commodity that they hired to its owner in the same state, natural wear and tear excepted, at the end of the hire period.

Suppose that, consistently with generalised production with wage-labour for continuous money maximisation and generalised purchase and sale, capitalists

---

uses the term in a more technical sense' (Gillis 2020). A 'contradiction between two reasonable claims' is not sufficient for an antinomy, because two reasonable but contradictory claims may leave some middle ground. An antinomy, by contrast, requires that we oscillate between two positions, and for this, 'it cannot appear to be the case that there is a third option different from them both' (Furner 2018, p. 125). The fact that on Gillis's report of the worker's and capitalist's claims, there is *no* antinomy, confirms why my 'more technical sense' of antinomy is required. Indeed, the reason why I criticised the official translations at length (Furner 2018, pp. 428–30) is that they encourage the widespread mistake that Gillis misattributes to me.

65   For an extensive critique of past interpretations of the rights-antinomy, see Furner 2018, ch. 12.

impose an amount of labour that is excessive. Capitalists may put a premium on labour in the present in order to make the most of what they see as a short-lived competitive advantage, or to do their best vis-à-vis other firms with this advantage; and the cheapest and easiest way to increase labour in the present, in terms of outlay on equipment and training, is to extend the hours of the existing workforce. By imposing excessive labour, the capitalist implicitly asserts a right that rests on the recognition of self-ownership premise and the value premise. The capitalist acts towards the worker as if to say: as you and I are self-owners, we each have the right to contract with one another over whatever is ours. A person's labour power is theirs to contract with for any stretch of time within a given time period. If I pay you an equivalent for means of reproduction for the period for which you agree to work for me, the use of your labour power in this period, for however long, is mine. If you unilaterally break off or slacken its use in this period, you steal what I have rightfully acquired from you.

It is in the worker's interest to resist the capitalist's imposition of excessive labour, by appeal to the *same* premises. In resisting the imposition of excessive labour, the worker acts towards the capitalist as if to say: as you and I are self-owners, our rights to hire out what is ours for one stretch of time cannot abrogate our rights to hire it out for a later stretch of time. Each of us is entitled to receive back any commodity, whose use we hire out, in the same state as before, natural wear and tear excepted, at the end of the hire period. Once your use of my labour power becomes excessive, you have to pay me accordingly. As you do not, you leave me no option but to unilaterally limit my work in the hire period, to directly put a stop to your theft of my property.

An antinomy therefore arises in capitalism's basic structure, of right against right, insofar as the chains of reasoning just outlined explicate views that lie behind the conduct of the capitalist and the worker when each seeks to ensure that labour power is used in accordance with the end that each pursues in capitalism's basic structure. The capitalist's conduct vis-à-vis the worker is as if they believe that there is a right to an unlimited working-day, while the worker's conduct vis-à-vis the capitalist is as if they believe, on the same premises, that there is a right to a limited working-day. As such, the irrationality of 'an antinomy occurs here in the general relation itself'.[66] Faced with this rights-antinomy, it is a rational requirement to resolve it, or as Marx urged as early as 1843, to 'develop new principles for the world out of the world's own principles'.[67]

---

66   *MEW*, 43, p. 172; *MECW*, 30, p. 184.
67   *MEW*, 1, pp. 345; *MECW*, 3, pp. 144.

10   Resolving the Rights-Antinomy

We have offered a simple, hopefully uncontroversial account of capitalism's basic structure; explained the premises that its actors can be taken to accept, and described the antinomy of rights that this basic structure and its related premises produce. By the antinomy premise, actors in capitalism are rationally required to resolve this antinomy. Actors in capitalism are rationally required to apply a principle to remove this antinomy-exhibiting conduct, provided that any need expressed in but separable from the antinomy's premises can still be satisfied. These needs are for recognition, and for producers to receive means of consumption. For now, we shall simply assume that these needs can be met in forms other than that of the recognition of self-ownership, and the purchase of labour power by a capitalist. We return to these matters later on. Our focus for now is on the principle whose application is to remove the antinomy-exhibiting conduct.

Capitalism's basic structure exhibits an antinomy due to the imposition of excessive labour, and the reaction to its imposition by the worker. If it is to be possible to remove this antinomy from capitalism's basic structure, that can only be because it is possible either to prevent the capitalist from imposing excessive labour, or else to prevent the worker from resisting its imposition. As it is impossible to prevent the expression of exhaustion, a resolution of the antinomy depends on the possibility of prohibiting excessive labour. Actors in capitalism are rationally required to apply the principle: excessive labour is prohibited. This principle does not abolish capitalism's basic structure. It merely modifies it.

The principle that excessive labour is prohibited can be implemented by a law that prohibits excessive labour. A general, enforceable law is necessary, as competition between capitalists gives each an interest in imposing excessive labour. The law of capitalist society prevents the capitalist from imposing excessive labour if it clearly formulates an adequate limit on the maximum daily and weekly hours of labour that it is permissible to work; if it puts sanctions in place that are an adequate deterrent; and, finally, if these limits are policed and the sanctions are reliably and timely enforced. If all this is achieved, and production with wage-labour for continuous money maximisation remains lawful, there is no reason to deny that the basic structure of production remains capitalist. So, excessive labour may be prevented consistently with the basic structure remaining capitalist; and if there is no excessive labour, no conduct in this structure appears to exhibit the aforementioned antinomy. This may seem to cast doubt on the prospect of using an antinomy-based strategy to ground an ultimate value that can condemn capitalism.

There are two reasons why this is not the end of the matter, however. Firstly, a commitment to the principle that excessive labour is prohibited is *rational* only if it avoids and undermines antinomy, by rejecting at least one premise of the rights-antinomy. Actors in capitalism are not merely rationally required to prohibit excessive labour on principle, but to do so on grounds that avoid and undermine antinomy. Secondly, the principle that excessive labour is prohibited reflects an underlying value. It reflects the value of guaranteeing the reproduction of the current population of producers for no further reason than that they are producers. Capitalism's basic structure may continue to tend to violate this value even if excessive labour is prohibited. Let us expand on each of these points.

A foundational argument identifies agents related to an intuition-independent fact who accept certain premises, and asks what these agents are rationally committed to. If actors in capitalism's basic structure accept premises that produce an antinomy in this structure, then they are rationally committed not just to remove the antinomy, but to do so on grounds that avoid and undermine antinomy. As regards avoidance, if the grounds for prohibiting excessive labour themselves produce an antinomy, then an irrationality remains. A commitment to the principle that excessive labour is prohibited is only rational, therefore, if its defence does not rely on premises, such as the recognition of self-ownership and value premises, that lead to antinomy. Its rational defence must avoid, or be *distinct* from, premises sufficient to produce antinomy. As regards the undermining of antinomy, if a rational defence of a prohibition on excessive labour is not combined with a *rejection* of at least one of the premises of the rights-antinomy, the call for this prohibition, and its retention, still remain vulnerable to an unchallenged irrationality, for capitalism's basic structure continues to produce the beliefs behind the antinomy.

On the one hand, if coordinated action by a social movement must occur for the call for a law against excessive labour to be heeded, then the intellectual position it must assume is only rationally resolute if it includes a rational response to any criticism it faces as a result of beliefs produced by capitalism's basic structure. Such criticism includes the criticism that the recognition of self-ownership and value premises dictate that there be no limits on the working day, as well as the criticism that the call for a prohibition on excessive labour is based on premises that lead to an antinomy. The comprehensively rational response to such criticism includes a rational rejection of any false premise of the rights-antinomy. As an antinomy must rest on at least one false premise, the comprehensively rational response is to adopt a principle with which to reject at least one of its premises.

On the other hand, even if excessive labour is prohibited, this does not remove the conditions that produce a belief in the premises of the rights-antinomy. Capitalists who resent the legal limits that suspend excessive labour may be expected to articulate their claim that there is a right to an unlimited working day. Pressure could arise to repeal laws that stood in the way of excessive labour, or to cease to police them stringently. The comprehensively rational response to this threat includes a rational rejection of any false premise of the antinomy. So, again, at least one premise of the rights-antinomy must be rejected, on rational grounds. The rights-antinomy in capitalism's basic structure commits actors not simply to a principle with which to prohibit excessive labour, but to a defence of this principle that avoids antinomy, and to a principle with which to reject at least one of the antinomy's premises.

Consider, secondly, the value that underlies the principle of prohibiting excessive labour. The aim of a prohibition on excessive labour is to prevent the imposition of excessive labour. But why is the imposition of excessive labour to be prevented? To protect the current population of wage-labourers from labour that would deprive them of their long-term capacity to work. Their work is to be limited to hours consistent with their continued employment as wage-labourers, until the end of their working life. Indeed, a prohibition on excessive labour is rationally applied whether or not the labour is performed for a capitalist. If a prohibition on excessive labour is a rational response to the capitalist's imposition of excessive labour, it is a rational response to *any* employer who, acting on the recognition of self-ownership and value premises, seeks to impose an unlimited working day. So, the value underlying the principle that excessive labour is prohibited is the value of guaranteeing the reproduction of the current population of producers for no further reason than that they are producers.

Capitalism's basic structure may continue to tend to lead to violations of this value, however, even if excessive labour is prohibited. This insight is available from the perspective of actors in capitalism. It can be voiced by a participant in a working-class movement for legal limits on the working day – a movement that must have formed for the call for a prohibition on excessive labour to be heeded. (This is merely a probabilistic claim, based on an assessment of class interest, not a strict rational requirement.)

To demand legal limits on the working day, a working-*class* movement must have formed out of a learning process that includes a failure of more immediate workplace and trade-specific struggles to limit working hours in particular workplaces or specific trades, in opposition to capitalist firms who, appealing to the premises of value and self-ownership, use their power to refuse these limits in their own interests. As Marx writes in *Capital* Volume I:

> For protection from the serpent of their sorrows, labourers must ... as a class, compel a state law, an irresistible social shackle, which prevents them, by voluntary contract with capital, from selling themselves, and their kin, into death and slavery. In place of the grandiose catalogue of 'inalienable human rights' comes the modest Magna Carta of a legally limited working day.[68]

Any non-statutory, voluntarily agreed limits on working hours in individual workplaces or trades will tend to unravel, owing to the competitive handicap that a given capitalist firm or branch of capitalist firms suffers, if it is an exception among capitalist firms in not imposing excessive labour. Through the formation of a working-class movement for legal limits on the working-day, its participants show that they have learnt, from the failure of workplace and trade-specific struggles against excessive labour, that each capitalist firm is indifferent to whom they hire, as long as one individual's labour is as good a means of continuous money maximisation as that of the next.[69] But to be aware of this indifference is to have a reason to believe that capitalist firms, both individually and collectively, will never cease to oppose statutory restrictions on contracts of labour or taxes on their profits that aim to guarantee the reproduction of the current population of producers for no further reason than that they are producers – which is to say, *whether or not* conditions in the labour market leave capitalist firms reliant on re-hiring them. By implication, any movement to guarantee producers' reproduction for no further reason than that they are producers can be expected to encounter capitalist opposition. As Marx comments in *Instructions for the Delegates of the Provisional General Council*:

> Trades' Unions originally sprang up from the *spontaneous* attempts of workmen at removing or at least checking that competition [competition among themselves – JF], in order to conquer such terms of contract as might raise them at least above the condition of mere slaves. The immediate object of Trades' Unions was therefore confined to everyday necessities, to expediencies for the obstruction of the incessant encroachments of

---

68   *MEW*, 23, p. 320; *MECW*, 35, pp. 306–7; Marx 1976, p. 416.
69   Indeed, if there are enough bodies to sacrifice, excessive labour is in the capitalist *class*'s interest: 'the history of modern industry has shown that a continuous overpopulation is possible, even though it is a stream formed of human generations who are quickly ruined, swiftly succeed one another, and are picked unripe, so to speak' (*MEW*, 43, p. 173; *MECW*, 30, p. 185; see also *MEW*, 43, p. 297; *MECW*, 30, p. 302).

capital, in one word, to questions of wages and time of labour. This activity of the Trades' Unions is not only legitimate, it is necessary. It cannot be dispensed with so long as the present system of production lasts.[70]

As long as there is production with wage-labour for continuous money maximisation, movements to guarantee current producers' reproduction for no further reason than that they are producers can be expected to have to struggle against its effects.[71] A movement for legal limits that prohibit excessive labour is just one such type of movement for an association of unions to support. Even if excessive labour is prohibited, any other such measure will have to face capitalist opposition. To end the cause of such struggles, it would be necessary to abolish capitalism's basic structure itself.

Capitalism's basic structure may not exhibit an antinomy once excessive labour is prohibited. But if actors are committed to the principle that excessive labour is prohibited, then they are rationally required to uphold its underlying value in other contexts too. As capitalism's basic structure can be expected to persistently violate this value, a commitment to this value is also a reason to condemn capitalism. To be sure, it is conceivable that, for each issue that renews the conflict between production with wage-labour for continuous money maximisation and the value of guaranteeing current producers' reproduction for no further reason than that they are producers, a law can be enacted so as to remove the conflict. But corrections after the fact of a whole period of predictable capitalist opposition to them do not prevent violations in this potentially quite prolonged period. To be reconciled to only making corrections after the fact on each and every issue is to be reconciled to ongoing violations. To be committed to the value underlying the principle that excessive labour is prohibited is thus to be committed to condemn capitalism's basic structure, as a cause of violations of this value.

One might suppose that this completes the negative part of a Marxist foundational argument. For according to the argument thus far, actors in capitalism are committed to a value with which to condemn capitalism's basic structure. But this does not exhaust all of the rational requirements arising from the antinomy. There remain the rational requirements to avoid and undermine the rights-antinomy, by rejecting at least one of its premises. The value of guaranteeing current producers' reproduction for no further reason than that they are producers is not sufficient for this. It might be affirmed by affirming the

---

70   *MECW*, 20, p. 191.
71   In these everyday struggles, Marx writes in *Value, Price and Profit*, workers are 'fighting with effects, but not with the causes of those effects' (*MECW*, 20, p. 148).

versions of the recognition of self-ownership premise and the value premise that lie behind the worker's assertion of a right to a limited working day. We require a further principle, both to defend a prohibition on excessive labour on a basis that is clearly distinct from antinomy, and to reject at least one premise of the rights-antinomy. This principle must also be consistent with conceiving of freedom as to be enjoyed by all, a prohibition on excessive labour, the value underlying this prohibition, and the condemnation of capitalism implied by this value.

11 The System Universalisability Principle of Justice

To avoid and undermine the rights-antinomy consistently with these conditions, it is rational to adopt the system universalisability principle of justice:

> The system universalisability principle of justice: a system in which advantages are obtained by pursuing system-reinforced ends that cannot be universalised is unjust (the *system universalisability principle*, for short).

The system universalisability principle directly condemns certain systems as unjust, where a system consists of generalised interactions that enable and constrain one another. It can also support a condemnation of certain system-reinforced conduct in systems that are unjust:

> advantages (money, leisure, honour, power) obtained by pursuing system-reinforced ends that cannot be universalised are unjust.

Even without further elaboration, it is apparent how the system universalisability principle can be used to reject the premises of the rights-antinomy. Firstly, it can be used to reject the recognition of self-ownership premise, which says: commodity exchangers are to recognise one another as self-owners. The system universalisability principle requires that self-ownership not be recognised. It implies that no one has the right, through a system, to benefit from the pursuit of an end that not everyone can conceivably achieve, even if self-ownership is not infringed, because this would contradict the value of community. The system universalisability principle instead establishes a duty to remove systems that enable and constrain ends that cannot be universalised. As rights limited by the system universalisability principle are limited for a purpose other than that of protecting rights, rights cannot take the form of self-ownership rights, consistently with this principle.

The system universalisability principle may also be used to reject the value premise of the rights-antinomy. The value premise says: labour power can only be purchased for money sufficient to purchase its means of reproduction. This premise can be rejected if its realisation must belong to a system that promotes an end that cannot be universalised. We argue below that capitalism's basic structure is a system of this kind. So, if the value premise cannot be realised except in capitalism's basic structure, the system universalisability principle can be used to reject this premise, in addition to the recognition of self-ownership premise.

Further, if (as argued below) capitalism's basic structure systematically reinforces an end that cannot be universalised, then the system universalisability principle can be used to defend a prohibition on excessive labour in a way that avoids antinomy. The system universalisability principle can be used to defend this prohibition on the basis that it limits the pursuit of an end that no one has a right to pursue, and that it is just to prohibit.

The system universalisability principle incorporates a type of universalisability test. This test is a test of a system, rather than a test of purely individual conduct. In this respect, it differs from Kant's Formula of the Law of Nature, and from Kant's other formulas of the categorical imperative, which are addressed to a finite rational being. We may recall Kant's Formula of the End in Itself (FEI):

> So act that you use humanity, in your own person as well as in the person of any other, always at the same time as an end, never merely as a means.[72]

An evaluation in terms of FEI must rest entirely on the conduct of an agent, or associating agents. There must be an agent (or associating agents) whose conduct is evaluated, because only an agent can act on an end; and third party influences that impact on the addressee's overall situation are not relevant simply by virtue of that. Even if third party influences result from the pursuit of ends, these ends are not the ends of the agent(s) whose conduct is under evaluation. In applying FEI, the evaluation of conduct by A addressed to B is not constituted even partly by an evaluation of conduct by C addressed to B, unless A is associated with C.

By contrast, the system universalisability principle condemns systems. A human ethics takes cognisance of the fact that humans are interdependent, needy beings who must develop their capacities if they are to improve themselves and their conditions so as to allow everyone to enjoy freedom. Systems

---

72   *GMS*, 4: 429.

bear directly on this development. What is evaluated, by the system universalisability principle, is not an end, but a type of end that is socially enabled and constrained. Its application does not require us to show that the systematic nature of conduct is part of anyone's end. No particular agent need be responsible for the fact that an end is system-reinforced. Nor is it necessary to establish an association between the actors who enable and constrain each other's ends. To apply the system universalisability principle to capitalism's basic structure, it is not necessary to show that a particular agent is responsible for the fact that continuous money maximisation is a system-reinforced end, or that capitalist firms who pursue continuous money maximisation are joined by an association.

To ask whether a system-reinforced end can be universalised is to perform a counterfactual thought experiment. The first step is to describe the conditions, means and end of conduct whose end is system-reinforced, and that yields an advantage for its agent. The second step is to imagine that this conduct is legislated by a public power, and universally adopted. The thought of publicly legislated, universally adopted conduct is the thought of a universal law of human nature. The third step is to ask whether the conception of any human world that includes this universal law of human nature is contradictory. We ask whether everyone who satisfies its conditions can adopt its means to achieve its end. If, in any world in which some actors satisfy its conditions, at least one cannot adopt its means, or cannot achieve its end by adopting these means, the conception of such a world is contradictory.

If the conception of such a world is contradictory, the system universalisability principle condemns the system as unjust. To condemn a system as unjust is to condemn it, on impartial grounds, as a system that ought not to be enforced. The system universalisability principle can be defended on impartial grounds if capitalism's basic structure contains an antinomy that actors are rationally required to remove, avoid and undermine; and if these requirements, given the other four conditions that an antinomy-resolving principle must satisfy, commit to the system universalisability principle.

These conditions, we said, are that the principle must be consistent with freedom for all, a prohibition on excessive labour, the value underlying this prohibition, and the condemnation of capitalism implied by this value. The system universalisability principle is consistent with the idea that freedom is to be conceived as enjoyed by everyone, because it is a duty that reflects the value of a community of equal social beings. It is consistent with a prohibition on excessive labour, because a prohibition on excessive labour does not necessitate a system that reinforces ends that cannot be universalised. For the same reason, the system universalisability principle is consistent with the value of guaranteeing the reproduction of the current population of producers for no further reason than that they are producers. This guarantee can be provided independently of such systems.

The remaining condition is that the system universalisability principle must be compatible with the condemnation of capitalism's basic structure implied by the value of this guarantee. The system universalisability principle offers a *complementary* condemnation of capitalism, if it can be applied to condemn a system that reinforces continuous money-maximisation as unjust. While the value of guaranteeing current producers' reproduction simply because they are producers is a value with which to condemn capitalism on account of the pressures its basic structure tends to effect (through delays to and erosions of measures to limit working hours, raise taxes on profits, or remove dangerous or unhealthy conditions of work that protect existing producers as producers, independently of market demand for *their* labour power), the system universalisability principle can condemn capitalism's basic structure as the system that it is.

To apply the system universalisability principle to capitalism's basic structure, we first formulate the end that this system reinforces. We ask: by what type of system-reinforced end imposed on what type of actor does capitalism's basic structure shape human development? The answer is: by continuous money maximisation, imposed on each capitalist firm. Competition between capitalist firms imposes an imperative to pursue continuous money maximisation on each, so as to be able to accumulate, reinvest, and out-compete its rivals.

We must also describe the conditions and means of this end. To determine its means, we ask: if all actors on whom a type of system-reinforced end is imposed are to achieve this end, what general type of means is it necessary for them to adopt? The general means by which all the firms of capitalism's basic structure can pursue continuous money maximisation is: production with wage-labour. If all firms are to maximise their monetary wealth, then they must produce something, for otherwise, any gain by one is counterbalanced by another's loss; and the most responsible, and therefore profitable, type of producer to employ, is a wage-labourer. The conditions of any maximising conduct are simply: whenever it is possible to do so. The capitalist firm's conduct can therefore be described as: continuous maximisation of its monetary wealth by means of production with wage-labour whenever its monetary wealth is at stake.

Having described this conduct, we can identify the types of actor who must be thought to populate any hypothetical human world that contains the corresponding universal law. We ask: if all capitalist firms engage in production with wage-labour to the end of continuous money maximisation, what other types of actor must exist, as necessary conditions of this conduct? Besides capitalist firms, one other type of actor that must exist is: wage-labourers. Any hypothetical human world that is to include a universal law of money maximisation must be thought to contain wage-labourers, as well as capitalist firms. It might be argued that a managerial group is also necessary, to administer a capitalist firm's decisions. But we may ignore this issue here, as well as other candidates. It is sufficient that any hypothetical human world in which money maximisation is a universal law must contain capitalist firms and wage-labourers, to arrive at a judgment of a system that reinforces money maximisation. To show that any hypothetical human world in which money maximisation is a universal law is contradictory in conception, it is sufficient to argue that not all wage-labourers are able to maximise their monetary wealth in any such world.

We can now formulate the universal law. Its means need not be identical with those of the system-reinforced conduct, because the universal law is thought of as universally adopted. Its means must reflect the fact that all hypothetical actors satisfying its conditions are to be thought of as pursuing its end, with all available means. These means need not be identical with the means adopted by real-life actors on whom the end is systematically reinforced. The means of a universal law of money maximisation must be formulated so as to allow us to conceive of all wage-labourers as adopting it, and wage-labourers do not possess the means of capitalist firms. Hiring the wage-labour of others is not a means that is available to wage-labourers, in their function as wage-labourers, to achieve any end.

To obtain a sufficiently general statement of the means of a universal law, we ask: what is the most general description of what a rational human being must do to pursue an end, provided merely that its means, if they were really adopted, would not disrupt the system of reinforced conduct that is to be evaluated? In this case, we ask: what is the most general description of what a rational human being must do to the end of continuously maximising their monetary wealth, provided that these means would not disrupt continuous money maximisation by capitalist firms if actors in capitalism adopted them? All disruptive, non-economic means (violent crime, for example) are ruled out. What we are left with, as the means of a universal law of money maximisation, is the means of putting one's possessions to economic use.

This allows us to say that a universal law of money maximisation is the public legislation of the following, universally adopted conduct:

> Everyone, when their monetary wealth is at stake, puts their possessions to economic use, and thereby maximises their monetary wealth

A capitalist firm acts on this universal law by hiring wage-labourers to produce for it. Wage-labourers act on this universal law by maximising the time for
which they sell their labour power, performing the labour, and minimising their
expenditures. A hypothetical world that contains the universal law of money
maximisation is contradictory in conception if not all wage-labourers can maximise their monetary wealth by performing these functions. Marx indicates the
answer to this question in the *Grundrisse* when, in reference to the injunction
to maximise labour and to maximize savings, Marx suggests that

> if workers *generally* were to act on these demands, that is, as *workers*
> (what the individual worker does, or can do, in contrast to their genus,
> can only exist as an *exception*, not as a *rule*, because it does not lie in the
> nature of the relation itself), that is, as a *rule*, then (aside from the damage
> they would do to general consumption – the drop would be enormous –
> and hence to production as well, thus also to the number and volume of
> exchanges they could perform with capital, hence to themselves as work-
> ers) the worker would employ, absolutely, means that abolish their own
> end [*er absolut Mittel anwendete, die ihren eignen Zweck aufheben*], and
> which must directly degrade him to an Irishman, to a level of wage-labour
> at which the most brutal minimum of needs and means of subsistence
> appear as the sole object and end of his exchange with capital.[73]

Some conduct cannot be universalised because it relies on instrumental action
to the performer of the conduct that can then no longer be forthcoming. Not
everyone can achieve a goal by purely parasitic means, such as by living entirely
off the work of others while doing nothing. Nor can everyone lay claim to a
status whose assertion denies it to others, such as the status of slaveholder, if
slaves cannot possess the property rights required to own slaves. The problem,

---

73   *MEW*, 42, p. 211; *MECW*, 28, p. 215; Marx 1973, p. 285. The Marx 1973 translation of the brack-
     eted phrase, 'the worker would be employing means which absolutely contradict their
     purpose' (which translates as: '*er Mittel anwendete, die ihren Zweck absolut widersprechen*'),
     contains a number of inaccuracies. The main problem is that to say that 'means ... con-
     tradict their purpose' is to convey a mistake in the choice of means to an end, that, for all
     this phrase says, may be a possible end. If all Christians treat Christmas as an occasion to
     get drunk, they might be said to 'contradict the purpose' they have as Christians, to reflect
     on Christ's birth. But this is not to say that it is inconceivable for them all to use Christmas
     as a time to reflect on Christ's birth, if only they adopted more suitable means to this end.
     Marx's claim is that, if capitalists and wage-labourers all seek to maximise their monet-
     ary wealth, wage-labourers cannot achieve this end, however unmistaken they may be in
     their choice of means.

in these types of case, is that any actor who acts on the universal law relies on action towards them that cannot go as planned, once their conduct is universally adopted.

The same applies to a universal law of money maximisation. This law requires two types of actor to succeed in competing, money-maximising uses of labour power. Workers cannot succeed in maximising their monetary wealth by extending the hire and use of their labour power in each period, and restricting the purchases that they make to maintain themselves as workers in each period, owing to capitalist firms' money maximising response:

> If all or the majority are extra hard-working ..., they do not increase the value of their commodity, but merely its quantity, and thus the demands placed upon it as a use-value. If they all save, a general reduction of the wage will put them back on the right track; for the general saving would show the capitalist that their wage is generally too high, that they receive more than their equivalent for their commodity, for the capacity to dispose over their labour.[74]

Every general increase in the amount of labour performed in a given period allows each capitalist firm to impose that increased standard on their workforce as the norm. Every general saving by wage-labourers reveals that labour power can be reproduced with fewer purchases. Capitalist firms can reduce what they pay their workers, and still pay them enough to purchase the means of reproduction of their labour power. Exhausted by these responses, workers may reach a point at which they lack the will to continue to maximise their monetary wealth, if minimally rewarded excessive labour deprives them of this self-control. But even if workers retain enough self-control, capitalist firms' money-maximising response condemns workers to fail to maximise their monetary wealth. Any hypothetical world containing the universal law of money-maximisation is therefore contradictory in conception. As any such world is contradictory in conception, capitalism's basic structure is condemned as unjust.

The system universalisability principle thereby satisfies the remaining condition required of any principle for undermining the rights-antinomy. It is consistent with the condemnation of capitalism that is implied by the value of guaranteeing current producers' reproduction for no further reason than that they are producers. Indeed, the fact that the system universalisability principle

---

74 *MEW*, 42, p. 211; *MECW*, 28, pp. 215–16; Marx 1973, p. 285.

condemns the universal law of money-maximisation means that this principle can also be used to reject the value premise of the rights-antinomy, as well as the recognition of self-ownership premise. It can be used to reject the value premise on the basis that the latter is a means for distributing means of consumption to producers so as to facilitate capitalists' money-maximisation, whose pursuit is constitutive of an unjust system. This end is inherent to the realisation of the value premise, for in the absence of this end, there is no reason to distribute means of consumption to producers by the measure of what reproduces producers' labour power as a commodity. In sum, the system universalisability principle provides both (a) a condemnation of capitalism that complements the condemnation provided by the value of guaranteeing current producers' reproduction, and (b) a basis for rejecting the premises of the rights-antinomy, while defending a prohibition on excessive labour in a way that avoids antinomy. It is a principle to which actors in capitalism are committed, by the rational requirement to resolve an antinomy in capitalism's basic structure.

12   The Autonomy of a Human Community

Although an antinomy is an irrationality, a premise of an antinomy may give expression to a need that is separable from the form of its articulation in this premise. Even if it is a rational requirement to implement a principle to remove antinomy-exhibiting conduct from the world, it may only be rational, all things considered, to do so if any need separable from its premises can be satisfied once this conduct is removed.

This applies to the rights-antinomy in capitalism's basic structure. The recognition of self-ownership premise gives expression to the need for recognition, while the value premise gives expression to the need for producers to receive means of consumption. It is only rational, all things considered, to implement a principle to remove the rights-antinomy, if needs for recognition and for producers to receive means of consumption can be satisfied even in the absence of the antinomy-exhibiting conduct. By implication, it is only rational, all things considered, to defend the implementation of this principle on grounds that avoid and undermine antinomy, if these needs can be satisfied without such conduct, and consistently with this defence.

A review of the principles and values that actors in capitalism are already committed to, on the above argument, will reveal whether these two needs commit to anything further. We have argued that actors in capitalism are rationally committed to: a principle that excessive labour is prohibited; the value of guaranteeing current producers' reproduction for no further reason than that they are producers; and the system universalisability principle. If current producers' reproduction is guaranteed, they receive means of consumption. So, the need for producers to receive means of consumption commits to nothing further. But the need for recognition does commit to something further. It is not satisfied, just by these principles and value. So, it is rational, all things considered, to adopt principles to remove the rights-antinomy and to defend its removal on grounds that avoid and undermine antinomy only if the system universalisability principle can be combined with a principle (or principles) that reflects the value of guaranteeing current producers' reproduction for no further reason than that they are producers, and satisfies the need for recognition. If a value underlies this combination of principles, actors in capitalism are rationally committed to it. This value, we argue, is the value of the autonomy of a human community, understood as the co-legislation of public principles that expressly endorse harmonious social dynamics.

An attempt to ground the value of autonomy raises two preliminary issues. Firstly, if a value commitment is a commitment to a version of autonomy, our commitment to it cannot rest on chance or desire. A commitment to it must be shown to arise from the nature of the subjects who are thereby committed to it. A grounding argument for the autonomy of a human community must show that our nature as interdependent, needy, developing beings commits us to it. The foundational argument defended here purports to do this, insofar as it proceeds from facts about a historically necessary form of human society. Secondly, if this value commitment is to be fundamental, it must have a positive content that can regulate the actions of those who are committed to it. The foundational argument presented here can do this, if it can show that the value of the autonomy of a human community underlies a combination of principles which include not merely the negative, system universalisability principle, but also a positive principle for recognition and for providing producers with means of consumption.

Thus, in this argument, the relation between the system universalisability principle and the value of the autonomy of a human community is not a relation between a fundamental principle and a fundamental value. To say that a principle is fundamental is to say that it is a *full* expression of a fundamental value, that it merely gives imperative form to the fundamental value. For example, in Kant's ethics, 'always treat humanity in a person as an end' is a fundamental principle: it fully expresses the fundamental value of the exclusive absolute worth of humanity in a person. A fundamental principle cannot be grounded without establishing that we are required to regard something as of fundamental value. The Formula of the End in Itself cannot be grounded without establishing that we are required to regard only humanity in a person as having absolute worth.

On the view defended here, the system universalisability principle does not fully express the value that is fundamental. It is just one of the principles that this value underlies. Their justification therefore occurs in distinct steps. A commitment to the system universalisability principle arises from a rational requirement to avoid and undermine an antinomy, consistently with other conditions. A commitment to the value of the autonomy of a human community arises from the rational requirement for a value that underlies the combination of the system universalisability principle and a principle that, consistently with it, satisfies the need for recognition and for producers to receive means of consumption. The system universalisability principle cannot itself satisfy these needs, as it is entirely negative.

The system universalisability principle reflects, if only partially, the value of the autonomy of a human community, on three counts. First, it incorporates a thought experiment that asks us to conceive of a universal law of human nature. A principle that incorporates a thought experiment can only require us to conceive of ourselves in a position that is appropriate to the value underlying the principle. As human beings can only conceive of themselves as bringing about a universal law through a public power, the system universalisability principle rests on a value that can be reflected in the exercise of a public law-making power. As public law-making power is exercised in the name of a human community, the system universalisability principle rests on the value of a co-legislating human community. Second, the system universalisability principle assesses systems which are a feature of a human community. A principle that condemns certain systems as unjust, and thereby justifies their removal, presupposes that we value the kind of entity from which such systems are removed: a human community. Third, the system universalisability principle condemns systems that divide a community by enabling and constraining actors to adopt an end that cannot be universalised. It condemns as unjust any system that enables some part of a community to act as if it were superior to the community as a whole, by enabling it to adopt an end that not everyone can conceivably adopt. Through these features, the system universalisability principle reflects the value of the co-legislation of public principles that do not endorse disharmonious social dynamics.

A commitment to a more positive value arises from thinking of the system universalisability principle as combined with a principle that satisfies the needs for recognition and for producers to receive means of consumption. Both needs can be satisfied consistently with the system universalisability principle (and a prohibition on excessive labour) through a principle of rewarding and rewarded productive activity; that is, a principle of meaningful work. In that this principle rewards productive activity, it satisfies the need for producers to receive means of consumption. As a principle of ensuring that productive activity is rewarding, it satisfies the need for recognition. If each is aware that meaningful work is a public principle, each can assume that everyone, in having co-legislated this principle, puts a value on productive activities being reward-ing and rewarded. But if so, each can assume, on account of their work and this awareness, that they have a valued status in valued others' ends. This satisfies the need for recognition, in the form of recognition as a member of a human community. As this recognition depends on the affirmation and implementa-tion of meaningful work for all, it rests on the co-legislation of a principle that expressly endorses a harmonious social dynamic.

This, finally, brings us to the value of the autonomy of a human community. Since it is a rational requirement to remove an antinomy, as well as to avoid and undermine it in thought, and since it is rational, all things considered, to do so if the system universalisability principle and the principle of meaningful work are thought of as combined, actors in capitalism are rationally committed to this combination of principles. As their combination rests on the value of the autonomy of a human community, we are rationally committed to this value.

One issue remains. We have seen how this value can support a condemna-tion of capitalism, on account of the system universalisability principle. But does this value also recommend socialism? At issue, here, is not the mammoth task of explaining how a detailed vision of socialism can be realised, but simply whether socialism can exhibit a commitment to this value. In Staudinger's terms, the issue is whether 'the socialisation of production' can be thought to provide the basis for 'a unified regulation of the human community'.[75] To this simpler question, the straightforward answer is: yes. The socialisation of productive resources under the control of a public power is a means to pro-mote the system universalisability principle and the principle of meaningful work. Regarding the former principle, unjust systems need no longer arise and persist without any organisational capacity being prepared to dismantle them. As Marx and Engels write in *The German Ideology*: through its regulation of material production, '[t]he reality that communism creates is just the concrete basis for the making impossible of all reality independent of the individuals, insofar as this reality is nevertheless nothing but a product of individuals' past intercourse'.[76] Regarding the latter principle, public control of the allocation

---

75   Staudinger 1899, p. 159; compare the longer passage of text translated in ch. 2, sec. 1.
76   *MEJ*, 2003, p. 79; *MEW*, 3, p. 70; *MECW*, 5, p. 81.

of productive resources offers a way to direct a harmonious dynamic of development. The value of the autonomy of a human community is therefore not merely a value with which to condemn capitalism, but also a value with which to recommend socialism.

13   Summary

In summary, the structure of a Marxist foundational argument can be represented as follows:

(1) Freedom, however it is to be conceived, is to be conceived of as enjoyed by all

(2) There is no capitalism-free route to freedom

(3) Capitalism has a basic structure that combines generalised purchase and sale with generalised production with wage-labour for continuous money-maximisation

(4) Capitalism's basic structure explains actors' acceptance of two premises: commodity exchangers are to recognise one another as self-owners, and labour power can only be purchased for money sufficient to purchase its means of reproduction

(5) Conduct in line with these premises in capitalism's basic structure exhibits an antinomy: the assertion of a right to an unlimited working day, and the assertion of a right to a limited working day

(6) Antinomies in the social world ought to be resolved

(7) Therefore, it is a rational requirement to apply a principle to remove this antinomy-exhibiting conduct, provided that any need expressed in but separable from its premises (recognition and means of consumption for producers) can still be satisfied

(8) This principle must be: excessive labour is prohibited

(9) A commitment to this principle is rational only if it avoids antinomy and undermines the rights-antinomy by rejecting at least one of its premises

(10) Therefore, it is a rational requirement to affirm a principle with which to defend a prohibition on excessive labour on a basis distinct from antinomy, and to reject one or more premises of the rights-antinomy

(11) The value underlying the principle that excessive labour is prohibited is the value of guaranteeing the reproduction of the current population of producers for no further reason than that they are producers

(12) Even if excessive labour is prohibited, capitalism's basic structure tends to produce violations of this value

(13) Therefore, it is a rational requirement to condemn capitalism

(14) Therefore, it is a rational requirement to affirm a principle with which to defend a prohibition on excessive labour on a basis distinct from anti-nomy and to reject one or more premises of the rights-antinomy (per (10)) consistent with freedom for all (per (1)), a prohibition on excessive labour (per (8)), the value underlying this prohibition (per (11)) and the condem-nation of capitalism implied by this value (per (13))

(15) This principle must be the system universalisability principle: a system in which advantages are obtained by pursuing system-reinforced ends that cannot be universalised is unjust

(16) Needs for recognition and for producers to receive means of consumption can be satisfied consistently with the implementation of a prohibition on excessive labour and the system universalisability principle through the principle of meaningful work

(17) To affirm the system universalisability principle and the principle of meaningful work is to be committed to a value that can underlie this com-bination of principles

(18) This value must be the autonomy of a human community

(19) This value can only be realised in socialism, at least as distinct from cap-italism

(20) Therefore, it is mandatory to realise socialism, at least as compared with retaining capitalism

All of the above premises have support in Marx's texts, or follow logically from what Marx's texts support.[77] Marx's early and later writings are recon-ciled insofar as the rights-antinomy that Marx describes in *Capital* Volume I is incorporated into the form of argument that Marx first suggests in *Letters from the Deutsch-Französische Jahrbücher*. In content, the argument preserves the spirit of Marx's declaration of a '*categorical imperative to overthrow all rela-tions* in which the human being is a debased, enslaved, abandoned, despicable being',[78] insofar as it satisfies the conditions set out at the start of this chapter. It condemns capitalism as unjust, and recommends socialism as just. It is not a timeless argument, but appeals to facts about capitalism. It can evaluate sys-tems, using the system universalisability principle. It grounds the value of the autonomy of a human community, by appeal to an antinomy. It can support

---

77 Although no direct argument was made for Marx's commitment to (6), this is surely uncontroversial in light of the tone of Marx's account of the rights-antinomy in *Capital* Volume I. Marx's *Critique of Hegel's Doctrine of the State* also criticises Hegel repeatedly for failing to resolve antinomies; see *MEW*, 1, p. 204, pp. 257–8, p. 295, p. 300; *MECW*, 3, p. 6, p. 55, p. 91, p. 95.

78 *MEW*, 1, p. 385; *MECW*, 3, p. 182.

the claim that existing society ought to be revolutionised because the class oppression in it is in one way bad for everyone, by appeal to the absence of community resulting from the pursuit of continuous money maximisation, on which existing class oppression rests. It can also support the claim that social arrangements that promote rational self-transparency ought to be adopted because false consciousness is in one way bad for everyone. If by the autonomy of a human community we understand the co-legislation of public principles that expressly endorse harmonious social dynamics, then, in an autonomous human community, knowledge of the principles adopted by a public power is a guide to the relation of one's action to social life as a whole. The only condition whose satisfaction is not apparent is that a Marxist foundational argument should not preclude action necessary to achieve socialism. We now consider this question.

14   The Justification of Socialist Strategy

An ethics that recommends socialism, but precludes the necessary means to achieve it, is not of much practical use. We need to show that the grounding argument just summarised does not have implications that preclude the means to achieve socialism. We need to argue that the principles and values that it grounds cannot be applied to capitalism to object to a strategy of class struggle, if the latter is necessary to achieve socialism.

An ethics may be called a *conditional ethics* if it commands us to act in a certain way if a condition is met, but to act to bring about that condition if it is not met. If the condition is not met, then the thing to do is to bring it about, even perhaps by doing what it is not permissible to do, once the condition is brought about.

On this understanding, the ethics that Staudinger proposes in *Wirtschaftliche Grundlagen der Moral* is a conditional ethics:

> In practice, Kant's morality in its entirety is therefore useless, suited at most as a moral shackle for those who have already grown out of the religious shackle. To make Kant's moral law useful, a correlate must be added that displays to human beings the community itself as the foundation, and says: where community links you with other human beings, act on Kant's imperative; but where there is as yet no community, seek to create it.[79]

---

79   Staudinger 1907, pp. 90–1.

One problem with Staudinger's proposal is that Kant ties the possibility of moral autonomy to the will's capacity to be self-determining. The will is self-determining, according to Kant, if it disregards material incentives, and determines itself a priori, purely out of respect for the moral law. Thus, on Kant's view of moral autonomy, no social conditions can be thought to preclude moral action. As Sartre notes, for Kant, 'moral activity is held to be independent of historical circumstances. It is pure positivity and can occur anywhere'.[80] As the incentives that social structures promote cannot be thought to prevent a finite rational agent from acting morally in Kant's terms, Kant's ethics is incompatible with the thought that a certain social state of affairs must first be brought about before we are commanded to obey the categorical imperative. Kant's view of moral autonomy does not allow us to revise Kant's ethics into the form of a conditional ethics.

Staudinger is nonetheless right to sense that Marxism requires a conditional ethics. It is impossible to honour the value of autonomy that recommends a classless society in the circumstances of class society. It is impossible to show respect for an autonomous human community as something existent if capitalism's basic structure is systematically divisive, and public power is used to cement this social division. The conception of moral action in a Marxist ethics of autonomy also permits a conditional ethics, in that it conceives of moral action not as the self-determination of the will a priori, but as the resolution of an antinomy premised on an existing form of recognition.

It is clear, too, that a society characterised by class struggle does not instantiate the value of the autonomy of a human community. To engage in class struggle is to prosecute the interests of one or more classes against those of another. Such antagonistic confrontations exhibit a disharmony. If a commitment to the value of the autonomy of a human community is not to preclude class struggle as a means to achieve a society in which autonomy can be realised, this value must support a conditional ethics that allows autonomy to be brought about by means that an autonomous human community excludes.[81]

---

80   Sartre 1983, p. 173; Sartre 1992, p. 165.

81   Steven Lukes claims that 'marxism is deeply and unremittingly anti-deontological ... marxism and orthodox Marxist thought require an exclusive, single-minded preoccupation with the attainment of emancipation' (Lukes 1985, p. 142). A 'single-minded preoccupation with the attainment of emancipation' presupposes a conditional ethics. However, it does not imply that this conditional ethics has some particular character, consequentialist or deontological. Its character depends on what is of value once its condition, 'the attainment of emancipation', is met. A conditional ethics is only consequentialist if, once this condition is met, the only things that are regarded as of value are actions' resultant states of affairs (compare Wood 2014, p. 146). As a conditional ethics need not be con-

A Marxist foundational argument permits an ethics of autonomy to be a conditional ethics. This argument is not a priori, but rests on facts about a specific, necessary form of society, capitalism. If a commitment to a value rests on facts about capitalism, a normative evaluation of such facts may impact on a basic statement of what this value requires agents to do in the context of these facts. On the above argument, a commitment to the value of autonomy is held to follow on from a commitment to a principle (the system universalisability principle) that condemns capitalism's basic structure as unjust. So, this argument allows the judgment of capitalism's basic structure as unjust to impact on a basic statement of what the value of autonomy requires agents in capitalism to do. This is relevant, because justice is a good that permits action that abolishes injustice not to instantiate or 'pre-figure' justice. An action's suitability as a means to ending an injustice is, as such, relevant for determining whether justice permits it. So, if the system universalisability principle condemns capitalism's basic structure as unjust, a foundational argument for autonomy on which this value commitment follows on from a commitment to this principle cannot preclude a socialist strategy simply on the basis that it does not instantiate the value of autonomy. In capitalism, the ethically valuable and permissible thing to do is to remove unjust systems, as a condition for bringing about a community that can exhibit autonomy. On this argument, a Marxist ethics of autonomy is a conditional ethics insofar as it commands actors to respect the autonomy of a human community if it exists, but to bring about its social conditions if it does not exist, by dismantling systems that violate the system universalisability principle of justice.

Take, for instance, the desire of *The Communist Manifesto* that '[t]he proletariat will use its political rule to progressively wrest all capital from the bourgeoisie', and its suggestion that first among its other priorities will be: '1. Expropriation of landed property and use of ground rent for state expenditures'.[82] If a Marxist ethics of autonomy is a conditional ethics, then its evaluation of such uses of public power will rest on a judgment of whether or not they serve to bring about the conditions of an autonomous human community. In this evaluation, the system universalisability principle is key. Such uses of public power can be affirmed, on this principle, if they dismantle systems that reinforce ends that cannot be universalised, such as continuous money maximisation, or living while doing nothing, provided that they do not replace them with other unjust systems.

---

sequentialist, Lukes has no reason to claim that 'marxism is deeply and unremittingly anti-deontological'.

82   *MEW*, 4, p. 481; *MECW*, 6, pp. 504–5.

To say that a socialist ethics is a conditional ethics is not, therefore, to imply that it does not constrain action to achieve socialism in any way.[83] First of all, on the above argument for autonomy, a commitment to replace capitalism's basic structure with socialist relations of production is a consequence of the system universalisability principle. This principle requires *any* system that violates it to be dismantled. A socialist commitment is therefore inseparable from a commitment to refrain from promoting systems that violate the system universalisability principle. Given this principle's grounding, a socialist commitment is also inseparable from a commitment to avoid *any* antinomy-exhibiting conduct. Further, we began from the premise that freedom is to be conceived of as enjoyed by all. If a radical transformation of society is to be a vehicle for a defensible socialism, it must prepare people for a community in which everyone is to be free. Popular acceptance of this idea can only arise from a process generally conducted in a spirit of equality. Among other things, this rules out a coup supported only by a small minority. These are not insignificant constraints.

These constraints do not, however, include positive duties to aid capitalists or their political representatives, if their power derives from systematic injustice; or to treat individuals of these groups far better than they treat others (on any realistic account of how capitalists and their government representatives act) by never treating them merely as means. While Kant's Formula of the End in Itself carries these implications, which preclude class struggle as a means to achieve socialism,[84] a Marxist ethics of autonomy does not, as it grounds the value of autonomy upon a principle of justice that condemns their ends.

This argument for regarding a Marxist ethics of autonomy as a conditional ethics is based on principle. It rests on the non-timeless character of its foundational argument, and its judgment of capitalism's basic structure as unjust. As a Marxist ethics of autonomy is a conditional ethics, it does not preclude a class struggle strategy to achieve socialism merely on account of the fact that a society characterised by class struggle fails to instantiate the value of autonomy. It does not preclude any strategy simply by virtue of the fact that this strategy does not exhibit the value of autonomy.

To this, we can add a further claim: insofar as a strategy can bring socialism about, a Marxist foundational argument for an ethics of autonomy implies that

---

83   Lukes suggests that a Marxist ethics 'has no basis for resisting any measures taken that appear to promote such consequences [the attainment of socialism – JF]' (Lukes 1985, p. 147).

84   See chs 2–3.

there is a (pro tanto) reason to think that it is permissible. Again, this relates to the fact that a Marxist foundational argument condemns capitalism's basic structure as unjust while recommending socialism as just, and that the suitability of an action as a means to the end of removing an injustice belongs to a judgment of its permissibility. In the context of self-defence, the quality of an action as a means for repulsing an aggression is relevant for determining whether it is permissible. Similarly, it is a reason to think that a strategy that replaces capitalism with socialism is permissible, if it is a means to the end of getting rid of the injustice of capitalism's basic structure. As an ethics of autonomy allows us to say that a strategy that is a means to replace capitalism with socialism serves to get rid of an injustice, it gives us a reason to say that any strategy that can achieve socialism is permissible. It therefore gives us a reason to say that any class struggle strategy that can bring socialism about is permissible.

We have suggested two reasons as to why a Marxist foundational argument does not preclude action necessary to achieve socialism. First, action to achieve socialism is not required to instantiate the value of autonomy, so no socialist strategy is precluded by failing to instantiate this value. Second, action that replaces capitalism with socialism is viewed as removing an injustice, so the fact that action is a means for this is a reason to hold that it is permissible. This is all that we need argue. For an ethics to qualify as Marxist, it is sufficient that it offers a pro tanto justification of any effective class struggle strategy for achieving socialism. To quality as Marxist, an ethics does not have to offer a view on when or when not one ought finally (all things considered) to embark on action viewed as a means to achieve socialism. Marxism can accommodate different views on this issue. Views on this issue need not mark off a Marxist ethics from a non-Marxist ethics.

By implication, to defend the Marxist status of a foundational argument for autonomy, we do not need to offer a solution to the problem of a revolutionary ethical code. Norman Geras offers a well-known analysis of this problem in an article entitled 'Our Morals: the Ethics of Revolution'.[85] While it is not necessary, here, to offer a solution to this problem, we may indicate the framework for addressing it that is suggested by a Marxist foundational argument for autonomy.

A Marxist ethics of autonomy is a conditional ethics. It says: act so as to respect the value of an autonomous human community (where co-legislated public principles expressly endorse harmonious social dynamics); or, if this

---

85   Geras 1989.

community does not exist, act so as to bring it about. It defines the ethical task, for now, in consequentialist terms: the present-day task is to bring about the conditions for an autonomous human community. This implies that, if actors were to accept this ethics of autonomy, then, while they would have a pro tanto reason to adopt any means to bring socialism about, when they proceed to a final, all things considered judgment about whether to adopt some particular strategy viewed as a means to achieve socialism, they are to make a consequentialist calculation.

This calculation might be summarised as follows: if a potentially successful strategy would (if successful) abolish capitalism's basic structure and replace it with socialism, then, provided that less injustice is contained in this strategy and the state of affairs it produces (if successful) than if capitalism's basic structure survives across this entire period, the strategy is justified. On this view, the strategy is defended on the grounds that less injustice is involved in its use and in socialism, than is involved in the continuation of capitalism. We consider the costs (in terms of injustice) of means used to attain an end *only* insofar as they are measured *together* with the costs and benefits (in terms of justice) of the end itself. The overall result, in terms of the avoidance of injustice, is compared to the continuation of the status quo, and the comparison must favour socialism. Of this calculation, it is inaccurate to say that the end justifies the means. Rather, the end and the means (as compared to the status quo alternative) justify the means. We shall call this the consequentialism of justice framework.

Geras objects that the consequentialism of justice framework is ethically unsound, because it gives actors too great a license to do wrong. Geras's objection proceeds from two premises. The first premise is that the consequentialism of justice is not a 'determinate'[86] ethical code. By this, Geras means to say that it neither prohibits specific means (for instance, specific weaponry), nor limits any means to a particular category of persons (for instance, combatants, as distinct from non-combatants).[87] If a consequentialist calculation weighs up all benefits and costs in a single calculation, and if there is no a priori reason why a specific means or action against a particular category of persons cannot 'turn out in some circumstances to be efficacious even in a just cause',[88] the consequentialism of justice framework cannot rule out any specific measure. For Geras, an ethical code that cannot rule out any specific measure is not determinate. Geras's second premise is that, with a good determinate ethical

---

86 Geras 1989, p. 193.
87 Geras 1989, pp. 196–7.
88 Geras 1989, p. 191.

code, its 'definite rules ... are observed often enough to be of value'.[89] The definite rules of a determinate code will be observed often enough *just because* they are definite rules. If the acceptance of an ethical code with definite rules makes a difference to what people do because of its definite rules, an ethical code with good definite rules will prevent some moral wrong, just because it contains good definite rules.

From these two premises, it follows that, as the consequentialism of justice framework is not determinate, it is, to the extent that it is not determinate, not optimally wrong-preventing. In respect of its indeterminacy, it is not an optimal revolutionary ethical code for ensuring that socialists avoid moral wrongs. But it hardly follows that socialists should accept Geras's alternative, whose 'basis is a principle that individuals have rights ... that may not, in general, be set aside; unless they forfeit them by making war themselves'.[90] 'These individual rights', Geras says, 'constitute a limit upon consequentialist calculation'.[91] Geras explains the qualification that rights may not 'in general' be set aside by saying that rights may not be set aside, unless setting rights aside is 'the sole means of averting imminent and certain disaster'.[92]

Geras's alternative does not follow from his objection to the consequentialism of justice framework, as his alternative lacks a distinction that would make it more discriminating. If introducing the distinction into Geras's alternative would make it more discriminating, then Geras cannot resist its introduction by sticking to his more indeterminate formulation when indeterminacy is the basis of his objection to the consequentialism of justice framework. Once the distinction is introduced, however, we have left Geras's own view behind.

Geras's view is crude, in two ways: it limits the class of combatants to 'leaders, soldiers, police, security agents, jailers, torturers'[93] while considering *everyone else* as non-combatants *and* while treating *all* rights that are violated in the 'violation of individuals and of lives'[94] as limits upon consequentialist calculation. His class of non-combatants includes capitalists and senior managers acting on their instruction on the one hand, and members of all other classes on the other. His category of limiting rights includes non-violent and non-life-threatening violations of personal rights, such as enforced detention at home, as well as violent and/or life-threatening violations of personal rights.

---

89   Geras 1989, p. 197.
90   Geras 1989, p. 202.
91   Geras 1989, p. 203.
92   Geras 1989, p. 204.
93   Geras 1989, p. 198.
94   Geras 1989, p. 203.

We adopt a view distinct from and more determinate than Geras's if we distinguish, among 'non-combatants', persons implicated in systems of injustice by the advantages that they obtain, and persons not so implicated. If capitalism's basic structure is unjust, an ethical socialist may see little reason to refrain from action to achieve socialism that violates a capitalist's personal rights in a non-violent and non-life-threatening way, especially if these 'non-combatants' can avoid this by renouncing their unjustly held resources.

More fundamentally, Geras's alternative produces an *antinomy*, because it requires socialists to prioritise the avoidance of wrongful violations of non-combatants' personal rights over the use of the most minimally bad efficacious means of socialist transformation that include these violations, even if such means and their result are less bad than restoring capitalism, and necessary to prevent its restoration. It is unclear how Geras can defend this implication of his view. As a socialist, Geras believes that capitalism is unjust. Presumably, he believes that capitalism is unjust because it, too, leads to violations of 'rights ... that may not, in general, be set aside'. But if so, this premise leads, in the aforementioned scenario, to an antinomy. Either the rights of non-combatants are not set aside, in which case we may foreseeably be setting aside the rights of victims of a restored capitalism; or else the latter's rights are not ignored, in which case we are back to setting aside non-combatants' rights. It is unclear how Geras can avoid this antinomy outside of the consequentialism of justice framework, which (unlike Geras's alternative) may include the following principle: action necessary to end a greater wrong than the wrong that this action would constitute if it were instead done in the absence of wrong, is not wrong.

If this antinomy returns us to the consequentialism of justice framework, it is worth noting a way for this framework to address the problem that Geras identifies: indeterminacy. The consequentialism of justice view is compatible with a recognition of the need to develop a socialist strategy and tactics for any context in which socialism is on the agenda. It is also compatible with a belief that, once this strategy and tactics are developed, more specific rules can be formulated to concretise the consequentialism of justice framework into a determinate code for a given context.[95] If so, one may adopt the consequentialism of justice framework, and believe that any socialist agency requires a more determinate ethical code than is provided merely by this framework in the abstract. This seems to offer a basis for addressing Geras's worry that, if ethical constraints 'are too general to yield any more precise guidance, they

---

95   This is one way to understand Trotsky's remark that '[p]roblems of revolutionary morality are fused with the problems of revolutionary strategy and tactics' (Trotsky 1973, p. 49). Geras (1989, p. 190) cites the remark, but does not consider its possible significance.

may well come to nothing under the pressures of revolutionary conflict'.[96] If the specific rules of a socialist ethics for a revolutionary situation in a particular time and place presuppose a revolutionary strategy and tactics for that time and place, a charge of indeterminacy is not properly raised against the consequentialism of justice framework itself, but only against actors who adopt it without concretising it with more specific rules suited to the strategy and tactics of their context.

Clearly much more could be said about the application of the consequentialism of justice framework to revolutionary situations. The aim here was not to offer an exhaustive defence of this application, but to argue that a Marxist ethics of autonomy permits actors to adopt the consequentialism of justice framework, and that Geras's objections to this framework are far from convincing. A Marxist ethics of autonomy allows actors to adopt the consequentialism of justice framework (where justice is not reduced to rights but includes duties to the whole) for making all things considered decisions in a revolutionary context, because it is a conditional ethics. This framework is difficult to do without, if the alternative leads to antinomy. It need not be viewed as inadequately determinate, moreover, if it is open to concretisation. Once the strategies and tactics for promoting a cause regarded as just in a given context are developed, more specific rules regarding the different kinds of intervention permitted in respect of various categories of person can be formulated.

15   Conclusion

The aim in this chapter was to offer a grounding argument for a Marxist ethics of autonomy. We may conclude by highlighting some implications of its use of impartial reasoning. This ethics is distinguished from liberal egalitarianism not just by its institutional recommendation to replace rather than to reform capitalism, but also by its use of impartial reasoning, which is not fundamentally tied to personal equality. If the options in political philosophy are presented as limited to those political philosophies whose use of impartial reasoning is fundamentally tied to a personal equality of some kind, it can appear as if liberal political philosophies are all we modern egalitarians have to choose from.

The foundational argument we outlined proceeds from capitalism's basic structure, and a type of irrationality in it. Because capitalism's basic structure

---

96   Geras 1989, p. 191; see, similarly, Lukes 1985, p. 146.

exhibits an antinomy, each actor in this structure has a reason to disvalue a state of affairs common to everyone. This gives each actor a reason to apply a principle to remove the antinomy, and to affirm a principle with which to reject at least one of its premises. As such, the argument exhibits a commitment to equality and impartial reasoning. Each actor in capitalism is regarded as someone who ought to be able to live in a form of society that is not irrational, and that implements the principles that are rational requirements of resolving an antinomy. It is not merely some actors in capitalism's basic structure who are owed this, but all of them, on grounds that are presented as acceptable to all.

Yet what each is owed, on this foundational argument, is irreducible to a particular share of something of which each is thought to have their own separate share, or to the valuing of a personal attribute. Each is owed the enjoyment of a common social situation. Each is owed an antinomy-free form of society that exhibits the values and principles rationally connected to the resolution of antinomy. Insofar as what each is owed is a common social situation, the argument's use of impartial reasoning is *non-personal*: each actor is treated as equally worthy of consideration qua reasoner on what principles are rationally required, but this cannot be reduced to saying that each actor is treated as equally worthy in respect of a personal share of something, or in respect of the valuing of a personal attribute.

The possibility of a grounding argument whose use of impartial reasoning is not completely wedded to a personal share or personal attribute confounds some assumptions about the options in political philosophy. These assumptions are reflected in the following passages in Amartya Sen's *Inequality Reexamined*:

> a common characteristic of virtually all the approaches to the ethics of social arrangements that have stood the test of time is to want equality of *something* – something that has an important place in the particular theory. Not only do income-egalitarians (if I may call them that) demand equal incomes, and welfare-egalitarians ask for equal welfare levels, but also classical utilitarians insist on equal weights on the utilities of all, and pure libertarians demand equality with respect to an entire class of rights and liberties. They are all 'egalitarians' in some essential way – arguing resolutely for equality of something which everyone should have and which is quite crucial to their own particular approach. To see the battle as one between those 'in favour of' and those 'against' equality (as the problem is often posed in the literature) is to miss something central to the subject.

I also argue that this common feature of being egalitarian in some significant way relates to the need to have equal concern, at some level, for all the persons involved – the absence of which would tend to make a proposal lack social plausibility.

... Indeed, the answers that are given to the question 'equality of what?' can serve as the basis of classifying different ethical theories of social arrangements. This classificatory principle brings out in each case what the invariant properties are and what are merely conditional or incidental connections.[97]

And again:

Equality is judged by comparing some particular aspect of a person (such as income, or wealth, or happiness, or liberty, or opportunities, or rights, or need-fulfilments) with the same aspect of another person. Thus, the judgement and measurement of inequality is thoroughly dependent on the choice of the variable (income, wealth, happiness, etc.) in terms of which comparisons are made. I shall call it the 'focal variable' – the variable on which the analysis focuses, in comparing different people.[98]

Sen concludes:

What do we conclude from this fact? One obvious conclusion is that being egalitarian (i.e. egalitarian in *some space or other* to which great importance is attached) is not really a 'uniting' feature.[99]

According to Sen, every modern 'ethics of social arrangements' selects a 'particular aspect of a person' as the main variable or space for examining equality. To propose to use this choice of space as 'the basis of classifying' different ethical theories is to suppose that this choice is the fundamental marker of every modern ethics. This is not, of course, to say that a concern with equality in some or other personal space exhausts a modern ethics. To treat something as fundamental is distinct from treating it as exhaustive. A modern ethics may also defend other values, such as efficiency, as part of its general approach. But an egalitarian commitment to equality in some specific personal space remains

---

97   Sen 1992, pp. ix–x; see similarly Sen 2009, pp. 291–2.
98   Sen 1992, p. 2.
99   Sen 1992, p. 14.

the fundamental and therefore classificatory feature of every modern social ethics, according to Sen.

Sen links the equal concern for persons shown by valuing equality in some personal space to the use of impartial reasoning. For Sen, 'impartiality and equal concern, in some form or other, provide a shared background to all the major ethical and political proposals'.[100] More specifically,

> even before a specific space is chosen, the general requirement of the need to value equality *in some space that is seen to be particularly important* is not an empty demand. This relates to the discipline imposed by the need for some impartiality, some form of equal concern.[101]

Sen suggests that, if an impartial reason is to be given in support of an ethics, this impartial reason must refer to the fact that this ethics values equality in some personal space:

> If a claim that inequality in some significant space is right (or good, or acceptable, or tolerable) is to be defended by reason (not by, say, shooting the dissenters), the argument takes the form of showing this inequality to be a consequence of *equality* in some other – more centrally important – space. Given the broad agreement on the need to have equality in the 'base', and also the connection of that broad agreement with this deep need for impartiality between individuals (discussed earlier), the crucial arguments have to be about the reasonableness of the 'bases' chosen.[102]

In other words, egalitarianism *in a personal space* is said to be what allows a social ethics to be presented as an impartial theory. Indeed, the reason Sen offers for why any modern ethics must treat equality in a personal space as fundamental is that an ethics must be impartially defensible, or based on 'non-discrimination',[103] to survive in modern conditions, and any such defence is assumed to have to take the form of a defence of the fundamental value of equality in a personal space.

Read against the foundational argument just presented, Sen offers an overly narrow account of what an ethics has to maintain, to be impartially defensible. If an ethics is to be impartially defensible, it must offer everyone a good

---

100   Sen 1992, pp. 18–19.
101   Sen 1992, p. 24.
102   Sen 1992, p. 21.
103   Sen 2009, p. 293.

reason to accept its claim about what is of value. But this is not to say that it must identify a personal space as of fundamental value. Even if persons are to *accept* a claim, the claim need not be *about* persons. Claims about values in social life need not be confined to claims concerning what it is of value for each person to get their own equal share of (be it rights or capabilities or resources or something else) or to claims concerning what it is about each person that should be counted equally for distributive purposes (for utilitarianism, equally intense desires). Claims about values in social life include claims about the rationality of systems. As claims about values need not be claims about persons, it does not follow from the fact that a modern ethics must be impartially defensible that it must treat equality in a personal space as of fundamental value. A modern ethics qualifies as impartially defensible – it upholds non-discrimination – just by treating the presence or absence of certain kinds of system as of fundamental value. But as such an ethics does not treat equality in a personal space as of fundamental value, it will not be appropriately classified by any personal space it favours, to treat persons equally. Given this possibility, Sen's proposed classification may not be nuanced enough to adequately accommodate every modern ethics.

Indeed, on Sen's proposed classification, a Marxist foundational argument for autonomy will not properly register as an option. This argument identifies a common social situation that is rationally disvalued by all, and shows that certain values and principles follow from the need to resolve an antinomy. As each actor in capitalism's basic structure is said to have a reason to disvalue a common social situation, the argument is presented as impartial. But as its use of impartial reasoning is not fundamentally tied to some personal space that is equally valued in each person, Sen's proposed classification cannot capture it adequately.

To be sure, a Marxist ethics of autonomy can include a commitment to valuing a personal space equally in each person. Just as the ethics that register on Sen's proposed classification are committed to other values besides the personal equality that each treats as fundamental, so an ethics whose fundamental use of impartial reasoning grounds a duty to the whole can also value equality in a personal space; for example, the opportunity for meaningful work. But if the valuing of a personal space is not exhaustively fundamental to its use of impartial reasoning, it cannot be described satisfactorily within Sen's classificatory scheme.

Sen's scheme is, in fact, a scheme for classifying positions in liberal political philosophy masquerading as a scheme for classifying positions in political philosophy tout court. What makes liberal political philosophy liberal is a form of argument that says: the *fundamental* thing to do is to count something about each person equally, or to distribute something to each person equally. As Sen's scheme classifies every modern ethics by its appeal to equality in a personal space, it assumes that the only options in political philosophy are liberal options. One consequence of this assumption is that it becomes impossible to identify anything distinctively about liberal political philosophy. Sure enough, Sen fails to see that being egalitarian in a personal space and attaching fundamental value to this is 'really a "uniting" feature' of liberal political philosophy.

To be sure, Marx's normative position is sometimes presented as falling within the liberal tradition. According to Tony Smith, 'Marx fully embraced the normative individualism of liberal egalitarian thought',[104] and differed only on his assessment of its institutional consequences. Likewise, for Igor Shoikhedbrod, 'the insight that liberalism cannot realize its own ideals of freedom and equality' is 'at the heart of Marx's critique of liberalism'.[105] It is notable, however, that both Smith and Shoikhedbrod offer rather underspecified accounts of what they take liberal egalitarian thought or liberalism to be. Consider the following pair of statements:

> As a first approximation we may define 'liberal egalitarianism' negatively as a rejection of the thesis that some individuals are inherently of greater worth than others. More positively, 'liberal egalitarianism' can provisionally be taken to refer to positions in normative social theory accepting the 'Moral Equality Principle' that all persons are of equal moral worth as ends in themselves.[106]

> Liberalism is of course a broad term that usually encompasses a diversity of political outlooks and movements, but it will be understood here according to its commitment to the freedom and equality of individuals, whose dignity and moral worth are secured primarily through the device of rights.[107]

Liberals (or liberal egalitarians) characteristically do not *only* say that all persons are of equal moral worth. They characteristically say that this worth is *fundamental*. For Rawls, individual freedoms have 'a high priority'.[108] Personal

---

104   Smith 2017, p. 58.
105   Shoikhedbrod 2019, p. 6.
106   Smith 2017, pp. 1–2.
107   Shoikhedbrod 2019, p. 56.
108   Rawls 1993, p. 43.

liberty is a good that can be 'restricted only for the sake of liberty itself'.[109] For Ronald Dworkin, 'rights are best understood as trumps'.[110] Certainly, a political philosophy is non-liberal (or non-*liberal*-egalitarian) if it does not value persons equally in any way. But a political philosophy is also non-liberal (or non-*liberal*-egalitarian) if it treats what it values about persons equally as subordinate to something else that it values more fundamentally, and that is based on non-discrimination. A society that respects individual agency and wellbeing is not a society that liberal (egalitarian) philosophy can recommend, if this respect is subordinate to duties to the whole, such as that expressed by the system universalisability principle of justice, that liberals cannot defend, because duty-to-the-whole-based principles restrict liberty not for the sake of liberty, but for the sake of community. In a world where systems reinforce ends that cannot be universalised, we lack community because there is too much liberty. Contrary to Rawls, we can indeed 'suffer from a greater liberty'.[111] To adopt the system universalisability principle of justice to deflate our bloated liberty is to cross, at least in one point, what Marx called 'the narrow, bourgeois horizon of right',[112] by subordinating individual rights to a negative duty to the whole.

The case for a Marxist ethics of autonomy is thus, at the same time, an argument against a number of views. It is an argument not to allow Kantian constructivists to claim a monopoly on the options in political philosophy that appeal to our normative conceptions; not to allow liberals to claim a monopoly on impartial reasoning by treating appeals to personal equality as definitive of impartial reasoning; and not to allow Marxists to require a Marxist ethics to fit the mould of a liberal egalitarian philosophy.

More positively, we have tried to show how, on the basis of a focal concern with capitalism as an irrational system, it is possible to identify with a working-class-based movement on impartial grounds even without an exact conception of the society it may bring about. We have sought not merely to identify values and principles that a Marxist can use to condemn capitalism and recommend socialism, but also to address the neglected issue of how they can be grounded. Only on this condition is a Marxist ethics possible.

---

109   Rawls 1971, p. 244.
110   Dworkin 1984, p. 153.
111   Rawls 1971, p. 143.
112   *MEW*, 19, p. 21; MECW, 24, p. 87. On the translation of this phrase, see Furner 2018, pp. 48–50.

Bibliography

Adler, Max 1912, 'Marxismus und Ethik', *Archiv für Sozialwissenschaft*, 34: 184–91.

Allen, Derek P.H. 1973, 'The Utilitarianism of Marx and Engels', *American Philosophical Quarterly*, 10, 3: 189–99.

Allison, Henry E. 1990, *Kant's Theory of Freedom*, Cambridge: Cambridge University Press.

Allison, Henry E. 2011, *Kant's* Groundwork for the Metaphysics of Morals. A Commentary, Oxford: Oxford University Press.

Ameriks, Karl 2003, *Interpreting Kant's* Critiques, Oxford: Clarendon Press.

Aune, Bruce 1979, *Kant's Theory of Morals*, Princeton: Princeton University Press.

Bauer, Otto 1906, 'Marxismus und Ethik', *Die Neue Zeit*, 24, 2: 485–99.

Beck, Lewis White 1960, *A Commentary on Kant's Critique of Practical Reason*, Chicago: University of Chicago Press.

Bernstein, Eduard 1899, *Die Voraussetzung des Sozialismus und die Aufgaben der Sozialdemokratie*, Stuttgart: J.H.W. Dietz.

Bernstein, Eduard 1901. *Wie ist wissenschaftlicher Sozialismus möglich?* Berlin: Verlag der socialistischen Monatshefte.

Bernstein, Eduard 1993 [1899], *The Preconditions of Socialism*, edited and translated by Henry Tudor, Cambridge: Cambridge University Press.

Booth, William James 1989, 'Gone Fishing. Making Sense of Marx's Concept of Communism', *Political Theory*, 17, 2: 205–22.

Brudney, David 1998, *Marx's Attempt to Leave Philosophy*, Cambridge, Mass.: Harvard University Press.

Callinicos, Alex 2006, *The Resources of Critique*, Cambridge: Polity.

Callinicos, Alex 2013, 'Marxism and Contemporary Political Thought', in *The Routledge Companion to Social and Political Philosophy*, edited by Gerald F. Gaus and Fred D'Agostino, Oxon: Routledge.

Chojnacki, Pierre 1924, *Die Ethik Kants und die Ethik des Sozialismus. Ein Vermittlungsversuch der Marburger Schule*, Freiburg: Studia Friburgensia.

Cohen, Gerry A. 1978, *Karl Marx's Theory of History*, Oxford: Oxford University Press.

Cohen, Gerry A. 1981, 'Freedom, Justice and Capitalism', *New Left Review*, I/126: 3–16.

Cohen, Gerry A. 1983, 'Karl Marx. By Allen W. Wood', *Mind*, 92, 367: 440–5.

Cohen, Gerry A. 1988, *History, Labour, and Freedom. Themes from Marx*, Oxford: Oxford University Press.

Cohen, Gerry A. 1995, *Self-Ownership, Freedom and Equality*, Cambridge: Cambridge University Press.

Cohen, Gerry A. 2001, *If You're an Egalitarian, How Come You're So Rich?*, Cambridge, MA: Harvard University Press.

Cohen, Gerry A. 2008, *Rescuing Justice and Equality*, Cambridge, MA.: Harvard University Press.

Cohen, Gerry A. 2013, *Finding Oneself in the Other*, Princeton: Princeton University Press.

Cohen, Hermann 1889, *Kants Begründung der Aesthetik*, Berlin: Ferdinand Dümmler.

Cohen, Hermann 1904, *Ethik des reinen Willens*, Berlin: Bruno Cassirer.

Cureton, Adam 2013, 'A Contractualist Reading of Kant's Proof of the Formula of Humanity', *Kantian Review*, 18, 3: 363–86.

Deacon, Terrence W. 2012, *Incomplete Nature. How Mind Emerged from Matter*, New York: Norton.

Deligiorgi, Katerina 2002, 'Universalisability, Publicity, and Communication: Kant's Conception of Reason', *European Journal of Philosophy*, 10, 2: 143–59.

Dewey, John 1973 [1938], 'Means and Ends' in Leon Trotsky, John Dewey, George Novak, *Their Morals and Ours: Marxist Versus Liberal Views on Morality*, New York: Pathfinder.

Dietrichson, Paul 1964, 'When Is a Maxim Fully Universalizable?', *Kant-Studien*, 55: 143–70.

Dworkin, Ronald 1984, 'Rights as Trumps', in *Theories of Rights*, edited by Jeremy Waldron, Oxford: Oxford University Press.

Ellerman, David P. 1988, 'The Kantian Person/Thing Principle in Political Economy', *Journal of Economic Issues*, 22, 4: 1109–22.

Elster, J. 1978, *Logic and Society. Contradictions and Possible Worlds*, Chichester: John Wiley & Sons.

Elster, Jon 1983, 'Exploitation, Freedom and Justice', *Nomos*, 26: 277–304.

Engstrom, Stephen 2009, *The Form of Practical Knowledge. A Study of the Categorical Imperative*, Cambridge, Mass.: Harvard University Press.

Feenberg, Andrew 1981, *Marx, Lukács and the Sources of Critical Theory*, Totowa, NJ: Rowman and Littlefield.

Forst, Rainer 2017, 'Noumenal Alienation: Rousseau, Kant and Marx on the Dialectics of Self-Determination', *Kantian Review*, 22, 4: 523–51.

Furner, James 2011, 'Marx's Sketch of Communist Society in *The German Ideology* and the Problems of Occupational Identity and Occupational Confinement', *Philosophy and Social Criticism*, 37, 2: 189–215.

Furner, James 2017a, 'Kant's Contradiction in Conception Test: A Causal-Teleological Version of the Logical Contradiction Interpretation', *Theoria*, 64, 152: 1–23.

Furner, James 2017b, 'Kant's Contradiction in the Will Test: An Extravagant Imperfect Nature Interpretation', *The Philosophical Forum*, 48, 3: 307–23.

Furner, James 2018, *Marx on Capitalism: The Interaction-Recognition-Antinomy Thesis*, Leiden: Brill.

Furner, James 2020. 'Recovering the Social Interpretation of Disability', *Disability and Society*, 35, 10: 1535–55.

Galvin, Richard 1991, 'Ethical Formalism: The Contradiction in Conception Test', *History of Philosophy Quarterly*, 8, 4: 387–408.

Galvin, Richard 2011, 'Maxims and Practical Contradictions', *History of Philosophy Quarterly*, 28, 4: 407–19.

Galvin, Richard 2013, 'Practical Uncertainty, Practical Contradiction, and Logical Contradiction', *History of Philosophy Quarterly*, 30, 4: 349–66.

Geras, Norman 1985, 'The Controversy about Marx and Justice', *New Left Review*, I/150: 47–85.

Geras, Norman 1989, 'Our Morals: The Ethics of Revolution', *Socialist Register*, 25, 185–211.

Geras, Norman 1992, 'Bringing Marx to Justice: an Addendum and Rejoinder', *New Left Review*, I/195: 37–69.

Giesecke, Peter 1991. *Kant und der Sozialismus. Studien zum Marburger Neukantianismus, philosophischen Kritizismus und kritischen Rationalismus*, Inaugural Dissertation, Ludwig-Maximilians-Universität München.

Gilabert, Pablo 2017, 'Kantian Dignity and Marxian Socialism', *Kantian Review*, 22, 4: 553–77.

Gillis, Rory 2020, 'Marx on Capitalism: The Interaction-Recognition-Antinomy Thesis, reviewed by Rory Gillis', available at: https://marxandphilosophy.org.uk/reviews/18346_marx-on-capitalism-the-interaction-recognition-antinomy-thesis-by-james-furner-reviewed-by-rory-gillis/

Goldmann, Lucien 1971 [1945], *Immanuel Kant*, translated by Robert Black, London: New Left Books.

Gould, Stephen Jay 1982, *The Panda's Thumb. More Reflections in Natural History*, New York: Norton.

Grau, Bernhard 2017, *Kurt Eisner 1867–1919. Eine Biographie*, München: C.H. Beck

Guyer, Paul 2007, *Kant's Groundwork for the Metaphysics of Morals*, London: Continuum.

Haezrahi, Pepita 1962, 'The Concept of Man as End-In-Himself', *Kant-Studien*, 53, 1–4: 209–24.

Hall, Everett W. 1949, 'The "Proof" of Utility in Bentham and Mill', *Ethics*, 60, 1: 1–18.

Harrison, Jonathan 1957, 'Kant's Examples of the First Formulation of the Categorical Imperative', *Philosophical Quarterly*, 26, 7: 50–62.

Hegel, Georg Wilhelm Friedrich 1986 [1821], *Werke 7: Grundlinien der Philosophie des Rechts*, Frankfurt am Main: Suhrkamp.

Hegel, Georg Wilhelm Friedrich 1991 [1821], *Elements of the Philosophy of Right*, edited by Allen W. Wood, translated by Hugh B. Nisbet, Cambridge: Cambridge University Press.

Heinrich, Michael 2005 [2004], *Kritik der politischen Ökonomie. Ein Einführung*, Stuttgart: Schmetterling.

Heinrich, Michael 2012 [2004], *An Introduction to the Three Volumes of Karl Marx's* Capital, translated by Alexander Locascio, New York: Monthly Review Press.

Herman, Barbara 1990, *Morality as Rationality*, New York: Garland.

Herman, Barbara 1993, *The Practice of Moral Judgment*, Cambridge, Mass.: Harvard University Press.

Herman, Barbara 2011, 'The Difference that Ends make', in *Perfecting Virtue. New Essays on Kantian Ethics and Virtue Ethics*, edited by Lawrence Jost and Julian Wuerth, Cambridge: Cambridge University Press.

Holzhey, Helmut (ed.) 1994, *Ethischer Sozialismus. Zur politischen Philosophie des Neukantianismus*, Frankfurt am Main: Suhrkamp.

Horn, Christoph 2006, 'Kant on Ends in Nature and in Human Agency', in *Groundwork for the Metaphysics of Morals*, edited by Christoph Horn and Dieter Schönecker, Berlin: de Gruyter.

Intergovernmental Panel on Climate Change 2018, *Global Warming of 1.5 °C. An IPCC Special Report on the Impacts of Global Warming of 1.5 °C above Pre-Industrial Levels and Related Global Greenhouse Gas Emission Pathways, in the Context of Strengthening the Global Response to the Threat of Climate Change, Sustainable Development, and Efforts to Eradicate Poverty. Summary for Policymakers*, available at: https://www.ipcc.ch/site/assets/uploads/2018/10/SR15_SPM_version_stand_alone_LR.pdf

James, David 2017, 'The Compatibility of Freedom and Necessity in Marx's Idea of Communist Society', *European Journal of Philosophy*, 25, 2: 270–93.

Johnson, Robert N. 2011, *Self-Improvement. An Essay in Kantian Ethics*, Oxford: Oxford University Press.

Kahn, Samuel 2019, 'Defending the Traditional Interpretations of Kant's Formula of a Law of Nature', *Theoria*, 66, 158: 76–102.

Kain, Philip J. 1988, *Marx and Ethics*, Oxford: Clarendon Press.

Kant, Immanuel 1830 [1817], *Vorlesungen über die philosophische Religionslehre*, zweite Auflage, Leipzig: Taubertsche Buchhandlung.

Kant, Immanuel 1956 [1788], *Critique of Practical Reason*, translated by Lewis White Beck, New York: Liberal Arts Press.

Kant, Immanuel 1978 [1817], *Lectures on Philosophical Theology*, translated by Allen W. Wood and Gertrude M. Clark, Ithaca: Cornell University Press.

Kant, Immanuel 1987 [1790], *Critique of Judgment*, translated by Werner S. Pluhar, Indianapolis: Hackett.

Kant, Immanuel 1991a [1784], 'Idea for a Universal History with a Cosmopolitan Purpose', in *Political Writings*, edited by Hans S. Reiss, translated by Hugh B. Nisbet, Cambridge: Cambridge University Press.

Kant, Immanuel 1991b [1797], *The Metaphysics of Morals*, translated by Mary Gregor, Cambridge: Cambridge University Press.

Kant, Immanuel 1992 [1800], 'The Jäsche logic', in *Lectures on Logic*, edited and translated by J. Michael Young, Cambridge: Cambridge University Press.

Kant, Immanuel 1996a [1784], 'An Answer to the Question: What is Enlightenment?', in *Practical Philosophy*, edited and translated by Mary G. Gregor, Cambridge: Cambridge University Press.

Kant, Immanuel 1996b [1793], 'On the Common Saying: That may be Correct in Theory, But it is of No Use in Practice', in *Practical Philosophy*, edited and translated by Mary G. Gregor, Cambridge: Cambridge University Press.

Kant, Immanuel 1996c [1795], 'Toward Perpetual Peace', in *Practical Philosophy*, edited and translated by Mary G. Gregor, Cambridge: Cambridge University Press.

Kant, Immanuel 1997a [1785], *Groundwork of the Metaphysics of Morals*, edited and translated by Mary Gregor, Cambridge: Cambridge University Press.

Kant, Immanuel 1997b [1974], 'Moral Philosophy: Collins's Lecture Notes', in *Lectures on Ethics*, edited by Peter Heath and Jerome B. Schneewind, translated by Peter Heath, Cambridge: Cambridge University Press.

Kant, Immanuel 1997c [1783], *Prolegomena to Any Future Metaphysics That Will Be Able to Come Forward as Science, with Selections from the Critique of Pure Reason*, edited and translated by Gary Hatfield, Cambridge: Cambridge University Press.

Kant, Immanuel 1998 [1781], *Critique of Pure Reason*, edited and translated by Paul Guyer and Allen W. Wood, Cambridge: Cambridge University Press.

Kant, Immanuel 2002 [1788], *Critique of Practical Reason*, translated by Werner S. Pluhar, Indianapolis: Hackett.

Kant, Immanuel 2006 [1798], *Anthropology from a Pragmatic Point of View*, edited and translated by Robert B. Louden, Cambridge: Cambridge University Press.

Kant, Immanuel 2009 [1793], *Religion within the Bounds of Bare Reason*, translated by Werner S. Pluhar, Indianapolis: Hackett.

Kant, Immanuel 2011 [1785], *Groundwork of the Metaphysics of Morals: A German-English Edition*, edited and translated by Mary Gregor and Jens Timmermann, Cambridge: Cambridge University Press.

Kant, Immanuel 2013 [1788], 'On the Use of Teleological Principles in Philosophy', in *Kant and the Concept of Race. Late Eighteenth-Century Writings*, edited and translated by Jon M. Mikkelsen, New York: State University of New York Press.

Kautsky, Karl 1901, 'Problematischer gegen wissenschaftlichen Sozialismus', *Die neue Zeit*, 20, 2, 38: 355–64.

Kemp, John 1958, 'Kant's Examples of the Categorical Imperative', *The Philosophical Quarterly*, 8, 30: 63–71.

Kerstein, Samuel J. 2013, *How To Treat Persons*, Oxford: Oxford University Press.

Klagge, James C. 1986, 'Marx's Realms of "Freedom" and "Necessity"', *Canadian Journal of Philosophy*, 16, 4: 769–78.

Korsgaard, Christine M. 1986, 'Kant's Formula of Humanity', *Kant-Studien*, 77: 183–202.

Korsgaard, Christine M. 1990, *The Standpoint of Practical Reason*, New York: Garland.

Korsgaard, Christine M. 1996, *Creating the Kingdom of Ends*, Cambridge: Cambridge University Press.

Korsgaard, Christine M. 1997, 'Introduction', in *Groundwork of the Metaphysics of Morals*, edited and translated by Mary Gregor, Cambridge: Cambridge University Press.

Korsgaard, Christine M. 2011, 'Valuing Our Humanity', Unpublished manuscript, available at http://www.people.fas.harvard.edu/~korsgaar/CMK.Valuing.Our.Humanity .pdf.

Leibholz, Gerhard 1966 [1929], *Das Wesen der Repräsentation und der Gestaltwandel der Demokratie im 20. Jahrhundert*, Berlin: Walter de Gruyter.

Leiter, Brian 2015, 'Why Marxism Still Does Not Need Normative Theory', *Analyse & Kritik*, 37, 1–2: 23–50.

Leopold, David 2007, *The Young Karl Marx: German Philosophy, Modern Politics, and Human Flourishing*, Cambridge: Cambridge University Press.

Lessing, Gotthold Ephraim 1777, *Ueber den Beweis des Geistes und der Kraft*, Braunschweig.

Lessing, Gotthold Ephraim 2005 [1777], 'On the Proof of the Spirit and of Power', in *Philosophical and Theological Writings*, edited and translated by Hugh B. Nisbet, Cambridge: Cambridge University Press.

Linden, Harry van der 1988, *Kantian Ethics and Socialism*, Indianapolis: Hackett.

Linden, Harry van der 1994, 'Cohens sozialistische Rekonstruktion der Ethik Kants', in *Ethischer Sozialismus. Zur politischen Philosophie des Neukantianismus*, edited by Helmut Holzhey, Frankfurt am Main: Suhrkamp.

Lukács, Georg 1968 [1923], *History and Class Consciousness*, translated by Rodney Livingstone, London: Merlin Press.

Lukács, Georg 1977 [1968], *Werke Band 2. Frühschriften II. Geschichte und Klassenbewußtsein*, Darmstandt und Neuwied: Luchterhand.

Lukes, Steven 1982, 'Marxism, Morality and Justice', *Royal Institute of Philosophy Lecture Series*, 14: 177–205.

Lukes, Steven 1985, *Marxism and Morality*, Oxford: Oxford University Press.

Martin, Adrienne M. 2006, 'How to Argue for the Value of Humanity', *Pacific Philosophical Quarterly*, 87: 96–125.

Marx, Karl 1973 [1939], *Grundrisse: Foundations of the Critique of Political Economy (Rough Draft)*, translated by Martin Nicolaus, Harmondsworth: Penguin Books.

Marx, Karl 1975, *Early Writings*, translated by Rodney Livingstone and Gregor Benton, Harmondsworth: Penguin Books.

Marx, Karl 1976 [1867], *Capital. A Critique of Political Economy. Volume 1*, translated by Ben Fowkes, Harmondsworth: Penguin Books.

Marx, Karl 1981 [1894], *Capital: A Critique of Political Economy. Volume 3*, translated by David Fernbach, Harmondsworth: Penguin Books.

Marx, Karl 1994, *Early Political Writings*, edited and translated by Joseph O'Malley, Cambridge: Cambridge University Press.

Marx, Karl and Friedrich Engels 1956–2018, *Werke*, Berlin: Dietz Verlag.

Marx, Karl and Friedrich Engels 1975–2005, *Collected Works*, London: Lawrence and Wishart.

Marx, Karl and Friedrich Engels 1975–, *Marx-Engels-Gesamtausgabe (MEGA)*, herausgegeben von der Internationalen Marx-Engels-Stiftung, Berlin: Akademie Verlag.

Marx, Karl, Friedrich Engels and Joseph Weydemeyer 2004, *Marx-Engels-Jahrbuch 2003. Die deutsche Ideologie. Artikel, Druckvorlagen, Entwürfe, Reinschriftenfragmente und Notizen zu* I. Feuerbach *und* II. Sankt Bruno, edited by Inge Taubert and Hans Pelger, Berlin: Akademie Verlag.

McFarland, John D. 1970, *Kant's Concept of Teleology*, Edinburgh: Edinburgh University Press.

McNair, Ted 2000, 'Universal Necessity and Contradictions in Conception', *Kant-Studien*, 91, 1: 25–41.

Mehring, Franz 1898, 'Aesthetische Streifzüge', *Die Neue Zeit*, 17, 1, 9: 281–8.

Mikkelsen, Jon M. 2013, *Kant and the Concept of Race*, New York: State University of New York Press.

Mill, John Stuart 1962 [1910], *Utilitarianism, Liberty, Representative Government*, London: Dent.

Miller, Richard W. 1981, 'Marx and Aristotle: A Kind of Consequentialism', *Canadian Journal of Philosophy*, Supplementary Volume, 7: 323–52.

Miller, Richard W. 1984, *Analyzing Marx: Morality, Power and History*, Princeton: Princeton University Press.

Natorp, Paul 1923, *Philosophie und Pädagogik. Untersuchungen auf ihrem Grenzgebiet*, *2. verbesserte Auflage*, Marburg: N.G. Elwert'sche Verlagsbuchhandlung.

Nelson, Leonard 1917, *Vorlesungen über die Grundlagen der Ethik. Erster Band. Kritik der praktischen Vernunft*, Leipzig: Veit und Comp.

Nielsen, Kai 1989, *Marxism and the Moral Point of View: Morality, Ideology, and Historical Materialism*, Boulder, CO: Westview Press.

O'Neill, Onora 1989, *Constructions of Reason*, Cambridge: Cambridge University Press.

O'Neill, Onora 2013 [1975], *Acting on Principle. An Essay on Kantian Ethics. Second Edition*, Cambridge: Cambridge University Press.

Paton, Herbert James 1953, *The Categorical Imperative. A Study in Kant's Moral Philosophy*, London: Hutchinson's.

Peffer, Rodney G. 1990, *Marxism, Morality, and Social Justice*, Princeton: Princeton University Press.

Pogge, Thomas W. 1998, 'The Categorical Imperative', in *Groundwork of the Metaphysics of Morals. Critical Essays*, edited by Paul Guyer, Oxford: Rowman and Littlefield.

Postone, Moishe 1993, *Time, Labor, and Social Domination. A Reinterpretation of Marx's Social Theory*, Cambridge: Cambridge University Press.

Rattansi, Ali 1982, *Marx and the Division of Labour*, London: Macmillan.

Rawls, John 1971, *A Theory of Justice*, Cambridge, Mass.: Harvard University Press.

Rawls, John 1980, 'Kantian Constructivism in Moral Theory', *The Journal of Philosophy*, 77, 9: 515–72.

Rawls, John 1989, 'Themes in Kant's Moral Philosophy', in *Kant's Transcendental Deductions*, edited by Eckart Forster, Stanford: Stanford University Press.

Rawls, John 1993, 'The Law of Peoples', *Critical Inquiry*, 20, 36–68.

Rawls, John 2000, *Lectures on the History of Moral Philosophy*, Cambridge, Mass.: Harvard University Press.

Rawls, John 2007, *Lectures on the History of Political Philosophy*, Cambridge, MA: Harvard University Press.

Reath, Andrews 2006, *Agency and Autonomy in Kant's Moral Theory*, Oxford: Clarendon.

Reiman, Jeffrey E. 1987, 'Exploitation, Force, and the Moral Assessment of Capitalism: Thoughts on Roemer and Cohen', *Philosophy and Public Affairs*, 16, 1: 3–41.

Reisner, Andrew E. 2013, '*Prima Facie* and *Pro Tanto* Oughts', in *The International Encyclopedia of Ethics*, edited by H. Lafollette, Oxford: Blackwell.

Roberts, William Clare 2017, *Marx's Inferno: The Political Theory of* Capital, Princeton: Princeton University Press.

Roemer, John E. 1982, *A General Theory of Exploitation and Class*, Cambridge: Harvard University Press.

Rousseau, Jean-Jacques 1790 [1762], *Du contract social, ou principes du droit politique*, Lyon: J.B. Delamollière.

Rousseau, Jean-Jacques 1997 [1762], The Social Contract *and Other Later Political Writings*, edited and translated by Victor Gourevitch, Cambridge: Cambridge University Press.

Sartre, Jean-Paul 1983, *Cahiers pour une morale*, Paris: Gallimard.

Sartre, Jean-Paul 1992 [1983], *Notebooks for an Ethics*, translated by David Pellauer, Chicago: University of Chicago Press.

Sayre-McCord, Geoffrey 2001, 'Mill's "Proof" of the Principle of Utility: A More Than Half-Hearted Defense', *Social Philosophy and Policy*, 18, 2: 330–60.

Scanlon, Thomas M. 2008, *Moral Dimensions: Permissibility, Meaning, Blame*, Cambridge, Mass.: Harvard University Press.

Schefold, Christoph 1972, *Die Rechtsphilosophie des jungen Marx von 1842. Mit einer Interpretation der "Pariser Schriften" von 1844*, München: C.H. Beck.

Schwartz, Justin 1995a, 'In Defence of Exploitation', *Economics and Philosophy*, 11: 275–307.

Schwartz, Justin 1995b, 'What's Wrong with Exploitation?', *Noûs*, 29, 2: 158–88.

Sen, Amartya 1992, *Inequality Reexamined*, Oxford: Clarendon Press.

Sen, Amartya 2009, *The Idea of Justice*, Cambridge, Mass.: Harvard University Press.

Shoikhedbrod, Igor 2019, *Revisiting Marx's Critique of Liberalism. Rethinking Justice, Legality and Rights*, London: Palgrave Macmillan.

Sidgwick, Henry 1962 [1874], *The Methods of Ethics. Seventh Edition*, London: Palgrave Macmillan.

Smith, Tony 2017, *Beyond Liberal Egalitarianism: Marx and Normative Social Theory in the Twenty-First Century*, Leiden: Brill.

Stammler, Rudolf 1896, *Wirtschaft und Recht nach der materialistischen Geschichtsauffaussung. Eine sozialphilosophische Untersuchung*, Leipzig: Veit und Comp.

Stammler, Rudolf 1914 [1896], *Wirtschaft und Recht nach der materialistischen Geschichtsauffaussung. Eine sozialphilosophische Untersuchung*, dritte verbesserte Auflage, Leipzig: Veit und Comp.

Staudinger, Franz 1899, *Ethik und Politik*, Berlin: Ferdinand Dümmler.

Staudinger, Franz 1906, 'Cohen und Kautsky', *Sozialistische Monatshefte*, 12, 4: 315–22.

Staudinger, Franz 1907, *Wirtschaftliche Grundlagen der Moral*, Darmstadt: Eduard Roether.

Stebbins, Samuel, Suneson, Grant 2020, 'Jeff Bezos, Elon Musk among US Billionaires Getting Richer during Coronavirus Pandemic', *USA Today* (1 December), available at https://www.usatoday.com/story/money/2020/12/01/american-billionaires-that-got-richer-during-covid/43205617/

Steinbüchel, Theodor 1921, *Der Sozialismus als sittliche Idee. Ein Beitrag zur christlichen Sozialethik*, Düsseldorf: Schwann.

Timmermann, Jens 2006, 'Value without Regress: Kants "Formula of Humanity" Revisited', *European Journal of Philosophy*, 14, 1: 69–93.

Timmermann, Jens 2007, *Kant's Groundwork of the Metaphysics of Morals*, Cambridge: Cambridge University Press.

Tönnies, Ferdinand 1909, 'Ethik und Sozialismus', *Archiv für Sozialwissenschaft und Sozialpolitik*, 29: 895–930.

Tronto, Joan C. 1993, *Moral Boundaries: a Political Argument for an Ethic of Care*, London: Routledge.

Tronto, Joan C. 2015, *Who Cares? How to Reshape a Democratic Politics*, Ithaca: Cornell University Press.

Trotsky, Leon, John Dewey, George Novak 1973, *Their Morals and Ours: Marxist Versus Liberal Views on Morality*, New York: Pathfinder.

Tugan-Baranowsky, Michael 1901 [1894], *Studien zur Theorie und Geschichte der Handelskrisen in England*. Jena: Gustav Fischer.

Tugan-Baranowsky, Michael 1905, *Theoretische Grundlagen des Marxismus*. Leipzig: Duncker & Humblot.

Tugan-Baranowsky, Michael 1908, *Der moderne Sozialismus in seiner geschichtlichen Entwicklung*, Dresden: O.V. Böhmert.

Tugan-Baranowsky, Michael 1910, *Modern Socialism in its Historical Development*, translated by M.I. Redmount, London: Swan Sonnenschein.

Vogel, Jeffrey S. 1994, 'Is Marx a Moral Consequentialist?', *Canadian Journal of Philosophy*, 24, 4: 541–63.

Vorländer, Karl 1900, *Kant und der Sozialismus, unter besonderer Berücksichtigung der neuesten theoretischen Bewegung innerhalb des Marxismus*, Berlin: Reuther & Reichard.

Vorländer, Karl 1904, *Marx und Kant. Vortrag gehalten im Wien am 8. April 1904*, Wien: E. Pernerstorfer.

Vorländer, Karl 1911, *Kant und Marx. Ein Beitrag zur Philosophie des Sozialismus*, Tübingen: J.C.B. Mohr.

Vorländer, Karl 1920, *Kant, Fichte, Hegel und der Sozialismus*, Berlin: Paul Cassirer.

Vorländer, Karl 1926 [1911], *Kant und Marx. Ein Beitrag zur Philosophie des Sozialismus*, zweite neubearbeitete Auflage, Tübingen: J.C.B. Mohr.

Waldron, Jeremy (ed.) 1984, *Theories of Rights*, Oxford: Oxford University Press.

Wolff, Jonathan 1999, 'Marx and Exploitation', *Journal of Ethics*, 3, 2: 105–20.

Wolff, Robert Paul 1973, *The Autonomy of Reason: A Commentary on Kant's* Groundwork of the Metaphysic of Morals, New York: Harper & Row.

Woltmann, Ludwig 1900, *Der historische Materialismus. Darstellung und Kritik der marxistischen Weltanschauung*, Düsseldorf: Hermann Michels.

Wood, Allen W. 1970, *Kant's Moral Religion*, Ithaca: Cornell University Press.

Wood, Allen W. 1972, 'Kant on False Promises', in *Proceedings of the Third International Kant Congress*, edited by Lewis White Beck, Dordrecht: Reidel.

Wood, Allen W. 1978, 'Translator's Introduction', in *Lectures on Philosophical Theology*, translated by Allen W. Wood and Gertrude M. Clark, Ithaca: Cornell University Press.

Wood, Allen W. 1981, *Karl Marx*, London: Routledge.

Wood, Allen W. 1984, 'Justice and Class Interests', *Philosophica*, 33, 1: 9–32.

Wood, Allen W. 1990, *Hegel's Ethical Thought*, Cambridge: Cambridge University Press.

Wood, Allen W. 1991, 'Marx Against Morality', in *A Companion to Ethics*, edited by Peter Singer, Oxford: Blackwell.

Wood, Allen W. 1993, 'Hegel and Marxism', in *The Cambridge Companion to Hegel*, edited by Frederick C. Beiser, Cambridge: Cambridge University Press.

Wood, Allen W. 1995a, 'Humanity as End in Itself', *Proceedings of the Eighth International Kant Congress*, Vol. 1, Issue Part 1: 301–19.

Wood, Allen W. 1995b, 'What is Exploitation?' *Social Philosophy and Policy*, 12, 2: 136–58.

Wood, Allen W. 1999, *Kant's Ethical Thought*, Cambridge: Cambridge University Press.

Wood, Allen W. 2004 [1981], *Karl Marx*, Second Edition, London: Routledge.

Wood, Allen W. 2008, *Kantian Ethics*, Cambridge: Cambridge University Press.

Wood, Allen W. 2014, *The Free Development of Each. Studies on Freedom, Right, and Ethics in Classical German Philosophy*, Oxford: Oxford University Press.

Wood, Allen W. 2017, 'Marx and Kant on Capitalist Exploitation', *Kantian Review*, 22, 4: 641–59.

Wood, Ellen Meiksins 1989, 'Rational Choice Marxism: Is the Game Worth the Candle?', *New Left Review*, I/177: 41–88.

Index

www.ingramcontent.com/pod-product-compliance
Lightning Source LLC
Chambersburg PA
CBHW071137130626
46553CB00004B/1404